GUY SIMONIS

Lottery Lore

...A personal journey through the development of lotteries and casinos

Lottery Lore

Mr. Guy Simonis

2019

ISBN: 9781095210796

To Ina:

Without her encouragement, this tale would
never have seen the light of day.

FOREWORD

This is my story of the trials and tribulations in the development of government licensed games of chance in Canada and elsewhere. The story is not intended to be a scholarly tome but rather an array of narratives — a singular description of how games of chance developed into an industry. In my search, there appears to be no other personal essay that depicts the series of events that elevated Canada to one of the leading countries in lotteries and casinos.

My career in games of chance started in 1972 a small sports betting game with an annual turnover of $250,000 and ended in the year 2000 with $1.4 billion in sales. The worldwide growth in games of chance has continued to grow exponentially since then but this account is about the first steps of lottery development.

Strange as it may sound, I got into the business of gaming via the sport of water polo. As a so-so active player and President of the Canadian Water Polo Association, I was asked to head the water polo section of the 1967 Pan American Games. It was there that I met the leaders of most amateur sports in Manitoba. To foster growth of sport, we together formed the Manitoba Sports Federation (MSF: now morphed into "Sport Manitoba")

While the objective of the MSF was to improve the quality of amateur sports, the means to achieve that goal was money. In the early '70s, the three levels of government began to show a tepid interest in promoting sports. The city councils and the Province of Manitoba focused on stimulating participation at the beginner level. Prime Minister Pierre Trudeau created Sport Canada that funded athletes to strive for excellence. But it wasn't enough.

It was the need for additional funding that led your lottery scribe to become involved in the development of games of chance. Lotteries entered the picture.

On a note: In a story about oneself, the frequent use of the pronoun "I" becomes annoying. The expression, "Your lottery scribe" will supplant "I" from time to time. Thank you for bearing with me.

Spring of 2019

RECOGNITION: A shout-out to some of my colleagues who were an important part of this story but didn't make it into this much curtailed saga.

Sandra Marotto

Doug Penrose

Cluny Macpherson

Heather Brandorst

Sanam Bakhtiar

Shirley MacAllister

THE PIONEERING YEARS
1971-1985

THE PARADOX OF LOTTERIES

In 1971, I entered the lottery business. At that time, it was an enterprise that was considered by many Canadians as sinful.

Many of today's lottery colleagues cannot imagine how difficult the political and religious environment was for the lottery business in the early '70s. Pronouncements by two historical figures serve to illustrate the contradictions that we will see appear again and again as the story unfolds:

"A Lottery is properly a Tax upon unfortunate self-conceited fools." **William Petty, British Economist,1893**

"These lotteries bring in 100 million francs each year. I will certainly forbid it at once — as soon as someone can name a virtue that brings in as many francs." **Napoleon Bonaparte, 1814**

IN THE BEGINNING

In the 1950s, when the federal government realized that Canada was a nonentity in the world of international competitive sport, leaders of the day began to show interest in enhancing its development.

What prompted that awareness was the poor showing by Canada in the 1954 World Hockey Championships. The final game of that tournament pitted Canada's entry — the senior amateur club East York Lyndhursts — against the USSR, both teams being undefeated. Most believed the Canadians would cruise to their seventh straight championship but the heretofore-unknown Soviet players passed, checked and skated so fast that they thoroughly dominated the World Championship game in a 7—2 win before 16,000 fans.

Two years later, at the 1956 Winter Olympics, Canada's hockey team was defeated once again by the Soviets, and for the third time at the 1960 Olympic Games in Squaw Valley California. This riled Canadian sports fans who believed Canada had an undeniable right to the world championship in hockey.

After that national loss of face, calls for government funding of sports activities increased. In 1961, Parliament enacted the Fitness and Amateur Sport Act (C-131) to "encourage the development of fitness and amateur sport in

1

Canada." That legislation was of some benefit to national sports organizations but did nothing for the development of athletes at the local and provincial level.

I entered this story through the sport of water polo. Through the years I morphed from a utility player (a nice word for a worker bee) to a volunteer executive in the sport in Canada. In 1965, I was elected as national president of the Canadian Water Polo Association. In turn I was named Chairman of the Water Polo section of the 1967 Pan American Games in Winnipeg.

The Canadian water polo team didn't do very well at those Games. Neither did the teams in any of the other 26 sports competitions. Canada won not one of the many gold medals on its own turf. The public's reaction to this embarrassment was a muted anger.

To soothe the shame, the Government of Canada funded a small training program for a few elite athletes who would not embarrass Canada too much in international competitions. The majority of the responsibility for the development of athletes of the future was left to the provinces.

In ideal circumstances government support should have started at the local club and provincial level but the public demanded achievement at the international stage — now! In this political climate, the provinces would have to initiate development programs on their own.

PROVINCES TO DEVELOP ATHLETES

PAN-AMERICAN GAMES
WINNIPEG CANADA 1967

The 1967 Pan-Am Games in Winnipeg showed that the various sports in Manitoba had many problems in common. Parental pockets funded coaches, travel expenses, facilities, equipment, uniforms and other essentials. The government of Manitoba helped out in a way. Each of the sport-governing bodies was granted the annual sum of $500 towards these costs. These meagre contributions were not comparable to the support of athletic development in other countries, especially in Eastern Europe.

After the poor showing at the Pan-Am Games, the Manitoba Government's Recreation Branch gauged interest in the creation of an umbrella organization of sports groups that would focus on common projects such a Manitoba Games (similar to the Canada Games). A meeting of leaders in sports was arranged. Those early discussions exposed fear that an association of sports, endowed with substantial funds, might interfere with the fiercely guarded self-determination of the individual sports associations. The prevailing opinion was that the sport-governing bodies didn't need any help other than receiving money without strings attached. Give us the money, then leave us alone. Please?

At those meetings in Manitoba and speaking as the representative for water polo, I emphasized the value of a sports federation which I had learned about in the Netherlands. A sports federation could not only emphasize the value of co-operation between sports but could wield more political influence when speaking to government as one voice. Last but not least, I spoke of the capability of the Netherlands Sports Federation to raise funds through a lottery on behalf of sports. None of these co-operative efforts diminish the power of the sports organizations to manage their respective activities.

After a speech by your lottery scribe, the fears of the provincial sport federations were somewhat dispelled and a set of agreed objectives emerged. While the most urgent need was — surprise — money, the concept of a Manitoba Games, with regions of Manitoba representing participating "nations," found some favour. While those games appeared to be the priority of the Government's Recreation Branch, for the sports organizations it remained an idea for another day.

One of the stumbling blocks in the relationship between the sport organizations and the government's Recreation Branch was that its director and staff saw the creation of a province-wide federation of sports as a potential threat to their mandate. Similar to government people anywhere, they wanted allies to support their aims, not usurpers of their perceived powers.

A formal meeting of the heads of the sport-governing bodies was arranged. **Vaughn Baird**, a representative of Diving, well-known lawyer and good friend, led the opening session. He proposed that your sporting scribe be named as interim chairman of the formative group. And so I was.

At that initial meeting we agreed that a presentation should be made to the Minister of Recreation, urging the government to consider separating support for organized competitive sports from recreational activities. The Recreation Branch maintained that their mandate was to support recreational activities for the masses, not the improvement of athletes at a national or international level.

The creation of a formal association of provincial sport-governing bodies was endorsed. The membership was to be limited to those organizations that were a provincial branch of a federally recognized sport.

Immediately, the old bug-bear of an umbrella organization exercising control of all activities raised its head again. As interim leader, my task was to convince the fearful ones that a sports federation would assist in raising funds and in the co-ordination of multi-sports activities. It was stressed again that there was no intent to interfere with the conduct of their respective sports.

A first measure of faith was achieved when the Manitoba sport-governing organizations unanimously committed to contributing their $500 annual provincial grant towards the creation of a provincial federation.

Vaughn Baird undertook responsibility to see that the Manitoba Legislature would pass an Act creating a federation of sport-governing bodies in Manitoba. The name Manitoba Sports Federation was adopted over objections by the Recreation Branch. Their argument was that the word "sport" without the addition of "amateur" was reserved for professional sports. The Branch's view carried the meeting but not the day. That evening, over a late coffee, the majority of attendees agreed that they'd been too subservient and decided to retain the name Manitoba Sports Federation.

MANITOBA SPORTS FEDERATION INCORPORATED

Vaughn Baird created the legal entity. On January 20, 1970, the Manitoba Legislature voted to incorporate the Manitoba Sports Federation (MSF). Listed as founding directors were: **Guy Simonis** (Water Polo), Vaughn Baird (Diving), Bill Addison (Hockey), Ernie Draffin (Soccer), Art Kolisnyk (Football), Fred Law (Curling), Anne Doherty (Figure Skating), Jim Trifunov (Wrestling) and Eric Oland (Cycling).

At the first official meeting of the Manitoba Sports Federation, your lottery scribe was elected President. To flesh out the aims and objectives of the MSF, a weekend-long seminar was convened at the government's Recreation Complex in Gimli, with all the heads of Manitoba's sport-governing bodies in attendance.

4

While there was lukewarm interest in joint administration services and coaching seminars, the main concern was MONEY. It was evident to all — even with the thousands of volunteers who kept sports running — that administration comes at a cost, especially when the desired goals move beyond mere recreation and reach for higher levels of accomplishment.

Government was seen as the desired source of funding but in reality, no one believed government would hand over taxpayers' money in sufficient amounts to satisfy the requirements of the sports community. Old fashioned fund-raising efforts couldn't deliver enough revenue. The consensus of the organizations present was that they had to raise a steady stream of funds themselves.

COULD A LOTTERY PROVIDE SUFFICIENT FUNDS?

Given the recent buzz about lotteries, it was no surprise that the meeting soon turned to the idea of the MSF conducting a lottery for the benefit of its member organizations.

Everyone knew of the Irish Sweepstakes but your lottery scribe presented a lottery game called SPORT TOTO. During my frequent business trips to Europe on behalf of the Manitoba Immigration Department, I had spent my free time gathering information about lotteries for the benefit of sport. My files still bulge from the massive amount of papers collected.

I had some excellent contacts in Europe. I should immediately acknowledge the assistance by my childhood friend, **Joop van der Reijden** who — at that time — was Minister of Sport in the Netherlands. He provided detailed information about the SPORTS TOTO operation as did Paul Lut, my former water polo teammate, who was the Managing Director of the Dutch TOTO operation.

Lothar (Pete) Lammers of the West German SPORTTOTO told me that in 1950, the #1 priority of the Deutsche Bundesrepublik was to rebuild its ruined sports infrastructure. The government delegated responsibility for sport development to the West German States (Laender), allowing them to conduct lotteries based on soccer competitions (TOTO). After the first two decades, with many sports facilities rebuilt, a larger share of TOTO revenue was dedicated to the development of athletes rather than bricks and mortar.

TOTO was distinct from the German state lottery. In that centuries' old game, lottery players bought a ticket and months later checked the winning numbers list. TOTO, on the other hand, required active involvement by predicting the outcome (win, lose or tie) of a dozen or more soccer games.

The main difference between the Dutch and German operations was that in Germany, retail stores (mostly tobacconists) collected the TOTO entries; the Netherlands depended on sports clubs and door-to-door volunteer sellers.

The format of TOTO offered in the various European countries was the same. Retailers/sellers accepted entry slips marked with predictions on the outcome of 12 or 13 soccer games. To be more precise, players were required to predict a win, tie or loss for each of a number of weekend soccer games. The prizes were based on a *pari-mutuel* basis which means that the players shared the available prize fund. (Usually 45% of the total amount bet by the participants)

That prize fund was divided into three equal prize pools. One prize pool was shared equally by the players who had all predictions correct. The second pool was shared by those who missed only one prediction and those who missed only two predictions shared the third pool. If there was no winner in one of the pools, the prize would be transferred down to the lower pool.

 In Canada, where hockey is the national obsession, a TOTO lottery based on soccer was of little interest. By substituting NHL hockey for soccer, your stumbling scribe made a big mistake by ignoring the difference in the number of tie games in hockey vs. soccer. In soccer, tie games occur in about 30% of games played. Ties in NHL hockey were less than 10% in the '70s. That difference turned out to be a serious impediment to the lack of success of the TOTO scheme in Manitoba.

Given the Canadian public's tepid acceptance of gambling, it was clear that a business like the TOTO operating in other countries was politically unacceptable.

The operation of a Canadian TOTO had to be conducted by volunteers — club members, armed with entry forms, would approach friends, family and supporters and persuade them to take a little gamble in support of sport.

The profit for the selling club would be 30% of their sales. The Sports Federation would earn 25%.

The TOTO concept met with many questions but once the model was understood by the leaders of the sports federation, they passed a motion that the MSF would apply for a lottery license. A letter was forwarded to the provincial Minister of Recreation but, oddly, no response came.

Two reasons explain the reluctance to respond to the request. One was the murky history of gambling that still bothered many politicians. More importantly, the government didn't like the thought of competition for the Irish-Sweepstakes they were planning to fund celebrations of the province's 100th Anniversary in 1970. And then there was federal musing of a national lottery.

LOTTERIES ON THE NATIONAL AGENDA

To go back to the national level... Hansard records that on September 12, 1967, the Minister of Justice, Pierre Trudeau announced in Parliament that article 179 of the upcoming Omnibus Bill was about lotteries. In non-legal language the bill said:

1) The federal government has the right to manage and conduct a nation-wide lottery system.

2) The government of a province may authorize a lottery within its territory pursuant to an existing enabling provincial law.

3) A lottery licensed by a provincial government is forbidden to sell tickets outside its territory without a negotiated agreement with the affected provinces.

4) An interprovincial lottery is authorized.

The legislation was introduced but it got bogged down in long studies by committees and a flood of amendments. A year later, Pierre Trudeau became Prime Minister and the file was handed to the new Minister of Justice, John Turner. In Parliament, the lottery legislation was continually being picked apart.

Meanwhile...a lottery of questionable legality had started elsewhere. Well before Ottawa's deliberations about lotteries, **Jean Drapeau**, the Mayor of Montreal, on April 2, 1968, launched a "voluntary tax"— a scheme that looked a lot like a lottery.

The City of Montreal invited people from anywhere to pay a tax of $2 with the freedom to pay as many $2 taxes as they desired. The generosity of these voluntary tax payers would be rewarded. Each month, the $2 tax receipts would be entered in a draw for a chance at a "tax refund" of one of the 151 silver bars in the prize pool, valued at around $1,000 each. One lucky taxpayer would receive a "grand refund" of $100,000. (How silver bars could be valued at $1000 was never explained.)

The profit of the scheme, as estimated by the City, was a strange amount of $2,666,666 per month. According to Mayor Drapeau, this scheme was not a lottery, because the prizes were paid out in silver bars (Silver is not a prize?) But that wasn't the only strange aspect. The lucky taxpayer so drawn to receive a "Grand Refund", would have to correctly answer four questions about Montreal — a hurdle that sounded a lot more difficult than it was, because the answers were printed on the back of every lottery ticket... sorry, I meant "tax receipt." In all later draws only one poor winner couldn't read the answer on his ticket. The city fathers immediately set up a "Help Fund" so that the loser could obtain the prize he had missed out on.

Drapeau's "voluntary tax" caused dismay in both Ottawa and Quebec City. After four draws, the Quebec Minister of Justice Jean-Jacques Bertrand made short shrift of the issue: "It's a lottery, pure and simple," he said. In September 1968 the Quebec Appeal Court rendered its judgment. Montreal's voluntary tax was illegal. It was dead!

SUDDENLY LOTTERIES ARE LEGAL

On May 14, 1969, the federal proposal permitting the conduct of lotteries was passed into law. The federal government and any provincial government alone or in co-operation with another province could conduct lotteries. Laws with respect to minor games of chance by charitable organizations and agricultural fairs were also addressed.

Meanwhile the cause for the lottery had shifted. All through, the emphasis had been on a lottery for a wide variety of "good causes." Now it appeared that the legalization of lotteries was intended for a specific purpose.

Montréal 1976

In 1970, after his lottery scheme was ditched, Mayor Drapeau convinced the International Olympic Committee to select Montreal as host for the 1976 Games. It was now clear that the lottery legislation was meant to be in support of Montreal's Olympic bid. The Liberal government didn't want to fund the Olympics from taxpayer pockets. Money raised by a lottery would lessen the demand on federal coffers and, more importantly, wouldn't incense the electorate.

In retrospect, the federal government didn't anticipate that the provincial governments would leap at the opportunity to get into the lottery business. The Liberal government assumed that only the Olympic Committee would take advantage of the opening. That the provincial governments of Quebec and the West — who for so long and so vehemently had opposed gambling — would be so eager to jump into the fray, must have been a surprise to the Feds.

THE FIRST LEGAL LOTTERIES APPEAR

The May 1969 passing of Ottawa's OMNIBUS ACT did indeed open the gate for lotteries. The province of Quebec, eager to fill in the demand created by Drapeau's lottery, was first out of the starting gate.

On December 23, 1969, the government of Quebec created a Crown Corporation named Loto Quebec to manage and conduct lotteries in the province. **Maurice Custeau**, the first president of Loto Quebec, took advantage of the public's wave of enthusiasm. He didn't care about market research; he wanted the lottery on the market as soon as possible.

Barely ten weeks later, on March 14, 1970, the first draw took place. Custeau, a wily politician, chose to retain the format of the tax scheme of the City of Montréal. In his shrewd opinion, familiarity was of the essence. There was no time to acquaint ticket buyers with a new lottery scheme. People who had prepaid for tickets in the now defunct Montreal lottery were offered a refund. So few asked for their money back that Loto Quebec had a substantial fund to draw from. From the very first day, participation exceeded expectations. Sales territories were designed. Private distributorships were appointed.

On March 14, 1970, the first lottery draw was televised province-wide. A preliminary draw had selected the names of the eventual prize winners. A card naming the winning candidate was stuffed into a huge balloon. Celebrities from sports and show business took turns bursting the balloons. Each lottery winner would receive a prize in order of magnitude. The last balloon busted contained the name of the winner who collected the top prize of $125,000.

Two months later, in May of 1970, the first weekly 50-cent Mini Lotto hit the counters of Quebec's retailers. Shortly after, the resurrected $2 Montreal lottery, now called Inter-Loto, became a monthly draw. Then the $4 Super Loto was launched, drawn every three months, with a top prize of $250,000.

MANTOBA GOLDEN SWEEPSTAKES

In the same month that Loto Quebec was created (January of 1970) the Manitoba government of Premier Walter Weir passed an Act creating the Manitoba Centennial Corporation and the Centennial Lottery, which went on to hold 9 draws within three years. The profits were to fund celebrations of the 1970 Manitoba Centennial, including many special projects and festivities. The draws of the $2.50 per-ticket were held in conjunction with the Canadian Curling Championships (March), the Manitoba Derby (August) and the CFL Championship, (November). The early financial results didn't match those of Quebec but nonetheless, the events caused enough of a commotion to consider making the lottery a permanent fixture. But I'll come back to that later.

1970 was Manitoba's Centennial. The overly-long tenured Conservative government viewed the milestone as an opportunity to present itself as a progressive, active promotor of the province. As other governments have done in their dying days, the Manitoba Conservatives decided to have a high-profile celebration with a lot of public participation in order to stir provincial pride.

The wily Premier Walter Weir did not want to create huge tax-funded festivities. Spending on frivolous pastimes is never a good idea prior to an election. Avoiding any hint that the lottery might be become permanent, plans were approved for three sweepstake drawings during the year 1970 and then, "Over and Out. No More." Due to the temporary aspect of this lottery program, investments in buildings or permanent staffing were out of the question. The Centennial Corporation under the formidable Minister Maitland Steinkopf, approved the lottery format, a clone of the Irish Sweepstakes — an unsound lottery scheme that offered several loopholes for fraudulent manipulation.

The name "Manitoba Golden Sweepstakes" was chosen because the sweepstakes format was well-known.

Although illegal in Canada, the Irish Hospital Sweepstakes had a significant player base. Furthermore, the name 'sweepstakes' would stifle any opposition because — despite being illegal — the Irish Sweepstakes had been popular for decades. Winners were openly published in the daily newspapers without any follow-up by police. It is intriguing that over so many years, this illegal, fraud-friendly scheme never caught the prying eye of Manitoba law enforcement.

Well before Manitoba initiated its Golden Sweepstakes, the U.S. Senate had paid attention to the Irish Sweepstakes scheme. In 1969, Senator Estes Kefauver chaired a senate inquiry that revealed many thousands of Irish Sweepstakes tickets bought by trusting Americans were regularly discarded by the Mob, the money stashed away. Those tickets never got into the draw. The Senate Commission's report cited that the mobsters sent "suitcases full" of ticket receipt stubs to Ireland-based cohorts, not to enter them in the draw but to mail acknowledgement receipts back to the buyers. The Irish postage-stamped postcard suggested that the buyer's ticket was indeed in the draw. Only a handful of buyers ever complained about this scam.

In the run-up to the implementation of the Manitoba Centennial Sweepstakes, the rancid smell of this compromised game was never aired publicly. Government involvement — however misplaced — instilled public trust. Your lottery scribe can attest that the lottery minister, **Maitland Steinkopf**, was made aware of the game's weaknesses but these warnings were waved off because Manitobans were not the New York mobster types and the lottery was a one-year fun event and would "never become permanent."

Premier Weir, counting on excitement for the upcoming Centennial festivities, called a general election for June 25, 1969, even though only three years had passed since the previous election. The date was important because the start of the Centennial was only six months away. The decision to go to the polls early proved to be a strategic error. In a surprise outcome, the New Democratic Party was elected with Edward Schreyer as its leader.

LOTTERIES: A HISTORIC PERSPECTIVE

It is now time for your lottery scribe to share perspective on Canada's history of gambling. Otherwise, you'll feel you've just been dropped into the middle of a story. The national shockwave of legalized lotteries was partly due to Canada's historical naiveté with respect to gambling. In Europe, games of chance had flourished for centuries, but it was only in the year 1900 that anything resembling a game of chance became vaguely legal in Canada. The Criminal Code was amended to permit small-scale raffles at bazaars held for a "charitable or religious objectives." That was good for church raffles but didn't allow for larger lotteries.

In 1906 revisions to the Criminal Code, the term "lottery scheme" was introduced. Since then, this simple legal phrase has been interpreted to encompass games like bingo, blackjack, roulette, slots, and raffles.

It took 20 years before the next amendment to the Criminal Code permitted "games of chance" and "games of mixed skill and chance" at annual agricultural fairs and exhibitions. This amendment was a result of lobbying by those who would benefit from the change — agricultural fairs and exhibitions. The words "games of mixed skill and chance" referred to such games as betting on horse races where knowledge of the horses' history was a factor in success.

In 1954, a joint committee of the Senate and House of Commons reported that illegal lotteries and other games of chance such as bingo were widely carried on in Canada. The report expressed concerns that schemes of this nature posed "the most acute problem of control."

However, significant public support still existed for lotteries and bingos on behalf of charitable organizations. The turning point of Canadian gambling policy occurred in 1969 in response to public and political pressures.

On the surface, gambling was associated with the rich and sophisticated but it was also strongly linked to loose morals and organized crime. Related to every kind of excess, gambling had a seedy reputation and, perhaps that was part of the appeal. While this mix of glamour and seediness was exciting to some, gambling was still largely viewed as a vice.

A national consensus on gambling couldn't be established because Canada's regions held contradictory views. Let's look at those differences.

FIRST NATIONS

First nation tribes were the earliest gamblers in North America. The indigenous games of chance were mostly contests of skill and guessing games. Gambling was popular due to the belief that supernatural forces influenced the outcomes of unpredictable events.

Among indigenous people of Western Canada, 'dice' games were the favorite. At community events, dice games provoked great celebration and shouting. Entire villages bet on the individuals chosen to play a game. Yet there was a consensus among many first nations that gambling — outside of ceremonial context — was frowned upon and could lead to excess.

BRITISH COLUMBIA

In 1867, at the time of Confederation, gambling in British Columbia was limited to lumberjack dorms, mining camps and the occasional church raffle.

More intense gambling was found in Chinese neighborhoods. Mysterious **Chinese games of chance** were indecipherable to the average settler. One BC newspaper editor wrote, "One of the things that is the most mysterious about Chinese gambling, is the lottery ticket itself. It is a piece of paper covered with hieroglyphics of which no person can make head or tail unless you understand these Chinese characters. One-hundred well-known sayings are listed on a sort of entry form. The buyer may choose ten of these phrases by putting a pen stroke though them. At the final drawing, pieces of paper with the names of the hundred sayings are stored in a ceremonial-looking urn. If the ten phrases drawn from the urn match those the buyer had chosen, he or she wins the grand prize. The Chinese ethos holds that the integrity of the lottery is not in the slightest doubt. Shockingly, the odds of getting the ten phrases out of a hundred correct, is one in 17 trillion, 310 billion. Fortunately for the bettors there are secondary prizes."

THE PRAIRIES

In contrast to Chinese culture, the ethnic-European population of the prairies favored simple games of chance such as local raffles with names drawn from a hat, conducted in a small social setting. The illegality of gambling was ignored because the intent was to provide funds for local good causes.

The prairie view of lotteries was best summarized by **Gerald R. Craig**, a Presbyterian clergyman who said, "Lotteries destroy all moral values and wherever they have come into existence, they have proven to be too costly to operate, and have a pernicious effect, of doubtful value to the beneficiaries and with sinister results for the population. They also destroy the authentic philanthropic spirit." Yes, the prairie people were primed to resist all major gambling.

ONTARIO AND THE MARITIMES

Ontario and Atlantic Canada showed no particular interest in allowing anything more daring than church raffles and harness racing. The Catholic parishes near the Ontario/Quebec border showed a fondness for church bingos.

QUEBEC

It has always been an interesting question why Quebec is more fascinated by gambling than any other Canadian region. In a poll conducted in 1965, 87% of Quebecois thought lotteries should be legal. Ontario was less certain at 71%, while Westerners were even less enthusiastic at 52%. Quebec's infatuation with gambling was in no small measure due to the attitude of the Catholic Church.

One Catholic historian of the day expressed the views of the Catholic Church this way: "Gambling in and of itself is not a sin. No more so than drinking alcohol. Drinking when under age or getting drunk to the point where one causes harm to oneself or others, that is sinful. Gambling can become an addiction but each person must choose for themselves. If a person spends food or rent money on the lottery that would harm themselves and likely others, then it would be sinful. Individual persons must be accountable for their own actions. The position of the Church is that one should avoid the temptation to sin. Every individual should determine what is too much temptation for them."

THE PROTESTANT VIEW

An Ontario minister of the United Church, **Reverend Hawthorn**, described Quebec as a priest-ridden society and warned: "We may expect that the province of Quebec under duress of the Catholic hierarchy will become a North American gambling center. One is loathe to refer to the religious monopoly of lotteries in South America but once such an activity is declared to be a moral practice, its reversal is unthinkable."

The United Church Observer, the Protestant organ of the day, ran an editorial that "Quebec's Roman Catholic churches' dependence on gambling revenue affected its views on the legalization of games of chance." It was all too true. In the early 1850s the profits of gambling were viewed by the Catholic clergy as a voluntary contribution to the Church.

At the same time in North America, hundreds of lotteries were being conducted by unscrupulous individuals. An estimated 80% of those schemes were run for the sole benefit of the operators. In 1840, a committee commissioned by eight U.S. states concluded that the total take of illegal lotteries exceeded $54 million— $10 million more than the entire administration budget for the United States.

In 1892, the 23-year old Dominion of Canada banned all forms of gambling. Despite this ban, in Quebec, games of chance sprang up like weeds in a pristine garden. Pressure was brought on the Quebec government to make exceptions for "charitable" causes, a code-word for the Catholic Church.

During the 1930s Depression, the old points of view were hauled out to support the creation of a Quebec provincial lottery. A lottery would:

- be for good causes
- allow people do legally what they now do illegally
- follow the example of most countries that allow lotteries
- bring legislation in harmony with overwhelming public opinion
- bring an end to an ineffectual law
- provide for a lottery to be run under government supervision
- attract foreign dollars to Canada
- bring additional revenue to the tax coffers

CANADA-WIDE

While Quebec's population supported the idea of a provincial lottery, in the rest of Canada there was little interest in legalizing games of chance. After World War II, opinions changed. In a 1962 survey by the Canadian Institute of Public Opinion, 70% of Canadians wanted a government lottery, including 80% of Quebeckers, 72% of Ontarians and 63% of Westerners. Atlantic Canada was not polled. In November, 1962, MPs of all parties supported "Bill C 36" that called for a national lottery. Public support came from all sides: the Canadian Chamber of Commerce, municipalities, societies, and the Canadian Legion. The pressure was in vain. The bill was "talked out."

Despite public support, the federal government turned a deaf ear. Canadians, illegally so, were spending tens of millions of dollars on lotteries from countries such as Switzerland, Austria, Japan, Israel Portugal, France, Sweden, Germany, Norway, Spain, and the Netherlands. The most successful of them all was the Irish Sweepstakes, which found buyers all over Canada. The activity was widely tolerated by authorities — even the names of winners were reported by newspapers without causing any investigation by the authorities.

NEW GOVERNMENT. NEW SUPPORTERS.

Let me take you back to Manitoba. On June 25, 1969, **Ed Schreyer**, at age 33 and a charismatic figure from the centrist wing of the NDP, became the youngest premier in Canada. His party had won the support of many center-left voters. The NDP won 28 seats, the Tories 22. On election night, Walter Weir, the outgoing Premier told his supporters "The people have spoken and the people are wrong."

It was the first time the NDP had held power in the province. Aware of the NDP's negative view on lotteries, all bets were off on launching the Manitoba Centennial Lottery since gambling was the bane of socialists everywhere. Media speculation was rife that the entire celebration of the 1970 Centennial was on hold. Fortunately, Premier Schreyer, a rational man, left Maitland Steinkopf, Chairman of the Centennial lottery, in place and did not interfere with the planned proceedings.

 **Laurent (Larry) Desjardins** was a Liberal MLA from Saint Boniface. While the NDP party had the most seats, they were one seat short of a majority. Desjardins crossed the floor. Desjardins, liking the idea of a lottery, found himself against the grain of the cabinet. Many cabinet members deemed the lottery to be a pestilence but Desjardins, who had a great relationship with Schreyer — almost as father and son — convinced the new premier that a lottery was a "Good Thing."

Busy with the implementation of the government's car insurance scheme, Desjardins waited for the "one-time-only" Sweepstakes to end. He had plans for a lottery to fund sport in Manitoba but wasn't in a position to reveal them.

The Centennial Sweepstakes enjoyed popular support however, the Manitoba Sports Federation had no role whatsoever in the management of the Centennial lottery. This didn't deter the MSF from selling Sweepstakes tickets. In fact, in 1970, the MSF earned in excess of $30,000 in commissions.

CENTENNIAL SWEEPSTAKES EXPLAINED

 Manitoba Sweepstakes tickets were selling well, even though the system couldn't be considered to be secure. The lottery featured three draws per year. The Spring Draw was based on the Brier, the Curling Championship of Canada. The Summer Draw winners were announced at the Manitoba Derby and the Fall Draw winners were announced at the Grey Cup. The formats of the three events were similar; the prizes ranged from $100 to $100,000.

To illustrate the Curling draw, 10 lottery entrants were drawn from among the $2.50 entries. Each participant chosen was then matched with a provincial rink in the bonspiel. The winner's prizes corresponded to the final placement of the rinks in the tournament. The lottery player who was matched with the winning rink would win $100,000, a considerable amount at that time. The other nine finalists won substantial prizes and 2,000 other prizewinners collected small amounts. Today's percentage devoted to prizes is in the range of 45% to 60% but the Manitoba Sweepstakes prize-pot was around 17% and the highest it ever got was 23%. Today, such a percentage would be called a rip-off. Neither the public nor the press asked any penetrating questions. Naivety reigned. But it was fun time for all.

Ticket distribution was a ramshackle affair. Thousands of booklets, each containing 12 tickets, were issued to any organization qualified as a selling agency. In turn, the selling agencies issued lottery booklets to anybody who promised to sell them. No formal marketing system was adopted; most tickets were sold by individuals to individuals. Once a seller found a willing buyer, the name, address and phone number were to be filled in on the attached stub, not once but twice.

Any *sold* booklet, that contained the names of buyers, was to be returned to the Sweepstakes office accompanied with a $15.00 payment i.e. the $30.00 face amount of the tickets less a commission of $5.00 (the value of 2 tickets) for the seller and $10.00 commission for the distributor.

THE AGE OF INNOCENCE

When the money and the tickets were turned into the lottery office, the system worked as planned. Eagle-eyed auditors watched every dollar that came in. Yet they didn't feel responsible for tickets that may have been sold but where the seller kept the money and threw the ticket stubs away. The auditors would quibble with complaints by your critical scribe. They'd counter my accusation by re-explaining the "security system," which consisted of the lottery mailing the self-addressed ticket stub back to the buyer as a confirmation within 21 days. Unfortunately, many players didn't know this or forgot about it. Crooks mailed the stubs back to the buyer themselves thereby "certifying" that the buyer's ticket was entered in the draw. The government only cared about money received. Unsold booklets were to be returned after the draw but... if the distributing club hadn't kept them ... well... no problem. Just sign here attesting the lost booklets.

Today, it would occur to any cynical mind that such a scheme was ready to be ripped off by unscrupulous sellers. And it was. It was an age of innocence and expecting the best of people. Part of the problem was that before 1970, lotteries were forbidden in Canada and there was no public concept what constituted a secure lottery program.

Meanwhile, my work in government-sponsored immigration was changing. The Schreyer government decided that immigration to fill specific jobs should end. The NDP subscribed to the policy that if business needed qualified tradesmen such as tool and die makers, the industry should train them, rather than bring in qualified people from abroad.

It was an ideal that invited failure. There was no government-sponsored program to train specific trades. Apprentices had to learn on the job, bad habits included. The sad experience with any apprentice program is that when well-trained-apprentices are ready for prime time, employers in locations — with better climates and salaries — hire them away at higher pay.

My employment at Industry and Commerce was not at risk. The upside of the change in policy was that I would spend many more nights at home with the family instead of extensive travel in Europe for weeks on end. As a substitute for importing skilled workers, I was asked to determine the interest of the Manitoba steel-fabricating industry to commit to a European-type apprentice system. After six months of convincing and gaining the industry's commitment, I managed to get an agreement between the trade association and the commerce department to launch a pilot-project of apprentice training. It was lauded as one of the first cooperative apprentice systems in Western Canada.

The appreciative industry group organized a dinner to thank Industry Minister Sidney Spivak for creating this new opportunity. The minister was pleased and reflected all the thanks back to me. It was an achievement of sorts but the work didn't excite me. The idea of creating a lottery for sport had become far more interesting.

SPORT AND LOTTERY AS A CAREER

The Manitoba Sports Federation (MSF) was looking forward to the end of the 1970 Centennial Sweepstakes, in the hope that the MSF would then be licensed to conduct SPORTS TOTO. The Centennial Sweepstakes had been so popular that the Schreyer government decided to make it a permanent operation. (Surprise!) A Crown Corporation named the Manitoba Lottery Commission was created to keep the sweepstake-style lottery going.

Government had no intention to license the SPORTS TOTO to be a second provincial lottery. However, in the federal Omnibus legislation of 1969, another level of government, municipalities, was empowered to license lotteries. Vaughn Baird, volunteer legal-beagle, mentor and friend, found a way. As a lawyer he provided legal counsel to the City of Transcona, a suburb of Winnipeg. He convinced its City Council to license SPORTS TOTO.

It would be a license for only one weekend, followed by a second license for the following weekend and so on for the rest of the year. Al Mackling, the Manitoba Attorney General, in his wisdom (and his appreciation for sport) couldn't let the apparent bending of the law go unnoticed. A new government branch was created to license lotteries. Its Chairman was Charles Bachman, an optometrist and father of two members of the Bachman-Turner Overdrive rock band. Quietly, the board issued a license for SPORTS TOTO for a year, starting in October 1971. The fee amounted to $10, a sum which I paid, on the spot, from my own pocket.

 The lottery license caused a major change to the serene administration of the MSF. Someone dedicated full-time was required. After a brief search, **Brian Horton**, my protégé in water polo, was hired as the first Executive Director of the Manitoba Sports Federation. Brian had a Bachelor of Physical Education degree from the University of Manitoba and a Master of Sciences from the Pennsylvania State University. A small office was established in Winnipeg at 520 Hargrave to house the administration. Barb Smith, a colleague of your lottery scribe at the Department of Industry and Commerce quit her job there and looked after the MSF office chores.

Having learned so much about lotteries for the benefit of sport, I wanted to be part of that development in the province. I had made a stupid move once before in my career when I started (and went broke in) the car-battery business. Now I was thinking again about a leap in the dark. Worrying about feeding four school-aged children and a mortgage on our home didn't help in the decision.

20

Moreover, this perilous job was to introduce a Toto game in a land that had little or no history of lotteries and was still quite puritanical about the "sin of gambling." My Wife Ina and I talked about the great risk. She said that our move to Canada had also been a risk. She supported the move but I suspect with fingers crossed. It would not have been possible for your apprehensive scribe to take this blind leap without Ina's solid backing.

In fall of 1971, Vaughan Baird spoke to the MSF board of directors to set-up a fund to guarantee my salary for a year. It was set at $20,000, slightly more than what I was paid at my government job but there were no provisions for a pension or medical insurance. After nearly a four-decade career in the field of lotteries, the move could come to be seen as a brilliant decision but it could also have become a reckless plunge that would cause heartache and pain for my family. What had I done?

A SOMBRE INTRODUCTION OF SPORT TOTO

October of 1971, At the Recreation Centre in Gimli, the heads of the sport-governing bodies were assembled to celebrate the launch of the first sports toto lottery in North America. By Saturday afternoon, the meeting abruptly ended when the federal government proclaimed the War Measures Act. Quebec's High Commissioner of the United Kingdom, James Cross, had been abducted. All civil liberties were suspended.

The conference attendees clustered around the TV set. On Sunday, the news got worse. Quebec cabinet minister, Pierre Laporte, had been found murdered in the trunk of his car. The FLQ admitted to the crime. The next few days, Winnipeg Tribune sports pages published a series of friendly, informative articles about the launch of the SPORTS TOTO avoiding any mention of how the tragedy had affected the tone of the launch.

MSF OFFICE

The newly-rented MSF office on Hargrave Street, was now too small to handle the sports issues and the lottery. A bigger office was found on the second floor of the Pickles Tent and Awnings building on Ellice Avenue, one floor-up from the offices of the Liberal Party of Manitoba, whose Leader was the prominent entrepreneur Izzy Asper. His executive assistant was Peter Liba, a journalist who, 25 years later, became the 22nd Lieutenant Governor of Manitoba. I'm dropping names here. Despite the proximity of that political heft and frequent chats over coffee, it didn't help the Sports Federation at all.

THE LOTTERY BUSINESS

The job as a paid-president of the Manitoba Sports Federation was challenging with an uncertain future. Being out there on my own, leading a very precarious parade was daunting. The MSF board believed in your fearful scribe so strongly that whatever I suggested was accepted. I would have felt safer if I had been challenged more strenuously.

I feared that the sports journalists who had supported my efforts thus far would turn antagonistic. After all, I wasn't a noble volunteer anymore but a crass, paid fund-raiser. Gnawing away at me was an anxiety that there was no real public appetite for another lottery in addition to the Sweepstakes. Worse, public opinion might turn against an expansion in gambling.

To gain public support I staged a dinner for the top Manitoba business leaders and the sports-reporting fraternity. The turn-out of 120 honchos who came to listen to our pitch was most satisfying. The MSF was in there fighting for its survival. My walk-about speech, meandering through the audience was rehearsed over and over again until I could deliver the 25-minute sermon without notes.

My tale took place in the future, where the Montreal Olympics had just been completed to the world's applause. (This was four years before the Montreal Olympics) The facilities were superb, the organization flawless but Canada had not won a single gold medal (miraculous foresight since it turned out that way). As I hit the emotional tones, the tension in the room rose. I knew I was connecting with the audience. I asked for their endorsement to let sport help itself, through SPORTS TOTO. The MSF could create more trained athletes through funding of coaches leading to improved competition. That funding would not come just from government largesse but from profits of the lottery. When I finished, there was silence. It seemed to last for minutes. Then the audience stood and cheered. I felt exhilarated. The audience played a pretend-game of SPORTS TOTO by paying a quarter for each play. The winner got the whole pot. A crusty veteran of the press collected his $75.00. After that came the plea for support to launch SPORTS TOTO.

"Give us some seed money so we can get off the ground" was the pitch, "Do it now, this evening." The heads of big companies tossed in cheques of $500 to $1,000. What surprised me was that the group of sports reporters led by **Don Wittman** of CBC huddled together and contributed $200 — this at a time when you could get a superb dinner at a fine hotel for $8. We netted about $15,000 that evening. Later, the Government of Canada added a grant of $25,000. Off and running!

EARLY DISILLUSIONMENT

Participation in TOTO was lower than expected. In fact, it was terrible, despite free publicity by supportive media. Don Wittman, in particular, had been most helpful in giving his predictions on Friday evening's sports telecast and then showing results on Sunday in the same format as the TOTO entry form. It was so much different than the familiar sweepstakes.

Now there were competing lotteries. The familiar format of the Sweepstakes vs. this new Sports Toto game, where one had to think and consider game standings before entering a set of predictions. On the down side, the market for a lottery based on hockey was many times smaller than a familiar passive lottery game. There were far fewer people with knowledge of hockey than those who understood the concept of Sweepstakes. Whatever market existed for a hockey lottery was supported by the media but it wasn't enough.

IAN HOWARD AND SPORT CANADA

In the '70s, my friend and sometime lottery competitor came into the picture. **Ian Howard**, a true-red Liberal supporter had worked in Ottawa in the "high echelons of the Liberal government." By which he meant he worked in the office of Prime Minister Pierre Elliot Trudeau where he mingled with powerful people.

23

Over the years, most of the traits and tricks of these political operators had rubbed off on Ian. In 1972, when we first met, he had just been appointed as

 the BC representative for Ottawa's Amateur Sport Directorate. In that capacity he introduced me to **Ted Semmens** of the BC Ministry of the Provincial Secretary, a department responsible for sport. Ian sprung for a ticket on the float plane from Vancouver to Victoria. When we got to the Legislature, Ted Semmens and his crew were clueless about lotteries. Perhaps they didn't want to talk about it because BC was in the throes of an election. They offered coffee and listened politely. That was it.

Ian was very interested in the workings of our SPORTS TOTO, although now, after so many years, I suspect that he wasn't so much interested in promoting the lottery (which he was) as learning what the MSF was up to and feed that information up and down the federal tube.

MEETING THE HONORABLE JOHN MUNRO

 Another early supporter for SPORTS TOTO was Earl Dawson, a colleague of Ian Howard, whose territory for federal interest in sport encompassed the Prairies. He arranged to meet the Minister, **the Hon. John Munro** in his Ottawa office. The Minister appeared quite curious about this new sports-funding method and offered me a return ticket and hotel accommodation.

Once in the Minister's office Ian Howard appeared again. He and Earl Dawson were present at my explanation of the SPORTS TOTO game and how it would fund the sports organizations.

Minister Munro was persuaded to play a mini-Toto game. He pretended to be interested and asked how it worked in Europe. He was non-committal about any support by the federal government. The government photographer, slinking in the background, took some pictures of Munro filling out a SPORTS TOTO selection slip. His understanding of the game became evident minutes after I left the room. Ian Howard later told me that the Minister clasped his arms above his head, leaned back and exclaimed, "What the f*ck was that all about."

As a memento of the meeting, the photographs arrived in my mailbox with a nice note from Munro. Who could have foreseen that the photo would 10 years later (January 26, 1983) be filed in Superior Court as an exhibit in the case of Loto Quebec versus the federal government on the subject of whether the game of SPORTS TOTO was a lottery or a game of skill. Quebec won!

UNEVEN COMPETITION CREATES HAVOC

Looking back, the 1971/1972 hockey season was the worst time to launch a lottery involving NHL games. Earlier, the National Hockey League had expanded — practically overnight — by doubling its teams from six to 12. The new teams were poorly stocked with players thereby making a mockery of the desired parity between the OLD and NEW SIX.

In Winnipeg, interest in hockey was at a peak. The new World Hockey Association had signed the great **Bobby Hull.** Two professional hockey leagues provided an abundance of games to include in the SPORTS TOTO schedule.

Even under ideal circumstances, it would have been difficult for SPORTS TOTO to be successful but the NHL expansion that created six weak teams to compete with six well established teams proved to be a killer. When an "old" NHL team played an expansion team, the outcome was a near-foregone conclusion thereby impacting the odds. There were too many winners! On the other hand, when an expansion teams beat the "old" teams, the number of winners was so small as to cause player discontent.

The second problem was the World Hockey Association games —they played overtime in the event of tie, making predictions much easier. Obviously, predicting one out two possibilities is a great deal easier than one out of three. That obstacle was overcome by informing SPORTS TOTO players that results were considered final at the end of the regulation time. This angered the bettors, not only because it was counter to the rule of hockey but the media only reported the final score. Confusion and disappointment ensued.

Few expansion teams beat the "Original Six." In weeks when the experienced teams won, there were many winners each cashing only a few dollars. One week, 90% of the bettors had more than 10 games correct. The jackpot share was a miserly two dollars. The players didn't understand the impact of the uneven team-strengths and many soured on the SPORTS TOTO.

SPORTS TOTO - BUSTED

Because the first games on the entry form started at seven o'clock (CST) on Saturday evening, all predictions had to be in the possession of the MSF before that time. That was relatively easy for Winnipeg players but participants from rural areas had to use the mail. In the initial weeks, a substantial number of predictions missed the deadline. The MSF board, inexperienced in security pitfalls, insisted that if the postmark on the envelope showed that the envelope had been posted before the cut-off time, the entry should be accepted. I deemed it a mistake but didn't object to the ruling.

Trust and naïveté are dangerous traits in conducting games of chance. In the sixth week of the 1971/1972 season the schedule of games was a good mix of old and new-team games. Because the outcomes were difficult to predict, the expectation was that there would be few, if any winners. However, one postal entry bearing the postmark of the Thursday before the games had all 12 predictions correct. There were no other winners of 12, 11 or 10 correct. Freddie G, a local Winnipeg character, was the sole winner of the prize pot for 12 games correct. Upon our request, the Post Office investigated the possibility of fraud. The security chief at Canada Post — after a lecture on the hazards of failing to consult the Post Office prior to getting into the lottery business — illustrated how Freddie G. had achieved his "magic" trick.

This is the theory how it was done: On Thursday before the NHL weekend, the perpetrator had addressed an envelope in very faint pencil to his home address. Normally that envelope would be delivered Friday or Saturday morning. He didn't enclose anything nor even bother to seal it. His objective was to get an envelope with a postmark dated before the Saturday. On Sunday evening when the results were known, he filled-in the entry form with the correct outcomes. He took the envelope, erased the pencilled information and wrote the address of the MSF office, enclosing his prediction and the required fees. Early Monday morning, at about the same time that the postman duly delivered the genuine entries, he dropped his fraudulent entry in the mail slot at the lottery office.

The police weren't interested in laying charges. After deliberations of how to proceed, the MSF announced that in future, for "reasons of security," all entries had to be under lock and key before the start of the first game. Late mail would no longer be accepted. The lead story on all local media was the failing security of the SPORTS TOTO. The sports reporter's fraternity angered by Freddy's fraud took care of him. We released the name and address of Freddie G as a winner and subsequent sports reports —tongue in cheek — featured Freddy G. as the greatest hockey pundit ever, leaving Freddie to explain his amazing skill of prognosis.

We'd been snookered. Your distressed scribe vowed that from now on he would think like a crook and think of the ways fraud artists might try to cheat. The upside was that I had committed that blunder so early in my lottery career. In future years I would vigorously apply the lesson learned.

A NEAR-DEATH PROMOTION

Despite increased promotion by your lottery scribe, SPORTS TOTO sales were disappointing, so low in fact that expenses, salaries and rent were barely covered. Unless sales picked up, even the financial grants from Ottawa and the Winnipeg Foundation would be lost in running the lottery.

By November of 1971, it was clear that SPORTS TOTO needed to either boost participation or fold. Due to the lack of big winners, the game wasn't getting any headlines. As a last-ditch effort, the board approved my promotion that promised a big prize that was "nearly" impossible to win.

In regular SPORTS TOTO play one must predict a win, loss or tie for a dozen hockey games. There are more than a half-million possible outcomes. Of course, if the games are predictable and there is an absence of tied games, there are fewer than 8,000 possible outcomes. Add to this that many possibilities are eliminated because strong teams play weak ones and the SPORTS TOTO game becomes ridiculously easy to predict.

To raise interest, a promotion was planned that if a player predicted 12 correct outcomes in *two* successive weeks the prize would be a guaranteed

$100,000 to be shared by those who had all 24 predictions correct. People were sure to flock to the game, wouldn't they? To protect the possibility of losing $100,000, two weeks were selected where the teams were more or less evenly matched. The board, looking at the mathematical odds of 250 million to one, gave a nervous go ahead even though there was no $100,000 in the kitty to pay a winner. There was a desperate need to break into the headlines. SPORTS TOTO needed to compete with the Manitoba Government's Sweepstakes!

The hare-brained scheme, based on nearly impossible odds, was hatched by your loony scribe. Actuarially, there was an infinitesimal chance that someone could win this promotion. It was statistically close to impossible, but unfortunately not totally impossible.

Sales were good and sports reporters were talking it up. The first week was a bad omen. As a result of no upsets there were as many as 10 entries that had all 12 predictions correct. Statistically, there should have been a small possibility of only one winner. However, a commitment was made and if the game was to survive it was impossible to withdraw the promotion.

When the second week's contest began, I took photo copies of the 10 correct entries home. By Saturday evening, there were still three entries left that could win the big prize and Sunday's six games were yet to come.

Five of the six Sunday games were played in the Eastern time-zone and by nine o'clock that evening, there was one eligible entry remaining, Montreal at St. Louis in the central time zone. It was the only game between success and disaster. Your cowering scribe had a good chance of being convicted of fraud because there was no money to pay the winner if fate would have it so.

Public humiliation was near. The story of misleading and potentially fraudulent lottery offers would surely be headline news across the land. How could odds, 1 in 250-million, so stacked in favour go against your stupid scribe?

The game that would determine MSF's fate was the St. Louis Blues, a low-placed expansion team, playing the Stanley Cup-champions, the Montreal Canadiens. That game would decide if there was to be a winner of $100,000.

What was needed to save my lottery life was a win for St. Louis. No hockey fan in his right mind would predict that!

Of course, the single remaining entry predicted a win by the powerhouse Canadiens! I took our kitchen radio, attached it a home-made coat-hanger-antenna and found the St. Louis radio station that broadcast the game. In the last period the score was tied! My nerves were on edge. Ina was cowering in the kitchen. My life in the lottery business would be over. I might face jail time. The tremendous odds in favour of my scheme had beaten me!

Unexpectedly, St. Louis scored a fluke go-ahead goal. Five minutes to go! The crowd, anticipating the franchise's first win over the hated Canadiens, went crazy. I didn't go crazy; I was already crazy. Montreal pulled Jacques Plante, their famous goalie! 10-9-8.... seconds. IT WAS OVER! St. Louis won. A last-second reprieve! Your near-insane scribe lived to fight another day!

Ina, sitting at the kitchen with her head buried in her hands, yelled: "If you ever do something so stupid again, I will kill you!"

Twenty-five years later, I was to suffer a similar cliff-hanger. In basketball!

THE LUCKY 1971 GREY CUP

Even though it competed with the Manitoba Sweepstakes, the Sports Federation was also a selling agent for the big lottery. As a promotion, the Sweepstakes offered generous sales incentives in the form of seller's prizes. The seller who sold the winning ticket would get a bonus. Among three million tickets in the draw drum, it would be far-fetched to believe that such a windfall might ever come our way, but there is always hope. The MSF kitty was depleted and — unlikely as it was — such a win might fund my salary for a year!

At the Sweepstakes site, nine names of lottery finalists were drawn from the drum. Each was matched with one of the nine teams in the Canadian Football League. At that time, six teams were still in contention for the Grey Cup. The seller of the ticket that won the jackpot would earn a bonus of $25,000.

One of the tickets the MSF had sold was drawn and then matched with the Toronto Argonauts. It meant that we could be in for a prize, but how much?

The chances of Toronto winning a spot in the final was one-in-four. But luckily, Toronto won the Eastern Final. Now, the MSF was guaranteed to be in the money because even the losing team would win $10,000 for the ticket seller. At the 1971 Grey Cup, the Calgary Stampeders were ahead of Toronto until late in the fourth quarter when an interception put Toronto in front. At home in Winnipeg, the Simonis family was doing what no respectable Westerner would ever do under any circumstances — they were rooting for Toronto. Ina voiced her prediction that this lottery business would surely lead to an early death for her husband. The last minutes of the game were torture as Calgary threatened to win the game. But at the whistle, Toronto was still ahead and the MSF was the winner of the seller's prize of $25,000. My job, wobbly as it was, was safe for another year. And that was all it was going to be: one year.

JANUARY 1972: A FREE PRESS STORY

The first working day of 1972 began with a long article in *The Free Press* by **Kent Gilchrist**. With the MSF in such dire circumstances, your jittery scribe feared the worst.

The Free Press had learned that the Liberal Party's hatchet man for sport, Earl Dawson, was spreading rumours that Guy Simonis personally owned the SPORTS TOTO franchise and was siphoning off money for his own benefit.

The story raised the issue of my salary of $20,000, a similar amount to what I earned at the Manitoba Department of Industry and Commerce. What motivated Dawson to start the rumor, besides having a derisively sarcastic personality, was that he had found the federal copyright of the word SPORTS TOTO. The process of copyright requires an author and a beneficiary. My name appeared as the author of the name SPORTS TOTO but the profits belonged to the MSF. I immediately mailed out a photo-copy of the copyright document to all sports reporters. The story boomeranged on Earl Dawson. His person as a trustworthy federal liaison for sport was questioned by the sports media.

In the end Kent Gilchrist's story had its desired effect. The "in" group of Winnipeg's sports fraternity felt reassured that everything was fine. Kent didn't dwell on the fact that despite all the free publicity, the game was not catching on and MSF was living hand-to mouth.

Talking about that story many years later, Maurice Smith, the sports editor, explained that the aim was to assure the Winnipeg sports fraternity that the MSF was above board.

INTERNATIONAL CONTACTS AT MUNICH OLYMPICS

Internationally, our baby steps in SPORTS TOTO were unknown. Through Paul Lut, my old water polo friend and managing director of the Dutch Sport-Toto, I was invited to represent "Canada" at the **INTERTOTO** Annual Conference, the umbrella of TOTO organizations in the world. The meeting coincided with the 1972 Olympics.

The INTERTOTO members were pleased with the first inkling of interest in TOTO from North America. INTERTOTO had been formed in 1947 as an association of TOTO organizations to exchange information. Since each of the participating countries sold the TOTO as a monopoly within their own borders, there was no fear of divulging trade secrets or failures. Instead there was an open, unguarded exchange of experiences. For your curious scribe, it was an eye opener.

The generous invitation to attend INTERTOTO included free hotel, meals and local transportation. Now, the only requirement for your free-loading scribe was to pay for transportation to Munich. However, no matter how beneficial the results of the conference might turn-out to be, there was no travel money in the MSF kitty. Unexpectedly, John Munro, the federal Minister of Amateur Sport, offered to provide a free ride on a military aircraft from CFB Trenton to the Canadian air base in Lahr Germany — from there a four-hour bus ride to Munich.

Now the final hurdle was a ride from Winnipeg to Trenton, Ontario. **Phil Reimer** — later CBC's weatherman in Vancouver — was the PR person for TRANSAIR, a small Winnipeg-based airline with daily flights to Toronto. Phil immediately jumped to the rescue and issued a free pass to and from Toronto. The goodwill of so many supporters made it possible to attend this international gathering.

After a 22-hour journey from Winnipeg to the Anabel Hotel in Munich, the lone delegate from Canada was welcomed by a 28-year-old assistant to the General Secretary of INTERTOTO, Yvonne Schnyder. She immediately introduced me to President Lothar Lammers. His opening comment was that if one wanted to know anything about the business, he should consult "he-himself," Lothar

Lammers, because — as he confessed — he was the father of the world's LOTTO and TOTO games. "LOTTO will out-earn TOTO," he said, garnering pitying headshakes from his soccer-minded European colleagues within earshot.

It was stimulating to be among people who made these sports lotteries work so successfully. Even though I was a novice at this gathering, I was asked to address the session. I related the Canadian situation, our hope for success and also our failures. The thought of failure had, of course, never entered the minds of the audience. They were all operating in a soccer-mad world and they were convinced that in Canada, ice hockey would be just as successful.

The ambience of the conference had a whiff of old European class structure. The attendees were all chief executives whose employees treated them as minor nobility. Even the chiefs of the attending communist countries considered themselves to be someone of rank — certainly way above the workers. The amazing thing for me was that the old-world traditions still prevailed. All lottery directors had brought expensive gifts for the host director. A table was set aside where a stack of cardboard corporate name-tags were piled in a heap. They were the sort of stand-up engraved-printed name tags that one would find at an ambassadorial dinner. The gift-giving was to commence promptly at 16.00 hours (4.00 p.m.). As each director came forward with his gift (there were no women directors), it was placed on the table. Then, an attendant grabbed the appropriate name card and placed it with the gift. There were gifts of porcelain and crystal as well as clocks and beautiful tapestry.

Your nervous scribe saw the stack of remaining name cards getting smaller and smaller. I knew that at the end there was going to be a card for Canada but there would be no gift. **Yvonne Schnyder**, the Secretary General knew that there was no Canadian gift and, in a deft motion, she swiped the Canada card from the table and stuck it in my pocket.

The host director, an amiable Bavarian stood and smiled as the gifts piled up. He was probably tallying the value against what he was spending, because in those days the host organization paid all the bills including tickets for the Olympic events for everyone, spouses included.

The opening dinner was formal — women in gowns, men in dark suits. My light-coloured summer jacket stood out as a shiny memorial to North American bad taste. There was no hiding — four more such dinners were yet to come.

Numbingly boring and uncomfortable, the Munich dinners were devoid of any entertainment and accursed with long speeches. Those evenings were a punishment no one really deserved, but they were graciously accepted as the price of being considered an important official.

I confess, not all the dinners were that boring. One was a version of Oktoberfest, hosted under a huge canopy. An oompah band, tables full of beer steins, swaying patrons singing centuries-old drinking songs, waiters dressed in lederhosen; it was a blast. Still, my summer jacket stood out like a sore thumb.

The first bus ride of the Munich meeting proved to me that the old-world class-structure still pervaded. The executive committee members and spouses as well as INTERTOTO staff (one!) travelled in a separate luxury bus. Even though the entire assembly was small by today's standards, this special bus bore a huge sign "DIREKTORAT" to highlight that the passengers were people of standing! No others were allowed to ride with them.

The first business session was about game design, prize distribution, security, advertising and a lot of lottery politics. My naiveté in wanting to know everything must have been a pain for the conference. Your garish-but-lonely scribe was the first attendee from another continent. (It would be another 25 years before INTERTOTO would be led by someone from outside of Europe. As fate would have it, that person was ... wait for it... your lottery scribe.

München 1972 Attending the evening Olympic competitions was a nice perk. The Opening Ceremonies were impressive; several of the track events were world-record breaking and I even got the chance to see some old team mates of the Canadian water polo team at their practice. I was pleased that I was remembered and the recognition that it was my initiative that had gained Canadian water polo the necessary funding to attend its first Olympics.

Because of commitments for the military aircraft's return to Canada, I had to leave as soon as the conference was finished, although there was a whole week of Olympic activities yet to come. Boarding the bus for the RCAF airbase in

Lahr, it seemed that armed security was everywhere. Camouflage-clad German soldiers, machine guns at the ready made it look like World War II again. As we took off for Canada, the Canadian Air Force pilot announced that several Israeli athletes had been abducted from the athlete's village.

A lot more about this tragedy was learned when we arrived back home. Eleven Israeli Olympic team members had been taken hostage and eventually killed by the Palestinian terrorist group "Black September." The hostage-takers' demand was that 234 prisoners held in Israeli jails be released. Police officers killed five of the eight "Black September" members; three were captured and later traded for the passengers of a hijacked Lufthansa aircraft. Eventually Israel's Mossad tracked and killed the other three hijackers.

QUEBEC LAUNCHES PERFECTA

Although games of chance in Manitoba were limited to our TOTO and the thrice-a-year Manitoba Sweepstakes, Loto Quebec (still the only other lottery operation in Canada) was enjoying success with their three stalwart lottery games: the Mini, the Inter and the Super.

On August 10, 1971, Loto Quebec launched a new lottery game called **Loto Perfecta**, a title familiar to horse-racing fans. Before the start of the race, each of 10 horses in the race was adorned, randomly, with a number from 1 through 10.

Before the horses were numbered, the Perfecta player was to fill in a prediction slip and mark his choice of the first four finishers in the exact order of the finish. The chance of having the four winners in exact order of their finish was small compared to today's lotto. In reality, the horses were just replacing the role of a draw machine that was used in Loto Quebec's three other games.

The storm of publicity for this new game almost surpassed the launch of the Mini lottery in 1970. The Friday-night TV broadcast of the race was so popular that it continued for three years, but sales of the Perfecta didn't match the publicity. Players very soon realized that this was just another lottery and not a bet on horses. Fans of horse-betting fled.

The importance of Perfecta introduction was that in order to register the prediction slips, a computer system was required. A validator machine was placed on the retailer's counter to register the bets. Later in the day, the central system would electronically assemble the accumulated bets into one account.

The real desire of Loto Quebec was to launch a lotto game based on the great success of those in Europe. Quebec was now advancing into more active games where the player could determine his or her own fate. Manitoba had pioneered the active game of SPORTS TOTO in North America. Quebec officials were cautioned by their legal department that conducting a pari-mutuel game on sports results was illegal under the provisions of the Criminal Code. Yet, here was little Manitoba doing what Quebec's legal people held to be unlawful.

Loto Quebec executive, **Denis Vendry,** a storied lottery pioneer, came to see our simple operation. His main concern was how Manitoba could operate a TOTO game without the Justice Department coming down hard, insisting that pari-mutuel games were illegal. Your innocent scribe informed Denis of the old maxim that is easier to ask for forgiveness than for permission. He left shaking his head, either in wonder or pity.

THE PRINCE AND THE TOTO

It was late August of 1972 when Vaughn Baird called me with good news. He was so excited he stumbled over his words. After successful Manitoba Sports Federation dinners of 1970 and 1971, he had prevailed upon his acquaintances both political and diplomatic, to cause an invitation to be extended to Prince Bernhard of the Netherlands to address the MSF annual dinner. Unlikely as it

seems today, Queen Juliana's husband accepted. Perhaps he acceded because, at home, he was in deep trouble and wanted to rebuild his international status. Because **Prince Bernhard** had accepted kick-backs from Lockheed Aircraft Company for the purchase of fighter planes for the Dutch Air Force, the Dutch Government had banned him from acting as a commercial representative of the Netherlands and/or the House of Orange.

Prince Bernhard combined his desire for rehabilitation with an opportunity to earn some money from the Dutch aircraft industry. The Fokker Aircraft

Company had just launched the Fokker Friendship, a short-haul passenger jet. The Prince agreed to fly the Fokker Friendship to Winnipeg to gain some international exposure. I had learned from my Dutch friends that the Prince was under the impression that the sports dinner was tied-in with the '76 Montreal Olympics. Your sheepish scribe suspected that his acceptance to speak at the MSF dinner also served as part of his efforts to be re-instated as a member of the International Olympic Committee. Never mind, it served our objective. The Prince would get his exposure; the MSF would bask in his reflected celebrity.

At the Winnipeg Airport, reporters, cameramen and photographers were lined up three deep as the Fokker Friendship taxied to the gate. The pilot's window opened, an arm came out and a small flag with the coat of arms of the House of Orange was placed on the tiny mast of the aircraft. The press waited for the doors to open. They did not notice that the pilot putting out the flag was the Prince himself. This gesture was obviously designed to provide a photo-op but none of the photographers realized it.

Vaughn ran to the cluster of photographers, yelling, "The Prince is the pilot." The angle of every camera changed immediately. As the aircraft door opened and Prince Bernhard descended the stairs, the Mayor, aldermen, MLAs, consuls-general and ministers both federal and provincial lined up to greet His Highness. Vaughn and I stood far off to the side, all by ourselves. Vaughn was philosophical. "Let them have the glory," he grinned happily.

The highlight of the Sports Dinner was of course, the Prince's address. A month before, the Dutch Foreign Office had requested a draft of the Prince's address; the call slithered down the diplomatic pipe to Vaughn Baird.

"What do you want him to say?" Vaughn asked me. I thought it would be useful if the Prince explained how the TOTO funded sports in the Netherlands. The subject wasn't the average run-of-the-mill speech for the Foreign Office so — back in The Hague — the officials asked the head of the Dutch Lotto, my old Dutch friend Paul Lut, to draft a speech for the Prince.

Paul Lut phoned me in frustration: "You invited him. You know what you want him to say. You write a draft and send it to me." My draft depicted the Dutch Toto as the financial saviour of Dutch sports development with the added hint that perhaps Canada should emulate the Dutch example. The bureaucrats in Holland appeared to be satisfied with my draft and sent it on to the Palace.

36

At this point, the tale takes a surrealistic turn. The Prince and Queen Juliana were in Gstaad, Switzerland for their annual skiing holiday. The Prince had brought his speech along because he knew one of the regulars in the Gstaad ski community namely, Lothar (Pete) Lammers, the Director of the West German Lottery and a friend of your very fortunate scribe.

One of Bernhard's aides approached Lammers at the Gstaad hotel and asked him to fact-check the speech since it pertained to lotteries. Now the circle was complete. Lammers telexed me a copy of the Prince' speech (faxes were unknown). An alteration was made to my draft. It put the speech about TOTO in the context of the Montréal Olympics rather than sport development in Manitoba. So much the better!

MY DINNER WITH THE PRINCE

All earlier efforts to put SPORTS TOTO in the limelight didn't compare to the publicity that the Prince Bernhard dinner gathered. The head table was groaning under the heavyweights of the Winnipeg elite, the Lt.-Governor (Hon. John McKay), Premier (Ed Schreyer), the Minister for Sport (Larry Desjardins), the Mayor of Winnipeg (Robert Steen) the angels of financial support for community affairs, the owners of Sony Canada (the Cohen brothers).

I don't recall all the obligatory pre-amble speeches. I do remember that Bernhard received a Hudson's Bay blanket-coat as a gift.

The Prince read the script word for word. The audience, amazed that a blueblood would speak words of approval for a lottery, applauded in all the right places.

After dinner, the head table guests were invited to a reception at Government House where Prince Bernhard stayed for the night. The Premier and Larry Desjardins congratulated Vaughn and me on our "catch" of the Prince.

Bernhard was late in joining the reception. The Lt. Governor confided that the Prince was getting an injection for the pain in his back. A while later he walked in, all smiles, his lapel adorned with his trademark red carnation.

When your awestruck scribe (the one on the right with the bought hair) finally got the chance to speak with **Prince Bernhard** I reminded him that in summer of 1953, I had been his Dutch escort on his car-trip from the Allied Airforce Headquarters in Fontainebleau to the walled-off luxurious Paris apartment of Madame Hélène Grinda (a socialite with whom he later had an illegitimate daughter named Alexia). After I blurted out my memories, he looked pleased and convincingly smiled, "Ach, ja... Paris," probably happily remembering his extra-curricular activities! On the other hand, he might not have listened at all and just uttered an inanity.

Doubling down on our tenuous connection, I told him about our meeting at the 1968 Olympics where just before my introduction to him I tore the crotch out of my Olympic uniform trousers. He seemed oblivious to the Paris story but the Mexico pants-ripping made him chuckle.

In Simonis circles, the incident of the torn-pants-crotch is still the most humorous memory of the 1968 Mexico Olympics. The pants of the uniform were made of a clinging nylon and were really uncomfortable in the crotch. The official uniform had been issued just hours before they were required to be worn and there was insufficient time to have them altered. My weird way of walking was somewhat embarrassing but no one seemed to notice. The event was an opportunity for Prince Bernhard to greet Dutch "ex-patriates" now part of other countries' delegations.

The ceremony, seemingly casual, was carefully scripted. Bernhard met the former Dutch water-polo players first and afterwards, we officials were admitted to the enclosure. To get there, one had to step over a small hedge. Bob Dunn, the reporter for the Winnipeg Tribune, had great fun in his next day's sports column relating how — as I stepped over the hedge — the crotch of my Mexico-issued pants split wide open. Luckily, protocol didn't demand that I bow before his Royal Highness. I studiously kept myself from being exposed by carefully avoiding any angle that might provide a glimpse of my underwear.

A week after the Prince's dinner speech, Vaughn and I met with the **Lt. Governor John McKeag** to thank him for putting up our guest of honour. He didn't smile much. Actually, he seemed somewhat upset. He mentioned that at the morning breakfast after the dinner, Bernhard related that he and Prince Philip were heading the World Wildlife Fund and that all the well-known personages of the world were members. He thought John McKeag should be part of that. Apparently, our Vice-Regal agreed too hastily in accepting this honour because it turned out the membership fee was $10,000 per year. Lt.Gov. John was not amused.

The press had been full of pictures and praise of the Prince's address about SPORTS TOTO. The public, sportsmen and government saw the status of the

Sports Federation at an all-time high. The truth was the bank had loaned us substantial funds against no assets and now the account was drained. The payroll couldn't be met and the first salary to be sacrificed should be mine.

It was getting dark when I parked the car behind our home. Through the window I saw the children watching TV and Ina busily preparing supper. I stood for a long time, watching her working away in the realization that we would likely lose our house. I would have no job and would be retreating in shame. The lottery was doomed to go broke.

BUT THEN... OUT OF THE BLUE...

That evening came a call from **Larry Desjardins**, the Manitoba Minister of Sport. He was most complimentary about the organization of the Prince's dinner and said he'd like to talk to me the following week, preferably at his home on Ste. Anne's Road. I feared that the Royal Bank had expressed concerns about its loan to the MSF but it turned out to be a great turn in your scribe's fortunes.

The Desjardins house was situated in St. Vital on a huge lot with a great view of the historic Red River. The setting was a bit intimidating. The Minister put me at ease right away and asked how the MSF was doing. I told him the truth. The Toto game had not caught on. The MSF was broke. The bank was owed in excess of $50,000. Expenses had to be pared and our loan needed to be paid. The stark choice: improve TOTO or close up.

Instead of looking disturbed, he smiled, "They told me you were a straight shooter. If you'd come with a bullshit story that all was well, you'd have been out of here pretty quickly. I know the Sports Federation is in trouble. I know the size of your bank debt. The question is how can the MSF be saved? Competitive sport has always been a part of my life and I don't want to see the sports federation fail." He was an intimidating figure but I liked him instinctively. I had read that one of his fellow cabinet ministers had described him as a "Rabelaisian figure, a person who is marked by gross robust humor, extravagance of caricature and bold naturalism." That was so true.

Desjardins had been quite an athlete in his day. He was a left-handed pitcher and first baseman with St. Paul's College and played semi-professionally in the ManDak (Manitoba/Dakota) Baseball League. In football, Desjardins had played as a two-way tackle with the Winnipeg Blue Bombers and later coached a local junior football team, the Winnipeg Rods. He played hockey for the St. Boniface Juniors and became the president and general manager of the St. Boniface Junior Canadians. He was also a regional scout for the Montreal Canadiens and the Boston Bruins.

During our long afternoon chat he stressed that "Sport cannot get anywhere without government assistance, no matter how hard the struggle." He was silent for a moment and then blurted out, "If you really want to achieve something for sport you should to join my Department of Tourism and Recreation and help achieve the things you have talked about." I responded that while I was interested in the development of sport, my current focus was on obtaining steady financing for it.

"Well, you can't just pour money into sport without an administrative structure to dole out that money effectively. Structure first; money second."

I was tempted to accept his offer but I couldn't just abandon the organization I had created. "What happens to the Manitoba Sports federation and the TOTO if I join your Department," I asked.

"The first thing the MSF should do is get their books in order. The TOTO should perhaps be changed to a lottery format more familiar to the public. You can do that."

It sounded exciting. If I joined the Department I'd be back in government, with a salary and pension and I'd have the government backing to continue the development of sport. I didn't even ask what my rank or pay would be.

Larry (that's what he urged me to call him) had political concerns. "Your joining my Department may not be seen by the MSF as a friendly move," he cautioned. "Your friends and supporters may perceive you as selling out."

The news was received with mixed feelings. Betrayal might have been closer to the prevailing thought. A few board members saw the change as an opportunity for a spokesman within government; others feared a government "take-over" of MSF.

The board decided that Brian Horton would stay on as executive director but several staff members were let go. More volunteers would fill the gap.

Horton was thrilled that Desjardins offered the MSF a license for conducting a small sweepstakes kind of lottery, albeit with the top prize not exceeding $25,000. He seemed even more pleased that he would be the undisputed MSF boss. He and his board accepted the offer to conduct that familiar raffle-style lottery. It ran for a while but when the government of Manitoba began doling out substantial sports grants to MSF members, it disappeared because the MSF became one of the grantees.

A NEW OFFICE. A NEW JOB.

My relationship with the folks of the Recreation Branch was uneasy. As university graduates trained in recreation, they viewed that their responsibility lay in mass-recreational activity. Their workload encompassed practically all aspects of organized leisure time from tap dancing to flower arranging, to skating, to playground T-ball. Their objective was to get "the masses off their asses". Any activity that put a high emphasis on winning and thus creating losers was an anathema to them. The recreation professionals realized that their domain was under siege by the idea of "elite" sport. They were right. Your interloping scribe's directive from the Minister was for a separation between competitive sport and recreational activities.

On my initial walk through the office, it was evident that morale wasn't what it should be. Larry had just taken over and the staff he inherited had laboured under a stern by-the-rule-book Deputy Minister. Behind his back, the staff called the place Terrorism and Procreation.

The mandate of the Department of Tourism, Culture, Parks and Recreation  was an odd mix. Apart from the Recreation Branch, the Tourism section sent out brochures and placed ads about the wonders of Manitoba. The cultural component was under the fierce control of **Mary Liz Bayer** who looked after multicultural activities, as well as museums and the performing arts. The Parks side of the Department included all the provincial parks, campgrounds, wildlife protection, and so on. Sports, and its thousands of participants, occupied a niche in a neglected corner of the Department. To gain a higher profile for competitive sport would be quite a challenge. Minister Desjardins was the enthusiastic supporter of the latter and said he'd get it done.

Involvement in lotteries didn't make the list of my listed functions and I was told not to interfere with issues relating to funding of sport.

If not the lottery... why was I there?

THE SALARY

After the initial walk-through, Larry took me to the personnel administration. He told them the starting salary would be at the entry level of $14,000. That was a startling comedown from $20,000 at the MSF but hey...I had a mortgage and was happy to have a secure job again. Larry looked at me and beamed. I thanked him.

A little later when all the formalities were done, the Director of Administration called me into his office: "Larry was happy that you took the job and he is offering you a raise. Your salary is now $16,500." This was after only 30 minutes on the job. It was much later that I realized that Larry wanted that entry level salary of $14,000 on record if the press or politicians might say that he'd "bought" me away from the MSF. He wanted it to appear as if I had asked for the job at any salary. Larry knew where all this was heading. I was in the dark but a week later I received another raise to $20,000.

In the first few months, I was asked to perform boring tasks like reporting on the number of tourists visiting the province and a screed proposing a ban on motorized boats on the lakes of the pristine northern provincial parks. I was to write the rules governing the new Film Classification Board, an agency that would rule on what was art and what was pornography. I knew what direction that was going when Larry appointed a Catholic priest to be the chair.

 My first connection with sport in Larry's department was when the Winnipeg Blue Bombers came to ask for help in keeping the **World Football League** out of Canada. The newly minted American league had promised to set up a US league that included European and Canadian teams. Larry — a former Winnipeg Blue Bomber — was concerned that such a league would threaten the existence of the Canadian Football League. I was instructed to arrange a meeting at the Legislature with the top Blue Bomber executives, Paul Morton and Earl Lunsford, and listen to what they had to say.

Larry dropped in on the meeting, did his hellos and left the rest to me. I assured the football moguls that the Manitoba government would do what was within its power to protect the Blue Bomber franchise. I had no idea what that protection would be, nor had anyone authorized me to make such promises. Paul and Earl were happy with the government's assurances. In the end the World Football League never made a move to get established in Canada.

On the cultural side, Director Mary-Liz Bayer asked for help in writing a pamphlet about what culture meant to Manitobans. I confessed I didn't really know how to define culture. I had read somewhere that culture was "whatever turns your crank." Ms. Bayer loved it and had posters printed and displayed around the offices within her little fiefdom.

Larry was a bit of a doubter about "Culture." He understood the Winnipeg Ballet, the Manitoba Theatre Centre and the museums, but he was asked to devote government millions to something he couldn't quite grasp. He justified his great interest in sports by stating that if sports turned his crank, then that was culture, too! The cultural fans didn't like that! It was clear Larry was set on giving sport a place in the halls of government that it never had before.

SUPPORT FOR THE MANITOBA SPORTS FEDERATION

Larry's unique way of achieving his goals was by never clearly explaining what the objective was. I guess the strategy was that whatever the positive results were, he could say that's what he'd set out to do! It was hell on those of us who had to grope in the dark for signs of direction. He told me he wanted to have a report on the future financial support for sport in the province. Should it be solely private? Solely government? Or a mix?

Much later, I realized what he wanted: a firmly established non-government entity for the support of sport, funded by government and private sources... and executed under criteria set by government. In other words, he wanted to fund sport but within his guidelines.

The problem was that he created a lot of misdirection designed to have the plan unfold in such a manner that the public, his political colleagues and the sports community virtually had to force it upon him. He was very successful at that strategy.

His plan for my role began to unfold when I was directed to convene a commission of "Friends of Sport" — members of the sports media, schools, universities, professional sports and, as almost an afterthought, the Recreation Branch.

Both Winnipeg newspapers were represented, but **Jack Matheson** of the Tribune resigned early, replaced by Don Wittman of CBC Sports. Jack Matheson believed he was being used to undermine the MSF, whose participation was pointedly excluded. This particular selection of people wasn't overly enamoured of the sports federation that functioned mostly as a lottery. Their thinking was that in sport there should be two separate functions: the money makers and the sports administrators. The debate bade well for the future of sport. Meanwhile though, the Manitoba Sports Federation feared that they would be usurped by a new structure.

Desjardins was intent on finding out what the membership of the MSF wanted, not necessarily what the board of directors thought. Did the MSF wish to be primarily a funding arm (i.e. a lottery organization) or was their priority the improvement of sports activities, such as coach development, multi-sport training etc.?

The Minister invited me to come along to meet with the MSF executive committee, including the now very combative Brian Horton. It was unsettling for me to sit across from the group I had headed just a few months ago. They failed to understand Larry's position that if government was asked to foot the bill, it should have a large say in setting the objectives. No government hands over funds unless it approves the purposes for which it is intended. On the other hand, if the MSF wished to be a lottery organization, they should focus on that and hand over the profits to a separate structure that provided services for sports development.

Rather than participating in a rational discussion, the board took the stance that the MSF was a lamb being led to slaughter by the Machiavellian Desjardins. Soon the MSF would be dead or, at best, irrelevant. The MSF position was that it wanted to be both fundraisers and sport developers and thus government should hand over substantial grants.

Larry hinted that he would poll the various sports associations to see what they wanted. The MSF objected ferociously and maintained that if anyone was asking questions of their members it would be the MSF. They were obviously unsure how their members might react to such a government initiative. To explain the government's position, Larry had me organize a Saturday morning meeting at the Centennial Concert Hall with all the MSF members represented.

The minister chaired the tense meeting. The MSF had done a great job of rallying the troops with the war cry that "this socialist government was going to take over the running of sport in Manitoba." Rather than allowing for an orderly

debate, the new Chairman of the MSF launched a personal attack on your unsuspecting scribe. **Art Werier's** story was that Simonis had wasted MSF's resources. He declared that now, when the Federation was in trouble and I couldn't be the czar of sport within the MSF, I had switched sides in order to achieve my objective of being the supreme power in Manitoba sport.

Brian Horton had gathered some of my anti-government quotes of the past, especially where I condemned the Recreation Department's emphasis on playground activity and the inclusiveness of nearly all recreational activities. He even quoted some nasty things I had said in the past about government.

At one point in my MSF role, I had drafted an irate speech railing against the big umbrella concept of the Recreation Branch. Included in my diatribe was that their concept was so broad and watered down that it even contemplated adding native Indian dancing to their roster of inclusiveness. The draft speech was thrown in the waste basket and was never delivered but now — with the media present — Horton found it beneficial to publicize the screed.

Larry interrupted the tirade, rose and said: "At one point Guy worked for the MSF and was their spokesman and he did it well. Now he works for the government and he is my spokesman. You all know the concept in sport, you play for one team, then you get traded to another team and you do your best for them." The meeting accepted his point, but grudgingly.

In subsequent weeks, a mail poll of MSF members was held and the overwhelming majority of the sports fraternity wanted the MSF to continue to speak for them. Not surprisingly, on the question of government's financial support, they were in favour but the money should not be funnelled through the MSF but directly to them. It was a victory for both sides. Larry assured them again that a small traditional sweepstakes lottery format for the MSF would keep them busy enough to pay the debts and not to worry about sport programs for the time being.

DIRECTOR OF SPORT

In 1973, Manitoba was in an election mode and Larry was anxious to put his plans in place. It wasn't a sure bet that Premier Ed Schreyer would earn a second term for the NDP, nor any certainty that Larry — who had switched sides from Liberal to NDP right after the NDP victory — would win his old Liberal seat in St. Boniface under the socialist banner.

Larry Desjardins was loathed by the Winnipeg political establishment because he had switched to the NDP to support his friend Ed Schreyer whose middle-of-the-road values he shared. Without his switch, the NDP would not have had the seats to form the government. Desjardins was a Liberal through and through and certainly no socialist. He was a man who wanted certain things done and if he could get it done by being his own man within an NDP government, he would do it. He found himself in the unique position of being hated by the Liberals and Conservatives and distrusted by the leftish segment of the governing party, yet he continued to be a dominant force.

While right-wing Manitobans reviled him, he despised what he called the "Red Underwear Socialists" in his own party. While the election campaign was

46

still in progress, Larry dragged me out of the office and took me to a public school in North Kildonan where Premier Schreyer was speaking. Larry told me that he had to go and listen to the Premier's campaign speech. It made me uncomfortable to go in with him. I didn't want to be associated with any political party, not now, not ever. Vaughn Baird, the super Conservative was my friend and I had associated with Izzy Asper the Liberal Leader when we had neighbouring offices but I had no connections whatsoever with the NDP.

Larry told me I should wait in the car.

After a while Desjardins came out and motioned for me to come in. Premier Schreyer stood in the hallway extending his hand and said: "Congratulations on your appointment as the first Director of Sport in the Manitoba Government."

THE NEW TASK: SPORT

The task was clarified. I was to create two separate arms within the Sport Directorate. One, to establish the Sports Directorate with a broad mandate for development of competitive sport. Two, to create an administration centre for sport that would house the full-time executive directors of the respective sports governing bodies.

Almost as a side issue I was asked to talk with sports directors of the four western provinces to discuss a joint lottery for sport where the proceeds would be divided on a pro rata basis of participation.

When my role in lotteries became public, Larry caught a lot of flak from his own NDP that only the elite, healthy and wealthy citizens would be benefiting from lottery revenue. His action to neutralize the critics was immediate. Within days I was directed to approach The United Way of Manitoba to tell them that they could receive one-third of all lottery profits. Sport would get a third and Culture and Recreation would share the rest.

The United Way declined on the grounds that publicizing this generous gift might reduce donations. Their board agreed reluctantly after I suggested that the United Way could use the money to pay for its administrative costs which, in turn, would allow them to claim that *all* donations would go to the good cause with no money spent on administration. I recall the United Way's cynical remarks that the lottery money couldn't possibly cover their office cost and salaries (NOTE: In the first 5-years, the United Way's share of profits exceeded

$30 million; their operating expenses in the same 5-years were in the range of $8 million).

THE SPORTS ADMINISTRATION CENTRE

The Sports Federation and especially Brian Horton, its Executive Director, were pleased with their "new" old-fashioned sweepstakes lottery. They, too, issued books of tickets to anyone who cared to sell them but had no government auditors to check up on them. I was pleased that they were able to repay the money borrowed from the bank. It was a debt of honour for me.

A location for the Administration Centre was found on Cumberland Avenue, across from Central Park. It was now possible to offer tenancy to the sports associations. Due to budget restraints, there was only funding for ten paid executive-directors. The large-membership sports such as track and field and hockey had their own people in place but there had to be some sharing among the others. The easiest group that made sense was synchronized swimming, diving, swimming and water polo. Speed skating, figure skating and skiing had winter in common; soccer and field hockey also agreed to double up. When the Sport Administration Centre opened it had 10 sports offices, a print shop, meeting rooms, phones and office equipment for all. Don Fletcher was hired as the first manager. It all worked out quite well.

(NOTE: At the time of writing this memoir, the provincial government's 2018 lottery grant to the Manitoba Sports Federation's successor, SPORT MANITOBA, exceeds $25 Million.)

A JITTERY TIME

Your assiduous scribe had acquired adversaries in the Manitoba Sports Federation, inspired anxiety in sport-governing bodies, anger in the Recreation ranks and the scorn of the cultural faddists who felt they'd been sidelined.

It was an inopportune time to add more antagonists but it had to be done. Suddenly the subject of the Manitoba Lottery arose. Without any warning, the board of the Manitoba Sweepstakes was formally instructed by lottery Minister Desjardins that Guy Simonis was to be given free access to everything to do with the lottery business.

Up to that point, management and directors of the Manitoba Lottery had viewed your favourite narrator as the brash operator of the SPORTS TOTO, a game that was unique in the wide-world of lotteries in that it lost money. They had heard the bleats of the MSF folks and kind of enjoyed the impending demise of their sole competition in the lottery business. Now that Simonis was suddenly authorized to wade into what they considered their territory, the board and its managers feared for their fiefdom.

Naturally, the Manitoba Lottery officials adopted a defensive mode. The more they could undermine the government's plans for change, the more they could forestall any changes. Afraid to tackle Desjardins politically for fear he would fire them, they argued that Simonis didn't understand lotteries. They pointed at the failure of SPORTS TOTO. They were quite right to do so. If the situation had been reversed, I would have taken the same tack.

 **Ed Teillet**, the Executive Director of the Manitoba Sweepstakes fancied himself "part of the NDP establishment" because his brother Joe was the political aide of another cabinet minister. Ed was convinced that he was the ultimate repository of lottery knowledge. Feeling too secure in his position, he made a colossal mistake in attacking Larry Desjardins publicly, stating that the Minister's uninformed actions would kill the lottery and dry up all funding for those who currently shared in lottery profits.

He highlighted a victim of Larry's "foolhardiness": the St. Paul's Catholic High School, the Minister's alma mater. Teillet's criticism was duly reported in the press. One must know of Larry's lifelong fight to secure government funding support for Catholic schools — one of the most controversial issues in Manitoba's history — to understand his fury. Moreover, Mr. Teillet told the press that "the 'Westcan' Lottery should be killed and interred by a well-known funeral home in St. Boniface owned by Mr. Desjardins."

A few weeks later, an unannounced group of government auditors swooped down on the Sweepstakes office. The Ernst & Young report disclosed serious irregularities like awarding contracts to friends, costly dinners, gifts and expenses; within days, Ed Teillet was... poof... gone! The bonus for your bystanding scribe was that the board members of the Sweepstakes fell in line with the coming changes, albeit it with one reluctant foot still solidly placed in their old camp.

Desjardins was now well on his way to reshape sports funding. He envisaged a cooperative lottery of the four Western provinces. Fortunately, the political lay of the land was just right for such an implausible agreement. In 1973, Alberta had a Conservative government; the other three provinces were governed by NDP administrations. A ratio of three-to-one might be a huge help.

THE LAW, THE LOTTERY AND THE CHURCH

As he became more familiar with operation of the Sweepstakes, Larry was alarmed that the majority of profits were derived contrary to the provisions of the Criminal Code. He now realized that Manitoba lottery tickets were sold beyond the borders of the licensing province. An astounding 75% of Manitoba Sweepstakes sales originated outside the province.

In the Centennial year of 1970, the Manitoba Golden Sweepstakes had begun as a friendly people-selling-to-people operation but the picture wasn't so idyllic anymore. Ticket sales had morphed into a sort of boiler-room operation run by professional administrators who were fronting for various charities. One of these charities was Desjardins' alma mater, St. Paul's High School.

The school itself wasn't involved in handling lotteries. The aggressive entrepreneur acting on the school's behalf was **John Puchniak**, a graduate of St Paul's. There were five or six other "charities" doing the same kind of mass-mailing activities but Puchniak's operation was number one in terms of volume.

As a nice Polish-Catholic boy Puchniak had approached Father Boyle, the administrator of St. Paul's High School and proposed that if the school were to apply to be a distributor of lottery tickets and affirmed that the profits would be used to fund charitable purposes, they would receive profit cheques on a timely basis. "Profits in the range of $100,000 per year," as Father Boyle recalled. The deal was rather vague but what it boiled down to, was that the school shouldn't ask questions about how the business was run, just cash the cheques. The question of whether St. Paul's would get all the money earned in their name or merely a share remained unanswered.

Apart from the breach of the Criminal Code, Larry's concern was about the uncontrolled growth of the lottery. The massive sales beyond the borders of Manitoba would not go unnoticed by western provinces.

50

Father Boyle, of St. Paul's High School, who had heard the whispers of a lottery in Western Canada, summoned the former St. Paul's student, Laurent Desjardins to a meeting at the school.

To this day your mystified scribe doesn't know why Larry took him along to this meeting of Catholic biggies. Perhaps it was what he said: I knew the operation. Looking back, I think he needed me as a scape goat, one of his officials who made these bad things happen.

Father Boyle retraced the humiliations the Catholic school had suffered in the past century. How could the Minister, a former student, now act to take away funding of a Catholic High School? Larry responded that John Puchniak offended the Criminal Code of Canada. Father Boyle didn't buy it and accused the minister of joining anti-Catholic voices.

Desjardins replied, "Are you suggesting that I should condone criminal acts to benefit our schools? I have been fighting all my political life for government's support for Catholic Schools. My efforts are to fund our schools, legally. I will not stand for criminal acts to achieve that goal. There are legal ways to participate in Manitoba's lottery. You should help me to see what can be done about that."

I just sat and listened but I sensed that Father Boyle, while he admitted nothing, had lost the argument.

SUMMONED BY THE PREMIER

When Desjardins sat down with Premier Ed Schreyer to discuss the elimination of unproductive competition in lotteries between provinces, he asked your nervous scribe to attend. He argued that if each of the four Western Provinces ran a separate lottery and raided each other's territory, as Manitoba was now doing, there would be chaos, public criticism, increased expenses and an increase in offenses under the Criminal Code.

The Premier misunderstood Larry's proposal. He thought the idea was to create one huge unitary Western Lottery that would dole out money to applicants throughout Western Canada. He repeatedly returned to the issue how the profits would be distributed.

"A Western Lottery is a formula for internecine squabbles," he said dismissively. Larry pounced on the objection. He presented my idea of a cooperative scheme as a stroke of near-genius. Each province would have its own selling organization, keep its own revenue, pay for its own expenses and only contribute to the common prize pool and the operating expenses. There would be a central office for paying out prizes and some four-province-wide advertising but basically it was a cooperative scheme. "The head office will be based in Manitoba," he added as a bonus.

Schreyer warmed to the idea but countered that Manitoba's lottery profits would be severely reduced if they could only sell in Manitoba. Larry — a close friend of the Premier — told him that such thinking was like a criminal offered a chance to go straight and then complaining that since he couldn't commit crimes anymore, his income would be seriously reduced.

The inscrutable, stone-faced Schreyer just looked at Larry and said: "You can go ahead and try, but I think you won't convince the other provinces. If you do, it'll be a miracle." With this mandate, Larry sent me off on a trek that would result in a multi-billion-dollar enterprise.

TO EUROPE WITH THE DESJARDINS

Larry listened with interest to my stories about lotteries in Europe but he wanted to see these operations for himself. Many of his NDP caucus urged him to focus only on those jurisdictions who matched their social democratic values. Many of the 'Old Guard' couldn't believe that a true social-democratic government would allow lotteries to flourish.

Your travelling scribe was to be his tour guide. Larry, the stingiest minister in the cabinet, insisted on economy travel for him and his delightful wife Mel. Despite government rules that could provide for spouses' travel in business class, he insisted that he would pay for Mel's expenses and travel in economy.

Our first stop was the Sport Toto organization in The Hague, where my old water polo friend Paul Lut answered many of Larry's questions. He particularly liked the concept of club members selling the tickets. "That'll sell well in Cabinet," he grinned. At the lottery office he watched for an hour as the club volunteers brought in their supporter's soccer predictions. "That's excellent" he declared.

From there the trip went to Copenhagen where we visited my friends at the Dansk Tipstjeneste, the national lottery of Denmark. Of course, their story was the same as that in Holland. The Danes were great hosts and their explanations and their flattery about the knowledge of your rookie scribe did a great deal to enhance Desjardins' trust in my efforts.

PREMIER'S SUPPORT

Premier Schreyer had begun to like Larry's initiative of a Western Lottery. At the Western Premiers' conference in 1973, he convinced his colleagues to urge their sport and culture ministers to at least listen to what Desjardins had to say. Since there was no reason to discuss lotteries, the item was scheduled under the heading a "Proposed cooperative effort in sports development," an early indication that the word 'lottery' should be avoided. It had bad connotations in the government and public circles of the day.

It fell to your lottery scribe to send the invitations to the appropriate ministries on behalf of the Province of Manitoba. Surprisingly, the responses came quickly, eagerly, even. It was obvious that Manitoba's lottery raids on their territories had registered quite strongly.

At the formative meeting, Saskatchewan's Minister **Ed Tchorzewski** brought his Director of Recreation Bill Clarke, a former Saskatchewan Roughrider of note and national junior curling champion. BC's Minister Ernie Hall brought his deputy finance minister, Hugh Ferguson. Alberta's Minister Horst Schmidt brought his sports director and a government lawyer, neither of whom was allowed to say anything and were never seen at a lottery meeting again. Horst liked his own counsel best.

While the civil servants talked about the money the lottery could deliver and fantasized about what they could achieve with such riches, the four Minsters enjoyed a private dinner where they decided to explore how such a cooperative interprovincial venture — a structure unknown in Canadian legislative history — would work. The next morning the ministerial meeting resumed with all the civil servants included. Larry explained the four-Minister's agreement that implementation steps towards the creation of a lottery should commence. The other decision was in the realm of sports: a Western Canada Games was to be formed, based on the format of the Olympic Games.

An expert is often jokingly defined as "The only guy in the room who…" At that early 1973 meeting, I was the only person familiar with the national and international lottery scene. Larry, as chairman of the gathering described me as the "expert" and bragged about my "European lottery research" and "experience in the Olympics of '68 and '72" which impressed the provincial ministers sufficiently to designate your sporting scribe as the chairman of the "Implementation Task Force", a title I dreamed-up on the spot. If you think that my coronation to lead the lottery parade was due to my impressive talent, the reality was more likely that Larry wanted to keep the process close to himself. He didn't want the other provinces steering the lottery program in a direction he couldn't control.

To get the most influential civil servant involved on his side, Desjardins suggested that **Bill Clarke**, the ranking civil servant for Saskatchewan, should be in charge of the development of Bill's pet-project, the Western Canada Games. One catch was that the realization of the Western Canada Games was dependent on the availability of funds. In other words, the new lottery had to pay for the Games.

Overcoming the hurdles of creating a Western Canada lottery was so all-consuming that your frenzied scribe was relieved that the job of creating the Western Canada Games had landed in the capable hands of Bill Clarke. It was a sort of mutual assistance. I supported his positions on the Games and he backed my lottery efforts.

The Western ministers perceived (just as premier Schreyer did) that a single administration that ruled lotteries Western Canada-wide, was something none of the provinces wanted. Each desired to control its own province's marketing and retention of the profits.

After fighting small brushfires with those who believed that status would be lost, the ministers agreed to the Manitoba proposal that the Western Canada lottery would be a corporation owned by the four provinces that — together — would "manage and conduct" a lottery as per the provisions of the Criminal Code. The sale of tickets, with some minor exceptions, would be a responsibility for each province. In order to provide a unified public image, all advertising would be conducted by the Western Canada Lottery.

When this structure was presented it was received with enthusiasm by the Ministers. Every one realized that they would gain something new and retain what they had. The next issue to be solved was the enabling legislation in each of the provinces. As it turned out, that next step took some strange twists and lasted longer than expected.

The strong desire by each province to control its own ticket distribution was due to the fact that "lottery" was still a controversial term in Western Canada. Especially in BC, where the socialist-minded NDP old-guard, had to tread carefully to not offend their rank and file. **Ernie Hall,** the BC Lottery Minister presented the lottery as a clubby fundraiser— a fun thing for people who did folksy things with the little earnings from selling raffle tickets. In BC, any hint of a big-time lottery was to be avoided at all costs.

THE OLYMPIC LOTTERY

While the organising of Western Canada Lottery was going on, the Manitoba and Quebec lottery organizations faced an imminent, powerful competitor. In 1970, Montreal's Mayor Jean Drapeau had been awarded the hosting of the 1976 Olympics. A national outcry arose that the Olympics would lose money and that Drapeau would pickpocket the Canadian taxpayer to pay for an immense deficit. After presenting the budget for the Montreal Olympics Drapeau declared, "The Olympics can no more lose money than a man can have a baby." (NOTE: After the Olympics were over, the City of Montreal inherited a debt of $1 billion.)

Among Drapeau's many ways of self-financing the Games was — guess what — a lottery. "A Trans-Canadian Lottery," he called it. Drapeau had taken note of Germany's success in raising funds for the 1972 Games. In Germany, the organizing committee of the 1972 Munich Games had entrusted the conduct of the Olympic lottery to the combined Lotto-Toto organizations of the states (Laender) of the Federal Republic. A similar system was not viable in Canada because only Quebec and Manitoba had provincial lotteries. Hence, COJO (Comité Oganisateur des Jeux Olympiques) asked advice from Loto Quebec on how to handle things if such a nation-wide lottery were approved. Loto Quebec, ever-vigilant to protect its own interests, advised that a $10 lottery, far removed from their 50 cent MINI, the $2.00 INTER or the $5.00 SUPER lotteries, would be the right scheme to try.

Because there was no Canadian province-wide structure to conduct the Olympic Lottery on its behalf, COJO planned to set up its own operation but first it had to await enabling legislation from Ottawa. Prime Minister Pierre Trudeau was no friend of lotteries and let the matter mark time. In the end, to sell tickets, Trudeau told COJO to get permission from each individual province.

All this wrangling in 1972 delayed the Olympic lottery's operation for a year. It wasn't until the 3rd of August 1973 that the Olympic lottery finally received its federal go-ahead — seven months ahead of the incorporation of the Western Canada lottery.

 Julien Coté, the boss of the Olympic lottery, moved quickly to set up marketing offices in Atlantic Canada and Ontario, where no government lottery existed. The Western governments, busily preparing their own lottery saw the nascent Olympic lottery as something temporary and of little impact. It was an "Eastern Thing." Larry Desjardins, on the other hand saw the approaching problem very clearly. If the Olympic lottery established itself in the West, it would constitute a huge rival. He foresaw that the Olympic Lottery would be a hit.

"A lottery that raises money successfully and is popular with the public will not be discontinued," he argued. "Yes," he went on, "There are assurances from Ottawa that the Olympic Lottery will cease operations at the close of the Games in 1976 but there will be huge deficits. Mark my word, that lottery will continue in one form or another. They will not abandon this source of revenue. The political question is: are profits from lotteries a form of taxation for the benefit of the provinces or the federal government?" He further added, "I am of the opinion that the provinces are entitled to the tax revenue from gaming. I know my opinion is not unanimously accepted but I submit that we should not vacate this tax resource without strongly defending our position." The province of Quebec concurred completely with Desjardins' view. The other provinces hadn't yet acted to secure their share of the immense funds the lottery could deliver.

In the early seventies, Larry's strongly-worded assertion was astonishing to some Western finance ministers. "What is that man Desjardins talking about?" a senior BC civil servant asked your lottery scribe. "In BC, we are positioning the Western Canada lottery as a raffle on behalf of charities. This talk about of fields of taxation will irritate the old socialists in our party. The tiny revenue from lotteries for charitable purposes should in no way be portrayed as taxation."

(NOTE: A half a century later, profits from government-gaming in British Columbia now exceed $1billion per year)

Desjardins had a difficult time convincing his Western colleagues that the Olympic Lottery should not be allowed to set up a separate lottery structure within the jurisdiction of Western Canada, but they agreed. The west's position was firm: permission to sell Olympic tickets in the West was denied. The unspoken condition was that when the Western Canada Lottery was fully in operation, discussions to sell COJO's tickets might be re-opened, but for now, the door was closed!

MANITOBA AND THE WESTERN CANADA LOTTERY

It might be useful at this stage to review the state of games of chance in Canada while the Western Canada Lottery was emerging.

On June 28 1973, the Manitoba electorate returned Schreyer's NDP government. The constituents of St Boniface — Desjardins' territory — hadn't forgotten his defection to the NDP. The large majority he had enjoyed in previous elections had evaporated and his Liberal opponent Paul Marion won the seat by one vote (4301 vs 4300).

A judicial recount confirmed the election of Mr. Marion. Desjardins appealed under the Controverted Election Act. Premier Schreyer kept Desjardins in cabinet pending the outcome of the judicial recount.

Despite his weakened political state, Larry carried on with the lottery with the full backing of the NDP caucus. If Schreyer had had dismissed Desjardins, the drive for a Western Canada lottery would surely have collapsed because the position on lotteries of each province was so different. Furthermore, no political personality in the West had as driven a determination to see a Western Canada lottery come to fruition.

SASKATCHEWAN'S EARLY LOTTERY FORAY

Prior to any discussion of a Western Canada Lottery, the Saskatchewan government licensed a lottery to benefit the '71 Canada Winter Games in Saskatoon. Hugh Tate, a well-known mover-and-shaker, motivated a band of volunteers to run a lottery called Lucky Dog. Tickets were a dollar. When the Games were over, profit to the Winter Games was in excess of $300,000.

As in the history of all "temporary" and "one-time-only" lotteries, Hugh Tate felt Lucky Dog should continue after the Games. Saskatchewan's politicians were reluctant to authorize another lottery of any kind. It took a lot of persuading to get a licence approved.

The Saskatchewan Sweepstakes, based on a Saskatchewan horse race was born. As with the Manitoba Sweepstakes, community groups would earn commissions for selling tickets. Despite the Criminal Code provision that sales must be restricted to Saskatchewan, tickets were sold all over Canada and the U.S. Only small associations sold tickets to friends and family. The final result was too little revenue for a lot of hard work.

It wasn't easy going in Saskatchewan. Premier Allan Blakeney held that lotteries were a tax on the poor — a way to sell dreams that couldn't be realized. Despite his government's leanings, **Joe Kanuka**, the President of the Saskatchewan Sports Federation (Sask Sport) sought a license to manage and conduct a lottery and asked for a grant to hire a full-time Executive Director to run the lottery. The request remained unanswered for eight months until finally a meeting was convened with the Deputy Minister for Recreation. Sask Sport was awarded a one-year grant of $24,000 to hire an Executive Director and the use of an office. The Deputy Minister hinted that — in the near future — there would be a Western Canada lottery in Saskatchewan for the benefit of sport and culture. He stressed that it was *definitely not* going to be a government-run lottery.

In spring of 1973, Dick Teece was hired as Sask Sport's Executive Director. His mandate was clear. Joe Kanuka told him, "You can have all the dreams about sport you want but without money you can't do anything. So, concentrate on the lottery and get it going."

The first draw of the "Saskatchewan Sweetstakes" was held on January 3, 1974. By government edict, the Regina Exhibition was to share the lottery market. It was agreed that the Sweetstakes would operate in winter and the Exhibition's "Saskatchewan Sweepstakes" would sell in summer.

The first-year profit of Kanuka's Sweetstakes was $197,443 to be split between sport, culture and recreation. While these two rather small Sweepstakes alternated, the Saskatchewan bureaucracy was in discussions with their Western colleagues to create an interprovincial lottery. The problem of the Saskatchewan negotiators was that Cabinet shuddered at the thought that the electorate might suspect that it was enabling a large lottery. Government involvement in gambling was an abomination to the religious sections of Saskatchewan politics. The old guard socialists equally abhorred games of chance. In the past, the NDP parties in BC and Saskatchewan had taken a very strong stand against legalizing gambling.

In 1969, when Saskatchewan's Tommy Douglas spoke in the House of Commons he said: "If governments in Canada need more revenue, then that revenue ought to be collected from people on the basis of their ability to pay and according to the size of their income. It ought not to be obtained by appealing to the avarice of individuals or holding out hopes to people who have very little chance of improving their lot by buying lottery tickets. This is a complete reversal of the idea of taxation in Canada."

When the idea of a Western Canada lottery was introduced, Premier Allan Blakeney and others in his caucus were opposed to government involvement in gambling. However, given the overall public acceptance of lotteries in Saskatchewan he became convinced and slowly got on board.

In his memoirs **Premier Blakeney** recalls:

"In the 1970s when the western provinces were organizing the Western Canada Lottery, Saskatchewan declined to take part. It was not long before we found that there was a widespread sale of lottery tickets in Saskatchewan by agents acting for the Manitoba Sweepstakes. We felt we had to join in and we did. We declined to do it through any government department or agency."

When Bill No. 122, *an Act respecting Lotteries* was introduced Premier Blakeney expressed sympathy with members of the legislature who were uncomfortable promoting lotteries but his government had decided that the current situation was "as good a compromise as we can get." Blakeney emphasized that Government would not receive any revenue coming from lotteries. The only benefit to government would be indirectly in that organizations would receive funding from the provincial lottery system that otherwise might have been funded by the Treasury.

Sports Minister Tchorzewski added, "In passing this Bill there is an answer for many sports, recreation and cultural and leisure time agencies to secure their continual search for funds to finance improvements in programming."

The government named Sask Sport as a partner in the Western Canada Lottery. In doing so, the government committed an offense under the terms of the Criminal Code. The federal legislation was very clear that only the government of a province could combine with the government of another province. It didn't say that three provincial governments could join in with a sports federation — a distortion that the other provinces deliberately overlooked in order to proceed. However, the anomaly was amended a year or so later when the law of the land caught up with that sleight of hand. By then, the Saskatchewan public had accepted lotteries.

ALBERTA'S TWO CHARITABLE LOTTERIES

In the early '70s, despite opposition from the Bible Belt, Alberta was more open to lotteries than their neighbours. In 1973, when the idea of a Western Canada Lottery was discussed in government circles, Edmonton Klondike Days and Calgary Stampede both ran lotteries to support their respective festivals.

The schemes were similar to the Irish Sweepstakes. The first prize was $100,000. Edmonton's was called the "Canadian Derby" and Calgary dubbed it the "Stampede Futurity Race".

In 1973, with the Edmonton and Calgary lotteries humming along nicely, the shadow of an Olympic Lottery loomed. Alberta's delegates to the Western Lottery were arrogant and demanding. The free-enterprise boosters believed that civil servants couldn't possibly know as much about sales and marketing as

60

they did. Little did they suspect that when their exhibition-lotteries would encounter the Olympic Lottery and a Western Lottery, their sources of revenue would be headed for the scrapyard.

BRITISH COLUMBIA'S LOTTERY NOVICES

There was no significant lottery in BC in 1973. Anglo-Saxon settlers and their descendants were not in favour of gambling. However post-war immigration brought newcomers who were fans of games of chance and didn't condemn such harmless entertainment as raffles and bingo. BC's Provincial Secretary's office issued much-restricted lottery licenses to small charitable organizations. As a result of this sleepy situation, the two BC members named to the Implementation Task Force acted more as students of lotteries than spokesmen. They were caught between the Alberta firebrands and their own timid government.

ALBERTA BALKS

On August 3, a meeting was scheduled for the four Western lottery ministers and the Implementation Task Force. The agenda was dedicated to the progress of the Western Canada lottery. To everyone's stunning surprise, **Horst Schmidt**, Alberta's Minister, was a no-show. His officials were at a loss to explain. At that critical point, one of the four lottery ministers not showing-up for an important meeting was unsettling.

That morning's meeting between Larry Desjardins and the Federal Minister of Sport, John Munro, provided a hint that Alberta's Horst Schmidt was meeting with Jean Chrétien, the federal Finance Minister, to discuss the "future of the Olympic Lottery."

The Olympic Lottery had been a lifesaver for the financial sinkhole caused by Montreal's Olympics. When the Olympic Lottery Act was proclaimed, the Western provinces had stuck a stick in the spokes of the Olympic lottery wheel.

Prime Minister Trudeau had declared that any province that didn't want to sell Olympic tickets shouldn't be forced to. The West's refusal to sell the Olympic Lottery wasn't controversial. Rather, the idea of a lottery to fund "those Quebeckers" had been a real burr in the Western saddle. Bailing out the spend-happy Montreal Organizing Committee wasn't a popular idea either. Alberta, minding its own agenda, began to shy away from the Western position.

The Feds — as always in every provincial/federal controversy — picked on the neediest member of the pack to get their way. Alberta's position was that if Montreal got lottery funds for the Olympics, Edmonton should get funding for the 1978 Commonwealth Games.

In persuading Alberta to allow the Olympic Lottery to be sold in its province, the Feds' first argument was political. Why was a nice Conservative province like Alberta aligning with those three socialist NDP provinces? Secondly, and more importantly, was a vague promise that once the Olympic deficit was covered, Edmonton would get some funding for the 1978 Commonwealth Games.

Hearing the disconcerting news, the Vancouver meeting of the Western lottery ministers was in disarray. Larry, as Chairman and your lottery scribe were delegated to find the Alberta minister. We found him wandering the halls of the Hotel Vancouver, getting ready to participate in the opening ceremonies of the 1973 Canada Games. Larry — almost literally — dragged him into a hastily re-arranged meeting with the Western ministers. Horst looked uncomfortable and admitted that his Cabinet had ordered him to break off discussions about a Western Canada Lottery in order to get a better shot at Federal money for the 1978 Commonwealth Games.

The three NDP ministers told Horst that they would urge their respective premiers to contact Alberta's premier Peter Lougheed to complain about this turnabout. Horst was caught between the proverbial rock and the hard place, his premier being the rock. Nothing of importance was decided at that meeting except to bump the issue up to the Premiers. When it came time for the ministers to attend the opening ceremonies of the Games, the acrimonious atmosphere melted away.

OPENING CEREMONIES

1973 jeux canada games
new westminster · burnaby

The BC television schedule showed that the opening ceremony of the 1973 Canada Games was to be shown "live" at 9 pm Eastern Time, 6 pm Pacific. Television demanded a strict timetable. As part of the official program, limousines carrying the sports minister of each provincial government were to drive into the stadium in the order of the provinces' entry into Confederation and pull up at the VIP seating area at precisely 6:10 pm. Larry and his smiling wife represented Manitoba. The limos were pearly-white, brand-new Oldsmobiles driven by military personnel. Larry invited me to come along to the opening ceremonies; upon arrival at the stadium, I was to slink off into the stands while they headed to the VIP section.

One by one the limos left the Hotel Vancouver in the proper order. When it was Manitoba's turn, the next limousine bore the flag of Saskatchewan. The order of entry in Confederation wasn't known precisely to many but when the Saskatchewan car departed, the next limousine bore the Alberta flag followed by BC's. Sensing a problem, I headed for the army officer in charge of the VIP dispatch, who looked somewhat stricken. He was a large, nervous man whose black moustache kept twitching. It looked for all the world as if a small crow had flown up his nose and the fledgling was trying to get out.

"We are in radio touch with the driver of the Manitoba car," he mumbled under his twitch. "He's from New Brunswick and arrived in Vancouver only yesterday. He was a bit lost but he should be here soon."

When the BC car left and no other limousine was in sight, I decided to hail a cab. I motioned the vehicle to get into the VIP lineup and Larry and Mel hopped in the back. Seated next to the driver, I urged the cabbie to follow the motorcade as closely as possible. The scruffy cab driver needed no such encouragement. The tires shrieked as he closed the gap. I dared him to pass the Alberta limo and get ahead of the Saskatchewan. He grinned a crooked smile. He tried very hard, but at every intersection the motorcycle cop holding back the traffic did his best to force the mad cab driver out of the motorcade.

Larry enjoyed the commotion. Mel Desjardins, Larry's wife was nervous and lit a cigarette. The taxi driver stomped on the brakes so fiercely that the motorcycle cop behind him almost fell off his bike. The cab driver was enraged. "There'll be no goddamn smoking in my cab," he yelled. "Stop it or get out." All that Larry could utter was a prolonged, frustrated sigh: "Jeeezusss!"

Mel, still in shock of possibly being thrown-out of the cab, opened the car window and tossed the burning cigarette at a motorcycle cop, who managed to duck it. Satisfied that his no-smoking ultimatum was obeyed, the cabbie roared off to the stadium where the official cars were directed to enter the oval track leading to the VIP section. At the gate, police stopped the cab that in turn promptly blocked the RCMP car behind him from progressing. The cabbie wanted to be paid! He mumbled something about 21 dollars. All I had was twenties; I gave him two. Larry and Mel snuck out of the car found their seat on the podium without being caught by the camera.

Afterwards, Larry asked how much the fare was. I told him the fare was $21 but that I had given $40. "Well," Larry said. "Twenty-five would have been good enough!" He gave me $25 and told me to claim the $15 as a cab expense instead of my free ride to the stadium. The man was generous with his own money but a tightwad with government expenditures. Then again, it should be noted that it was Larry who okayed my expense account. He was not going to be on record as having given a cabby a 90% tip. Larry counted every public dollar to the last penny. Always. About everything. Even at the risk of looking silly.

The opening ceremonies went off fine and upon return to the hotel, the Manitoba limo stood in perfect formation. The driver gazed intensely at the steering wheel as the Minister and Mel got into the car. Larry, to his credit complimented the driver on finding his place in the motorcade. No dressing down or criticism. He was a rough and tumble politician but a gentle man.

WESTERN LOTTERY ALIVE AGAIN

Back in Alberta, lottery politics were aboil. The movers and shakers of the Calgary Stampede and the Edmonton Klondike Days were constantly knocking at Alberta's Cabinet door. Lottery Minister Horst Schmidt "had alienated the Western provinces by permitting the sale of Olympic lottery tickets," they claimed. "Alberta can't join the Western Canada Lottery," others shouted.

The managers of Alberta's exhibition lotteries feared that an Olympic Lottery would swamp their games. Their two annual lotteries with a $100,000 prize brought them more than a combined million dollars in net revenue. Given the choice of a partnership in the Western Lottery and nothing but trouble from a competing Olympic Lottery, they knew what was best for them.

Historically, the Edmonton and Calgary exhibitions were led by the Who's Who in their respective cities. Powerful business people who can demand that a minister of the provincial government should listen-up and listen closely! The wheeler-dealers conceded that the Alberta Commonwealth Games should benefit from any money that the Olympic Lottery might toss their way but they wanted a Western Canada lottery for their cherished exhibitions.

64

The Alberta Cabinet chose the best of both worlds. The Olympic Lottery was authorized to sell tickets in Alberta and the province agreed to participate in the Western Lottery through an organization jointly operated by the Calgary Stampede, the Edmonton Klondike Days *and* the organizing committee of the 1978 Commonwealth Games.

The three NDP provinces that were still holding the Olympic lottery at bay weren't overly happy with Alberta's participation in the Olympic lottery but Alberta's involvement in the Western lottery was of vital importance. In the end everything was settled to everyone's satisfaction more or less. Alberta was back in the Western corral. The Implementation Task Force could resume its efforts towards a cooperative lottery.

FIRST OLYMPIC LOTTERY DRAW

April 14, 1974. At lottery parties in homes all across Canada, folks crossed their fingers and held their $10 tickets tight. The 90-minute lottery program, shown live on CBC Television was titled *Mission Million...Possible.* It was an

attention-getter with dashing style and size. The show was presented simultaneously on both the French and English networks. Performers included Indian musician Ravi Shankar and opera star Maureen Forrester. Sports stars Maurice Richard and Barbara Ann Scott also took stage.

For the record: the winning number for the million-dollar prize was 3093734.

Nine lucky ladies from Quebec City shared a tax-free jackpot of $1 million — the largest lottery prize in history. A 48-year-old accountant from Guelph took home the second prize of $500,000 making him the largest *single* winner. Third prize ($250,000) went to a Quebec provincial police officer. In all, 25,000 ticket-buyers won prizes from $100 to $500,000, totaling over $8 million.

Two-and-a-half-million lottery tickets at $10 apiece had been sold in the first round. Given that the lottery had been on sale in only six provinces, those numbers were very high. The PR department of COJO bragged that the national broadcast had "surpassed anything of the kind that had ever been performed for the glory of the country and the Olympic ideal."

The financial forecast for the Olympic lottery was that it would net $35 million over its 3-year lifespan. To everyone's surprise the first draw had already earned $11.9 million. (At the end of the Olympic Games in 1976, the profit exceeded the original projection by a magnitude of 10. i.e. $392.0 million)

People who fancied themselves knowledgeable about lotteries (including your lottery scribe) were stunned to see those results. After all, the average hourly wage was $4.50 which meant that a worker had to work more than two hours of to buy a $10 ticket. With a success like that, it was highly unlikely that Olympic lottery would be shut down at the end of the Games, as promised.

On the technical side of the lottery operation, ticket distribution was a clone of the original (and now abandoned) system of Loto Quebec. Distributors (exclusively Liberal-Party supporters) bought tickets at a 10% discount, a fee they had to share with the seller. For the distributors, the business was a small goldmine. The average distributor's commission amounted to $50,000 in a few months. The excessive earnings by the distributors needed to be solved later.

MEETINGS, MEETINGS, MEETINGS

For your lottery scribe, spring and summer of '74 was one long, continuous series of meetings. I became a frequent traveller on Air Canada, either chairing lottery meetings or attending local sessions in any of the seven main population centres of Western Canada. Meetings included civil servants and charitable groups as well as the often-disdainful members of the Stampede and Klondike Days, who were still convinced that nothing worthwhile could be achieved by anyone in the employ of government. They were intelligent people but overly condescending and totally oblivious to the notion that leading inter-government relations is a high-wire act that can only be successful when an extreme balance of interests is attained.

One might expect that with Manitoba's Premier Schreyer and Larry Desjardins, acting as the initiators of a Western Canada Lottery, new lottery legislation in Manitoba would easily pass. However, the act to establish the Western Canada Lottery was fiercely opposed by members of the opposition, who — given the nature of their arguments — were obviously coached by professional lottery operators who would lose a large part of their illegal market. It is difficult to understand how legislators could so boldly defend acts that were very clearly offenses under the Criminal Code, but they did.

Excerpts from the Manitoba Hansard, of April 23, 1974, three weeks before the Western Lottery was incorporated, show the rear-guard actions to undo the new lottery. At the Manitoba Legislature, a chorus of badly informed MLAs ranted against the Western lottery, basically saying that the law that forbade lotteries to be sold outside the borders of the licensing province had never been enforced and therefore should be ignored. In effect, the objecting MLAs invited full-fledged competition from every other Canadian province, believing that Manitoba would be victorious in a Canadian lottery war. That was delusional. The selling agencies were satisfied that their case had been heard but most realized that the days of their rapacious marketing ploys were coming to an end.

Manitoba was not alone. All western provinces were being difficult. The delegates to the Implementation Task Force were mostly competent people but they brought four different perspectives to the table. I say "mostly" because the Calgary cowboys and Edmonton oilmen kept harping that that they had a great lottery system and the government couldn't improve on it. They didn't mind earning more revenue from the new lottery but didn't fancy the required cooperation. They demanded a guarantee from the other provinces that their exhibition organizations would make as much profit from the new scheme as they did from their old one. I boldly predicted that they would double their take. This shut them up for a while until they realized that no real guarantee was forthcoming. My response must have struck a chord because they became less ornery. (NOTE: Alberta's net revenue tripled in the first year of operation.)

Saskatchewan had been governed by the NDP for decades. The socialist party-line was that lotteries are a tax that weighs on the poor. In other words, the amount spent on a $1 lottery ticket as a percentage of income is greater for a poor man than for a rich one. So, of course, are bread and bus-fare but we didn't participate in polemics. Surprise! Saskatchewan sent two free spirits to the implementation group. Bill Clarke, the province's Director of Sport and well-known professional football player, who once had run for the Liberal Party. That's about as right-wing as you could get in the Saskatchewan '70s.

The other colorful character was Joe Kanuka, the volunteer-head of the Saskatchewan Sports Federation, lawyer by trade and comedian by inclination. With tongue-in-cheek, he explained to the Alberta oilmen that the Saskatchewan Minister of Sport gave him the freedom to vote as he saw fit. "The Minister has added only one limitation," he confessed with a serious face.

"The Minister told me that if I agree with Bill Clarke, I speak for the government. If I don't agree with Bill, I speak for myself."

These two clever people represented a government that didn't want anything to do with lotteries but the Sask Sport people did not stray very far from government's whispered dictates.

Manitoba's members on the Implementation Task Force consisted of a confused duo. Your lottery scribe was the Chair, so he couldn't be a Manitoba representative. To my surprise, Minister Desjardins assigned two unexpected delegates. The first was the Chair of the Manitoba Lottery Commission an NDP adherent. I objected that he was mostly interested in scuppering the Western Canada deal in favor of retaining the Manitoba sweepstakes. Desjardins — under pressure from his cabinet colleagues — just winked at me. He too had to compromise to achieve his goals.

The other was an NDP adherent, a naïve woman (a diplomatic way of saying that she was as dense as a sack full of hammers). Her inane comments were soon ignored by all. It must have been tough for her. She proudly crowed to the press that the Manitoba Sweepstakes was the best in the world and proclaimed that she would defend it and kill this "Westcan" deal. (Some folks had baptized the new scheme as the "Westcan." In a subsequent CBC-TV interview, I professed that I abhorred the nickname because it sounded like directions to an outhouse. After that, the moniker went rapidly into disuse.)

The official members of the Western Canada Lottery were now agreed. Manitoba named its crown corporation "Manitoba Lotteries Commission". Saskatchewan designated "Sask Sport" as its operating arm. The Alberta entity was a combination of the Calgary and Edmonton exhibitions plus the Commonwealth Games, to be called "Alberta Lotteries". British Columbia would operate as a government branch with the title "BC Lotteries".

The combination looked like anything but a successful lottery operation but as one of the more philosophical members said: "It is what it is."

IMPLEMENATION OF THE LOTTERY SCHEME

The only lottery scheme familiar to the new delegates to the Western Canada Lottery was the Irish Sweepstakes format. (The word "scheme" in the lottery provisions of the Criminal Code is not a pejorative word; it is the legal term used to describe a lottery format). The Sweepstake scheme is very simple. Reduced to its basic premise, one writes one's name on a piece of paper, puts it in a hat along with other entries, and a name is drawn from the hat to win. Rather than argue about sophisticated games operating in Europe, the Implementation Task Force chose the sweepstakes format because a quick start was a priority. Any other scheme would have been unfamiliar, caused delays and required a new distribution system.

Your lottery scribe's preference would have been to scuttle the existing, fault-ridden system but time was of the essence. The faster the scheme could be implemented, the less time there would be for objectors to rally. The most important advantage was that Manitoba had a working administration in place.

Ministerial direction was clear: Get the Western Lottery in operation. Once the interprovincial agreement was signed, my task in lotteries was at an end. I would return to my job of Director of Sport and someone would be hired to run the lottery and move it into the modern age.

In early autumn of 1973, at a Western Ministers' meeting in Edmonton, a 10-year agreement was signed, subject of course to the passing of enabling legislation in the respective provinces. Manitoba was designated as the site of the head office. The lone dissenter was **Jim Chabot** from British Columbia who insisted that the location of the Head Office should be reviewed in ten years. That seemed innocent enough and was quickly agreed to. Ten years later it would become a huge issue.

The principles of operation remained as they were initially agreed. The Western Canada Lottery would manage and conduct the lottery, issue lottery tickets to the provinces, conduct the draws, pay out prizes, and advertise across the four provinces. Provincial marketing offices (PMOs) were to sell the tickets and remit the proceeds minus commissions and office expenses to the Western Canada head office. Each provincial government would appoint two members to the Western Canada Lottery board of directors. The governments of the Yukon and Northwest Territories, with a combined population of less than that Medicine Hat, were admitted as associate members with the same marketing and financial benefits as the provinces but without a vote on anything.

Set to go!

LOTTERY OPERATIONS BEGIN 1974-1985

CORPORATION: NO! FOUNDATION: YES!

The lottery organization established somewhat precariously by the four western provinces, was now a reality but what to name this partnership? The Task Force recommended the name "Western Canada Lottery Corporation." BC Minister, Ernie Hall, objected strongly. "The name Corporation suggests a business enterprise when I am trying to sell it to British Columbians as a little fundraising raffle for community benefit." A suggestion was made to replace the word "Corporation" with "Foundation," a more noble word to indicate "funding" of community groups. Ernie loved it and no one else cared. "Foundation" it was, which established the initials as WCLF. Today it may seem to strange to argue about the title of an enterprise that would yield millions of dollars in revenue, but in those days a lottery was seen as a shady enterprise that only a few years earlier would have seen the operator incarcerated. Churches and moralists depicted a government-sanctioned lottery as a "paved road to hell." Toning down this gambling enterprise was the watchword.

In BC, as in the other provinces, most of the politicians ran for cover, proclaiming that they despised lotteries. Those who were in favour said it was a "fun thing" that would enable charities and community groups to obtain some much-needed funding. "Government won't really participate," a cabinet minister claimed, "We'll only keep a watchful eye." Those in opposition said they would dismantle this work of the devil as soon as they were in power.

The Alberta government pretended that nothing had changed. After all, the Stampede and Klondike Days had been running a lottery for a while. They were still running a lottery. Nothing to see here!

Saskatchewan's NDP government reminded everyone that Sask Sport ran the "tolerated but disliked gambling" in that province.

Manitoba, with a few years of the successful Manitoba Sweepstakes, was much braver and proudly proclaimed that this was a good government program. Perhaps the fact that the lottery was introduced by the Conservative party and then managed by the NDP made it difficult for the opposition to disown it.

Desjardins, due to the legalities of the controverted election, was not a Minister of the Crown any more but had moved to chair the Manitoba Health

Services Commission. While he was no longer the minister responsible for the lottery portfolio, he was still interested in guiding the development of the WCLF.

In Calgary, where the WCLF held its first formal board meeting, Desjardins put his name forward as a candidate for the (unpaid) position as Chair of the Board. The Alberta and the Saskatchewan members were distrustful of a high-profile former NDP politician in that role. Since the Head Office was to be based in Manitoba, other provinces wanted to feel a "source of influence".

Larry lobbied with the NDP government in BC to support his bid for Chair, but the Saskatchewan NDP legislators with their eyes covered (we-are-not-in-the lottery-business!) were reluctant to be up-front this early in the game. When the vote for Chair was held, Saskatchewan and Alberta voted for Bill Clarke. Manitoba and BC chose Desjardins. The tie was resolved when Bill and Larry withdrew to another room and emerged smiling, saying that a coin had been tossed: Desjardins had won. Years later it came out that Larry had said that he would call the premier of Saskatchewan to say that his position as chair was pre-empted by a civil servant. However, if Bill withdrew, Larry said he would support him as his successor in the near future. And so it was.

A POOR COPY OF A POOR GAME DESIGN

It was assumed by all that the lottery format initially introduced by Manitoba would be the first game for the WCLF, although some tweaking had to be done. The major changes apart from the name were two-fold. The main prize was increased from $100,000 to $250,000 and the frequency of the draws was increased from three to four draws a year.

Each Provincial Marketing Office (PMO) could license "charitable" ticket distributors, under a WCLF contract.

- Tickets, priced at $2.50, were bound in a booklet of 12. Total retail value per book: $30
- Of the $30, the seller could keep $5 (16.6%) as commission
- The licensed distributor would keep another $10 as commission (from which they would fund their charitable purposes)
- Of the remaining $15 as remitted to the WCLF: $3, went to advertising and administration and about $3.75 was dedicated to the prize fund.
- Hence the gross profit of a sold book would be $9.00 (30%)

By today's standards it is obvious that the lottery buyer was being royally screwed. Only 12.5% of every dollar went to prizes compared to an average of 55% today.

The term "rip-off" fitted this government-run program. The offer to the player was in essence: Give me a dollar. I'll put 12-1/2 cents in the prize pot for you and I'll keep the rest.

What was the title of that first game you ask? The name was: The Western Canada Lottery Foundation. Series AA. There was no specific game name.

CONTROLS AND ACCOUNTABILITY

The system the WCLF inherited from Manitoba had little or no accountability for all tickets released for sale. The smaller, truly community-based distributors received the requested number of ticket-booklets, making careful notes as to how many were issued to each individual seller and then returned all sold and unsold tickets along with the money to the lottery organization.

Of course, every once in a while — after carrying around a booklet for four months — a volunteer seller would lose a book of tickets or simply forget about it. In that case, a statement by the seller attesting to the loss was accepted by the WCLF.

The large distributors, run by professional administrators — seven of them — ran a type of boiler-room operation using "sucker lists" of names and addresses across North America. These targets were told that they could sell these books of tickets valued at $30 and that they could keep $5 or two tickets for themselves. The net to catch out-of-province buyers was spread widely. The United States Postal Service at one point notified the Manitoba Lottery Commission that a huge mail drop of booklets had been made in the Detroit area using the telephone directory to obtain recipients.

A huge percentage of these books never came back. Were they sold and the money kept by the seller? Were they idly tossed in the garbage? No one knew and few cared. In general, there was a naive belief in the goodness of mankind. The Manitoba Lottery's accountants — who took a different slant on things than your suspecting scribe — proudly announced in their audit report that every penny received was accounted for. That was true but not every book of tickets was accounted for. The auditors duly noted that formal statements were received from distributors listing the books that had not been returned to them or had never been issued. Well, that was okay then! No problem!

No one was auditing how much money these distributors — large and small — were devoting to their "good causes". Figures were accepted as presented, with no accounting for the tickets they might have sold and money they might have pocketed. Vague statements were issued with respect to salaries and expenses. The essential problem was that the Manitoba Lottery didn't have control of what happened to their tickets. The sole focus was on accounting for money received in the office and that was done very competently, without question.

Government would have been at a loss to explain if the press had inquired how much money that could have been received but was NOT received. Of course, there was no way of knowing how badly the system was compromised.

The fact that selling lottery tickets outside Manitoba was an offence under the Criminal Code of Canada didn't cause anyone any loss of sleep either.

That — in essence — was the system your lottery scribe inherited. It was not comfortable but it would have to suffice for a while. The plan was to keep fingers crossed that nothing untoward would happen and then install a modern, responsible system. So many people benefitted from this largely uncontrolled system — change wasn't going to come easily.

In late summer of 1974, your civil servant scribe phased out of the sports side of his government job and devoted most hours to the development of the lottery. The WCLF office was still housed in the Sports Administration Centre on Cumberland Avenue in Winnipeg. Lynn Norquay, the secretary on the sports end transferred to WCLF as well as my assistant **Billy Weissmann**. The initial task was clear. Administration of the Manitoba Sweepstakes was based in Selkirk and switching those employees to the WCLF presented no obstacles. The staff, building and equipment remained in the hands of the Province of Manitoba, its costs paid by WCLF.

Millions of lottery tickets needed to be printed to similar specifications as the Manitoba Sweepstakes. The WCLF board insisted on a tendering process for printing when my preference — given the short time span — would have been to do business with the incumbent, Bulman Brothers. It was agreed that we would do the first draw with Bulman and issue a Request for Proposal (RFP) for ticket printing before the second draw.

The draw schedule was now four draws per year instead of three. It was obvious that for timing purposes, the Manitoba Derby couldn't be used as a title, neither the Curling Championship nor the Grey Cup. Instead of having horses or football players decide the lottery winners, the decision was to create a televised draw show where pre-drawn winners would learn how much money each player would take home.

While there was some time to arrange details of the draw, distribution and sales were the priority.

At this point, let me take you back. It is summer of 1974; the Manitoba Lottery is selling tickets for the Manitoba Derby to be held in August.

The "Western Canada Lottery" was launched in mid-August. The format was new to the public. Eight finalists would be drawn to be the "contestants" on a TV show on December 11, 1974. To allow time for calling in unsold booklets and the finalists to make arrangements to attend the TV draw, sales would have to end seven weeks before that date i.e. October 23, 1974. That's how it was.

ADVERTISING CONTRACTS ARE POLITICAL

After a bit of a hassle at the board level, requests were issued for bids to be the lottery's advertising agency. It would be a plum assignment for the lucky bidder. Larry Desjardins, as WCLF Chairman was urged by the Manitoba NDP stalwarts to select a Montreal agency headed by Manny Dunsky, the godfather of NDP advertising throughout Canada. Manny's Manitoba representative was a bright young St. Boniface-born man named Richard Muller. Larry didn't care that much for Dunsky but he liked Rick, the son of the former St. Boniface Chief of Police. He told his not-so-swift Manitoba board members to vote for Dunsky, regardless of who presented the best advertising campaign. It was clear that the (NDP) BC lottery minister would also opt for Dunsky; after all, his agency had been instrumental in winning the BC election. The Saskatchewan NDP government was also a devoted client of Dunsky.

**Laurie Mainster** was the aggressive head of Foster Advertising in Winnipeg, a true, blue Conservative spear carrier who had enjoyed the benefits of his party's government advertising accounts until the NDP took charge. Laurie besieged the WCLF on an almost daily basis. For years, he had been on the receiving end of NDP complaints when he was rewarded with juicy government advertising accounts. Now he was intent to prove that the NDP played the same game. He promised he'd drag me into the political arena if I buckled under NDP pressure to hire Dunsky. It was not comfortable.

The WCLF board decided that the choice was between Foster and Dunsky.

At the advertising presentation, Laurie was cool and professional but Richard Muller, on behalf of Dunsky, showed a bit of stage fright. Larry had told me to butt out for this was a political decision. He explained that BC had agreed to endorse Dunsky and Saskatchewan would do the same. The NDP ministers hadn't bothered to consult Alberta; they were true blue Conservatives and everyone knew how they'd vote.

The planned collusion misfired and caused the first hullabaloo between the partners. The Saskatchewan government had given no instructions to Bill Clarke or Joe Kanuka, who assumed that they could make their own decision.

Ernie Hall, the BC minister had been vague in his instruction to his representatives, knowing that Saskatchewan and Manitoba would vote for the NDP agency. He told them to "vote with the majority." When the vote came, Bill Clarke chose the Conservative agency (Foster) and Joe Kanuka had been told to go along with whatever Bill said. Alberta chose Foster too. For the innocent and naïve bureaucrats from BC this was a "no-brainer." They went with the majority. It was 3-1 for Foster and so the Conservative agency was confirmed as the advertising agency of WCLF.

Desjardins was furious and called Ed Tchorzewski, the Saskatchewan minister, who phoned me before he returned Larry's call. "What the hell happened?" he snapped. I described Bill's and Joe's actions as neutrally as I could. "Bastards!" Ed shouted and hung up. Ernie Hall, the BC minister was next to call. When I told him that his bureaucrats had voted with the majority, he exploded, "Stupid assholes."

Thoroughly chastened from on high, the WCLF board met again and, following the vote of 3-1, your caught-in-the-middle scribe was directed to limit the Foster contract to "Series AA" only and award Dunsky the next three draws. The free-booting board members had learned a lesson:

- Governments appoint board members.
- If board members stray from government's direction, they will be dis-appointed.

DEFINITELY NOT INVITED

While WCLF was wrestling with its first controversy, the board of the Manitoba Lotteries Commission found a lifeline for their survival...or so they believed. During the 1974 provincial election, the Catholic Church hierarchy in St. Boniface reminded churchgoers that Larry Desjardins was elected as a Liberal but had defected to the godless NDP. The church's stance had its effect. Desjardins was defeated by a few votes. He was out of government until — four months later — a judicial recount put him back in the saddle. While he remained as Chair of WCLF, his absence in the Legislature during the critical stage of the young WCLF was nearly disastrous. In Cabinet, he had been replaced by a strangely inept Franco-Manitoban minister, Rene Toupin.

 Two of the largest lottery sales agencies were part of the French-Canadian milieu and **Rene Toupin** was the point man for the 'French Fact' in Manitoba. The lottery operators approached Toupin declaring that the Festival du Voyageur and the St. Boniface Mohawks hockey team would suffer if the Western Lottery was to be created. They were correct because a WCLF administration would run a proper, legal and accountable business and therefore they would suffer financial pain. Despite the Legislature's decision to create the Western Canada Lottery, Toupin did his best to undo the agreement. Fortunately, it was far too late and Desjardins was never far from Premier Schreyer's ear to negate Toupin's shenanigans.

Toupin met with the major lottery sales agencies and assured them that if he couldn't abort the Western Canada Lottery, he would prevent any attempt to enforce the provisions of the Criminal Code. Nor would he institute stronger accountability for the loss of tickets. Yes! This was a cabinet minister sworn to uphold the law and to promote peace, order and good government.

Hearing about this rebellious attitude, Larry called on Premier Schreyer and received assurances that the Province of Manitoba would not abandon the new partners it had so ardently wooed, nor would it tolerate any transgressions of the Criminal Code. After this, Toupin was chastened but didn't hide his dislike for your lottery scribe.

FAREWELL MANITOBA SWEEPSTAKES

On the August long weekend of 1974, the Winnipeg horse racing fraternity was out in its finery to celebrate the running of the Manitoba Derby.

It was already public knowledge that WCLF would abandon any lotteries based on sports events and this 1974 Derby would be the last turn in the lottery limelight. The horsey crowd was convinced that the glamour they brought to the Sweepstakes was the magic ingredient behind the lottery's success and quietly chortled that the WCLF would suffer dire financial losses without them. They were so naive about the new age of gambling.

A week later, on August 12th 1974, the Western Canada Lottery was launched in all seven major urban centres of the West. Rene Toupin — the minister who had tried to prevent, obstruct and delay the new lottery — was front and centre announcing this new "Lottery for Manitoba" that had raised its traditional first prize of $100,000 to $250.000.

Toupin urged the Manitoba Lottery management — which would soon be selling the WCLF lottery — to disinvite any WCLF people to the Winnipeg launch. Well, no matter; the public was invited and, as a spectator, your member-of-the-pubic scribe found a spot far in the back as Toupin rolled in a wheelbarrow filled with fake dollar bills to illustrate the size of the bonanza awaiting the winner. He then told the crowd that if there had been no Western Canada Lottery, the next Manitoba Sweepstakes issue would have been based on the Grey Cup football championship. In anticipation, the Manitoba lottery had bought a large number of toy footballs that were now "not relative to this launch, because of steps taken by the government." The crowd was invited to participate in what "would have been the greatest Grey Cup lottery." Aided by lottery staff, a thousand or more miniature footballs were tossed into the crowd. Your receiving scribe managed to snag a number for the kids and took them back to our summer-home on Matlock beach.

A few months later, Toupin came into bad odour when a newspaper article disclosed he had attended a late-night party where unnamed but questionable activities had taken place. Schreyer sent him off to Consumer and Corporate Affairs. Good riddance for the lottery.

In any event, the launch festivities in the seven cities had gone well and had created awareness in the media. Thousands of ticket-booklets had been shipped to the four Provincial Marketing Offices and issuing of tickets to distributors began. Each of the four offices had its own peculiar circumstances to deal with.

Manitoba carried on as if there hadn't been any change. More than 200 Manitoba community agencies, large and small, continued their distribution routine. The WCLF board concurred with my view that the introduction of strong controls should be delayed. The unfortunate result of that decision was that the three other provinces —by bad example — also introduced a lax system that needed to be harshly overhauled in the coming months. It would have been better for them to start with a proper distribution system but...

 When Jack Stewart, a Manitoba manager was transferred to run the BC operation, his deputy, **Len Gzebb** — a well-known veteran baseball player and radio man — took over. He knew the ropes and had a good relationship with the community agencies... so good, in fact, that in the beginning he was more on their side than the WCLF.

When the Manitoba Sweepstakes ended, many of the smaller distributors bowed out. The concept had changed from a one-time community raffle to a big ongoing business which was beyond their capacity. However, the big-business distributors who employed professional sales techniques, realizing the lottery was permanent and doubled down on their efforts.

Sask Sport had been named as Saskatchewan's provincial marketing operation within the WCLF. Remnants of their Sweetstakes lottery distribution system were used to create the WCLF marketing network. Moreover, Sask Sport was given a responsibility that the three other parties in the WCLF didn't have i.e. the ability to decide (in conjunction with sports and cultural government agencies) how lottery profits would be distributed.

Sask Sport had little money for its start-up. They relied on sheer grit and commitment by a large number of volunteers who were determined to prove that they could make the lottery go. Unbelievable these days, Sask Sport board members Cas Pielak and Joe Kanuka signed a personal promissory note for $100,000 as Saskatchewan's investment in the Western Canada Lottery Foundation.

 **Jim Burnett** — the ultimate leader of the Sask Sport lottery operations, now retired after more than four decades, recalls:

"My job in 1974, was to visit convenience stores to convince them to sell lottery tickets. Most of the stores were reluctant. The only proprietors who didn't chase me away were the Chinese store owners. They had been selling illegal Irish Sweepstakes tickets for a long time so they understood the attraction."

As the Western Canada lottery grew, people who had slammed the door in my face were now phoning and requesting another visit. We had hundreds of peddlers who haunted bars and streets. We'd sign anyone who showed up as long as they filled our minimum requirements —and they were minimal, believe me. People were selling on behalf of their sport clubs or charity. Many a sports supporter had a book of tickets to sell. It was a people vending machine."

Meanwhile in Alberta, you will recall that Olympic Lottery tickets were distributed there before the WCLF was introduced. The manager of the Olympic lottery in Alberta was a bombastic man — Gerry Lorente — someone who had earned his position by being a Liberal hanger-on (A rare bird in Alberta!).

His sales crew distributed some WCLF tickets but the best ready-to-go sales force was the staffs of the now-defunct Calgary Stampede and Klondike Days lotteries. They were united under the first manager of the Alberta Provincial Marketing Office, Andy Fraser. The sales staff included Bud Starr, Irene Shandera, Bill Mayson, Hugh Sangster, Clarence Riske, Ken Reeves and Dorothy Knowler, to name just a few Alberta's lottery pioneers.

The most supportive Albertan was Harry Hole — a larger-than-life oilman and a board member of both the Edmonton Exhibition and the WCLF. At one of your lottery scribe's appearances in Edmonton, a morning radio personality reported (untruthfully) that Simonis earned an indecently high commission on every ticket sold in Alberta. He added that I was the kind of person who should be investigated for illegal rip-offs.

Harry Hole didn't like the idea that anyone he supported was being described in those terms. A day after the accusation, Harry met me at the Edmonton Airport and drove me in his swanky Cadillac directly to the criticizing radio station. There, waiting in a bit of discomfort, was the manager of the broadcasting enterprise. Harry was invited to the poshest office in the building, where he politely addressed the nervous manager and told him about all the good things the lottery was doing for the people of Alberta. He then gently explained that anyone darkening such a civic service by uttering falsehoods should apologize and make amends. Harry mentioned neither the name of the radio host, nor what he had said, nor when he said it.

The manager, relieved that things weren't as dire as he feared, shook my hand and asked when I would be available for an interview on a program in prime time. A few weeks later I participated in an hour-long phone-in show, answering questions from listeners about the growing lottery business. Harry wrote me a nice note saying he had listened with interest.

British Columbia's newly-hired distribution staff, located in Victoria, had little experience in lotteries but had the backing of the government's civil service and the use of government premises. When the news release announced that the WCLF office was looking for community groups to become lottery distributors, Jack Stewart, the former Manitoba lottery manager was swamped with applications. One of the first in line — on behalf of Football BC — was **Larry Reda** and his wife Margaret-Anne. Other pioneers included Barry Auliffe, who sold tickets on behalf of the St. Joseph School Building Fund in Nelson and Nancy Bailey who toiled on behalf of the Hyack Festival. All these veterans became part of the lottery family for close to 30 years.

More about their experiences will be shared in later chapters.

FOUND A THRILL AT CHERRY HILL

September 15, 1974. In contrast to the aggravation of contracting advertising agencies, the appointment of auditors was not a political issue. **Bob Henderson** of the accounting firm Clarkson Gordon was handed the WCLF account. At first Bob considered his assignment a bit of a small operation but it would open up a new career path in lotteries that, 30 years later, would see him retire to a splendid home in Hilton Head, South Carolina.

In his first few weeks of working with the lottery, Bob didn't appear to be overly happy to be part of this "raffle business." At that time, there were only seven other state lottery jurisdictions in North America, six in the U.S. and one in Quebec. In the States a sort of club had emerged in order to exchange information between lotteries. The small group had the grand title of National Association of State Lotteries with Ralph Batch (Illinois) presiding. Duane Burke, an early lottery devotee and future great personal friend of your lottery scribe had formed a lottery publishing/consulting business named Public Gaming Institute with his wife Doris. He phoned from Seattle urging me to attend the annual meeting of U.S. lottery directors in Cherry Hill, Pennsylvania. It was a fine opportunity to bring myself and our new WCLF auditor up to date about the way the States administered their lotteries.

Before the trip, I convinced Bob Henderson that he should question the Manitoba Provincial Auditor about whether the accounts of the Sweepstakes Lottery were in good order. I explained some of the obvious gaps in control and security. After that, he readily accepted my invitation to join me at the Cherry Hill meeting to learn about the American operations.

The first stop on our visit was Springfield, Illinois, where the lottery had just become operational. We didn't meet the Superintendent **Ralph Batch**, the founding Godfather of the U.S. lotteries. However, he introduced us to his deputy, Richard Carlson, who would later succeed him. As it was, Carlson had more questions than answers. All we could tell him was *not* to do what Manitoba did. I'm not sure he listened. Ralph Batch might have been a much better mentor.

The lottery directors of Illinois, New Hampshire, New York, Pennsylvania and Michigan were gathered in Cherry Hill, New Jersey. At that time, I had no idea that this National Association of State Lotteries (NASL) would grow to encompass more than 40 lottery jurisdictions across North America, nor that I would become its first Canadian president. At a recent lottery conference attended by more than a thousand delegates, the joke circulated that those first meetings of NASL directors were held in a Volkswagen. That isn't true. The assembled lottery directors travelled in a Buick station wagon.

At the business sessions in Cherry Hill we got a good look at the U.S. system of pre-numbered lottery tickets, printed on state computers. Bob was impressed with the operation, called the 'Bearer System." There were no stubs to be filled in or transported. Tickets were printed with serialized numbers. Winning numbers were published and players holding a winning ticket had to step forward and claim their prize.

The task of your lottery scribe was as clear as it was difficult. The politicians in western Canada needed to be convinced that the old system had to go.

LOTO QUEBEC HOSTS AILE MEETING

October 15, 1974. In addition to the INTERTOTO organization which encompassed the world's sports betting and lotto companies (some of which had been around for centuries) another world-wide organization existed with the title of International Association of State Lotteries (AILE). This group included the old traditional government lotteries. Larry Desjardins, as Chairman of the Western Canada Lottery, was anxious to learn more about government-run lotteries. He readily accepted the invitation to attend the 10th Annual Congress of AILE in the Quebec City.

The first stop was Montreal where Loto Quebec had arranged for us to meet with officials of the Olympic lottery.

Olympic lottery tickets could be sold only in provinces that had granted permission to do so. The manager of the Olympic Lottery, Julien Coté, tried to persuade Desjardins to have Manitoba join the Olympic network but Larry turned a deaf ear. To allow the Olympic Lottery to operate in the three western provinces would put sales of WCLF tickets in direct competition with the $10

Olympic lottery. That in itself didn't bother Desjardins. He didn't mind marketing two lotteries, but he didn't want two lottery organizations.

"We have a distribution system," Larry kept repeating, "and if you guys want to sell your tickets in the West, we'll sell them on your behalf. Don't come out West and set up a bureaucracy because you will never leave." The Olympic people had a vision of a national Canadian lottery run by Ottawa. Larry wanted to preserve the provinces' "field of taxation" (aka taxation by gambling).

The Western NDP governments didn't really grasp his insight but they trusted Larry and kept their doors closed to the Olympic Lottery, while leaving the door open to sell Olympic tickets through the WCLF. Of course, no one in Eastern Canada could see the issue from the West's perspective. The refusal to let the Olympic lottery set up shop was painted in the media as Western odium for Quebec's moment in the sun: The 1976 Montreal Olympics.

The strains of the conflict didn't spoil Larry's enjoyment of his first international AILE conference. Delegates from 42 countries brought 224 delegates to participate in the discussions.

To meet people who administered lotteries that were decades, even centuries' old, was encouraging for Larry, since at home, he continued to take the brunt of criticism for "introducing gambling into our conservative society".

 The young man in charge of the conference details was **Jean-Marc Lafaille**, an up-and-coming Québec lawyer. Jean-Marc and I would go on to become long-time friends, colleagues and in later years co-authors of a notable reference work on lotteries.

THE WESTERN LOTTERY'S FIRST DRAW

Within weeks of the first Olympic lottery draw, Western Canada lottery tickets were released. When sales of the $2.50 Western Canada Lottery closed at the end of November 1974, more than $10 million worth of tickets had been sold. The people at the Selkirk lottery office worked overtime to get it all done. The secure storage area was filled with canvas mailbags stuffed with ticket stubs.

Each lottery ticket had two stubs attached. The buyer was required to write name, address and phone number on both of them. After registering the entry into one of those early new-fangled computers, the Selkirk staff members took one stub and stored it in one of a number of canvas post-office bags to be later entered into the draw machine. The other stub was glued to a pre-printed postcard that served as a confirmation to the buyer that the ticket was entered in the draw.

Of course, that statement wasn't necessarily true. The plain postcard only said that the stub was received by the lottery office. The postcard meant nothing! Did the lottery organization send the postcard? Or was it a rogue seller who had printed his own postcards and kept the money? Had the Selkirk folks stored the ticket in the proper place? Did the stored tickets actually make it into the draw drum? Both public and press were too naive to ask these kinds of questions. Trust was misplaced. The system needed to be changed!

The farce of the lottery's security became a little sillier when a huge draw drum was placed in the massive entry hall of Winnipeg's Pan Am Pool for the preliminary draw. Two Winnipeg policemen watched as ticket stubs were poured into the draw drum. In shifts, they would stand guard over the drum until the draw began. No one asked what they were watching for. Was there some fear that someone would throw an unpaid ticket stub into the drum? Or thieves might take tickets out? Anyway, it was a nice bit of show business.

At draw time, Vaughn Baird was scurrying about the hall. It was his idea to have the first draw at the Pan Am Pool as a symbol of the WCLF's contribution to sport. Volunteer ushers managed the crowd that would draw the 1,900 consolation tickets.

Your scribe's daughters **Joanne and Nadine,** clad in the light-coloured tracksuits of the Manitoba Games team, were thrilled to participate at this historic draw.

Local dignitaries — sleeves undone to show they weren't palming a ticket stub — drew the first eight winning tickets whose holders were guaranteed at least $25,000. The eight major prizes to be won ranged up to $250,000. A televised show slated for early December would decide who would win those amounts.

After that, spectators were lined up to draw the 1,900 ticket stubs that would pay the winner a hundred-dollar bill. It was a dreary, labour-intensive effort. As the draw continued, Vaughan Baird was on the PA system phoning the eight finalists to inform them of their $25,000 minimum win and invite them to attend the final draw in Lethbridge. They were required pay their own way to the Lethbridge draw or — if unable to travel — WCLF would appoint a stand-in.

At this point, it's important to remember that the Criminal Code forbade WCLF lottery tickets to be sold outside the borders of Western Canada. Yet Rene Toupin, the new Manitoba lottery minister, had assured the professional sales agencies that they could sell tickets in any country, state or province they chose.

Illegal sales became immediately evident when only four winners were western Canadians. Two were from Ontario, one from Quebec, one from Minnesota. A sampling of the $100 winners showed a similar pattern. No authority anywhere questioned the breach of the Criminal Code.

DECEMBER 11, 1974

Monty Hall, the famous Winnipeg-born game show host, came from his home in Palm Springs to emcee the first lottery draw-show at the Playhouse Theatre in Winnipeg. As a nice gesture to his home province, Monty requested that his performance-fee be donated to charity. The show, televised by the CBC network was based on a version of the show "Let's Make a Deal," where participants decide their own fate by choosing which door to open.

Wouldn't you know it? The first-prize winner ($250,000) was a lady from Minneapolis. Second prize went to a gentleman from Quebec and third prize to a ticket buyer from Ontario. The review in the Free Press the following day bitched that the show was boring for the home viewer but proudly proclaimed that people from across the North America had bought tickets by the millions. There was no mention that they did so illegally.

NEW OFFICES. NEW TROUBLES

On December 31, 1974, lottery use of the Sports Administration Centre came to an end. Sport and gambling were to separate.

A humble location for the lottery was found in a high-rise bachelor apartment on Hargrave Street. A huge Xerox machine took up most of the kitchen. Fortunately, one floor below was a similar-sized suite where Terry O'Rourke was installed to look after advertising. In turn, Terry hired a single mother to be his secretary. Her name was **Michelle McBride**. Her name will appear many, many times as this tale progresses. Michelle became a famous executive in the lottery business.

The WCLF board meeting in early 1975 was unruly. Manitoba had broken the agreement to solicit sales beyond its borders. The province's "professional" agencies had continued soliciting sales in North America, including a large percentage in the western provinces. To calculate the effect exactly, the remaining lottery stubs were randomly sample. Buyer names and addresses as well as the names of who sold them were known. For the first draw of the Western Lottery, Manitoba contributed 52% of total Western Canada sales compared to 14 % of the population. Three quarters of Manitoba's sales originated outside the province and half of that was sold in its WCLF partners' domain; those partners were angry.

Larry Desjardins, as WCLF Chair was livid about his colleague Toupin's behaviour but at the WCLF meeting he approached the subject calmly and said: "When Manitoba entered into the WCLF, I, as Minister responsible promised we'd be honourable partners who would not exploit our neighbors' markets. There is no doubt that my successor was instrumental in causing the current problem. On behalf of the Government of Manitoba, I regret the violation. We shall correct the problem. I hereby commit to paying out any and all profits that may have accrued to Manitoba from sales made in your respective provinces."

The subsequent payout from Manitoba profits exceeded $300,000. The WCLF board was satisfied that the partnership was an honourable enterprise.

WE'RE IN, BUT ON OUR TERMS

The standoff around the Olympic Lottery in western Canada was a matter of who would blink first. The West wasn't about to blink. After two draws, members of the Olympic Lottery management visited the WCLF office and explained that in the rest of Canada, commercial distributors (largely Liberal Party members) bought tickets at $9 and then sold them to retailers for $9.50. They explained over and over again that these distributors did a great job. If the West assented, western Canadians could be named as distributors, replacing Quebeckers. Larry stuck to his position that there would be only one western Canadian lottery distributor for the Olympic Lottery and it would be the WCLF.

"You won't make any money with those small margins," Julien Coté, COJO's lottery boss argued, in a vain effort to keep his distribution system alive. "We got him," Larry sniffed afterwards. "As long as we break even on the deal or even if we lose a little bit, we'll own that distribution function. The WCLF will only survive as a monopoly. If a federal lottery gets a foothold in our provinces, provincial lotteries would die across the country."

DROP IN SALES AND FAILED CONTROLS

Sales for the second draw of the *Western*, Series AB, were far less than for the first one. Manitoba's raids on the other provinces had ended, so overall sales suffered greatly. The selling period was also shorter by five weeks than Series AA. Nevertheless, media interest had reached a new high, fueled by the many lottery stories.

The preliminary draw for the Series AB was held in Brandon, Manitoba on January 31, 1975 where eight finalists were drawn.

On the coldest day of that January, we staged the ceremonial dumping of the contents of hundreds of canvas mailbags into the giant draw drum. A hundred or so Brandonites were present to watch and participate in draw of 2000 consolation prizes of $100. The Brandon policemen stared balefully at the rotating drum containing the millions of stubs. One of the spectators, looking at this spinning cauldron, whispered that the chances of her ticket being drawn were slim and none. In later years, chances of winning a prize were expressed numerically. People would read the odds of one-in-so-many millions and shrug their shoulders, but those who saw that big drum churning its four million tickets stubs were aghast at their small chance.

Emcee **Cliff Gardner's** superb chatter helped to make the dull drawing of names an amusing event. He talked with the aspirant-winners "live" via the amplification system so that the TV people would have their shots for the evening news and the audience could hear the winners' reactions. While Cliff was phoning and interviewing, the crowd lined up to draw winners of the $100 prizes.

Your relieved scribe looked at the spectacle with satisfaction; they were getting the hang of staging this show!

The Selkirk office manager, Phil Viau — not smiling — suddenly tugged at my sleeve. I turned and snapped at him to wait until the winner interviews were over. He didn't stop. Looking terribly concerned, he dragged me away from the draw area. "There are still six canvas bags of stubs in the truck," he croaked.

My mind was racing. This meant that the stubs of hundreds of eligible participants weren't in the drum and the ceremony was nearly complete. Worse... winners had been notified of their good fortune.

"I didn't hear that," I told Phil trying to stifle him. Phil thought I meant that I hadn't heard him.

"Six bags are still in the truck," he repeated.

I looked him in the eye. "I didn't hear that," I repeated. Phil looked stunned although the light began to dawn.

"Oh, yes," he mumbled as he wandered away.

The draw was complete and a great time was had by all. I didn't tell anyone what had happened. Months later when the subject of the Brandon draw came up, the discussion was about how cold it was that evening. "Not for me," said Phil. "There was a fire in the Brandon Hills."

That's the closest I ever came to knowing where those stubs went.

Decades later, at an educational seminar in lottery management, I presented the Brandon event as a fictional case study. Some participants answered that we should have phoned the winners and told them they weren't winners after all because the draw had to be redone. Other suggested that we let it be known that we goofed and that those names would be entered in the next draw.

Either of those solutions would have brought an avalanche of bad publicity. Governments and press alike would have zeroed-in on the idea that the lottery was run by idiots and your humble scribe would have been dubbed "the Greatest Idiot of them all." The ousted board members of the Manitoba Sweepstakes would crow that things like this didn't happen when they were at the helm. Never mind that we couldn't have apologized to the folks whose stubs weren't in their draw. They'd never know and we'd never know who they were. The ashes of their entries were blown across the snows of the cold prairie. May they rest in peace! But that rotten registered lottery system had to go!

LETHBRIDGE DRAW

Piggy-backing on the Canada Winter Games, the second televised lottery draw was scheduled for February 20th, 1975, "Live from Lethbridge." Your busy scribe wore two hats: one as Director of Sports of Manitoba and the other as the boss of the Western Canada Lottery.

Your sensitive scribe would normally refrain from relating a tale of a woman approaching him offering a drink and that I readily accepted, but I did. It was **Christie Blatchford** now a big-time columnist for the National Post but then a newbie sports reporter for the Globe and Mail. She was digging for intel about Ontario launching a lottery for the benefit of sports. I told her that I hoped Ontario would start off smarter than the WCLF because the Irish-Sweepstakes format lacked any of the current technology. She seemed quite satisfied with her "scoop". It later proved to be a positive support for the new Ontario Lottery Corporation.

A phone ringing in your hotel room at 4 a.m. never delivers good news. A voice instructed us to evacuate because it was on fire. The cold Lethbridge night left me shivering in nothing warmer than a Manitoba team jacket. It was finally announced that a small electric fire had been limited to a single room and the freezing guests were allowed to re-enter the hotel.

The star emcee for the televised draw was Conrad Bain, known for his TV roles in *Maude* and *Different Strokes*. A twist in the show was that near the end — to Conrad's great surprise — we brought his identical twin from Edmonton on stage, dressed in an identical white tuxedo. The brothers hadn't seen each other for a long time. It was a nice touch.

A week later, Conrad Bain appeared on the Johnnie Carson Show. He raised oohs and aahs from the audience about the -31 Celsius temperature in Lethbridge, the hotel fire and meeting his twin brother again under those unusual circumstances. I have often wondered if the stories that these celebrities tell on these late-night TV shows are real. This story was true.

THE DEBUT OF ALEX TREBEK

The third televised draw, series AC, was slated for the Jubilee Theatre in Calgary on May 8th, 1975. By now the staging of the show was routine but the new emcee, engaged for next fiscal year, was not content with the old format. **Alex Trebek** had only a bit of national TV experience but he was a performing genius to behold. While Monty Hall and Conrad Bain had needed scripts to lean on, this man memorized the whole thing and although the teleprompter was there, he never used it. His interviews with the winners were courteous, informative and funny. This Alex Trebek could go far, I thought.

VISITORS FROM ONTARIO

At Trebek's debut as emcee of the Western Canada Lottery, the Board, local politicians and special guests were looked after by Billy Weissmann. Among the invitees was the man who — just three weeks earlier on April 17, 1975 — had launched the Ontario Lottery. **Marshall Pollock**, whom I introduced as a visitor from the East appeared to be a cocksure person. After many years I still count him among my best friends but there should be no doubt that — although being a man of high intelligence — in his early years he often lacked empathy for those around him. At this gathering he loudly condemned WCLF's ticket system and his comments were somewhat personal. I think he failed to appreciate the advantage he had in Ontario. The Wintario Lottery was launched in a market unsullied by the flaws of the Sweepstakes scheme. He missed the point that the West had to tear down the old before the new could be built. Now, many decades later Marshall has mellowed; our friendship continues and your scribe asked him to recall some stories about the start of Ontario's Lottery.

Writing in the third person, he wrote

"For Marshall Pollack it all began on a Friday evening in October of 1974 when he was invited to a Sports Awards Dinner in Toronto. As fortune had it, he was seated between Ontario Premier William Davis and Deputy Minister of Community & Social Services, Dorothea "Crit" Crittenden, whose ministry was responsible for amateur sports. During the dinner, Crittenden was pressing Davis for an Ontario lottery similar to the Olympic Lottery that would generate funds for sports in Ontario. At one point, Davis leaned forward during that conversation and said: 'Pollock, you are the government's expert on gambling,' ... Those words had consequences."

Among Marshall's duties as the Assistant Deputy Attorney General, he served as Director of the Strike Force Against Organized Crime that sought to coordinate anti-crime efforts of the Ontario Provincial Police, Regional Police Forces and the RCMP with the FBI and the US Attorney in Upstate New York.

In those days, before the plague of narcotics, organized crime was primarily involved in illegal gambling. The focus was on bookmaking. Law enforcement targeted the cross-border influence of the Magadino Crime family in Buffalo, the

largest "layoff center" for bookmaking in North America, next to Las Vegas. For those not hip to the jargon, "layoff" refers to a bookmaker placing a wager with another bookmaker in order to help reduce a liability or to balance books. Marshall welcomed the Premier's remarks because had just completed a task force study on off-track betting. **Premier Bill Davis** told Marshall, "Crit has been bending my ear about launching a lottery in Ontario to support sports. Do you think it would be successful?"

"Probably," Marshall replied casually, "My mother buys Irish Sweepstakes tickets all the time and I am sure that she is not alone."

And that was the end of it.

The following Monday, Marshall was summoned to the Premier's Office and was asked to head up a task force to determine the feasibility of an Ontario lottery. His first call on that assignment was to Gus Harrison, the Director of the Michigan Lottery, who, in a previous role, had been the Commissioner of Penitentiaries. A meeting was arranged with the Director of the Ohio Lottery and a few days later with Maurice Cousteau who was then President of Loto Quebec. Marshall recalls that it seemed to him that "Cousteau didn't know too much about the lottery, but at lunch he certainly had a good eye for wine."

From those brief meetings it became very clear that with a profit margin of 40%, the lottery business could be a profitable enterprise for Ontario.

On December 4th, 1974, invited to attend a Cabinet meeting, Marshall delivered his report accompanied with charts and slides. In his presentation he was assisted by his friend Peter Szego, who had been a policy advisor to Ms. Crittenden. His report confirmed an Ontario lottery was feasible.

"How long do you think it would take to implement," asked the Premier.

"That all depends on who does it and how much government interference is involved," Marshall replied in his bold manner.

"Well, you are going to do it," replied the Premier, "... So, how long?"

Marshall let his bravado get the better of him and said that it probably could be done within six months.

"No way," grumbled Alan Grossman, the Minister of Revenue, "Nothing in government can be done that quickly."

By this time, Marshall had met with Gaston Boulanger of British American Banknote, who was the guiding light in the success of the provincial lotteries, so Marshall confidently declared: "Well, without too much interference, I think it can be done."

"It will never happen," scoffed Grossman.

"Why don't you bet him, Alan?" offered Roy McMurtry, the Attorney General.

"OK, I'll bet you five bucks that you can't do it in six months", said Grossman proffering his hand across the table.

"Done", Marshall agreed and began his race for a lottery launch. With a repayable advance of $300,000 from the provincial Treasurer, Peter Szego, Barbara Jesson, David Galloway (a brilliant Harvard Business School-trained consultant), joined in to make it happen. Legislation was drafted and passed in February 1975; the Ontario Lottery Corporation board was appointed shortly thereafter. On April 3rd, 1975 (120 days after December 4th) 1.4 million lottery tickets for a bi-weekly lottery called WINTARIO went on sale, using a makeshift crew of distributors. It was sold out in three days. Marshall won his $5 bet.

SWEEPSTAKES SYSTEM CAUSES TROUBLE

On April 30th 1975, after the first two draws of the Western Canada Lottery, attendance at the third draw in Saskatoon had diminished. People weren't that excited to see little pieces of paper drawn from a drum. WCLF staff and the auditors handled the 2000 $100 prizes by themselves. One of the eight winners was a Saskatchewan-sold ticket which bore the legendary musical name of Les Paul, the guitar genius. Billy Weissmann could not contact him.

The telephone company told Billy that the phone number shown on the ticket had been disconnected but Billy — ingenious as ever — persuaded SaskTel to give him the current phone number at the address on the ticket.

An older voice with a heavy eastern European accent came on the line. Billy told the man that he was the lottery representative and had good news. He then asked if there was someone there by the name of Paul.

"Ja," the man growled, "Dat's me, Pawluk." He pronounced it "Paul Look".

Billy asked: "On your lottery ticket, did you write your last name as Paul to make it easier to understand?"

"Ja," the man confirmed.

It can be argued that Billy should have asked more questions but all of us were naïve in the world of gambling and grifters. You may wonder why this unremarkable incident found a spot in this tale. Stay tuned.

THE VANCOUVER TV SHOW

The May 10th 1975 televised draw for the third issue of the Western Canada Lottery in Vancouver made a big splash. Ginette Reno, a feted Quebec songstress, was the guest star. Maurice Cousteau the Loto Quebec boss and Jean-Marc Lafaille, the young lawyer, were invited as guests of honour. These two men — aware that your lottery scribe wanted to change the system — brought along **Gaston Boulanger**, the president of the printing firm that printed the Quebec and Olympic lottery tickets.

On the afternoon before the evening's draw, WCLF board members and spouses were invited to sail around Coal Harbour in a yacht; well, maybe not a yacht, but a well-appointed motorboat. Gaston's objective was to schmooze his potential customers. Regretfully his plan went awry: 300 metres from shore, the engine stalled and the boat was adrift.

Apart from Gaston Boulanger, this incident didn't bother anyone because food and drink were available in abundance. Gaston was in the engine room, splattered in oil, trying to revive the machinery. He stayed there for most of the afternoon and finally agreed to call for a tow back to the Bayshore Marina.

Meanwhile rehearsals for the televised draw were underway at Vancouver's Queen Elizabeth Theatre. Joe Kanuka, the WCLF lawyer sauntered into the temporary lottery office and watched the graphic artist calligraph the eight oversized cheques made of thick card-stock. The pretty cheques were authentic and would serve as a promotional device at the prize presentation. After the show, the winners' names and the amount of the respective prizes would be entered.

Instead of making the cheque out to Les Paul which was the name on the winning ticket, Billy Weissmann, a generous young man, planned to make it easier for Bill Pawluk to cash the cheque by inserting Pawluk's name on the cheque and not his 'nom de plume', Les Paul. This panicked Joe Kanuka the lawyer and he set out to correct matters.

He found Mr. Pawluk in his hotel room and asked for proof that the name Les Paul was somehow connected to Bill Pawluk. The man opened a suitcase and tossed a pile of tickets stubs on the bed. Joe spoke in Ukrainian to the man, who swore that Les Paul was his "pen name."

Joe met with Alex Trebek, the show's emcee and instructed him introduce Bill Pawluk as playing on behalf of Les Paul. Trebek objected. "That's awful," he protested. "I'll sound as if I have my head up my ass." But Joe was adamant and Alex did what was asked of him which only added to the problems to come.

When it was Pawluk's turn to speak on the show, Alex asked him how many tickets he had bought. "I buy two hoonderd ebberry time," he said. Alex, off-camera rolled his eyes. Pawluk didn't win the jackpot. He drew the lowest prize category: $25,000. He accepted his fancy calligraphed cheque with the name Les Paul as the payee. His family was elated.

Lawyers are supposed to keep their clients out of trouble. By insisting that we issue the cheque to Les Paul, Joe Kanuka had gotten the WCLF in trouble. Later, that lottery chicken would come home to roost.

1975 WESTERN CANADA GAMES

In August 1975, the first Western Canada Summer Games were officially launched in Regina. The initiative had sprung from the Implementation Task Force that had spawned the Western Canada Lottery. The connection of the Games to the lottery was obvious. Lottery profits would provide the funding. The Games were to convene every four years, one year ahead of the summer Olympics. The roster of sports included 23 summer-sport disciplines, similar to the Olympics. The objective was to provide promising athletes with the opportunity to compete at a national level in a sports-festival setting.

To get this new Western sports event to be shown on television, some financial incentives were needed. Telecasting from remote sites is a costly enterprise. Therefore, combining the Western Canada Games with the drawing of the series AD of the WCLF was a smart move.

At the opening of the first Western Canada Games at Taylor Field in Regina, your lottery scribe and his spouse were seated in the VIP section. It was a treat to see each province parade its 400 top-athletes in the Opening Ceremonies.

Our son, **Leonard** (at age 20) was part of the Manitoba water polo team. As he marched past the VIP section, he suddenly leaped across the low-level barrier and ran towards his mother who was seated in the VIP section. He handed her a little Manitoba flag. He was obviously stirred by the occasion. It was a precious gift to us, a public compliment by a son to his parents.

THE CHICKEN COMES HOME TO ROOST

The morning after the opening ceremony, at breakfast at the Regina Inn, trouble announced itself. A gentleman with distinct South-East Asian features and accent to match approached our table. He pointed to a shifty-looking man standing at the back of the restaurant. "That is Mr. Les Paul," he proclaimed in his Mumbai English. "Mr. Paul never received his winnings from the August draw in Vancouver and Mr. Paul would like to have his cheque presented to him as soon as possible."

I wondered what he meant when he said Mr. Paul wanted his cheque "presented." It turned out that Billy Weissmann was a too-high achiever at Public Relations. Not only had he prepared calligraphed cheques for the winners, when the bank returned the cashed cheques (they did that back then), Billy forwarded them to the winners as a souvenir of their good luck.

To mail the cheques, he used the address given on the ticket stubs. The cheque for Les Paul had been addressed to Les Paul at the home of Bill Pawluk just as it read on the lottery stub. However, the post office had a forwarding address for Les Paul in Hudson Bay, Saskatchewan.

Les Paul — souvenir cheque in hand — stood at the back of the restaurant. When I introduced myself, Mr. Paul explained that he had been a lodger at Bill Pawluk's place for several years and then moved "Up North."

On the back of that huge lottery cheque, the endorsement, "Les Paul" was written in the same elegant lettering as the calligraphed name on the front. I wondered, how in the hell could the bank have not noticed that there was something amiss. Later, at the trial, the manager of the TD Bank where Pawluk cashed the cheque testified that he had watched the televised draw and saw Bill Pawluk. He needed no further proof of identity.

THE TRIAL

The trial was held in the Provincial Court in Melfort, Saskatchewan. The judge found that the WCLF had violated its own rules. When Pawluk couldn't prove that he was Les Paul, the lottery should have advertised in the newspapers. As the judge pointed out, if the lottery had mailed a notice of the win, the postman would have found him, even though Billy Weissmann couldn't.

As soon as Les Paul stepped forward with his claim, the TD bank closed Pawluk's account. It still had a $5,000 balance. The judge ordered that the WCLF pay Les Paul $25,000 and ordered the TD Bank to return the $5,000 to Pawluk.

During the trial, both Pawluk and Paul were shifty and gave evasive answers. To this day, I still have a quiet notion that Pawluk and Paul were in cahoots so that each would get the prize. Joe Kanuka, our lawyer, admitted to the Court that WCLF was remiss. Later, over a drink, I told him that if he hadn't advised us to make the cheque out to Les Paul, the PR problem would have never arisen, but the wrong person would have been enriched.

THE COMPROMISED REGISTERED SYSTEM

The push for an improved lottery system was going nowhere. Despite news reports about flaws in the registered lottery system, the professional agencies strongly objected to any change. The Olympic Lottery had clearly demonstrated that the public understood the "bearer" system where the player buys a ticket with a serial number and then checks the winning numbers after the draw.

The professional agencies sent thousands of lottery tickets far and wide to names and addresses on mailing lists that can be purchased from various sources. Each agency guarded these purchased names with great care. What the professional distributors worried about most was that the bearer ticket system required them to pay for their tickets in advance. While they could obtain a refund for any unsold tickets, they realized that if they pre-paid the tickets they couldn't very well spread them indiscriminately across the continent. They'd never get their money back!

Their public argument against a bearer system was that — unlike the registered system — winners had to declare themselves. They depicted the ticket-buying public as naïfs, who — once they had invested in a lottery ticket — would forget all about it, leaving prizes unclaimed.

It was clear that if the WCLF wanted to introduce the bearer system, the weakness of the current system had to be exposed. When the public grasped the inherent problems, there would be a groundswell in favour of a more secure system. The obvious targets for supporting such a change were the political leaders and the press, in that order.

THE BATTLE FOR A BEARER SYSTEM

Manitoba had the largest number of lottery agencies objecting to change. Their political connections were strong enough to convince several Cabinet Ministers to oppose any changes. I approached Larry Desjardins with a rather tricky scheme that might convince his cabinet colleagues that the current system was far from secure. He chortled about the deviousness of my plan. I took some of the free-floating Western Canada Lottery tickets and — using Larry's private phone index — I copied names and addresses of key members of Cabinet on the phony ticket stubs. I didn't pay for the tickets because I didn't intend to put them in the drum.

The phoney stubs were glued on an ordinary postcard. On the back was typed: "The ticket stub is your proof of entry in the Western Canada Lottery draw on October 11, 1975." The design and wording on the real WCLF post card was much more professional, but the whole thing was intended to look fishy.

Feedback came quickly. Saul Cherniak and Sid Green, both conscientious socialists and senior Cabinet Ministers, approached Larry after a Cabinet meeting and informed him that neither one had ever bought a ticket, so what was this notice of purchase? Larry, delighted in his role as provocateur, looked at the postcard, said that it didn't look very official and undertook to get back to them. He already knew the answer, of course, but he wanted to respond to them at a full cabinet meeting with the Premier and the Attorney-General in attendance. He first got both ministers to assert that they believed the receipt to be real. He then revealed the hoax.

"My colleagues were not happy that I had made them look a bit naive," he told me later. "They were not in a mood to agree to a change."

Then some help from an unexpected source arrived. The RCMP reported that a locker at the bus-depot, opened after its 30-day expiry period, contained 700 tickets stubs sold by someone who kept the money and abandoned the stubs. The draw had been held weeks earlier and the holders of these tickets were not in the draw. None of them complained that they had never received a receipt. They probably didn't even know they were supposed to get one.

Larry took this "gift" and played it at Cabinet for all it was worth. He pointed out that ordinary crooks could sell tickets and keep the money but that smarter crooks would send out phoney receipts so that people wouldn't get suspicious. Larry immediately issued a news release of the RCMP's findings and announced that, although he expected fierce opposition from the major selling agencies, he couldn't let the current lottery scheme continue.

Larry kept the ministers in the other provinces abreast of the progress at his own cabinet table. He convinced his western colleagues that the current system was untenable and told them in his own immortal words: "We're sitting on a powder keg that's gonna blow up in our face." His presentation of the various frauds perpetrated during the first year of lottery draws convinced the Manitoba ministers to approve the new system.

PUBLIC CRITICISM HURTS

The professional selling agencies were ready for combat and they trained their guns on your lottery scribe. There were whispers to the media that Simonis had bankrupted SPORTS TOTO. A bit of a rabble-rouser, *Tribune* reporter **Vic Grant** did a hatchet job. Previously, whenever my name had appeared in the sports press it was always in a positive way. For the first time I was being criticized and made out to be a scheming, underhanded conniver—a shill for an incompetent government. It bothered me greatly and I dreaded that my friends and family were reading these accusations.

Over lunch at the Charterhouse, a group of friends — Bruce Wardrope, Co Lammens and **Joe Giczi** — listened to my fears and facts. They were very

supportive and in the next few weeks, I learned a very important lesson about the limelight. You might be obsessed with what people say or write but the public reads it and forgets. George Kent, the CBC producer, asked: "I saw something about you in a front-page story in the Free Press. What was all that about? Water polo?"

Despite the furor about the registered system versus the bearer system, it became publicly clear that the bearer system provided full accountability of tickets, a higher return to the prize pot, and lower administration costs— all leading to higher contributions to good causes.

THE "BOMB THREAT"

As the face of the WCLF, I had incurred the wrath of the big lottery agencies. Among harassing phone calls, a picture postcard of a headstone imprinted with my name on it was delivered to our family home. I had no fear of physical harm until, one day, my **wife Ina** phoned me at work, yelling that she didn't dare go into the house because something black and suspicious was attached to the doorknob. It looked like a bomb!

When I got home, I saw that the package looked like a man's sock. It felt as if there was something hard inside but when I opened the package, there was no explosion. It contained a chocolate gift from Dale Nelson, the producer of the television show. It seems hilarious now but we were often in a state of anxiety in those days. Even our children didn't escape public harangue. Son Leonard, at a get-together with his friends met a priest/teacher from St. Paul's High School. Upon learning Len's last name, the cleric told him in accusing terms how his father was harming the church's programs. Fortunately, Len shrugged it off.

CHANGE IS DIFFICULT

While Larry Desjardins fought an honourable battle for change at the Cabinet table, the professional distributors were not so morally constrained. It was easy to dismiss agency leaders as people who would do or say anything to keep their livelihood, but complaints by the "Good Causes" that benefitted from their profits were more difficult to counter.

As the Minister of the Crown who had fought for the funding of religious (Catholic) schools, Desjardins was under pressure from his alma mater, St. Paul's High School, a major Catholic educational institution. The governing board of the school was loaded with influential Winnipeggers.

Father Stephen Boyle was the priest in charge of fundraising. When the new lottery system was announced, he pushed Desjardin's guilt button. As Cabinet Minister, Larry was charged with upholding the law and the St. Paul's lottery distributor was one of the major offenders of the Criminal Code.

"But it is for a good cause," Father Boyle argued.

"With that attitude there is an easier way to make money for the school. Why not rob a bank?" Larry retorted.

"I am not speaking only for St Paul's," Father Boyle said. "I am appealing on behalf of all the major lottery distributors."

"Same for them! The province will no longer tolerate transgressions of the laws," Larry thundered.

CHARITABLE DISTRIBUTORS SIDELINED

The ministerial edict didn't slow the lottery sellers for long. Father Boyle and the heads of the major distributors brushed past Larry and called directly upon Premier Schreyer. A week later, Larry announced a compromise. A Manitoba-only charitable lottery would be licensed, distinct and separate from the WCLF.

 It would be called Total Community Involvement (TCI) and was to be organized by the former distributors themselves. The participating members included all former sellers of the Manitoba Sweepstakes including the Manitoba Sports Federation. Their license was limited to a $1 ticket price and a maximum first prize of $100,000. In addition, TCI was explicitly forbidden to sell tickets in the three other Western provinces. (There was no mention of the rest of North America).

After this, the Total Community Involvement agencies organized themselves, did reasonably well and disappeared from your frazzled scribe's radar. They carried on for a year or so but, in the face of competition by the Western Canada Lottery and the Olympic Lottery they soon ceased operations and began applying for lottery grants from government.

It was a pyrrhic victory for WCLF in Manitoba — a win in the sense of neutralizing the hostile sales agencies but a loss of a formidable, albeit illegal, marketing machine. While the distribution systems of the other provinces were growing, Manitoba had to start anew. The days of selling lottery tickets to friends and co-workers from a booklet in your coat pocket were over.

DESIGNING A HORSE BY COMMITTEE

Now that the ministers and the board had approved a new system, the question was: which lottery system? The bearer systems employed by Quebec and Ontario were the simplest and successful. For your scribe it was a no-brainer: Copy them! However, the board was leery of a change to a simple system. The thinking was that several features of the old system should be retained, especially such goodies as board members traveling to other cities to attend the TV Show on the lottery's nickel.

As a result, the design of the first bearer game, dubbed the $3 WESTERN, was a result of bad inputs by board members who didn't fully understand games of chance. It was a perfect example of "A camel is a horse designed by a committee." Your lottery scribe was outnumbered in the desired to clone Wintario and Quebec's Mini-Loto.

The old guard of the WCLF board wanted to keep familiar features of the old system. First, there was the cost of the ticket. Your brave scribe pushed for the price of the ticket that every other jurisdiction in North America offered, i.e. $1.50. Those of the mindset of pleasing the professional, charitable distributors insisted that the $2.50 price should be maintained. However, the greatest need was to raise the prize percentage that still hovered around 12-15% of sales. Another absolute requirement was to lower the commissions. After a desperate plea to conform to other North American lottery systems, the controversy ended in a slightly reduced commission.

Thus, on October 1975, the $3 WESTERN was born — an improvement in terms of security but as a game design, it landed with a thud. An abomination. A disaster in the making. A 7-digit piece of misery.

The conventional bearer system draws a five or six-digit winning number that spins off subsidiary prizes. For example, in a six-digit game, tickets that match only the last three digits of that number win a prize. Those matching only the last four digits win a bigger prize. The last five digits would win more and matching all six got the main prize.

If you're wondering at the awkward wording, "Tickets matching ONLY the last…", those winners who have four matching numbers have also a three-match and if the world ONLY was omitted, those having four digits correct would also have a legal claim on having three digits correct.

Another problem for those yearning for the old system was that drawing only one winning number meant that the draw process would last about two minutes. The board members abhorred this short cut. What would happen to the one-hour TV show that was a four-times-a-year party for the board members? The benefits included travelling throughout the West, being spotted in the TV audience, socializing with winners and schmoozing with Alex Trebek. Those features shouldn't be eliminated, should they? The shortened version would be efficient and cost less but people should have fun seeing an entertaining TV show. Right?

Board members who had grown-up with the Irish Sweepstakes couldn't bring themselves to appreciate the simple features of the bearer system. When a winning number was drawn in a bearer system, there was a chance that that ticket bearing that number isn't sold. Hence, no winner. The subsidiary numbers of that winning number may not have all been sold. So, what to do with the prizes those tickets would not pay out?

This is where the reasoning of the inexperienced board members went awry. The basis of the bearer system is that 45% of ticket sold is devoted to the prize fund. When all prize claims have been paid (from that 45% fund) and there is money left over, that amount is added to an unclaimed prize fund from which bonus prizes are added from time to time. Well, that was too foreign a concept for the board. They ruled that all numbers drawn MUST have the proper prizes attached. I yelled my frustration but I couldn't convince the board, not even my very own Minister, Larry Desjardins.

The argument was lost. The idea of a TV show had to continue.

In keeping with the old format, there would be eight tickets drawn and the holders of those tickets would be part of the TV show. As a gesture toward the concept of lotteries in Ontario and Quebec, one extra 7-digit number would be drawn that would yield subsidiary prizes.

BE CAREFUL WHAT YOU ASK FOR!

The board members were smugly satisfied with over-riding management's recommendation but they hadn't fully grasped that, in order to draw winning tickets from sold ticket-numbers only, the unsold tickets needed to be removed from the draw. Larry proved to be as uncomprehending as the rest. "Just take the unsold tickets out of the draw," he suggested cheerfully.

To draw numbers only from tickets that are sold, the lottery operator must wait until all unsold tickets have been returned and refunded, something that takes many days. The unsold numbers are then removed from the original list by a simple computer program but with frustrating results when it comes to the draw for winning numbers.

Gaston Boulanger, our printer, shared a sigh with me and joined in figuring how to achieve this complicated task.

To begin: 2.5 million ticket numbers are printed, sequentially numbered from 1,000,000 to 3,499,999. The aim is to delete all unsold numbers, leaving only sold numbers — in sequence, but with large gaps of unsold numbers in between. The draw machine with the balls doesn't know which numbers have been deleted. A scheme has to be devised. To draw a winning number, the eligible numbers are sorted by last digits in 9 different lists numbered from 1-9.

To explain it in a different way, there will be a (long) list containing all the eligible numbers that end in 0, a second list with the last digits ending in 1, a third one with the last digit ending in 2 and so on.

The draw for last digit is first. One draw machine is loaded with balls (size 90 mm width) numbered 0 through 9. One smaller draw machine sits empty. It holds balls of 50mm width). To simulate a draw:

- The first digit drawn will be the LAST digit of the winning lottery number: Let's say that was number 9.
- Backstage, all numbers other than those ending in 9 are discarded.
- Every ball so drawn is re-inserted in the draw machine.
- Only tickets ending in 9 are now in play.
- The second digit drawn is: Let's say number 5. Backstage, all numbers other than ending in 59 are discarded.
- The third number drawn is 6. Backstage, all numbers other than ending in 659 are discarded.
- The fourth digit drawn is 1. Back stage all numbers other than ending in 1659 are discarded.
- The fifth digit drawn is 5. Only the list with sold tickets ending 51659 is left.

But there are two digits still needed to complete a 7-digit winning number.

Since the ticket numbers issued ran from 1,000,000 to 3,499,999, we need to check to see how many first-two-digits survived in this procedure. (The draw drum with the 50mm balls (the smaller ones) is filled with the balls that correspond to the ticket numbers still alive)

If you've read this far you and followed it, you qualify as a lottery expert. The draw was a stinker imposed by people who didn't understand. I should have resigned when they imposed it but I had a family to feed. The consequences of this weird draw scheme are yet to come. Wait for it.

At the televised draw in Victoria, BC on May 14, 1976, only six holders of the eight winning numbers stepped forward. Minor BC celebrities were invited to stand in for the two no-shows, who — despite their absence — would collect whatever their substitutes won for them.

Bob Henderson, the draw's auditor remembers: "The show was running long, with only 70 seconds remaining to draw the final two digits of a seven-digit number. There were only two eligible tickets and their prefixes were 21 and 31. Those two balls were put into the draw drum where they wildly jumped around.

Experience suggested when there were so few balls in the machine, it might take as long as 90 seconds for one ball to drop."

The audience waited. The CTV Nightly news was next. With three seconds to go, ball number 21 dropped. Alex Trebek yelled: "Good night!" The credits rolled as Bob ran backstage and barfed into a fireman's bucket. Later, Bob said that he toyed with the idea of holding the two balls behind his back and ask one of the winners on stage to choose the left hand or the right. It would have been much quicker and would have been a nice news story.

NEW MANITOBA DISTRIBUTOR

At the end of March 1976, when the charitable distributors were winding up the sales of the Series AE, the Province of Manitoba incorporated the Western Lottery Manitoba Distributors (WLMD). It was a new course that would put Manitoba behind the eight-ball for a while but the other Western provinces had to follow sooner or later. (BC didn't get around to it until six years later)

Changes in personnel caused **Terry O'Rourke**, WCLF's advertising manager to be traded for Len Gzebb, the interim manager of the Manitoba Sweepstakes. Michelle McBride left WCLF to join the new WLMD. The rest of the staff were offered positions either within the civil service or the administration of the new WLMD. A few joined the Head Office of the WCLF. None lost their employment.

The most noteworthy appointment by Larry Desjardins was the WLMD manager: his son-in-law **Leonard Bye,** whose sole prior experience was as an apprentice embalmer at a funeral home. "Watch out for him, please?" Desjardins asked me. "Leonard hasn't even managed a lemonade stand." In the long run the nepotism didn't work out. More on that later.

New sales people were brought in to sign-up retailers. It was a tough sell. It was 1975 and lottery tickets were still considered a bit shady— certainly not an item that would one would readily find on a store counter. A raggedy network of pioneering hardware stores, bicycle repairs and corner groceries was cobbled together. Many of the outlets who had previously sold Manitoba Sweepstakes on behalf of a club, balked at the idea of paying for tickets in advance.

Those merchants who refused a retail license were correct in calculating financial returns. Investing in a product that doesn't move off the shelves for three months isn't worth the 10% commission that it yields.

The new Manitoba distribution staff was asked to sell a bastardized bearer-ticket format to a disturbed market. Sales slumped to a record low. Dark clouds were gathering. Manitoba was in trouble.

UNCLAIMED PRIZES

Many US lotteries implemented the simplest solution for unclaimed prizes. If after a certain period of time a prize is not claimed, the state confiscates the amount. One may argue whether that is fair. The prize was initially part of an amount dedicated to be paid-out as prize. Already in the early years of lotteries in Canada, it was established that when the lottery promises to pay out 45% of sales in prizes, the lottery will pay out 45% and not enrich itself by keeping unclaimed prizes for itself.

Ontario took this promise literally. Every prize, large or small was registered and if not claimed within the time period it was dedicated to the extra prize fund — a labour-intensive accounting.

Your lottery scribe, with ministerial assent, established a policy in Western Canada that 45% of total sales would be dedicated to the Prize Fund. All prize-claims would be paid from that account. After the claim period had expired, the remaining funds in the account would be returned to players in bonus prizes. Hence a stable prize percentage was guaranteed. Soon the other provincial lottery corporations instituted the same policy.

NEW DRAW MACHINES

With the change from drawing names to drawing numbers, the submarine-shaped draw machine that used to carry millions of stubs was rendered obsolete. Gaston Boulanger, the boss of BA Banknote, owned the franchise for the most popular number-drawing draw machine. The Ryo-Catteau machine's best feature is that, when it is in operation, it mixes the balls thoroughly. The machine is controlled by a hand-held device that allows the draw-master to control how many balls will be released based on the game being played.

Your lottery scribe accompanied Boulanger to the manufacturer in northern France. It was my third trip to Europe on behalf of the lottery business. When we got to the small border town of Wattrelos, the business turned out to be a carpet-weaving factory, typical of the industry in that area.

What did a carpet factory have to do with a lottery? The technician who maintained the carpet weaving equipment had hit upon the idea to convert the principals of mechanical weaving to a device that randomly mixed rubber balls in a Plexiglas bowl. WCLF ordered seven units. It proved to be the correct decision; the machines looked impressive and lasted for many years.

NEW TICKET

Fears that the public wouldn't understand the format of the new $3 WESTERN were quickly laid to rest. The explanation was rather simple. Whoever held a ticket with a number that matched a winning number drawn would get the prize attached to that number. Names of winners wouldn't be known until they stepped forward to claim their prize. The bearer-ticket was like owning a $10 bill. If you lost it, the finder would own it, unless you wrote your name on the back of the lottery ticket as soon as you bought it. Then it was yours and no one else could claim the prize.

In the 1970s, security demanded that lottery tickets couldn't be copied without resorting to buying a security printing plant. BA Banknote, one of Canada's banknote printers, applied the same printing technique for lottery tickets as it did for Canadian currency. In "Intaglio," as the printing technique is called, the image is engraved upon special paper. As part of the security paper, planchettes (tiny removable dots) are embedded, a well-known security feature used for many years on Canadian dollar bills.

THE LAUNCH

The $3 WESTERN was launched in November of 1975. The ticket price was divided into four categories: If all tickets issued were sold, the percentages worked out as:

- Prize fund 45%
- Retailer commissions 10%
- Distributor commission 10%
- Gross profit to WCLF 35%

To repeat: If all tickets issued were sold. If they weren't all sold the percentages would change up or down depending which prizes were won.

The faulty game design came back to haunt. Eight winners were guaranteed prizes ranging from S10,000 to $500,000. By order of the Board, there would be no prizes on unsold tickets, thus — in the early draws — the prize fund amounted sometimes to 55% and produced a gross profit of 25% profit rather than the projected 35%.

The reduction came as a shock to board members who hadn't understood the system they had forced on management. Many believed that the projected 35% profit margin was etched in stone — a guarantee. board members of the three provinces west of Manitoba were looking for a scapegoat. "If only Manitoba had pulled its weight… the issue would have been sold out."

Looking for a solution, the board agreed that each province should contribute to the prize fund on a per-capita basis and not an amount corresponding to sales. Holy cow! In that arrangement, Manitoba's sales would not even cover its compulsory share of the prize fund. Manitoba would actually have to spend tax revenue to run a lottery. But majority rules! The compulsory prize contribution was imposed retroactively! Manitoba would have to pay!

Upon learning about this most unfair decision, Desjardins — who had moved over to be the Minister for Health and was not on the board—phoned his former colleagues: the Western lottery ministers. He argued that Manitoba had changed its distribution system for a better future. He further added that the WCLF was one entity and should act as such.

A couple of days later, Chairman Bill Clarke (forced by his Minister) called an urgent board conference call and the compulsory prize contribution was reversed. The lottery was returned to a partnership. One for all; all for one. A lesson learned.

HOW TO LIE WITH STATISTICS

Brian Horton, manager of the Manitoba Sports Federation was still upset that his organization's lottery was dying. He set out to portray the WESTERN as a losing proposition.

Although he thoroughly understood the concept of prizes and profits, he decided to launch a guerrilla attack. He purloined some WCLF stationary and published a fictitious accounting of the first draw of the $3 WESTERN including an illustration of what the profit numbers would have looked like if all tickets had been sold. In that ideal scenario the profit would amount to 35% of sales. (The entire series was NOT sold out and the profit was 25%.)

He compared the profit numbers if all tickets had been sold with the actual sales and presto...he manufactured a loss! He knew that the draw hadn't made the ideal 35% profit of sales but only 25% profit. He referred to the difference an $840,000 loss. A fictional loss!

Horton sent his sham accounting anonymously to **Fred Cleverley** (an oxymoron if there ever was one)— a reporter at the *Winnipeg Free Press* who promptly published a front-page story: "Lottery loses $840,000." All other media immediately jumped on this stunning revelation.

Operating on the age-old newspaper maxim that facts tend to spoil a good story, Fred Cleverley hadn't bothered to talk to me or anyone else in the organization. Larry Desjardins tried to contact him after the fact but Mr. Cleverley didn't return the call.

A brash young WCLF board member from Saskatchewan, Casper Pilak, did manage to contact Cleverley and tried to explain to him that a reduction in projected profit cannot be called a loss.

"Besides" Pilak added, "the reduction in projected profits wasn't $840,000 as your article stated, it was $760,000." The next day's Free Press headline read: "Lottery losses grow to $760,000."

Lawrie Pollard of Pollard Banknote, vying for the WCLF's ticket printing contract, noticed your sad scribe's agony and offered to call upon his friend, the publisher of the Free Press. Lawrie Pollard laid it all out, proving that the accounting was a gross misrepresentation.

Lawrie later reported that the publisher just smiled and said, "You've got to keep the government's feet to the fire, just to keep them honest. I think that lotteries should be outlawed."

While the story upset many people in the lottery business, the public forgot about it very quickly.

BIRTH OF THE WESTERN EXPRESS

It was frustrating to see lottery organizations in the US, Quebec and Ontario enjoying success with their weekly, low priced lotteries at $1 while your vexed scribe had to deal with a rapidly declining, hybrid $3 scheme.

Most board members and lottery ministers viewed the old-world Sweepstakes format as the one-and-only feasible lottery system. They were either blind to the economic benefits of more frequent draws or knew it and resisted any further growth of lotteries.

A great number of legislators in the Western provinces were afraid to support lotteries. Your astonished scribe had seen that phenomenon in the first year, when elected officials would condemn the lottery publicly and then — in private — take delight in the growing profits to fund their favourite projects. Most politicians — except for Desjardins — still didn't view lotteries as a legitimate product to be sold in convenience stores.

For a weekly lottery to be successful, it needed retail distribution. Yet, the community-at-large wasn't ready to embrace modern lottery marketing.

"Lottery tickets are bought from people's jacket pockets and that's how it has always been," wrote the *Lethbridge Herald*.

"Selling lottery tickets in stores would commercialize a social activity such as a raffle," the *Vancouver Province* declared. There was also great concern about additional lottery games.

A BC lottery minister once asked me, "Once you have one lottery why do you need two?" He found it quite normal that 14 different brands of toothpaste were available in stores throughout the province but the concept of consumer choice in lotteries escaped him.

Larry Desjardins was different. Manitoba had opted to abandon community agencies as distributors and settled for retail distribution. The new Manitoba sales organizations badly needed more products than the four-times-a-year WESTERN and the infrequent Olympic Lottery. Moreover, the Olympic lottery would end within a few months.

I told Larry that retail stores need products with rapid turnover. He took my word that the $3 WESTERN could not survive by itself. In an off-handed manner he told me to get everything ready for a bi-weekly lottery for Manitoba only. He had tried and failed to convince his Western colleagues of the necessity for a more frequently-drawn, low-prized game.

The new *Western Express* (so baptized by Richard Muller, our advertising guru) was based on an issue of 90,000 tickets (called a series) numbered from 10,000 to 99,999. The market would decide how many series should be sold.

Tickets were issued in booklets of five. Once the secure pouch that held the five tickets was opened, those tickets couldn't be returned for a refund.

For this initial issue, for a Manitoba market of a million people, two series were issued. Individual tickets within a series were marked on the pouches with Series # 1, Series # 2 etc. This may seem obvious but just wait — even such little things can come back and bite you in the ass.

Prize calculations were easy to follow:

- Tickets holders with ONLY the last 3-digits correct win $10;
- Those with ONLY the last 4-digits correct win $100;
- All 5-digits correct wins $1,000.
- A series number would be drawn and the ticket holder who had the 5 digits correct AND the series number would win $50,000.

Only unopened pouches could be bought back. However, for the first draw there were no returns. The issue had sold out. For the third draw there would be a Series #3 in play.

POUCHES

As mentioned before, tickets were sold in secure opaque pouches that contained five tickets. The "secure" pouches were quite secure. Once opened and the tickets removed, the little envelope would somewhat adhere to itself, making it impossible to re-insert losing tickets after the draw and get a refund. Many buyers bought the $5 pouch for themselves. Another feature of the pouch was that it didn't have to be turned in for a refund, thereby making it an instant-win game after the winning numbers were drawn.

HE DIDN'T SAY NO

Since responsibility for the Western EXPRESS rested with Manitoba, the WCLF board could only watch. At every step of the way — ticket printing, advertising and investing in material and equipment, your lottery scribe informed Minister Desjardins and his colleagues what was going on.

Finally, everything was in place. Time for "Go" or "No Go".

Your brave scribe realized that the little-known government concept of *"Absence of disapproval"* was in operation. One cannot find a description of this phenomenon in any text book. It has to be grasped and assimilated. I asked Larry Desjardins directly: "Do I have your permission to launch the EXPRESS in Manitoba on the first of April of 1976?"

He responded that he wasn't able to give me an answer. I asked Larry what I was supposed to do. Money was spent. Wheels were spinning. Clocks were ticking. Then, I suddenly understood that "Absence of Disapproval" was in operation. He looked at me directly and said: "I didn't say no!"

What he meant was: Go ahead. If things go sideways, I'll help but if it becomes controversial, I will castigate you publicly because I haven't given you approval. Then we will go from there." Not everyone dares to launch a government program under such vague circumstances and —if you're faced with such a dilemma, my recommendation is to be careful. And make sure the boss knows everything you are going to do; no surprises!

The Western EXPRESS went on sale — in Manitoba only — on April 21, 1976. CKY TV, Manitoba's independent TV channel, agreed to produce a television show for the *WESTERN EXPRESS* on Saturdays at 7.30 PM.

The show, supported by a small production budget, was done in a cheap but folksy way. **Don Wittman**, the CBC Sportscaster was engaged as the *"EXPRESS draw-master,"* a position he was to fill for nearly two decades. With only five single-digit numbers to draw and one series number, the show needed added patter to fill the available 22 minutes. The format was that a well-known citizen, with something to tell about anything of interest, was interviewed and then invited to push the remote button for the lottery ball to drop.

David Jandrisch, a versatile musician, supplied the music. David would go on to work for the lottery show as musical conductor for a decade or more.

THERE'S A TIE IN YOUR COFFEE

As in any business, the relationship between a lottery and its banks is important. Banking funds and paying cheques is the easy part for the bank but the WCLF needed a distribution function for its bi-weekly tickets. Throughout the West more than 600 selling agencies needed to buy their allotment of tickets of the Olympic Lottery, the $3 WESTERN and the new $1 WESTERN EXPRESS. Functionaries of the Canadian Imperial Bank of Commerce visited our offices to discuss their reluctance to act as a distribution service. CIBC, an old-fashioned firm wanted as little as possible to do with gambling. They'd been forced by the Canadian government to handle the Olympic tickets but they were glad that it was almost over.

In addition to distributing tickets, we also wanted the bank to pay out all prizes of $1,000 or less.

The meeting grew quite heated. Len Gzebb remembered the meeting very well. He recalled your lottery scribe getting up from his chair, removing his jacket and launching into a tirade, loudly questioning the recalcitrance of the bank. As he told it, I was standing behind my desk, leaning forward on both hands, so as to better intimidate the bankers opposite.

Leaning forward in an "in-your-face" mode, the tip of my wool-knit tie slowly dipped into the cup of coffee. I noticed that the bank official repeatedly switched his glance from my face to the desk but I believed that to be the effect

of my rant. Of course, he was looking at the coffee slowly soaking its way up my tie. He sputtered a bit and then suddenly pointed at my chest. I looked down and promptly spilled the rest of the coffee over the desk. My argument was lost in the clean up. (Months later, after seeing the potential financial rewards, the banks were outbidding each other for the lottery account!). The staff gave me a fake photo of the event.

PRIZE PAYOUT WITH POSTCARD STANDS

Today when company cheques are required, a button is pushed and a printer produces the document, signed and ready to go. Not so in 1976. As soon as the winning EXPRESS numbers were known, Pollard Banknote began printing a cheque for every winning ticket whether it had been sold or not. Each cheque bore the corresponding winning ticket number. That amounted to 90 cheques for every single series of 90,000 tickets issued. When winners come to collect their prize, keeping that many cheques in a pile wasn't very efficient. One of our people had the idea to purchase carousels like those used to display scenic post cards. It worked. Plus, it gave us an early assessment on how many prizes were claimed, although the slow lottery winners had a year to claim their prize.

ADVERTISING RE-ARRANGED

Since the second draw of the $2.50 Western lottery, Winnipeg's MHG Advertising had held the WCLF advertising account. But now, voices in the other provinces were claiming that their favourite agencies should have a chance at the lucrative lottery account. Larry Desjardins insisted that **Richard Muller**, the owner of MHG, should retain the account. The demand for the advertising bonanza was strong, especially from BC and Alberta who favoured the agency of Baker Lovick. I told Richard that it was impossible for him to retain the whole Western account but that a compromise could be worked out.

The idea was rather simple. A new lottery agency could be created where each provincially designated advertising group would be a partner. WCLF would have a steady lottery advertising group and if any one of the governments

118

would — at some point — want to change its nominee, no problem. There was some skepticism in the viability of the compromise but, under Richard Muller's leadership, the Lottery Agency Group (LAG) was formed. The acronym LAG wasn't inspiring but it was a one-client operation and didn't require publicity.

Many months later, LAG participants lauded Richard's effort. They recognized that having a great account and then seeing 75% of it being divided among others would have been a heart-breaking experience but Richard bit the bullet and stayed in the lottery business for more than two decades.

THE JIG-SAW PUZZLE

The WINTARIO game, launched in May of 1975, was very similar to the *WESTERN EXPRESS*. It also featured a secure pouch that, once opened, glued itself shut. After several draws of WINTARIO, Mr. Gooday, a tradesman in the flooring business walked into the news department of the CBC in Toronto and claimed that given enough pouches, he could predict which ones contained winning tickets. Marshall Pollack, accompanied by Gaston Boulanger, the president of the lottery printing company, visited Mr. Gooday's office.

Mr. Gooday agreed to demonstrate how he located winning tickets. He opened a box of 25 sealed pouches (from a past draw and supplied by the lottery) and arranged them on a table which allowed him to match the overprinted pattern of repeating logos that ran in a diagonal pattern on the plastic packaging.

The man, whose skill was matching carpet patterns had surmised that the pouches were cut from a much larger sheet and once he determined the decorative pattern and the ticket numbering sequence, he could locate the winning pouches.

"How long have you known this?" Marshall asked.

"I only figured it out over the weekend," Gooday said.

"Why didn't you keep quiet and use the system for your personal gain?"

"Oh, I was too pleased to show you my finding," he said. "It's a thrill to beat the lottery."

After this revelation, Gaston Boulanger, the printer, chucked the system of printing ticket numbers in sequence and literally threw 90,000 tickets of a series in a big hopper, shook them thoroughly and packed them—five random-numbered tickets to a pouch.

LOOKING FOR AN EDGE

Mr. Gooday was a model citizen. Regrettably, not all those who found a fault in lottery security were so community-minded. In Manitoba, at about the same time, two series of Western *EXPRESS* were issued — a total of 180,000 tickets. The sealed pouches could be sold right up to draw time and even afterwards, thereby making it an instant game. Unsold, unopened pouches could be returned by retailers for a refund.

In one of the draws of the Western *EXPRESS*, the top prize of $50,000 remained unclaimed. The winning ticket was in series #2.

About 200 pouches remained unsold and of those, 80 were numbered "Series #2." Staff members reported that someone had come into the Manitoba sales office and offered to buy all the returned pouches from series. Even though there was a policy forbidding selling returned pouches after the draw, an eager but naive young employee thought he was doing a great thing... getting a $400 sale for the lottery instead of having them dumped into the shredder.

The buyer, not related or known to anyone in the lottery, opened all pouches and found the winning $50,000 number. It was a risk on the part of the buyer. It was possible that someone out there had that winning ticket but hadn't yet come forward to claim the prize. But, for an investment of $400, for a very reasonable chance at $50,000, it wasn't a great risk.

The press smelled a good story and told a tale of the hapless sales guy at the lottery who didn't have a clue. Your lottery scribe defended the sale of the tickets rather than hang a young employee out to dry. I pointed out that players had a year to claim their prize; therefore, the man had no assurance that in buying the tickets he had a certain winner.

The story kept going and the press loved it. Even my critics in the media said that my response was correct — intellectually — but the public wouldn't buy it. They smelled a conspiracy. Another lesson was learned.

120

When the legislature recessed for lunch, Minister Desjardins was questioned by a TV reporter. Larry looked straight into the camera and said that the incident of selling pouches after the draw was a mistake: "We shall fix it. It will not ever be a problem again." And with those words the story was over. The moral: If you're in trouble, "Fessin' up" is the right thing to do.

THE LOTTERY IS DEAD! LONG LIVE THE LOTTERY!

The Olympic Lottery was legally dead in 1976 but the feds had other intentions. A new state-owned company Loto Canada was incorporated by Parliament on June 7, 1976 to provide funds for "the improvement of sports". The legislation decreed that 82.5% of the profits would be applied to the 1976 Olympic deficit, to a maximum of $300 million. In addition, it would assist the 1978 Edmonton Commonwealth Games to the tune of $100 million. A further 12.5% of the profits would go to the provinces and the remaining 5% would be used by the federal government to fund amateur sport programs. The lottery's format was similar to the Olympic Lottery — a ticket price of $10 with a top prize of $1 million, drawn bi-monthly. The kicker was that it was to be sold everywhere in the country whether the provinces wanted it or not. This was worrisome for the Western provinces who distributed the Olympic Lottery. The $10 game that the WCLF had promoted and distributed was lost and became its competition.

QUEBEC TORN BUT, IN THE END, CHOOSES LOTO CANADA

Some interesting political dynamics were at work. Some of Quebec's Liberal politicians were in favour of continuing the Olympic Lottery until the last nickel of the Olympic deficit had been paid. The Quebec government wanted the Feds to help fund the deficit, but it didn't want to see a national lottery that might crush its own provincial lottery organization, Loto-Quebec.

The creation of Loto Canada vexed the provinces of Ontario and the West. There were cries of scandal and jurisdictional interference. Wheeling, dealing, scheming and lobbying were orders of the day. To cut to the chase, a meeting was scheduled to discuss the provincial options.

In July 1976, the ministers responsible for lotteries in western Canada and Ontario met in Montreal. **Grace McCarthy**, the BC Minister, and Larry Desjardins of

Manitoba were there as was Horst Schmidt for Alberta. Loto-Québec was represented by one of its senior officers, Denis Vendry. Saskatchewan sent Bill Clarke. Ontario's Minister Ruben Baetz was late but joined in forcefully.

The Ministers discussed the problem of a national lottery competing with their provincial programs. The problem was rooted in the Criminal Code that allowed both the federal government *and* the provinces to conduct lotteries. Naturally, the provinces wanted that income for themselves. So did the federal government.

The meeting agreed that the provinces (Quebec' representative didn't say a word) would undertake to match the federal government's offer by guaranteeing the $300 million contribution towards the Montreal deficit. This meant there was no need to create a national lottery. This offer was, of course, dependent on the acceptance of the deal by the Quebec government.

My Quebec colleague **Denis Vendry** was asked to phone his Quebec Minister of Finance for direction. He came back rather quickly saying that he didn't have a dime for the pay phone. Those at the meeting collected a handful of dimes after which Denis returned saying he was unable to contact the minister. Years later, Vendry confessed that he did talk to Raymond Garneau, his minister, who told him it was too late. Quebec had struck a deal with lottery minister Jean Chretien. A Federal Crown Corporation called Loto Canada was to take the place of the Olympic Lottery and continue operations for the benefit of the Quebec deficit until a $300-million profit level was reached or three years, whichever occurred first. This meant the competition between the Feds and the provinces would carry on at least for another three years.

At a CBC interview Prime Minster Trudeau spoke of the lottery as a unifying force that would bind the country together. He made the provinces appear to be undermining national unity for the price of $300 million. Quebec government officials didn't react publicly. They avoided a controversy because they were preparing for a tough election campaign where Rene Levesque, the leader of the Party Quebecois, was expected to bring a separatist party to power.

LOTO CANADA FALTERS

Because the provinces operated a solid retail network that offered popular games, Loto Canada sales volume was a far cry from the success of the Olympic Lottery. Later, in its annual report for 1977-78, Loto Canada spoke in grand terms about their efforts in anticipating consumer tastes and future expansion of their product line. They proudly pointed out that even in the face of what they called "aggressive competition by the provinces" a national distribution network was developed, which included most of the country's financial institutions. While the words were colourful, this was an annual auditor-approved report and there was no disguising the actual numbers. Loto Canada had to admit that sales for its second draw of March 1977 barely covered the costs of operation.

Shrinking profits did not prevent the federal government from launching an advertising blitz to sell Loto Canada tickets. This led many to speculate that the federal government had other motives than merely raising money for sports. Former Quebec lottery colleagues still maintain that given the looming threat of Parti-Quebecois, the federal government's aim was to "sell" Canada to Quebec. Paying off the Olympic debt and raising money for amateur sport became almost a secondary objective. "Conquering the hearts of Quebec," was the gist of an opinion piece in a Toronto newspaper. In the West Loto Canada went almost unnoticed.

Loto Canada did create a huge presence in Quebec. As one chronicler of the period noted: the federal crown had "beaten the drum and raised its banners at all major sports events." Loto Canada went even further by signing a deal with the CBC to create a series of lottery specials in the high-profile time-slot of the Tommy Hunter Show (12 shows, each in French and English), at a cost of $2 million plus in-house salaries.

Responding to criticism of Loto Canada's funding of hundreds of Quebec events such as festivals and concerts, Jean Chretien stated publicly that he didn't care whether Loto Canada lost millions in its lottery battles with the provinces; he believed the lottery was a weapon to strengthen Quebecers' attachment to Canada.

ATLANTIC PROVINCES JOIN

This lottery story has so far ignored the Atlantic Provinces. Back in 1974, the four eastern-most provinces had acceded to the request by the Olympic Organizing Committee (COJO) to allow sales of the Olympic Lottery. It was an easy decision. No involvement by the provinces was required, save for cashing the cheques of 5% of all lottery sales in the Atlantic Provinces. But now, when they noticed the other provinces getting more deeply involved in the lottery business, Atlantic Canada began to eye the COJO-built distribution system as a basis for a lottery in their four provinces.

The Maritime Council was the body that took the initiative to create an Atlantic lottery corporation. Your lottery scribe was invited to meet in Halifax with the council to acquaint them with the ups and downs the Western Canada Lottery Corporation had faced. The most valuable advice I could give them: Don't copy the Western Canada Lottery. I related the problematic conversion from hundreds of charitable lottery groups to a professional system. When they heard that the job of building a new system wasn't yet complete after two years of struggle, the Council had heard enough and decided to keep charitable organizations far away from any role in lotteries.

THE MAYOR GOES TO COURT

To divert from the national lottery scene for a moment, I want to tell you the tale of a Saskatchewan mayor. One of the staffers of the Western Canada prize-payout department — a kind-hearted, grey-haired lady — stood forlorn in the doorway of my office. She was close to tears. It's about the Mayor," she whispered.

"What about the Mayor? Which Mayor?" I asked looking up from my work.

"The Mayor of Weyburn. He's waiting in the lounge," she sniffled.

It turned out that the mayor of a Saskatchewan mid-sized city was claiming the $100,000 main prize in the Western EXPRESS.

"We have already paid out that prize to someone else," she said, "But the first digit of the mayor's ticket has been altered." She gave me the ticket and indeed, a quite clever alteration had changed the first digit "5" to the number "8". I accompanied her to the lounge where the man was reading one of the magazines. He rose and offered his hand to me.

"I hear you are claiming the $100,000 prize," I said. He smiled and offered his business card that showed he was the Mayor of Weyburn. I barged right in and told the man, "There is a problem with the ticket. Is there any reason why this ticket might not be genuine?" He looked surprised and said he wasn't aware of anything being wrong.

If he had said something like… "I am a city official and I wanted to test the security of your prize payout practices," he would have been off the hook. Instead, we called the police.

Weeks later he appeared before a judge with an anti-gambling bias who listened to the prosecution's charge. The mayor responded that he was in dire financial straits and the lottery claim was his desperate attempt to get out of debt. After hearing the man's response, the judge rattled on about the evils of gambling and how the state creates victims. The mayor went free.

I am not sure that the soon-to-resign mayor realized that by altering the ticket, he had forfeited the $1,000 prize that his ticket had won.

LOTTERY WARS BEGIN

Back to that Minister's meeting in Montreal, when Quebec's Denis Vendry couldn't get a positive response to the provinces' offer to fund the $300 million Olympic debt.

The meeting decided — whether Quebec was in or out — that a counterbalance to Loto Canada had to be created. It was to be a two-party agreement. The Western Canada Lottery and the Ontario Lottery would join in an Interprovincial Lottery Corporation to conduct a lottery called The PROVINCIAL to be priced at half the cost of the $10 Loto Canada ticket but offering the same $1 million prize.

The PROVINCIAL was packaged in a secure pouch similar to Wintario and the Western EXPRESS which allowed the ticket to remain in the market until after the draw. The initial game design was rather simple: a 7-digit number, decomposed to the last 3, 4, 5 and 6 digits. Contrary to normal game design, most of the prize fund was dedicated to fund the five $1 million prizes, thereby limiting the money available for the smaller prizes. But hey…we were competing for the attention of players who always focused on the top prizes. At 5%, commissions in the East were similar to Loto Canada but the West went even further and doubled the retailer commission to 10%.

The new Global TV network was to televise the first draw from London Ontario in November 1976, around the same time as the first draw of the new Loto Canada.

The lottery wars began. As Marshall Pollack said, "A new political concept was born: Government by competition."

GAME REALIGNMENTS

The birth of The PROVINCIAL triggered a change in western Canada's lottery line-up. The Olympic Lottery was dropped from store counters and replaced by the $5 PROVINCIAL. For the Western Canada Lottery Foundation, the introduction of the $5 PROVINCIAL provided the opportunity to rid itself of the ill-engineered $3 WESTERN. The last draw of that mongrel lottery was held on October 30th 1976. The three Western provinces now had only one game which made it politically acceptable to introduce the *WESTERN EXPRESS* that Manitoba had pioneered a few months earlier.

These changes required ministerial signatures. Speed was of the essence. Tickets had to be printed, new distribution systems created and advertising booked. Instead of awaiting signatures via bureaucratic snails, your travel-ready scribe decided to do it all in a single day.

Manitoba's signature was in my pocket when I arrived at 10.a.m at the Victoria Legislature where Grace McCarthy was kind enough to sign the documents in time for me to take the lunch time flight to Edmonton. Horst Schmidt left his seat in the Alberta legislature to sign the documents in the ornate entrance hall. At the Regina Airport Bill Clarke stood ready to drive me to the legislative office of Ed Tchorzewski who put on his coat on while signing the document at going-home time. I made it home for a late supper after 4,000 km jaunt. The Western EXPRESS was now fully western.

LET'S DO IT TOGETHER

It was December of 1976 when the three Western provinces joined the *EXPRESS.* The game proved so successful that ticket supplies ran out several days before the draw date. Most retailers were sold out, but there were always a few who had some to return. Because of these sell-outs, it was unusual that a winner of $100,000 remained unclaimed.

But... Late at home I received a phone-call from Jack Stewart, manager of the BC office. He told me that someone, who wanted to remain anonymous, had presented him with a photocopy of the winning ticket. The holder of the ticket was ready to claim the $100,000 prize but wished to avoid publicity.

It sounded very fishy to me. I snarled, "Jack. Tell these people to go screw themselves. Just tell them: No ticket, no money!" An hour later, he called again.

"It's my secretary," he whimpered. "We have a staff agreement here at the office. When the pouches are returned and there is no immediate claim for the big prize, the staff pool their money and buy up the unsold pouches."

I told him I didn't understand his comment for fear he'd implicate me in the scheme. What he told me would surely be grounds for dismissal but he went on spilling the beans. He requested that the conversation to be kept confidential. I told him I would think about it, which was a cowardly answer because I had no choice but to report the incident to the lottery minister in BC.

The result? Jack was fired and Eva the secretary — when she produced the actual ticket — got her $100,000 but only after completion of a long investigation. The BC Government Employees Union fought on Eva's behalf and eventually she was allowed to keep her job. But Jack Stewart was gone.

A MONTH TO REMEMBER

September of 1976 was a month of important developments. In addition to the federal government's announcement on Loto Canada:

- Quebec elected the first Parti-Quebecois government with René Lévesque as Premier.
- Atlantic Canada Lottery was incorporated. Jean-Marc Lafaille was appointed as G.M. Its first $1 lottery named A1 was launched.
- The first draw of the "The PROVINCIAL" was held in Toronto.
- The WCLF moved its Head Office to much larger premises at Lakeview Square in Winnipeg.

HOISTED WITH HIS OWN PETARD

The structure of the Interprovincial Lottery Corporation was becoming a Rube Goldberg design. When the initial corporation was formed by the four Western provinces and Ontario, each province wanted a director on the Board. This meant there would be four Western directors and one from Ontario.

Ontario's Marshall Pollock argued that while the five participating provinces were shareholders, the corporation was really a cooperative venture of two lottery organizations that should have equal representation. Thus, upon his insistence, the board was structured with eight directors — one from each of the Western provinces and four from Ontario. This decision proved to be a stumbling block in later years, but in the beginning, everyone was full of goodwill... Sort of...

Marshall championed the idea that an "instant scratch" addition to the $5 PROVINCIAL would put us farther ahead in the competition with Loto Canada. The detachable scratch portion of the ticket would allow the player to cash a win immediately and still have a ticket in the $1 million draw. The four Western board members thought it was a good idea but weren't sure of their lottery ministers' reaction. In the minds of some Western legislators the word "instant" created an image of a slot machine.

Marshall dismissed the western Canadian concerns. During the lunch-break he talked of backward governments, stuck-in-the-mud minds and general lack of pluck. Back in the formal meeting, he declared that the West's mettle would be put to the test at the next meeting of the board where Ontario would propose the addition of an instant scratch portion to the $5 PROVINCIAL ticket.

Unknown to Marshall, there had been a question in the Ontario Legislature of whether or not the minister responsible for lotteries was going to introduce an instant lottery. Unfortunately, Marshall had kept his boss in the dark about his intentions for the PROVINCIAL, which caused the **Hon. Robert Welch** to thunder in the House: "There will be no slot machines in the milk stores of Ontario!" A friend in the Ontario lottery office told me later that when Marshall approached Bob Welch for approval of the instant feature, he was forbidden to go ahead.

Marshall didn't relish the idea that he had to face his western colleagues at the next meeting and admit that, while he had previously castigated them for their reluctance, he couldn't deliver the goods himself. Admitting to being wrong was not Marshall's forte.

Minutes before the meeting, I met one of the Ontario board members — a dear, saintly Anglican minister — who told me that everything was a go and Marshall would introduce the motion to approve the instant scratch. Oops! Marshall had not told his board members of his minister's disapproval.

With the meeting about to start, I cautioned the Western board members that Marshall was going to propose the instant scratch portion, certain in the knowledge that the West would vote against it. When the vote came, Ontario's four Directors voted "Yes." Bill Clarke put on his best poor-boy face and…. voted "Yes" on behalf of the West. Two Ontario board members, unaware that Marshall was bluffing, applauded. Marshall knew the decision would be negated by the Ontario minister but it wasn't until he got back to his Toronto office that he called me and said that his minister was opposed and he needed time to convince him. I talked to the ministers of Manitoba and BC while Bill took on Saskatchewan and Alberta to explain that the WCLF voted for the instant portion of the game. All four western ministers concurred.

Now the shoe was on the other foot. Marshall had to confess to Bob Welch that he had bluffed, expecting the West would say no. The minister was torn. He could either kill the approved proposal or wriggle his way out of the "no-slot-machines-in-the-milk-store" declaration. He opted for increased lottery profits. The instant scratch — the first in Canada — was approved. In the Ontario Legislature, Bob Welch explained that the West had forced the issue.

ADVERTISING NOT UNIVERSALLY UNDERSTOOD

To launch the new scratch portion of the PROVINCIAL, Richard Muller, our point man for advertising in the West, produced a newspaper ad with an enlarged replica of the PROVINCIAL ticket, pointing to various parts the part of the ticket included the section that read "SCRATCH HERE," the specific area the player needed to scratch to discover if he or she had won a prize.

One of the less intuitive players called a hotline radio-station to report that the advertising was a fraud! The radio-host told him to call the lottery office. Our receptionist asked the caller to come in and bring his ticket. "I don't have a ticket," the heavily accented voice declared. After a series of confusing exchanges, it became clear that the person had scratched the picture in the newspaper ad and had torn the newspaper. It only confirmed that the madcap fringe is also part of the lottery business.

WINSDAY STORIES

On September 13, 1978, the *EXPRESS* introduced a major enhancement. The frequency of the draw would change from once every-two-weeks to once-a-week. While two of the lottery ministers feared a backlash, at the end of the fiscal year 1979, the sales volume of the *EXPRESS* had nearly doubled — from $40 million to $75 million.

The Nielsen ratings for the *Western Express* Lottery show on the CTV network were quite good. In order to infuse the show with some western Canadian flavour, Dale Nelson, the producer introduced a new feature. His first effort was the BC radio-morning-man Rick Honey, who brought a huge, fresh salmon that he deposited on Don Wittman's lectern during the drawing of the winning numbers. He wanted to tell a story about his fishing experience. Hilarity ensued, as they say. Your cautious scribe didn't think it would go over well but the public response was favourable.

A STRANGE NUMBER

As a born Nervous Nellie, Dale Nelson abhorred ad-lib comments by guests or even Don Wittman. One week the number 10000 was drawn. Don cooed, "Ooh! What are the odds of that number coming up?"

The following morning, his innocent remark brought inquiries questioning the integrity and fairness of the draw. Many players were quite content to see any wild combination of five digits, but 10000 looked too neat — skulduggery was suspected.

To the relief of our PR person, the holder of the winning ticket came forward. He admitted that when he bought the ticket and saw all those zeros, he was disappointed because he too believed it didn't have a chance.

THE UKRAINIAN LEI

At one of the WINSDAY shows the guest — a popular radio announcer from Northern Alberta — did a take-off on the Hawaiian custom of welcoming visitors with leis. On the show he related how visitors to his town were welcomed with home-made leis made of Ukrainian sausages. To make things worse, he performed his entire 'shtick' in a thick Ukrainian accent. It was funny.

The next day Horst Schmidt, the lottery minister from Alberta, called me from his speaker phone. He was outraged; he ranted about the show mocking Ukrainian culture, insulting a whole segment of society that made such a great contribution to life in Alberta. The sausage lei, he said, was insulting, degrading and deeply offensive. I explained that the initiative for this gag had come from a well-known radio personality within the Ukrainian community. This appeared to enrage Horst even more. He said that if anything like this type of insult was ever used again on the Winsday draw, I should realize what the consequences were for me personally.

I was upset. Whenever a minister threatens you with dismissal over a humorous skit, you have to think of alternate employment. A few hours later, Horst called again. He giggled with glee. "How did I do, Guy?" he tee-heed, "Did I sound convincing?" He explained that at the time of his phone call he had a delegation of an Edmonton Ukrainian dance group in his office, demanding an increase in cultural funding. Horst was in the process of toning down their expectations when the head of the delegation cynically commented that while there was no money for true cultural expression, there appeared to be lots of lottery money to ridicule Ukrainian culture. In the eyes of the Ukrainian delegation, this was not just some local guy on a TV show. This man appeared on a show put on by an agency under direct the control of Cultural Affairs Minister Horst Schmidt himself.

"You know, Guy," he explained. "I am also the Minister of Cultural Affairs. Not only that, but a large number of my constituents are of Ukrainian descent. I needed to show some action on behalf of my constituents, so I grabbed the speaker phone and gave you hell. I have to tell you that the delegation was most impressed. I just want to tell you that I saw your show and I thought it was funny. My office staff thought so, too, and all but two of them are Ukrainian. I am sorry if I upset you. You're doing a terrific job."

IF YOU HAVE EYES YOU CAN CLAIM THE PRIZE

In fall of 1978, Bill Clarke as Chairman of the WCLF sacrificed his precious vacation days to attend the annual meeting of AILE in the City of Lights. Marshall Pollock and Jean-Marc Lafaille also travelled to Paris. I felt quite comfortable that I was the lone senior lottery executive left in Canada. It turned out to be one of the more intense incidents in lotteries.

The call came from Peter Warren, the hard-nosed, highly-rated investigative broadcaster of radio station CJOB in Winnipeg.

"I've got a guy wanting to come on the program to explain how to beat the instant-scratch feature on the PROVINCIAL lottery," he told me. "Do you want to meet him before we go to air?"

Knowing he might kill a good story by getting a rational explanation, this was a pretty decent offer by Warren. While many of the media clobbered us with myths and misunderstandings, here was a man who had taken the time to understood lotteries and wanted to give us a fair shake.

The nicely-dressed young man waiting for me in the studio said that a buddy in Saskatchewan had told him how to "break" the instant scratch game. He showed me how simple it was.

The PROVINCIAL featured a detachable stub that contained a scratch area. When scratched, the strip would reveal either the amount of the prize or "Bonne chance/Good luck" as in "Get lost, you won nothing!"

In the early stages of instant lottery development, we learned very quickly that if winning tickets and losing instant tickets were printed in separate print runs, there was bound to be some distinguishing mark between winning and non-winning tickets. Sharp operators looking for such differences can compromise a lottery by buying only winning tickets.

Some years before, in the '70s, an RCMP officer called on Winnipeg Banknote and asked that he be given a large box of pull-tab tickets and a room to himself. Twenty minutes later he emerged with two piles of tickets: a stack of non-winners and a pile of winning tickets. The tickets had not been marked or damaged in any way.

The officer showed that the non-winning tickets, after being printed, were trimmed a different way than the winners. All he had done was stand the tickets next to each other and spot the minute differences in height and length.

But, this PROVINCIAL ticket in question was not a cheap break-open ticket. It was printed by the same company that prints Canadian dollar-bills. Security is their priority. The problem wasn't with the ticket itself — it had many of the features of a banknote. The cause of the trouble was simple. In order to make sure that the latex cover over the prize area would adhere to the paper, vertical lines were printed around the edge of the scratch area. The overprint looked like this: //////////////. That is, the losing tickets showed those markings. The winning tickets were overprinted with \\\\\\\\\\\\\.

Quite upset, I informed Peter Warren that if that information was released, the lottery would incur serious losses. After learning what the actual problem was, he agreed to sit on the scoop for a while.

Of course, the problem wasn't just restricted to the West. Your anxious scribe had to handle the Canada-wide fallout of this hot potato. The first step was to convince the printer that there was indeed a problem. Printers of the nation's currency are loath to admit their product could be counterfeited or compromised. Fortunately, this event happened just before the Thanksgiving Day long weekend. The press would be digging into turkey instead of news.

 **Jim Trask** of British American Bank Note agreed to bring a randomly selected box of 1000 tickets to your lottery scribe's home. I opened the box and made two piles of tickets: the left-slanted slashes and the right-leaning ones. Jim scratched the first ticket with the //// markings. It was a $5 winner, the second a $25 winner, the third a "Free Ticket." Jim was convinced.

What to do? We could perhaps retrieve all the tickets from the retailers. They would ask why. We could tell them it was for security reasons but what if the media explained the flaw? Once the retailers understood the problem, many of them might only return losing tickets and keep the winners for themselves. If we went public with the problem, the press across Canada would give us a deserved black-eye. Trust in the system would be undermined. Could we stick it out and say nothing until the day of the draw, five long days away?

There were no lottery chiefs or influential board members to consult; they were wining and dining in Paris.

A CBC talk show-host insisted that I should participate in a nation-wide broadcast to talk about the problem. I acceded. During the interview I agreed that there was a lot of talk about how to break the game. One rumour had it that you could take the ticket to an airport scanner and it would tell you, winner or loser. Others claimed you could read the prize by putting the ticket on top of a flashlight. I even related the rumour that if you daubed scotch on the scratch area, the symbols would bleed through. (I didn't mention an anonymous player's advice that rubbing urine on the latex strip would reveal the prize.)

The host laughed, not realizing or not caring that the real issue hadn't been addressed. Several radio interviews from across Canada accepted my humorous answers. The only bad break came from Marshall Pollock's assistant, who confessed to the Canadian Press that there was a problem and management knew what it was. Canadian Press checked and I responded that if the young lady knew how to break the ticket, she should reveal it. After hearing this, the poor thing went into hiding until it was all over. We escaped unscratched! The printer did not.

LOTTERY WARS HEAT UP

In 1978, with the end of Loto Canada in sight, the lottery wars escalated. It reached a peak of madness when Loto Canada offered 20 prizes of $1 million and The PROVINCIAL offered 22. The lesson learned was that offering multiple prizes of $1 million did not increase sales proportionally. While lottery game designers believed that offering many $1 million prizes was an attraction, the player still only thought of winning a single $1 million bonanza. For those who grasped the odds of winning, it made some difference. It was true that the chance to win the big prize was enhanced, but for most, the dream of what they would do with a million dollars had not changed.

Later it was proven that if one single prize of $22 million had been offered instead of 22 of $1 million, sales would have gone through the roof. Not so long before, a top-prize of $100,000 was seen as the ultimate dream prize. As the lottery wars dragged on, the $1-million draw that only a few years ago emptied the bars had lost its sheen. What size of the prize would move the needle? Would it creep up as the years passed?

Loto Canada's legal life was to expire in August 1979. The executives were acutely aware that their "liberal" expense-account nirvana would soon end.

Their fear was, as Mel Brooks told his underlings in the film *Blazing Saddles,* "All your phony baloney jobs will be lost."

IT'S NOT OVER 'TIL IT'S OVER... OVER THERE

Your lottery scribe, having his ear to the ground, heard persistent rumours that the federal government planned to launch a Canada-wide lotto game to replace Loto Canada. If the rumours were true, it was clear that the Feds had no intention to vacate the lottery business. It was said they were planning to introduce the successful European game of Lotto. A game of that scale would overpower the smaller provincial lotteries and depress provincial net revenues.

To get ahead of the competition, Loto Quebec planned to launch its existing LOTTO 6/36 using a direct online system because it would yield greater revenue over the long-term. It would even be better if there was a larger purchase base for terminals. That's why Loto Quebec agreed to team up with Ontario —also ready to launch a lotto game — to introduce their respective lottos in the spring of 1978. Bids for the joint purchase of central computers and lottery terminals closed on July 7, 1979.

Five months later, in November of 1979, Ontario launched a 6/39 lotto game called LOTTARIO while Quebec updated its existing LOTTO 6/36. Western Canada didn't want to be left behind, but your intrepid scribe had four governments to persuade. The idea that a "raffle" — a "fun thing" — would actually put computer terminals on retail counters was too much for most politicians, who were still trying to survive the shock of having a lottery at all. The concept of a community-wide Irish-Sweepstake system was still the ideal game held by many Westerners; unfortunately, those included at least two of the four WCLF lottery Ministers.

RUMOURS OF RENEWED LOTTERY WARS

Meanwhile back in Ottawa: To keep federal hopes alive for a permanent national lottery, the Feds planned a pre-emptive strike. In early 1979, the Ottawa bureaucrats convinced Liberal Lottery Minister **Iona Compagnolo** to issue a secret RFP (Request for Proposal) for the installation of a Canada-wide computer-based lottery system that would house a lotto game in which 6 numbers were drawn from a field of 49. The secrecy was necessary to keep the provinces from finding out that the Liberal government had no intention of vacating the lottery field as promised. If the secret manipulations were to become known, the provinces would raise hell about the breach.

The plotters forgot the old truism that secrecy cannot protect a house of cards from falling apart. The soon-to-be-unemployed Loto Canada operatives signed a contract with U.S. based General Instrument and its subsidiary AmTote, to provide a computer system and retail lotto terminals to connect 10,000 retail-stores throughout Canada. In addition to the contracted expenditure of $20 million dollars in equipment — again all in secrecy — thousands upon thousands of brochures, signs and other promotional materials were produced. It was so secretive that the government's rules of public tendering were broken by awarding the contract without competing proposals.

The first unofficial announcement of the plot was at a meeting of Director/Members of the North American Association of State and Provincial Lotteries (NASPL) in Philadelphia, where all attendees were invited to an evening cocktail reception by General Instruments to celebrate their great coup in the North American lottery market.

The festively decorated tables, loaded with huge bowls of shrimp, were intended to impress the American lottery directors. General Instrument's management was obviously not aware that the meeting of NASPL Directors included Canadian lottery managers — the ones being victimized by the sinister stratagem. Your astounded scribe and his Canadian counterparts were shocked by the betrayal by the Government of Canada and decided to forego the shrimp in favour of urgent calls to their home offices.

Both public and political hell broke loose. The CBC tore into this controversy like a hungry piranha. It was close to federal election time and although the voters were tired of Pierre Trudeau, Joe Who (Clark) the newly-elected leader of the Conservative Party was not really expected to be prime minister any time soon. Nevertheless, Joe Clark got into the act and denounced the Liberal arrogance of secretly plotting to break the lottery agreement, not to mention the questionable action of awarding a $20-million contract without soliciting competing bids. Joe Clark tut-tutted that if he were elected, he'd cancel the whole "liberal-infested" Loto Canada organization.

The Honorable Iona Campagnolo's star had fallen. She was forced to cancel the deal with General Instrument and incur severe financial penalties. She maintained that the $20-million deal was a "strategy." By threatening to launch a national lotto game, the provinces would be so frightened that they would readily agree to keep the old Loto Canada going if only the Feds were to withdraw the massive lotto threat. In another interview she added that the move to a national 6/49 lotto was to get ahead of Ontario and Quebec which were ready to launch their respective lottos. The fact that this "strategy" cost Loto Canada and thus the taxpayers many millions of dollars seemed to escape many of the political commentators.

Most of Loto Canada's profit that year was blown by this nefarious plan. Iona asked for a meeting with the provinces to see what could be salvaged from her PR disaster but Trudeau — who obviously hadn't been aware of the scheme — didn't have enough confidence in his Minister to let her go alone. Marc Lalonde, the Finance Minister, headed the negotiations. At that meeting a truce was reached. Loto Canada could continue after 1979 but was limited to selling lotteries priced at $10 or higher while the provinces could price their tickets in the $1-$10 range.

The provinces had hoped for complete surrender but took comfort from Joe Clark's minions who promised that if the Conservatives were elected, Loto Canada would be dead anyway.

CONSERVATIVES ELECTED... AND CALLED ON THE CARPET

On May 22 1979, the Conservatives were elected. Loto Canada's cupboard was nearly bare. Net profit of the previous fiscal year was less than $24 million.

Prime Minister Joe Clark named **Steve Paproski** as the federal minister responsible for winding up Loto Canada. Steve was a good ole Alberta boy who was directed to "not give away the store" without getting something in return. He was smart in appointing my old friend, Ian Howard to head the dissolution of staff and assets.

On August 21, 1979, Paproski called a meeting of provincial lottery ministers in Ottawa. The senior lottery managers, including your lottery scribe, expected to attend the meeting in order to brief their respective ministers. After all, we knew the details. The ministers told us to go and pound pepper (as one Quebec official quaintly put it). The elected officials met by themselves.

In a surprise move, the ministers decided to bring in the feeling-neglected officials. One at a time. It was just about noon when Jean-Marc Lafaille of Quebec was called as the first "witness." The rest of us were a bit uptight about this unusual turn of events. Jean-Marc had barely closed the door behind him when the noon-hour cannon boomed on Parliament Hill.

The boom resonated though our little ante-room. Marshall Pollock got up, put his hand on the doorknob and announced in a loud voice, "NEXT!".

It turned out to be an amiable meeting. The lottery officials' role was to make sure the periods and commas in the draft agreement were properly placed.

Minister Paproski believed that he had negotiated a great deal when the provinces quickly accepted his terms for ending Loto Canada. The price was equal to the previous year's Loto Canada profit of $24 million, to be paid annually for as long as the provinces were in the lottery business. Annual increases were tied to inflation and, upon these conditions, the federal government would vacate the lottery field. The Feds were out! (Today, due to inflation, that $24 million has more than doubled.)

APPROVAL OF LOTTERIES SOARS

In 1979, a Weekend Magazine poll, conducted in the 32 largest Canadian communities, reported that lotteries enjoyed the approval of 84% of Canadians. The high rate confirmed the popular belief that lottery profits were used for Good Causes. Those who disapproved viewed lotteries a waste of money and exploitation of the poor. From a religious perspective, Roman Catholics tended to tolerate lotteries while fundamentalist Christians opposed gambling of any kind. Among non-Christians, Jews tended to tolerate lotteries while Buddhists, Muslims and Sikhs opposed them.

CONSERVATIVES DEFEATED

On December 13, 1979, the Conservative's budget came for a confidence vote. Whoever was charged with rallying the votes was poor at counting. Joe Clark's government, only nine-months old, (May 22, 1979 to Feb. 18, 1980) was defeated. Three weeks earlier Pierre Trudeau had taken his famous "Walk in The Snow" and announced he would step down as Liberal leader. However, with no new leader in place and a looming election, the Liberals convinced Trudeau to change his mind. Once the votes were tallied in the February election, Trudeau returned to 24 Sussex Drive with a majority Liberal government. The provinces thanked the lottery gods that Joe Clark had made good on his campaign pledge to cancel Loto Canada and leave lotteries to the provinces in return for a relative pittance.

WELCOME TO THE EIGHTIES

On February 20, 1980, the Liberal government took over and Pierre Trudeau was Prime Minister once again. He opened his victory speech with, "Welcome to the eighties!" To the provincial lottery executives, it sounded as "Welcome to more lottery trouble." As soon as the Liberals settled in their cushy offices in the Parliament Buildings, they fired their first lottery shot across the bow. Barely three months in office, Gerald Regan, the Minister for Fitness and Amateur Sport, presented a proposal to Cabinet that the federal government endorse a re-entry in the lottery field, either with a $10 Loto Canada game or a unique lottery such as a sports pool.

IAN HOWARD

In the Trudeau government Ian Howard had been a significant presence in Loto Canada. As a true government servant, he was loyal to the Conservatives when they dismantled the lottery and now that the Liberals were back in power, he was the point man in the effort to re-build a national lottery.

Ian knew Britain's judicial system tacitly allowed football pools to operate, even though in the U.K. there was a strong legal prohibition of lotteries. In the absence of a formal lottery, the pools were popular. The British courts, in recognition of the government's dilemma, held that footballs pools (named Sports Toto on the Continent) were contests of skill, not games of chance.

Ridiculous as it sounds, the governments of Sweden and Italy used the same rationale to let sports lotteries, ahem — I mean sports-skill games — proceed. Ian's idea was to sell this fancy interpretation of skill to the courts in Canada. If the courts agreed that Toto was a game of skill and not a lottery, the Feds could introduce it and not be found guilty of reneging on the lottery agreement.

According to the published annual report of Loto Canada, Ian's consulting company received $1.7 million to research how Sports Toto worked. A lot of money was devoted to high-priced lawyers who were to determine how the agreement with the provinces could be circumvented.

The federal government's re-entry into the lottery business alarmed the provinces. Less-rational provincial lottery managers across the country advocated ceasing paying the annually indexed $24 million. Luckily, saner heads prevailed as the Government of Canada would surely have taken the position that if the provinces failed to pay, the deal was dead.

Public opinion agreed that federal funding for the Calgary Olympics through a lottery was the way to go. For the provinces this effort was going to be an uphill battle again. In the end, the Feds would spend $4 million plus on research that a lottery based on sport wouldn't be deemed to be a lottery in the eyes of the law. (It took the Feds until May 1, 1984 to introduce a non-lottery lottery. But that was in the future, so you must wait until then to see how that complex plan turned out.)

SUPER LOTO APPEARS

During that turbulent period, the provincial lottery corporations were nurturing a game called SUPER LOTO that would supersede the terminated Loto Canada game. It was a modified clone of the Loto Canada game and retained its $10 price.

Michelle McBride, who had worked with Loto Canada for a year or so, read the tea leaves and figured Loto Canada wasn't likely to survive. Your lottery scribe welcomed her back into the Western fold. Western Canada Lottery games were once again the only ones in town. The new SUPER LOTO was now part of the WCLF line-up in addition to the $1 EXPRESS and the $5 PROVINCIAL

On October 19, 1980, the lottery market became the provinces' domain. No more outsized ad budgets loudly proclaiming that "our" lottery was better than "theirs"; no more stealing retailers by offering increased commissions. No more tearing off "their" advertising posters and replacing them with "ours." Stability at last!

The provinces were now competing for the entertainment dollar rather than the lottery dollar. If boring games were offered or prizes skimped on, people wouldn't play. In short, the lottery market became rational.

SUPER LOTO was launched in the West with an award-winning TV commercial. It is the only television ad for which your lottery scribe earned a writer's credit. Do you remember seven-word commercial with three tycoons standing in front of a Bentley automobile?

The text? "Shipbuilding? Textiles? No! SUPER LOTO!"

It was quite popular!

HOW TO GET IT BACK AFTER YOU GAVE IT AWAY

Liberal Minister Responsible for Fitness and Amateur Sport, **Gerald Regan**, in an interview with the *Globe and Mail*, confirmed that the federal government was investigating options for getting back in the lottery business. Judging by the noise coming from Ottawa, the monopoly by the provinces was soon to end. In Parliament, the defeated Conservatives were accused of betraying the national interest by ceding the lottery field to the provinces for a pittance. "The flag of amateur sport was left abandoned at half mast," one Toronto Liberal dramatist declared.

The Liberals dedicated a large portion of Loto Canada's left-over prize funds to researching how to manipulate a feasible return to the lottery business — the cash-cow that had provided so much propaganda for the Liberal cause. The shenanigans didn't go unnoticed. The Auditor General, Kenneth M. Dye, later wrote of "unauthorized expenses that were contrary to the provisions of the Canada Business Corporation Act" and expressed concern about "heavy costs incurred by the continued existence of this non-operating corporation in researching lottery games." The auditor also pointed out that the money so squandered should have been turned over to the Receiver General rather than being used for arming lottery troops for another war.

The next Liberal approach was to question the legal validity of the 1979 federal/provincial lottery agreement. While a document was signed, a formal Order-in Council had never been issued. Parts of the agreement were described as "vague and incomplete." Government lawyers were charged with testing the legality of the agreement. To avoid legal missteps, the federal government stopped cashing the annual $24 million payment from the provinces. Steven Paproski, the former Tory cabinet minister who had been the chief negotiator for the 1979 deal with the provinces, questioned this tactic in an acerbic exchange with the Minister in the House of Commons.

"It is my understanding," suggested Paproski, "that the federal sports department is virtually bankrupt yet it won't cash provincial cheques for millions of dollars. The cultural and artistic communities also need money for symphonies and theatres."

The federal minister replied, "... the country's sport and cultural communities would be in a much better financial situation, if the Conservatives had not given away Loto Canada, which was netting $80 million a year." He added that the deal was "the most disastrous piece of negotiation since the sale of the Brooklyn Bridge."

But, eventually, the federal government was advised by its legal beagles that the Joe Clark agreement with the provinces withstood all legal tests. Reluctantly, the Feds began to cash the $24 million cheques.

On August 28, 1980, Federal Communications Minister Francis Fox announced that the government would not challenge the 1979 agreement.

In the House of Commons, the Liberals declared, almost tearfully, that sports and the arts were on the losing end — all because of that ill-conceived Conservative deal. After all the wailing, the government split the provincial money between sports and the arts, but emphasized that the $12 million for each of these sectors was nowhere near what Loto Canada might have earned if the Conservatives hadn't killed the goose that laid the golden eggs.

JAPAN

November 20, 1980. By now, you might be bored with tales of the tomfoolery of the federal/provincial lottery wars. Believe me, other exciting things were going on in the lottery world. The 1980 meeting of l'Association Internationale des Loteries d'Etat (AILE) was set for Japan. I had missed the '76 AILE meeting in France in order to hold the besieged fort for my Canadian colleagues. This time Ina and I were not going to miss the conference in Asia.

In 1980, travelling on business with a spouse wasn't as strict as it is today. I was assured by the board that taking **Ina** to Japan on the company's dime was quite okay. The travel included a 3-day stopover at the Honolulu landmark Royal Hawaiian Hotel, as well as a weekend visit on Fiji. Remarkably I remember absolutely nothing of the business sessions in Japan. They must have been business oriented; I just don't recall.

However, the tours for the benefit of the delegates were a great way to see Japan. On one of those trips, the urge to use the bathroom suddenly arose and the bus driver quickly found a massive complex where our twelve AILE buses parked to allow their passengers to use the facilities. It turned out that your lottery scribe was the only person in the entire congress who felt the need to respond to nature's call. The coordinator was duly concerned about my "loss of face". He didn't understand that — upon my return — the round of applause by the delegates was an appreciation by my colleagues that I had braved the bus tour. But the host was not yet finished in taking care of this perceived humiliation. A handsome car was idling behind the bus. Ina and I were gently escorted off the bus to address a bowing chauffeur who said in broken English that we had a choice. Proposition one was that we would travel in the bus and the car would follow closely. If nature called, the bus would stop and the car would dispatch me to the nearest toilet and then race to catch the bus again. We could also take the rest of the tour in the car. We chose the car.

As we came closer to where Mount Fuji was supposedly located, a dense fog surrounded us. The driver crawled along the narrow mountainous road. All AILE buses stopped. Mr. Japanese Host came outside and using the bullhorn, told us we wouldn't be able to see Mount Fuji. (See bought picture) Besides, it was late and we should head for the lunch at the Magic Lake. As the convoy pulled in, we could barely make out the restaurant; the fog had become that dense. The lottery crowd was kind of thrilled to be in such impenetrable surroundings due to a complete whiteout.

The atmosphere inside the hotel was delightful. Deliberately avoiding asking what we were offered as food, we ate some weird stuff but it tasted alright. After lunch the convoy drivers found a four-lane highway and when we approached Tokyo, the fog lifted. It had been a long trip to a mountain we didn't see, ate food we didn't recognize, at a restaurant without a view. But use of the bathroom had been a success.

BEGGING ON BEHALF OF THE PIANO PLAYER

Such lottery conferences always schedule an evening where suppliers can entertain clients. Scientific Games invited two dozen selected delegates to the ritziest roof-top, five-star restaurant in Tokyo. The service was impeccable; even my hamburger and fries were served with elegance. Bill Clarke, WCLF Chairman and our host Dan Bower sparred to decide who would order the wine.

The elaborate leather-bound menu must have cost a bundle in itself; it showed all the available choices but none of the prices. As the wine flowed freely, Lynn Nelson, Director of the Pennsylvania Lottery, got it into his head to tell the maître d' that our party included one of Canada's great jazz pianists and, if persuaded properly, this musical giant would likely deign to play a few songs. Within minutes, the resident piano player was shoved aside to make way. I played a few tunes to none of the diners' interest. Lynn upped the ante by stuffing a cognac glass with a U.S. dollar bill. Glass in hand, he solicited the nearby tables occupied by Japanese CEOs and their geishas. I never did learn how much he collected because Lynn kept the money.

When time came to pay the dinner bill, the maître d' whispered discreetly that the credit limit of Mr. Bower's American Express Gold card was not high enough to cover the bill. Dan muttered that his credit limit was $30,000 and all that he had charged thus far was his airline ticket. "No problem," the maître d' declared. He would just phone American Express in New York to get the credit limit raised. It was midnight in New York.

The problem was solved when the night manager of the hotel confirmed that Scientific Games' major shareholder was a guest at the dinner and everything was OK. It could also have been because Dan's shareholder threw his American Express Platinum card, with its six-figure limit, on the table.

INTRODUCTION OF INSTANT GAMES

While a version of an instant feature was attached to passive lotteries such as the PROVINCIAL and LOTO CANADA, there had never been an instant/scratch lottery in Western Canada. The reluctance was both technical and political, with political objections the most difficult to overcome. The concern was gambling addiction and the idea that instant lotteries were something like eating peanuts i.e. eat one and you can't stop until the bowl is empty.

In truth, gambling is addictive for a tiny number of players, but the major cause is casino-based slot machines and not scratch lotteries. However, back in 1983, anti-lottery warriors described instant-scratch games as a gateway to incite players into frenzied spending of the family's grocery budget.

For those unacquainted with lotteries, the instant/scratch ticket is a card with game details printed on it and then covered by a latex, rubber-based film. The original tickets, in the '70s, were covered with an environmentally unsafe solvent-based coating. In the early '80s, an improvement covered the hidden information with a water-based coating that can be scratched off relatively easily and was resistant to normal tears or damage.

The history of instant lottery games preceded the legalization of lotteries. In the '60s, grocery stores used to hand out free cards covered with a waxy coating that hid a small cash prize or a grocery item. To find out if you'd won, you either scratched off the coating or wiped it off with a rag dipped with a bit of butter. The prizes were small, as low as a dime, but customers loved them.

Dan Bower and his partner had a small business selling promotional cards. They decided that they could transform those promotional cards into games to be marketed by lottery corporations. But first, a technical problem needed to be solved. Promotional games contained thousands of tickets, of which only a handful would be winners. Security was practically non-existent. If one took a thousand tickets into a room and studied them for a few minutes, all winning tickets could be found. In those investigations, an abnormality, a special design, a stray printing mark or a serial number could expose the winners.

Such defects would not be acceptable to a government lottery system. Dan Bower had the idea to print much larger batches — 240,000 unique tickets at a time. There were so many differences among the tickets that it was difficult to find a pattern that would distinguish winners from losers. In the early '70s, Dan incorporated his business under the name Scientific Games. He approached the Massachusetts Lottery and presented the product as a secure ticket and nearly impossible to break. Scientific Games won the contract for the first instant/scratch lottery ticket in the world.

Retailers overcame their initial fear of having customers gather around their cash register scratching away and were further sold on the idea when customers bought multiple tickets. "Stores were demanding extra tickets," Bower recalled. "We had to print more tickets, and then, of course, all the other North American lottery companies took notice because sales were impressive."

PROVINCIAL INNOVATION

The once-a-month PROVINCIAL went weekly in early January of 1981. The novelty was that each weekly ticket was good for five subsequent weekly draws. The expectation was that players would buy a ticket each week and thus eventually would have five numbers in play on each draw date.

Another change was an instant feature that took the form of an attached check. It seemed like a good idea at the time...

SUPPLIERS CAN TURN ANGRY

On June 13, 1981, WCLF introduced its first instant/scratch game inspired by a well-known children's game — Tic-Tac-Toe — created by Scientific Games. A funny commercial by Richard Muller, emphasizing the motion and sound of scratching, rather than immediate winning, was introduced at a rather timid launch. Despite the modest ad campaign, the issue was sold out in days.

Although public acceptance was enthusiastic, a complaint came from an unexpected corner. Why were the tickets not printed in Canada, in Quebec, at Gaston Boulanger's printing firm? Larry Desjardins grabbed the opportunity and blasted me and the Western Canada Lottery for its "Anti Buy-Canadian stance." In a TV interview he promised that the tickets would soon appear on the retailer's counter, bearing the proud motto "Made in Canada." Very few complaints were received about the TIC TAC TOE game itself. The ever-wily Desjardins had managed to shift the public outrage away from the dread of instant games to the need for a Canadian ticket printer.

Once the Canadian-made Tic-Tac-Toe game was in circulation, Dan Bower appeared at my Winnipeg office. "There is a problem," he began, his "Good-old-Dan" manner missing.

He produced a package from his briefcase that contained a half-dozen Canadian-made TIC TAC TOE tickets. "The tickets can be compromised," he said, producing a sheet of paper on which the symbols hidden under the latex had popped up without damaging the ticket or the latex.

"In our lab, we poured some ordinary household chemical on the latex cover and pressed the paper on it. As you can see the ticket seems OK, but the symbols are clearly shown. A retailer, using this chemical, could separate winners from losers, sell all the losers and keep the winners for himself."

Your astounded scribe had two reactions. One was, "What a jerk, looking for faults in the tickets of a competitor." The other thought was, "I'm glad you told me; now I can be ready for the possibility." I didn't say anything like that to Dan but asked if I could have the compromised tickets. After that we went for lunch, where I was determined not to re-hash the subject. He seemed frustrated and finally said what I expected he'd say. "I may have to inform the press of the faulty ticket," he said. "You cannot offer them for sale."

I recall my response: "Until I know what chemical you're talking about and how it's applied, I won't change anything." Dan promised to follow up but never did. Years later, he confided that he wouldn't have gone to the press. He would have damaged the reputation of his own product in the process.

Meanwhile, Gaston Boulanger, our Canadian printer, was informed of his instant-scratch ticket problems. Gaston was upset but promised a cure. Other scratch-ticket problems cropped up in later years but the problem of markings leaching through the latex never happened again.

BACK TO THE LOTTERY WARS

In September '81, forced by Calgary's bod for the upcoming 1988 Winter Olympics, Federal Minister Regan formally announced that the government would establish a sports pool program for the benefit of the Games. This is what the news papers reported:

SPORTS AND RECREATION

Once again, lotteries emerged on the federal-provincial scene. The federal Conservative government in 1979 pulled out of the lottery business and left the field to provincial lotteries in return for an annual contribution from the remaining programs. In September, Gerald Regan, the federal minister responsible for sports, announced plans for a national sports wagering pool where people could win cash prizes for correctly predicting the scores of professional sports games. Regan argued the program was not a lottery because it required the application of skill. A new Crown corporation would be established and revenues would be used for amateur sports, cultural programs, medical research and special sports projects (Globe and Mail, September 15, 1981, p. 1).

Nothing more was heard from the feds for two years — except for many arguments about lottery profits. In 1983, the House of Commons passed the Athletic Contest and Events Pools Act, establishing the Canadian Sports Pool Corporation which had the power to conduct and manage virtually every type of lottery scheme in addition to sports pools. Charging that this constituted a breach of the 1979 agreement, in March 1984 the provinces commenced legal proceedings in federal court. But I'm getting ahead of myself...

PROMOTING THE ONLINE SYSTEM IN THE WEST

Discussions with WCLF board members about an online lottery system often went sideways because the impact wasn't fully understood by all. The concept that a machine on a retailer's counter could spit out a ticket based on the orders of a far-away computer was not easily grasped.

(We are in 1984 here, where there were still typewriters on every desk and the first Apple Macintosh computer was not yet publicly available.) The problem was that board members had to explain the system to their respective ministers. To get some board members to understand it before letting them loose on their political masters was an easy task. Fly them business class to Germany!

At the time, my friend Lothar Lammers — whom I first met in 1972 — operated the most successful LOTTO 6/49 system in the world. In the '70s he had made the game a cooperative scheme between four West German states (länder). The co-operative example was ideal for our four-province WCLF. My fellow-travellers included Joe Kanuka, Bill Clarke, Lou Hough, a board member of Sask Sport, Don Hamilton the Chair of Alberta Lotteries and George Geddes of BC.

Lothar Lammers was, as always, a most generous host. He received the large delegation in style and there seemed to be corporate gifts every hour. He was proud to show off his large operation. The weekly game, "Lotto 6 aus 49" had changed little in its 25-year existence, its popularity increasing each year.

I could leave it there and go on to the next topic but some hilarious scenes happened in Münster that are worth reminiscing. Your still-amused scribe has decided to provide a brief relief from the factual reports and tell of the mischief the Canadian guests got into.

Lothar Lammers was only 15 minutes into the presentation of his lottery company when the first gift arrived — an expensive cigarette-lighter, in various

colours. One for each of us. A photographer hovered around the table capturing photo opportunity. When our host took us on a tour through his massive complex, the lighters were left on the table. Upon return, Bill Clarke's lighter was gone. Joe Kanuka laughingly accused **George Geddes**, the BC delegate, of appropriating it. George's intense denial made us think he did protest too much.

George showed his yellow lighter as proof that he had only one. At the end of the day, when the photographer came to show his pictures, Kanuka pointed out that George originally had a blue lighter and Clarke's was yellow. George maintained his innocence, but his colleagues razzed him mercilessly. George was quite animated during the dinner and told a long story of how had fought his way with the Canadian Tank Corps in the Münster area at the end of the Second World War. I guess he hoped to regain some of his lost esteem.

WAR DAMAGE IN MÜNSTER

The following day, Lothar Lammers arranged a tour of Münster which included a tour of the historic Das Bonner Church that was heavily damaged during the war. The walls of the church were covered with photographs that showed the destruction by the Allies in the final months of the war and how the community had rebuilt the edifice to its original glory. There was even a small cinema that showed old newsreels of the actual 1945 battle for Münster.

The church was whisper quiet. Suddenly, Kanuka cried out: "He did it!" and pointed at George Geddes. "He took his tank through here and ruined this beautiful church!" The church visitors were aghast.

Joe, enjoying the attention, added: "Mr. Geddes has lived with this burden of guilt all his life and is now here to donate a stained-glass window as atonement for his wartime evil." The Germans applauded and vied to shake George's hand. In the midst of the commotion, Joe whispered to the hero: "Next time you're here to destroy the church you won't need a tank. All you need is that lighter to set fire to the place."

After coffee, tea, Coca Cola and free cigarettes and cigars at the late afternoon reception, Lothar Lammers, seated at his office desk announced that it was time for dinner. Well not so much dinner right now, but drinks before dinner. He led us through the small streets of the centuries-old city centre to our equally-historic eating place. In the middle of the sidewalk in front of the restaurant stood a life size cut-out of your sometime-musical scribe with a very funny sign that read that I will always fondly remember.

As I stood next to my name "in lights", a scruffy-looking hippy wearing a too-big army great coat wormed his way next to me. I asked him in German, nodding at the sign: "Who is this man?" The beatnik answered in a broad New York accent: "Beats the shit outta me man; never heard of the dude."

Inside the restaurant, the atmosphere, as the Germans say was "gemütlich," pleasantly comfortable. The waiter served pre-dinner schnapps in deep pewter spoons. He came around several times before asking for the dinner order.

It was Joe Kanuka's turn to steal something. He swiped a couple of the pewter spoons. Lammers noticed and whispered to the waiter to put the cost of the spoons on his bill. George busied himself lighting everyone's cigarettes.

LAMMERS AS HOST

Allow me one more anecdote. That story I just told you reminded me of an earlier visit to Münster. Whenever I found myself on business in Europe, I visited Lothar Lammers so frequently that he told people that I was able to conduct tours of the lottery buildings as well as he did. On a visit that included Pete and Sue Morrissey, Pete (Lammers) invited us to what seemed to be just another routine visit to the Münster office.

I smelled a ploy when we were detained at the entry to the parking lot. A huge sign hung over the entrance to the office complex congratulating me on my 50th birthday. We were led into the huge meeting room for a luxurious afternoon reception.

Lammers' management team was always uptight in the presence of the boss, but this time those gentlemen couldn't even muster a smile. They were stunned at the irreverent banter between their exalted leader, Herr Lammers and his North American guests. They had never seen him in his acquired North-American demeanour.

A small stage was decorated in the red and white of the Canadian flag and as a centrepiece stood an expensive grand piano. I realized that our host would ask me to play something. I could picture myself, with my back to the audience, playing for a mortified group of fear-ridden German managers who would not recognize any tunes beyond Oktoberfest drinking songs.

Sure enough, everyone was served several doses of schnapps. Lammers made an outrageous claim that not only was I the greatest person who ever lived, but the most talented jazz player as well. I protested that jazz players are never soloists; they play in small groups, trios or quartets but never alone.

"Oh, come on," Lammers exhorted, "you don't need a band. You're good all by yourself; play Sunny Side of the Street."

I gave-in to his wish but didn't feel happy about it. After struggling through the refrain, a big bass-fiddle joined from somewhere behind the stage. It sounded good. The drummer was pulled into the room on a moveable platform. Then from the other side of the room a baritone sax player strolled in. I extended the song to what seemed 10 minutes, with every musician doing an extensive solo. It was a great joy. The managers loosened up. In a most unusual development, two of the younger execs loosened their ties! It must have been the schnapps, although I'd like to think it was the happy music. It was certainly a most memorable 50th birthday surprise. Lammers was like that.

TRYING TO CO-OPERATE WITH LOTO CANADA

In early November of 1982, my long-time friend Ian Howard of Loto Canada approached me about the possibility that a Canada-wide sports-pool could be conducted through our inter-provincial system on behalf of the federal obligation to provide $100 million for the 1988 Calgary Winter Olympics. After that specific amount was reached, the federal government would have no further interest in lotteries. In short, to fund the Calgary Olympics, the intrusion of the federal government would not be required.

I liked the idea that the provinces would run such a lottery for the Calgary Games. Ian seemed to like it too, but neither the Federal Government nor the provincial ministers liked it. Sighs of relief were heard from all sides when the idea foundered on the rocks of self-interest. Later in this tale, when the wars were over, you will learn that the provinces ended up paying the $100 million anyway. As in any war, millions of dollars were wasted for no gain whatsoever.

One might wonder why the federal government wanted so desperately to hang onto the lottery business. It was often said that Pierre Trudeau, not a devotee of gambling, favoured a national lottery only because it would bring the government closer to the people. (Other than paying their taxes, very few people have any meaningful interaction with Ottawa.) However, there was a more practical reason. The political operators in the Liberal back room wanted a federal lottery because it meant "Jobs for the Boys" i.e. all the professionals, consultants and suppliers seeking favours from the Liberal Party.

Now that the Liberals were back in power, Ian Howard honed in on the dissatisfaction of the Liberal Party about the loss of Loto Canada. He convinced the Trudeau government to quietly keep Loto Canada on the books as an inactive Crown Corporation and above all to retain the $7 million in unclaimed prizes. The attractive situation for Ian was that the Feds could use those millions of dollars for research. In the year ahead, many thousands of dollars were spent trying to prove that their scheme wouldn't legally be deemed to be a lottery.

All the money spent researching a name for the game didn't yield the knowledge that the names SPORT SELECT BASEBALL and SPORT SELECT HOCKEY were protected trademarks of Loto Quebec. Yet — to the federal government's detriment — the lottery pool executives chose those names. The illegal use of trademarks and whether or not SPORT SELECT was a lottery, was not yet on the agenda. But it would be soon.

THE CASE OF THE PIN-STRIPED SUIT

Meanwhile, the Western Canada Lottery carried on producing a half-hour weekly TV show where the winning lottery numbers were drawn and the rest of the time was filled expounding on all the "good things" the lottery funded. The "Winsday" show was telecast across three time zones. It is not easy to generate the feeling of the lottery being "our lottery" when the players are dispersed over an area larger than Western Europe.

For the show's impact, it would be politically smart to present the draw "live" from various locations but it would simply cost too much to do a remote travelling show each week. So, why not pretend? The show would stay in Winnipeg and be transmitted on the western CTV network.

To create the sense of the show travelling around, local personalities from various areas were invited to co-host the show. In fairness, it was never said where the broadcast originated. The guest host bantered about "welcoming" us and showed vignettes featuring his home base. Even the Northwest Territories, where local lore has it that polar bears outnumber the people, received a turn.

The town of Tuktoyaktuk has a 1000-Watt radio station (CFCT) that flew its on-air personality from the Arctic hamlet to Winnipeg. Let us call him Thomas Jones, because that was his stage name.

Upon his arrival in Winnipeg, our WCLF's guest-relations staff member wanted to know what the celebrity's luggage looked like. Despite it being a chilly day in October, Jones appeared to have no luggage other than a toiletry kit. Our hero, badly in need of a haircut, was dressed in a shirt made fashionable in the Monty Python's sketch, "I'm a Lumberjack". The shirt material was a sturdy Mountie-red flannel with a prominent set of blue lines that divided his vast shirtfront in equal squares i.e. bushwhacker-style. The blue-grey denim jeans, suitably aged with appropriately scuffed kneeholes, tastefully complemented the bumpkin image.

That kind of dress may be "de rigueur" for appearances on today's late-night talk shows but this was 35 years ago, when TV folks still sported a dressed-up style. Our guest-relations person sprang into action, ordering a suit rental from the local stage-prop company. They had little in the way of business suits for our northern guest. A dark-brown-on-brown tux was the only garment available. A fully-frilled paisley shirtfront added a gay bohemian touch.

The scenario unfolds when we find Thomas Jones ensconced in the Viscount Gort Hotel, near the TV studio, awaiting his reincarnation as a well-dressed Northern celebrity. Also staying as a guest in the hotel is another T. Jones, an executive of one of North America's well-known department stores. Their Winnipeg store (Sears) is adjacent to the television station. This T. Jones is relaxing at the Viscount Gort in preparation for a dinner with the local department store's executives. He is here to read the riot act and he wants to make an impression!

The department-store Mr. Jones has asked the hotel to send out his perfectly tailored pinstriped suit to be pressed in time for his dinner party, which is delayed because of the final game of the World Series. When the bellhop delivers his suit, it turns out to be the ugliest suit since that movie "The Godfather", starring Marlon Brando. His invective directed at the hotel manager not only caused department store Mr. Jones to miss much of the game, it did not result in the delivery of his own fine suit.

Meanwhile, at the TV studio — a block away — the Winsday lottery show was being video-taped at the normal time but would not be aired until the World Series games was finished. The celebrity host, Mr. Tom Jones of Tuktoyaktuk, his hair neatly trimmed, looked resplendent in his expensive pinstriped suit, albeit a bit tight in the shoulders. He ventured the opinion that the lottery people are a first-class crowd. The guest relations guy agreed because he didn't realize the prop company had such expensive clothes to rent.

The lottery show over, Jones of the North goes back to the hotel. It'll be at least another 70 minutes before he can see himself on TV. He hangs the suit back on the hangers. Department-store Jones, meanwhile, lies on his bed in his underwear, nursing the double scotches the manager has sent over to soothe the businessman's frayed nerves. He waits in righteous anger, for he refuses to wear the dark-brown-on-brown tuxedo. The game's ending gives him no joy.

The hotel manager in his office, watching the game's end, suddenly realizes he has two Mr. Jones' staying with him and sends the bellhop to check out the northern guest's suit and bring it back if there was a switch. The bellhop is on his way back with the pinstriped suit when department-store Jones hears the opening strains of the lottery shows and hears the announcer loudly proclaim, "and from Tuktoyaktuk in the North, heeeerre isss your hoooost, Toooommmm Jooooones!"

Executive Jones, well into the sauce from the double scotches, grabs the phone and yells at the manager: "Some guy on television with my name has my suit and he is in Tuktoyaktuk."

The manager, slick as always, assures him he is mistaken and that the suit — re-wrapped in its clear plastic cover — will be delivered in a minute.

A TOUCH OF MURDER

On September 17, 1981, Paul Clear (22), son of a former colleague of your lottery scribe, was found murdered, buried in a shallow grave near Ste. Anne,

Manitoba. His convicted killers were two members of the Winnipeg police force who had committed a long streak of break-ins across the city. The loot included snowmobiles, boats, video players, and power tools.

The Western Canada Lottery came into the picture when police searched the summer cottage of one of the suspects during the investigation and found a camera. The camera's film showed a table strewn with *Western EXPRESS* lottery tickets. An enlargement showed that the serial numbers of the tickets matched those issued to a lottery salesman whose briefcase had been stolen from his car.

Leonard Bye, the sales manager of the Manitoba lottery division of the WCLF called at your friendly scribe's summer cottage in Matlock to inform me about the investigation into the murder and that he had — unknowingly — bought some of the goods involved in the case. He was crestfallen. My sole role in the murder trial was to testify that the ticket numbers featured in the photograph were part of the inventory issued to the salesman.

It was never alleged that lottery staff had been involved in the break-ins or the murder. Yet, the distributorship's board of directors found that serious offenses of company policies had occurred. The top two managers were fired.

ONLINE GAMING

Don't get bored and put the book down, but it is necessary to know how lotteries became part of the electronic age.

Back in the '70s, when U.S. state governments took over the mob's favorite racket — the numbers game — and turned it into a state-run lottery, moralists opposed the new frontier of gambling. Voices from the pulpits and newspaper editors' desks exclaimed that lotteries would lead to public scandals. Optimists, on the other hand, saw a chance to turn an age-old pastime to a good end. State lotteries could be modernized, computerized, and sanitized against rigging. Even if the odds of winning were remote, profits would fund good causes, not crime. With state-sanctioned outlets in convenience stores, lotteries could be big business. As a business, the industry was in its infancy, but it was poised to explode. The nation's growing anti-tax sentiment would make lottery revenue irresistible to politicians.

After years of simple, familiar games, paper-based lotteries had to make way for computerized systems.

In the fall of 1981, two years after Ontario and Quebec had evaluated various bids for online-lottery systems and installed their respective lotto games (6/36 and 6/39), **Pete Morrissey**, a representative of Gaming Systems came to visit me in Winnipeg.

Before entering the gaming business Pete had worked for Lear Siegler, a diverse technology supplier. In 1972, he had won a bid to supply the Michigan lottery with a computerized lottery system but Lear Siegler's directors were appalled at the idea of supporting gambling. They declined to honour the contract Pete had signed with Gus Harrison, Director of Michigan Lottery.

Rather than losing his sale, Pete got in touch with Gordon Graves, the President of Datatrol (a subsidiary of Applied Devices) where a man named Bob Stern was the Chairman.

Their first lottery terminal — Datatrol IDT 6000 —looked like an assembly of unrelated parts and was developed from a primitive retail terminal from Lord & Taylor (of the department store fame).

Meanwhile, among the diverse clients of a Princeton-based consulting company called Mathematica were the state lotteries of New Jersey, Pennsylvania and Rhode Island. Two of their employees specialized in lottery formats and distribution systems.

Guy Snowden, a husky, natural leader had worked for IBM.

Victor Markovicz, a Polish-born, immigrant from Israel was an introverted mathematician.

These two men recognized an opportunity in computerizing lotteries and left Mathematica to found a company called Gaming Dimensions where they would concentrate exclusively on supporting the business of government-sanctioned gambling.

The first home of Gaming Dimensions was a small building near the Arcade in Providence. Their first client was the lottery of Rhode Island headed by its bulldog-minded director Major P.J. O'Connell, a former State Police officer.

In 1981, Gaming Dimensions had two competitors (Automated Wagering and AmTote, both of which concentrated on horse racing) and three clients: the lottery organizations of Michigan, Connecticut and Rhode Island. Soon the lotteries for Quebec and Ontario would follow.

Eventually Snowden and Markovicz (with lottery clients) met Bob Stern, and Pete Morrisey (with the Datatrol system). The foursome formed a new company called Gaming Systems backed by the Texas-based Bass Brothers and their moneyman, Richard Rainwater.

As a test, the first lottery terminal was placed in The Olde Smoke Shoppe, a block away from the Gaming Dimensions office. For the new staff that included **Tim Nyman, Don Stanford** and Paul Bishop, the whole thing was a wild scramble. Whenever a problem arose with the terminal, every Gaming Dimensions employee would run to the smoke shop to examine the fault and fix it.

Gaming Systems went on to become GTECH, the largest supplier of lottery technology in the world, today known as IGT (International Game Technology) with more than 12,000 employees.

EQUIPMENT APPROVED BUT NOT THE LOTTERY

When Pete Morrissey — one of nature's true gentlemen — visited the WCLF offices to talk about online systems, he had difficulty imagining the winding road his prospective client had travelled to gain acceptance of lotteries.

I asked Pete if he would put a terminal in the reception area of the Winnipeg office so it would demonstrate to one and all what this online business was all about.

When the green-grass-hued terminal arrived, it came accompanied by an invoice for $3,000. We weren't buying a terminal; we needed one for show. Pete demonstrated his adaptability; the invoice rapidly disappeared and the staff was taught how to program the device so they could mimic online transactions for interested viewers.

To convince the WCLF board members and their respective ministers, the machine had to be presented as a necessary device to ensure integrity of the prize pay-out. I played on the politicians' apprehension that retailers were required to visibly determine whether a winning ticket was genuine or altered. If they failed to determine a fraudulent claim, it was at their expense. To overcome that weakness, the terminal was introduced to certify that winning tickets were truly winning tickets. Naturally — in my spiel — it followed that these terminals would need to be installed at the retailer counter and, of course, they needed to be connected by telephone to a central system.

Right there at the counter of the WCLF office, the demo terminal showed how the machine validated the winning tickets of our three lottery games. The board approved the concept of ticket validating machines and the money to buy them. The presentation made light of the fact that the equipment could also issue lottery tickets. Of course, the board members understood exactly what was going on, but they were now equipped to give their respective ministers a reason to allow the purchase to proceed. The implied bonus for the ministers was that if a Canada-wide game were approved, the system was ready to go.

LOTTO 6/49 ACROSS CANADA APPROVED

The NDP government in which Larry Desjardins had served as Minister of Lotteries was defeated in 1977, but in the Manitoba general election of November 17, 1981, the electorate decided that the New Democratic Party was the better of two bad choices. Larry was back in the lottery portfolio. In the four years he had been away, the Western Canada Lottery had quadrupled in sales. In his first week in office he told me he felt like an outsider in the business he had started.

The personal and business relationship between your lottery scribe and Minister Desjardins was not the same as it was before. He later told me that he was angry that I had not visited him socially after his defeat. He failed to recognize my point that, politically, I had to stay neutral to survive. I could not be seen socializing with a member of the opposition who —in Question Period — was likely to ask probing questions about the lottery.

Larry felt that during his four-year absence, the board and management had not served the lottery well. He suspected — despite evidence to the contrary — that overly generous expense accounts and needless travel had been approved. Unfortunately, time was not on WCLF's side. Larry had come back just at the time when all Canadian provinces agreed to jointly operate a nation-wide game, LOTTO 6/49. Larry, who hadn't gone through the lengthy step-by step analysis wanted to start from scratch. He threatened to withdraw Manitoba's participation.

The meeting of lottery ministers in Montreal, chaired by Jacques Parizeau, Quebec's Finance Minister, was to come to a final agreement for a Canada-wide lottery. Parizeau endorsed the concept, stayed for a while and then delegated Jean-Marc Lafaille to conduct the rest of the meeting.

Larry tried in vain to force re-examination of the 3-year study that resulted in the approval of LOTTO 6/49's launch. He didn't listen; he distrusted me as he distrusted anything that he hadn't nurtured himself from the outset. He obstructed proceedings for a while and hinted again that Manitoba might stay out of the LOTTO 6/49 game. However, given Manitoba's 5% of the country's population, no one at the meeting appeared overly concerned. The bigger problem was Ontario's sudden unwillingness to participate.

The cause of Ontario's unexpected position was due to the paranoia of the President of the Ontario Lottery Corporation, a self-professed Conservative-redneck and car dealer, **Norman Morris.** He feared that a Canada-wide lotto would kill his fledgling 6/45 Lottario game. It fell to Jean-Marc to explain that Quebec had a far more lucrative lotto game than Ontario and Quebec's studies showed that Quebec would make far more profit with LOTTO 6/49 in conjunction with their Lotto 6/36. In other words, the national Lotto 6/49 was not a threat to Quebec.

The final vote was at hand. Everyone was sure that Ontario would vote "No." If so, Manitoba would also bow out. Voting from east to west, Atlantic Lottery's four-man delegation voted YES. Quebec's four members voted YES. Norm Morris — who fancied himself a close confidante of Ontario's Premier — quickly voted NO, only to be contradicted by the Ontario Chairman of the Board who announced that he and the other two Ontario delegates voted for introduction of LOTTO 6/49. Ontario was in!

Larry conceded. It was unanimous. LOTTO 6/49 was to proceed. A little hassle about the name of the game in French and English was resolved when it was approved that the game would be called LOTTO 6/49. The ciphers of the 6-49 combination could be pronounced in whatever language one preferred but LOTTO was universal.

BUYING THE EQUIPMENT

After delivering his demonstration terminal, Pete Morrissey regularly visited the Winnipeg office filling gaps in your scribe's knowledge of online gaming so that the board could be kept up to date and its General Manager could appear to be a whiz in computerized gaming.

Thus far Pete Morrissey had dealt with the concept of facilities management, a system where the supplier essentially runs the gaming system and takes a very small a percentage of every transaction. I agreed with the advice of our technical people that we shouldn't go that way. It seemed obvious, that if the facilities manager could make a profit supplying the system and running it, WCLF could do it cheaper since there was no need for a profit margin. What was wanted was the lowest possible cost of the equipment.

The tab for the entire system of computers, retailer terminals and software amounted to around $14 million — a cost that could be earned back through lottery profits in less than five months. The required funds were in hand. Pete Morrissey brought his boss Victor Markovicz to seal the deal.

Bill Clarke, Joe Kanuka and your lottery scribe represented the buyer. After a lot of lame banter, Bill asked how big a cheque Victor wanted today in order to clinch the deal. Victor, keyed up to deliver a convincing sales pitch haltingly said, "Well, it isn't that easy, you know." We all waited to see how difficult it might be. A silence hung in the room.

"For one thing," he stuttered, "We need a contract."

Joe Kanuka chuckled a little lawyer's laugh. "Not really," he chortled. "We have your excellent submission in that big binder and since you hold yourselves out to be experts, we shall rely on your proposal!" Victor, who was used to signing extensive contracts nailing down every possible detail, couldn't take YES for an answer. He kept raising objections as if *he* were the buyer. Finally, Pete took him out in the hallway. Pete must have explained the lay of the land, for Victor came back in smiling, prepared to shake hands and said "$1 Million in US Dollars will do. The cheque was quickly written.

That evening Victor and Pete invited their new clients to dinner and brought along a local Winnipeg lawyer that Victor had engaged for legal advice. He had been hired in vain. The lawyer enjoyed the dinner and at the end he ordered some very expensive cigars that he kept for himself. He seemed content. He had just earned a healthy fee for having dinner.

Many years later, I can attest that it was a most rewarding deal for WCLF. We received what we expected and more. Soon after that Atlantic Canada followed in our footsteps. I know Victor accompanied Pete to the signing. I heard that he acted in a most laid-back manner and let Pete do the talking.

TEACHING THE POLITICIANS

The western Canadian lottery ministers who were asked to approve the LOTTO 6/49 game didn't have a clue how it worked. One reasonably intelligent deputy minister wondered why we would let people pick 6 numbers from 49 and pay them a heaping pile of money if they had all six correct. His mathematical calculation was that when one divided 49 by six, the outcome was close to one in eight. His angst was that in view of those odds WCLF would lose its shirt. I covered for his mathematical maladroitness by assuring him that such a calculation as he showed was the attraction of the game. It appeared so easy to win. He later figured out by himself that the odds of choosing all six numbers correctly were 1 in 13.9 million.

With four western Canadian governments required to sign-off, signatures to the agreement were hard to come by. There was to be no one-day tour of provincial capitols this time. Even though the lottery ministers had agreed to launch the game on June 12, 1982, several had to report back to their respective cabinet colleagues to get the "Final. Final." Each provincial cabinet had a particular nut to crack in approving that new lottery game.

Neither Alberta nor BC gave formal approval to the launch. I took refuge in the concept of Absence of Disapproval. I decided to proceed until someone stopped me. No one did!

LARRY NIXES MARKETING CHANGES

Larry Desjardins didn't like the fact that during his years of absence, WCLF's role had expanded while the activities of the province of Manitoba were diminishing. Before the advent of online systems, the provinces handled the entire operation from warehouse to player. Now, the 6/49 online system handled the entire transaction from beginning to end. Retailers paid WCLF directly and relied less on the provincial sales offices, whose task was limited to managing their retail network and delivering game supplies. But Larry worried unnecessarily. Retail contracts, delivery of instant and passive games and the encashment of smaller prizes were still important functions for the marketing offices.

To administer the new system the WCLF board approved the opening of WCLF branch offices: Three in BC (Richmond, Victoria and Kelowna), two in Alberta (Edmonton and Calgary) two in Saskatchewan (Saskatoon and Regina), and one in Winnipeg. These offices served as distribution centres and prize payout offices. The provinces went happily along, except Manitoba.

Larry had difficulty accepting that the activities of the WCLF head office would be more prominent in his province than those of the Manitoba distribution office, even though most lottery jobs (including the Data Centre) were based in Manitoba. He insisted that the Manitoba distributor would not be under the control of WCLF. Everyone agreed to his desire in the knowledge that the change would not make any difference other than in name. The six offices in the three western-most provinces were officially opened in spring of 1982.

Manitoba's obstructionist actions angered some of the other provinces, particularly BC, which contributed half the operating budget but had few of the jobs. They welcomed WCLF operating in BC and looked forward to creating jobs in their province.

The practical reason for lottery offices in the major cities was that LOTTO 6/49 could not be sold by volunteers selling tickets from their back pockets. The lottery terminal on the retailer's counter issued the tickets directly to the store and moreover, it enabled retailers to pay out prizes up to $200 directly.

Alberta had phased out volunteers years before in favour of a professional sales staff and had few problems in converting, but Saskatchewan and BC were still operating with a host of volunteer sellers.

Saskatchewan created a single distribution agency called Sask Sport Distributor Inc., which put the volunteer agencies out of business. Surprisingly, the agencies weren't unhappy. Back in '74 when they began to sell lottery tickets, there was a single draw every three months. Now there were more than 100 hundred draws a year. Most volunteer organizations were happy to escape the drudgery of selling while still receiving most of the profit. Saskatchewan treated its former distributors generously. A new program was created that enabled 800 communities, 23 regional recreation associations and eight zone sport councils to receive direct funding from Sask Sport.

LEARNING FROM PENNSYLVANIA

The Marketing Manager of the Pennsylvania Lottery, Owen Hickey, was an imposing personality. We had met a few times at meetings of the National Association of State Lotteries. His degree in Marketing from Temple University enabled him to match the distribution of lottery tickets with the practices of Coca Cola, Old Dutch Potato Chips, Procter& Gamble and the like.

"After an outlet becomes a retailer, delivery of the product is merely running a pre-destined route," Owen Hickey asserted. A regional manager could supervise a number of people and would respond to retailer problems. I liked his comparison. My view of a sales person was someone whose role was to convince a client to buy his wares —door-to-door salespeople, realtors and life insurance agents. Those who deliver bread, milk, and other staples to stores were called sales people out of habit, but selling was not their major skill.

Owen Hickey dismissed a system which meant that every sales person sold everything to anyone anywhere. The Pennsylvania manager preferred a planned, specific daily route for his lottery staff — a stop-by-stop, programmed visit to see every retailer on a regular basis. To carry out their function, delivery drivers carried substantial inventory and recorded their sales on a hand-held computer (an improvement on earlier handwritten-carbon-copied invoices). Fixed salaries became the norm rather than commissions, although small bonuses were paid for extra special efforts.

The British Columbia minister for lotteries, Evan Wolfe, new to this new type of distribution, agreed that this was to be the way to proceed, provided that salaries were not too divergent from the other three provinces.

Your lottery scribe was directed to keep a low profile in setting up a professional distributorship since the BC government was in the throes of a political war with Solidarity, the rebellious trade union movement.

CREATING WCLF OFFICES IN BC

Minister Evan Wolfe may not have realized the magnitude of his decision. On February 10, 1982, he agreed that the existing charitable lottery distributors should be paid off when they ended their services. That task, in itself, was daunting and fraught with potential political protests.

The first step was to establish the online system. Once LOTTO 6/49 was established, only then could the era of community groups selling lotteries could be ended. It is still amazing to me, after all these years, that this major change was devoid of major problems.

WCLF was fortunate that Michelle McBride, who by now lived in BC, was willing to head the new sales division in BC. She established Richmond and Victoria offices and a smaller sales office in Kelowna. She knew the business. She would build BC's lottery success.

Your lottery scribe will step aside and let Michelle tell the story of the beginnings of WCLF distribution in BC:

Michelle McBride writes:

"In comedy and life, timing is everything. Well it seems my timing was perfect back in 1982, as was my luck. I was living in BC when the decision was made to change the lottery ticket distribution in British Columbia. My six years of experience working at the Western Canada Lottery Foundation, Manitoba's Western Lottery Distributor and Loto Canada had prepared me for the opportunity. When Guy Simonis asked me to head the start-up of what was to one day become the British Columbia Lottery Corporation, I readily accepted.

"My task was to lease offices and warehouses in locations in the Lower Mainland, Kelowna and Victoria, hire and train employees, select and have sales agreements signed with hundreds of retailers, of which only 90 or so would be the first to go online. Oh yes, lottery terminals (TIVM) had to be installed. Within the retail location dedicated electric wiring and telephone lines had to be installed, dedicated bank accounts for each retailer established, training bondable retailers and training them on the new system. It was a big job.

"I accepted the job on March 15, 1982. The new distribution system had to be completed by the end of May — ready for the launch of LOTTO 6/49 on June 6. The budget to run the entire operation was not to exceed 2.5% of sales. My home in Richmond, specifically my kitchen and dining room, became the temporary office of the start-up and the staging location for the new terminals.

"As a relative newcomer to BC, I did not have a network of friends, family or acquaintances to draw upon. However, I had worked on another project with my husband and **Jacquie Goldberg Bayley**. I knew Jacquie had qualities and characteristics that complemented my own, so I offered her a chance to start something big and after considering the task, we vowed that we could deliver the job on time.

"Our direction was to work unobtrusively since there was still resistance in cabinet to have government operating the lottery. No promotional signs! No overt advertising! One of the first tasks was to locate and lease a non-descript location in Richmond's Elmbridge Way, a warehouse district. The first hire was

Leslie McCallister Hunter, full of energy and ambitious. Leslie became BC's first Retailer Trainer of the online system.

"The stage was set but we had no sense that what we were doing would become a multi-billion-dollar business decades later. The experience during those early years produced lifelong relationships, memories and amusing anecdotes.

"One of those stories involves an illegal mail-order operation that sold our lottery tickets.

"When the lottery operation moved from my home into the building on Elmbridge Way, we didn't know that the building housed an illegal lottery mail-order operation. Back in Winnipeg, at the Head Office of WCLF, alarm bells were ringing. A Winnipeg official, **Jack Ladobruk,** was sent to Vancouver to save us from a potential scandal worthy of front-page news.

"Meanwhile, Jacquie and I were conducting eight interviews a day in search of the perfect "route people" not to be confused with village people. Guy Simonis had this notion that if we identified the position as a sales role there would be higher salary expectations. There was no talking him out of this label and besides he reasoned, there was a synergy with the tracking and sales device — christened the 'route manager' — that each 'route person' carried. Three years later when the distribution system changed from WCLF to BCLC the lower salary became such a source of irritation to the people in the field that joining the BC Government Employees union began to look very attractive.

"As this was going on, the original distributors of the lottery, the non-profit organizations were waking up to the reality that technology was to replace them; they were facing dismissal as distributors. Needless to say, this wasn't received favorably by the charitable operators. It forced me to change my telephone number and dial up my survival instincts. Many years later I would face the same hostility when the charitable bingo business model was reinvented and subsequently displaced the non-profit organizations.

"By early May 1982, we were ready to go. The three offices were loading up selection slips and ticket stock. Each facility was deliberately separated (by walls) into two sections — "Sales" and "Warehouse." The Route Persons were hired but during their training it was realized that financial literacy was an important skill in the position. We had assumed that basic arithmetic skills were engrained in everyone. We were so sure that during the interview process not one candidate was tested on that subject. In fact, we discovered that filling out forms, balancing all products and cash at the end of the day would be critical as the employees would be responsible for any unexplained shortages. The depot Commandants, Marlene Thomas and Miles Pritchard were ruthless in their quest to fulfill the balancing act at the end of the day. Jacquie and I had to intervene regularly to avoid a mass uprising from within the sales force.

"The team that was created in spring of 1982 developed over the next few decades into an unusual combination of a real family and a high-performing team. We all have stories that will live with us forever and could fill a book, not just a chapter. Here is one anecdote which I'll call 'A Spy Among Us.'

"It was discovered that we had a plant in our midst which added a little more drama to our daily tasks. We suspected who he was, and our job was to impress him that we knew the business. We identified the undercover agent when someone within the team recognized him as a millionaire who owned a lot of Vancouver property. Moreover, he was a supporter of the government of the day. There could only be one reason that a millionaire was employed as a route person at a starting salary of $20,000 per year. Six months later at our first annual Christmas party, in a short speech, he presented me with a sewing box made of shells and complimented management and the staff for the stellar performance. He then resigned. Mission accomplished. I still have the box.

"Those were the "good old days!"

PARKSVILLE

Michelle has given you a glimpse of what it took to get the distribution machinery to work properly. But... we have gotten ahead of ourselves. Let's return to the weeks before the first LOTTO 6/49 ticket was sold.

On May 3, 1982 while the politicians were still hemming and hawing about a green light for LOTTO 6/49, several Interprovincial Lottery Corporation board members and national on-site managers didn't yet have a solid understanding of the game's intricacies. Knowing that people listen more attentively to experts from outside their immediate circle, board members from across Canada voted in favour of inviting **Lothar Lammers**, General Manager of the West Deutsche Lotterie to speak about his nearly four decades of experience in Lotto 6/49.

Lammers visited Quebec first, although Jean-Marc Lafaille and David Clark didn't need a lotto seminar. Loto Quebec board members were on-side with a nation-wide Lotto 6/49. No problems there. From Montreal, Lammers flew to Moncton to meet with the board and staff of Atlantic Lottery and then on to Winnipeg where he made a brief appearance before the board of the Manitoba lottery distributor. From there Lammers and I set out together for the Interprovincial Lottery Corporation meeting in Parksville, British Columbia.

Preparations for the launch of Lotto 6/49 were so advanced that Loto Quebec was able to show its TV commercial that featured a 747 aircraft bringing the LOTTO to Canada. The fact that Quebec had invested in a quality TV commercial solidified the confidence by the attendees that the launch was a certainty. After Lothar Lammers launched into his well-prepared speech and slide presentation about the overwhelming success of Lotto6/49 everyone was won over. There was no more "why," but a lot of "how."

Your lottery scribe remembers Parksville as one of the more enjoyable business meetings. Positive vibes remained throughout. The evening dinner morphed into a cabaret where each region of Canada contributed a funny skit about whatever subject they wanted. BC's skit was a hilarious show of unrelated slides showing random slides of people, animals, buildings and weird images.

Norm Grohmann, BCTV's funny weatherman was shown the slides at the same time as the audience. His 'shtick' was that he provided commentary when a slide appeared. He miraculously made a cohesive, comical story out of it. It was most amusing.

Loto Quebec management group prepared a fairy tale without the input from their President Jean-Marc Lafaille. The story was about the "King" (Lafaille) who was portrayed as a single-minded, yet beloved dictator. The emphasis was more about the follies of Jean-Marc than his benign treatment of his staff. It was all good fun. Jean-Marc laughed the loudest.

Chris French — the administrator of ILC —was written into the skit but at one point was jocularly banned from the dinner hall. Chris, expecting to be called back to return to his role in this fable, waited in the cloakroom. However, the performers got so into their improvisations that they forgot all about him. Chris missed his dinner before someone remembered that he had been banished. Chris was the only one who disliked the Parksville meeting.

A CHANGE OF NAME

Quite unexpectedly, someone in the BC Cabinet had a bright idea. Within the reigning Social Credit Party, lotteries weren't especially high on their agenda. Instead, the politicians were dealing with a much-debated issue i.e. the World Exposition and its cost. Public support for EXPO 86 was high but *only* if there would be no deficit left for the taxpayers to pick up. Premier Bill Bennett — no fan of lotteries — approved the introduction of 6/49 with one condition. To stifle his cabinet's lottery critics, he insisted — with only weeks to go before the national launch — that the name be changed to EXPO LOTTO.

It was an odd marketing strategy to call the game LOTTO 6/49 in nine provinces of Canada but another name in BC. Cheap-looking posters were quickly printed and each lotto terminal was plastered with a yellow sticker reading EXPO LOTTO. Of course, the Canadian news media, including those in BC, paid no attention to this BC quirk and referred to the game as LOTTO 6/49.

It was the jackpot prize that convinced British Columbians to play the game, not paying off the debt of EXPO '86. After a few weeks of this charade, the stickers began to fade and long before EXPO 86 closed its successful 6-month run, the EXPO LOTTO was forgotten. The then-newly-elected premier Bill Vander Zalm — standing in front of a huge LOTTO 6/49 logo — crowed that there was no EXPO deficit thanks to LOTTO6/49.

LOTTERY "TERMINALS" MAKE THEIR DEBUT

The task was now to educate the public on how the Lotto game worked at the retail counter.

Michelle McBride recalls: "I was sitting on my dining room floor in Richmond BC staring at a big blue box and breaking into a cold glow (ED: "Ladies don't sweat," as Michelle contends.)

"I was on the phone with a GTECH technician in Rhode Island as he patiently explained how to program the thing. Its debut before the media was to be held at the Robson Media Centre within hours. Evan Wolfe would be there to demonstrate the solution to financing EXPO '86. At the media center I diligently taped all the wires to the carpet. I wasn't as concerned about people hurting themselves as I was for the operation of the box — any break in the connection would wipe out the demonstration. On that day in May of '82, Minister Evan Wolfe demonstrated with flawless elegance how a store keeper would produce a lotto ticket." The press reports were flattering.

HIDING SIGNS IN ALBERTA

On June 1, 1982, with two days to go before the terminals would "go live", your panicked scribe received a call from the legislative assistant of the Alberta minister Mary LeMessurier that approval to launch LOTTO 6/49 was on the next day's agenda of the Cabinet. **Susan Green** thought it might be wise to remove all promotion to avoid the impression that Cabinet approval was a mere rubber stamp. It was not possible to blank out the massive TV and radio campaign, but a compromise was reached. WCLF received the home addresses of members of cabinet so that staff could remove signs along the MLAs personal driving routes to and from the Legislature. A posse of hastily-hired students hid or covered up the offending advertising material and waited for the "all clear" signal to bring the signs out of hiding. Cabinet approved LOTTO 6/49! All point-of-sale material was restored.

THE FIRST DRAW OF LOTTO 6/49 — IN DARKNESS

On June 12, 1982, the first LOTTO 6/49 draw was televised on CTV between program breaks on ABC's "Wide World of Sports" ("The thrill of victory and the agony of defeat" as the screen showed a skier flying off a jump). In the Eastern Time zone, sales across Canada ceased at 5 p.m. The fact that it was 2 p.m. on the west coast in the middle of the shopping day, was deemed not too important a barrier to our partners in the east.

Depending on the live action on the TV screen, the draw was slotted for around 6 p.m. Eastern time. WCLF staff and suppliers gathered at a reception at Winnipeg's Holiday Inn to witness the very first show together. The atmosphere was festive. Sales of the new game had surpassed expectations.

All those involved with the launch were excited. They had worked so many months, won so many battles, suffered some setbacks and now the climax was here. The game that would run for many decades was about to come to life.

At two minutes before six o'clock, a hush fell over the room. For a flashing instant the draw machine and the LOTTO 6/49 logo appeared, then the TV screen went dark. Our big moment was reduced to 50 seconds of dark screen and then an apology for technical difficulties. There was no technical difficulty. A switcher at the CTV studio in Toronto saw something on his screen that he had never seen before. He pulled the switch.

Some of the lost publicity was recouped that evening when Sandi Renaldo devoted two minutes on the CTV National News and replayed the draw. Few of those present at the Holiday Inn saw that piece on the late news. The party was on. It was a late night after that most memorable day.

LAUSANNE

September 24, 1982. The 1982 AILE Conference in Lausanne will be long remembered. Driving by car from Amsterdam your lottery scribe and spouse were accompanied by Pete and Sue Morrissey of GTECH and Richard Muller, WCLF's advertising guru. Hotel Krone in central Cologne was the first stopover.

The hotel owner/concierge/receptionist confessed that he also was the porter and therefore the North American guests would have to wait until everyone was checked in before the luggage could be brought up. In a demonstration of petulance, Pete took as many bags as he could carry and hang around his neck and headed for the door of the small elevator.

The door had a porthole at eye level. He was loaded down with bags and struggled to keep the door open. Finally, he used a suitcase as a door stop. We watched Pete suffer in the role as an over-loaded porter.

Once inside the cubicle, he looked up and realized what we already knew. He had stepped into a broom closet. For comic effect, he hauled his bags inside, closed the door and looked at us through the porthole. He ignored our howls of laughter, opened the door and checked the walls for imaginary up and down buttons. Then he announced: "The damned thing is broken."

The next morning the hotelkeeper was curious about our nationality. When he found out there were Manitobans amongst us, he told his guests that, immediately after the war, he had spent several years on a farm near Elkhorn. With Pete listening in, the man went into great detail of his life and how he went to Manitoba to make a new life and leave the devastation of bombed-out Cologne behind. "During the war, it was awful," he said. "One day the U.S. Air Force bombed Cologne for hours. They destroyed houses, hospitals, schools, churches and many people died. It was a spectacle, hundreds of American planes dropping bombs. Bombs!"

Pete couldn't stand it any longer. This was his first confrontation with a German who wanted to discuss the war. He asked in a most innocent voice: "Why did the Americans do that?" leaving the man speechless. He didn't attempt to answer.

Schaffhousen, a town on the Swiss side of the Rhine, was our next stop. **Sue Morrissey** was excited. She had stayed in Schaffhousen in her student days and still had the phone number of her lodgings at that time. Your lottery scribe was delegated to talk to whoever would answer the phone. The heavy Swiss accent was so foreign to my Dutch/English ears that I turned the phone over to Sue, who spoke English very loudly, a tactic I hadn't tried. Sue said the man had told her somebody died but she didn't know who.

No matter; Sue was intent on showing off Schaffhausen's highlights, at least those she could remember. Apart from the mighty river Rhine, there isn't a great deal to see in Schaffhousen but Sue did her best.

The next day we arrived in Lausanne at the majestic Hotel Beau Rivage to attend the Conference. I can't remember the business sessions. They must have been boring. For the final dinner, the conference delegates were taken on a lake vessel to the medieval Chateau de Chillon which is said to be among the best-preserved medieval castles in Europe. Arriving by boat, the first glimpse of the castle is really memorable.

However, the dinner was a bit of a disappointment. Some misguided lottery host had come up with the idea of arranging dinner partners by lot. Never mind that you had colleagues and friends you wanted to dine with; you had to dine where the luck of the draw told you sit.

Ina and I were seated in a drab panelled room along with a principal of Scientific Games, **John Koza,** one of nature's true bores and boors. He was mute most of the time and when he spoke, he exhorted me to buy his products. Ina and I left him alone, forgot about the food and took a walk around the castle which after a thousand years appeared to be solid enough to last another thousand.

We should have realized that the toilet facilities were state-of-the-art 10 centuries ago. A solid wooden cubicle was situated over a deep hole in the soil where, after completing your bodily functions, you were expected to shovel sand on your droppings.

As depressing as the dinner was for Ina and me, Richard Muller, our advertising guru had drawn delightful dinner companions. They were seated in one of the castle's charming candle-lit rooms. Conversation was great, the food superb, the laughter riotous, so much so that Richard reared back in his chair and, roaring with laughter, leaned back into the lit candles and promptly set his (remaining) hair on fire. Fear not. Richard was extinguished.

HOCKEY SELECT EXPLAINED

Loto Quebec and other Quebec crown corporations have always had excellent contacts in federal government circles. Not only does Ottawa border on Quebec but because of the bi-lingual requirements in Ottawa, a lot of Quebeckers were in places of importance. Some — it must be said — had Quebec first in their hearts and were quite willing to inform Quebec politicians what the federal government was planning, overtly or secretly.

To pre-empt the Feds going in to sports lotteries Loto Quebec launched a game called HOCKEY SELECT that was identical to the game that your lottery scribe introduced 10 year earlier. In 1972 it was called SPORTS TOTO. Let me

recall what I wrote some 100 pages ago. "The format is simple. The player is presented with a selection slip and is asked to mark Win, Loss or Tie of 13 hockey games to be played that week. Those players who have 13, 12 or 11 predictions correct share in the prize pool that amounts to 45% of the amount of dollars wagered."

Unlike in 1972, when the Government of Canada and indeed the NHL didn't object to Manitoba's tiny dip into the sports pool lottery, this time the NHL went to court to stop the use of "League Property" such as team names and the competition schedule. Your lottery scribe testified in that trial along with another person named Wayne Gretzky who had also used his team's city name in an unrelated contest. The outcome of the trial went against the NHL because the lottery identified the competing hockey teams by the names of the cities where they were located. City names are not the property of the NHL. Ergo, Vancouver-yes! Canucks-No!

However, the Feds found another bone to pick and brought out their legal hammers in an attempt to crush the hockey lottery. Their position was that the game HOCKEY SELECT was illegal because the pari-mutuel system used in the game applied exclusively to horse racing and not hockey.

On January 26, 1983, Justice Rene Hortubise of Quebec threw the out the request for an injunction. The federal hope for calling a halt to Quebec's HOCKEY SELECT vanished. The Feds appealed but lost again. A bonus for the provincial sports lotteries like SPORT TOTO and HOCKEY SELECT was that the Court deemed the games to be of **skill and chance** i.e. a lottery. A year later, that judgement came back to haunt the federal government once again.

While the win in the Appellate Court was good, sales of HOCKEY SELECT were bad. By the end of the hockey schedule, sales had dropped to $20,000 a week. If HOCKEY SELECT had been Quebec's only game, it would have caused a minor loss but the overall costs of Loto Quebec's other games easily absorbed the deficit without a ripple. No problem!

SHOWING CRACKS

As long as the four Western provinces needed each other to keep the lottery profits flowing, the wobbly organizational structure would remain intact. However, it was inevitable that as soon as one of them discovered it could operate a successful lottery by itself, the yoke of continuous compromise would be thrown-off in favour of being the boss in one's own house.

At a meeting of the western lottery provinces in the fall of 1983, Jim Chabot, BC's minister responsible for lotteries, demanded that a study be carried out to determine which location for a head office would be most cost effective. It didn't take a mathematical genius to figure out that the cost of so many communication lines from BC to Manitoba to handle online traffic were more expensive than if they were connected to somewhere more central.

Those in attendance knew why the subject was raised. The 1974 initial agreement that united the Western provinces in a lottery stipulated that the location of the WCLF Head Office would be in Winnipeg but reviewed in 1984. BC's economy was in dire straits and the re-location of the WCLF head-office from Winnipeg to BC would be a small blessing for the Interior of BC.

It wasn't easy for your lottery scribe — as WCLF's chief executive — to execute the evaluation because, no matter what my recommendation would be, at least one province would be upset. For the record, my initial report showed that it made no significant difference — in terms of operating expenses — where the Head Office was actually located.

The report made Manitoba happy however Chabot wasn't convinced. The case was not closed. It would rear its head again and soon.

IT WASN'T ALL BUSINESS ALL THE TIME

Believe it or not we had fun in those days too. **Barry Kelsey**, a long-time WCLF board member from BC contributed a story to this lottery tale that I had almost forgotten. I'll let Barry recount the occasion:

"We attended an Interprovincial Lottery Corporation meeting in St. John's NL. The board members had been entertained quite generously by our Newfoundland colleagues with traditional music, which — as I recall — didn't impress us that much, especially our General Manager Guy Simonis and board members Bill Clarke and Joe Kanuka. The Newfoundland ceremony of kissing the cod impressed them even less. I had lived in Labrador for a few years in the '60s, so I had a bit more background in local customs and enjoyed my colleagues' discomfort at seeing the dead fish they had to kiss. Back at the hotel in someone's room, a final set of drinks arrived from room service. Brandies were downed and the next thing I knew, Joe, Guy, Bill, and others, in the spirit of the evening, started tossing and crashing the empty glasses into the room's fireplace in riotous abandon. I recall joining in. It was an event to be remembered. The hotel staff must have wondered what was going on when they had to clean the fireplace.

"Some while later in Winnipeg there was a roast for Joe Kanuka's 50th birthday. Everyone had to contribute something that had been experienced at one of the many board meetings. Inspiration and desperation collided in my head. I gathered up all the glasses I could find, put them in a brown paper bag, went out onto the little balcony of the hotel, folded the top of the bag and dropped it repeatedly on the floor until there was a good clear sound of crushed glass. On stage later, my skit involved the incident from Newfoundland and Joe's role in instigating it. I gave him the bag saying, "Here you bastard, I had to clean up your bloody mess and return it to you." It may not sound so funny 35 years later, but the ensuing laughter is still with me."

SAVED BY THE METRIC SYSTEM

That particular Wednesday in July of 1983 had been a slow day at the lottery office. After hours, the Winsday EXPRESS show had just aired. As part of the usual security protocol, draw master Cliff Gardner had read the range of numbers that were eligible in the draw: WESTERN EXPRESS tickets numbered from 100000 to 439999. Michelle McBride called from Richmond to say a viewer reported that he had a ticket that showed the initial two numbers as 44. This was impossible because the numbers ended at 439999. There couldn't be a 44XXXX. The next morning, more phone calls came from people who had 44. The radio talk shows picked up the story and more folks called to report the oddity.

After a quick investigation, the people at the printing firm were hesitant to explain the problem. Apparently, the device that controls the numbering in the printing press had been printing 43 when it slipped a notch and printed 44 for a while only to click back to 43 again. The confusing advice from the printer was to publicly announce that anyone holding a ticket that started with 44 should read this as 43 and claim their prize.

In the dog days of summer, the media relished such a story. Suddenly the lottery office was inundated with requests for media interviews. On Friday afternoon, I did an interview for Winnipeg CBC TV be shown at supper time. I bravely explained the slipping of the numerator which probably made only sense to myself. My succinct summary was: "If you see a ticket starting with 44, it's a mistake; read it as 43." Pheww!

Walking from the Winnipeg CBC studio to our office in Lakeview Square, I found a cab driver waiting for me. Without any comment he handed me an EXPRESS ticket that began with 45. I refused to return his ticket until it had been checked out by the printer. The cabbie was angry. He thought he had gold or at least something that reeked of money in order to buy his silence. He said he would immediately drive over to the CBC studio. But it was almost six pm...on a Friday...in summer...in Winnipeg. Anyone at the office? Are you kidding?

I drove to our cottage in Matlock to join my family. I worried all day Saturday. I worried Sunday. What would the media have in store for me on Monday? What excuse could there be for a ticket starting with 45?

At 3:15 that Sunday afternoon, my worries vanished! The press would have a far better story on Monday. An Air Canada plane had just glided to a landing in Gimli after running out of gas over Kenora, Ontario. An aircraft worker in Ottawa had mixed-up the imperial measurements with the metric system. As a result, the plane had the prescribed number of gallons replaced by the same number of litres. No one called me about lotteries that Monday. The story died. I never asked what caused the number 45 to come up.

JACKPOT MANIA

By Christmas of 1983, the LOTTO 6/49 jackpot had rolled a few times and was approaching the $8 million mark. News coverage was relentless. This was the first of what was to become known as "Jackpot Mania." News media from across North America besieged our offices and even the homes of employees.

NBC Radio phoned me on a daily basis. The extent of this publicity didn't hit me until I received a call from a U.S. lottery colleague — on holidays with his family — that he had just listened to me on a beach in Naples, Florida.

The undisputed king of talk-show hosts in Canada was a Scot named **Jack Webster**. He was a holy terror for those who joined him on the air without knowing their stuff. He had wiped the floor with Joe Clark the Prime Minister, who thereafter refused to appear on his show again; Trudeau had battled him to a draw. This terrifying man wanted me for a full hour on his show, with its famous slogan *"9.00 o'clock prrrrecisely."*

The first Monday in January of 1984 at 9 am *prrrecisely,* I appeared on Webster's show. As the archived video tape of the interview shows, I managed not only to hold my own but scored a few points. Partway through the interview, I could see by the gleam in Webster's eye that he was enjoying the exchange whereupon he increased the bluster. I blustered back.

After the show, he asked me to stay and join him for a coffee and his second pack of cigarettes... of the morning. He complimented me on standing my ground and said I handled the interview well because I didn't try to bullshit my way out of difficult questions. In later years we did several more interviews and we kept in touch until his death in 1999.

While he might have been an intimidating bastard to many, he treated me as a professional who could share a laugh.

BC ANNOUNCES WITHDRAWAL FROM WCLF

British Columbia's rate of unemployment was high, especially in the interior of the province. The 1982 recession was nearly three times as devastating in BC as it was Canada. The economy had contracted by more than six percent. British Columbia needed jobs.

With 55% of ticket sales originating in BC, the province was very much aware that Manitoba had most of the lottery jobs —data centre, administration, software creation, printing plant and television production. Since BC had lived up to all the provisions of the 1974 agreement, it wanted a serious debate as to whether or not the head office and its spin-offs should remain in Winnipeg.

At the meeting of western ministers on March 31, 1983, **Jim Chabot**, handed his colleagues written notice that British Columbia wanted to move the WCLF head office to BC. (The 10-year agreement that Manitoba would be the head office was to expire on March 31, 1984). Failing that, BC would go it alone and establish its own lottery operation.

My report, endorsed by Clarkson Gordon, stated that from a cost perspective, it didn't matter whether the head office was in Manitoba or British Columbia. The Alberta and Saskatchewan board members were sympathetic towards BC's position and would agree to move the head office to BC, if that's what it took to keep the four provinces together. However, their political masters were not of the same view. Larry Desjardins, of course, argued for keeping the organization in Manitoba.

My task was two-fold. Provide data that would favour the status quo and draft procedures if BC were to withdraw.

"LUCK" MAKES ITS APPEARANCE

Despite the deliberations at the ministerial level, business went on as usual. After the deluge of media inquiries and increased interest public interest in lottery winners, two things happened almost simultaneously. For years WCLF had been spending close to $1 million per year to insert ads in the Western Canada newspapers, publishing winning numbers. Our sister organizations in Quebec, Ontario and Atlantic Canada made similar expensive expenditures to inform the public.

For many months I had been musing about the financial pages of the main-stream newspapers. Full pages showed the current value and up-and-downs of stocks, interest rates and commentary on market fluctuations. Who paid for publishing this information of benefit of investors? Answer: No one. Why were we paying to publish numbers while the investment crowd got a massive multi-page free ride every day?

I wrote letters to the newspapers in the West and announced we would no longer pay for publishing winning numbers but the general advertising of our lotteries would continue as usual. I received no letters but many phone calls saying that they would not consider publishing winning numbers for free.

The phone call I cherished was from Jack Webster of BCTV who chortled happily: "You're doing the right thing, lad. They'll come around."

They did come around when readers began to jam their phone lines asking what the winning numbers were.

With the expense of publishing winning numbers gone there was now a substantial budget for promotion. With the staff I mulled over the idea of publishing the winning numbers ourselves. The idea didn't gel until Bob Dunn, of my water polo days, called me out of the blue at a sales conference in Whistler. Bob had returned to Winnipeg after a long stint with the now-defunct Montreal Star. It was a welcome call. **Bob and Nancy Dunn** were fine journalists, a duo that was ideal to publish a weekly newspaper that presented winning numbers, articles about winners, upcoming promotions and other items of lottery interest. But the waters needed testing. Government is always looking over the shoulders of their Crown agencies.

The first issue called LUCK — so named after a similar magazine of our lottery colleagues in West-Germany — contained an opinion piece. I was slapped on the wrists about publishing anything that be controversial but was complimented on the innovation and the distribution of the newspaper via the WCLF retailers.

In April of 1984, there was enough confidence in LUCK's success that our very own weekly newspaper LUCK became available at every lotto retailer in the West. It would be published for two decades, close to a thousand issues.

LOTTO WEST

In summer of 1984, despite the threatening break-up, WCLF introduced a minor version of Keno but didn't dare refer to it as such. The name KENO had

such a Gambling/Las Vegas/Casino aura, that anti-gambling politicians might object to it. A stealth-like introduction was required in order for the game to find a solid place in the market.

Since our Eastern Canadian colleagues had no interest in experimenting with branches of the Keno family at that time, WCLF went it alone. Keno enthusiasts define the game as a unique concept, but really, it is a merely another version of lotto. The main difference, not realized by the average player, is that KENO is NOT a pari-mutuel format. It is really a bet on a certain set of numbers.

In Las Vegas, Keno provides a field of 80 numbers from which 20 numbers are drawn. If KENO was identical to Lotto, the jackpot would go to those who have all twenty numbers correct but such a massive field yields a near impossible number of permutations. Hence the Las Vegas Keno pays out on subsidiary prizes such as:

- 10 correct out of the 20 numbers drawn;
- 9 correct out of the 10 of the 20 numbers drawn;
- 8 correct out of the 10 etc. etc.

To come back to our first stab at KENO by another name, LOTTO WEST drew 8 numbers from a field of 56 numbers and paid prizes for matching 6 out of the 8 numbers drawn; lesser prizes for 5 and 6 correct out of the 8 drawn etc.

As this lottery tale enfolds, you will see how the game morphed into a "real" Keno game as years went by. The LOTTO WEST game launched in 1985 evolved over time — under various names — from being drawn twice-a-week to a huge, true KENO game, drawn every 5-minutes.

CHANGE COMING

In fall of 1984, WCLF employees were resigned to the fact that change was coming. Neither they nor I knew what it would be. Morale was at an all-time low. The issue could be resolved one of three ways. The hundred or so staff members hoped that BC would retract its threat to withdraw and things would stay as they were. The second possibility was that the office would move to BC, leaving all those tied to Winnipeg for family reasons, out of work. Those who might be transferred feared the high-priced Vancouver housing market. The third possibility was that BC would go it alone and the Western Canada lottery would be comprised of Manitoba, Saskatchewan and Alberta.

The choice was not for the board of directors to make. Political decisions were made way over our heads. I had seen BC's determination for change and knew that staying pat wasn't a real option. Larry Desjardins was furious about my neutral position. He felt I should insist on the status quo or failing that I should try to at least keep Saskatchewan and Alberta on side. However, my opinion didn't matter and neither did the Board's. This was politics.

A JOB OFFER?

To get away from the frustration of not being able to affect the outcome, it was a great opportunity for Ina and me to attend the Interprovincial Lottery conference in Quebec City. 1984 was the year of the "Tall Ships." The conference meant nothing of importance. We were all twiddling our thumbs, but companionship was great and the ships were impressive.

On the second day of the conference, **Barry Kelsey**, our board member from BC, invited Ina and me to join him for lunch. Usually a very erudite man, he double-talked and mumbled about BC going it alone and if so, how could it be done? I sketched a likely scenario He then asked whom I would recommend for the job of heading the BC Corporation. It took me 15 seconds to answer:

"Oh, I'd have to think about that... and OK... I have thought about it, and I'd say ME."

"Well that's good to know," said Barry, leaving it at that.

I turned to Ina and asked, "Was that a job offer?"

"Probably not, but I hope so," said my ever-optimistic spouse.

I was pleased about the interest of British Columbia. I could now straddle several opportunities. I began to look more carefully at the idea of BC's going it alone and found that apart from the much better climate, the job had many favourable aspects. In the Western Canada Lottery, a decision by the board of directors was never final. They'd all have to go back to their respective ministers, who often disagreed with their recommendations. Then it was back to the drawing board to revisit the issues. In the past, I have compared my job to that of the guy on the Ed Sullivan Show who twirled dinner plates on erect pool cues. One by one, he'd twirl a dozen plates and when he got a few spinning he had to run like hell to keep the first one from falling off. Then he hurried back to keep the rest going.

It was certain that no matter how long and how vicious the political battle was going to be, in the end, I would have to pick up the pieces. It would have been important for the business to be split up without damaging the financial situation of either side. Both lottery organizations had to be able to serve their players without interruption.

Our senior staff members, Vic Poleschuk and Ed Reger agreed that it would take a minimum of four months to establish a BC operation. A final decision at the meeting on December 9, 1984 would give us four months minus one week, not counting interruptions for the Christmas and New Year's celebrations. I'll tell you how that all worked out later... but first...

FINAL BATTLE WITH THE FEDS
HEADLINE: "THE FEDERAL GOVERNMENT INTRODUCES A NEW LOTTO"

Before I tell you the tale of SPORT SELECT BASEBALL that began and ended the Federal Government's third gamble in lotteries, let me begin by explaining what a weird game it was that they tried to fob off on players. Hang on, because it isn't easy... but let's try it. (If you're getting lost, try again. It is fun to see the Feds struggle.)

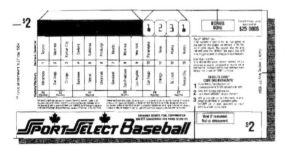

The weekly $2 game called SPORT SELECT BASEBALL was a strange combination of a lotto, combined with an instant game, coupled with a passive game and then turned into a SPORTS TOTO game.

The instant game component was located in the right-hand top corner of the ticket. After scratching the latex strip, the player would find the amount he/she would win...IF the results of the last four baseball games shown on the ticket matched the actual outcome of those games (Win, Tie or Loss).

Those visible four game outcomes were part of a 13-game series of baseball games to be played that week. Remember now: The player had no choice in

184

choosing the four outcomes because they were printed in advance and covered up by that latex strip.

The required predictions for SPORT SELECT BASEBALL weren't natural:

- The HOME team that won by MORE THAN ONE RUN was to be marked (1)
- The visiting team that won by MORE THAN ONE RUN was to be marked (2)
- The outcome decided BY ONLY ONE RUN was to be marked as a tied game (3) OR if the game was cancelled, postponed or not completed (3).

If the predictions of the LAST 12 games were correct, the player would win a share of the prize pool as did those who predicted the LAST ten, nine, eight, seven, six, five and four game outcomes correctly.

The lotto aspect of the game was that if the guaranteed jackpot ($250,000) for having all 13 predictions correct wasn't won, the entire sum would be added to the next jackpot.

In lotteries, or any other commercial enterprise, when customer preferences are forced to take a back seat to corporate considerations, it will likely be a bad product. Most of the few retailers who had agreed to sell the game detested SPORT SELECT BASEBALL. Customers rifled through their inventory to find outcomes of those four "open" games they liked, making a mess of sales counters in the process.

Because of those "open" predictions, unsold tickets had to be returned for a refund before the next game was played. Each weekly issue had to be printed and distributed across the land. Baseball games were rained out, cancelled and replayed at changed times. While the rules covered such events, confusion reigned, leaving the retailer to explain the weird rules to irate players. That is if they understood the games themselves. Regardless, the decision was made to launch this strange concoction.

Sports Pool Paris Sportifs

On May 1, 1984, six months after Parliament passed the enabling legislation to create SPORTS POOL CANADA, The Federal operatives entered the lottery market with the SPORT SELECT BASEBALL game, armed with a $1million advertising budget. Lottery War III had broken out.

The provincial governments immediately filed proceedings in federal court for a breach agreement of 1979 with a claim for reimbursement of the $120 million paid to the Feds to stay out of the lottery business.

After a heavy bombardment of advertising of the new game, public reaction was near unanimous: amazement and incomprehension but above all indifference. The reaction by the provincial lottery staff was astonishment. Expecting a formidable adversary that would launch a frontal attack on established positions, they were faced with a lottery scheme so obviously doomed to failure.

The provincial defence against SPORT SELECT BASEBALL was immediate: Deny access to our network of provincially licensed retailers! Our retailer contracts were exclusive, allowing them to sell only games approved by the provincial lottery organizations. It was made clear to the retailers that SPORT SELECT BASEBALL could not to be sold alongside provincial lottery tickets. Their choice was to sell either provincial games or the atrocious baseball game. Across the land — with some notable exceptions — the choice was obvious.

 In several provinces, a lone Liberal-minded retailer, financially supported by the Sports Pool Corporation, sued the respective provincial lottery organization for "restraint of trade." The WCLF lawyer, my now dear departed friend Joe Kanuka, handled the case of **Harry Bloy**, a BC retailer in New Westminster who was the most vocal adversary. Kanuka's charming attack in Court negated his harsh opponent. The Court found that if the Ford Motor Company could prohibit its licensed dealers from selling General Motor products, the same rules applied to contracted lottery retailers. Across Canada, in every instance, the courts rendered similar verdicts.

Contracted sellers of SPORT SELECT BASEBALL were the most unlikely outlets for lottery sales. Fish stores, carpet dealers and hardware stores that were signed up were not likely to be frequented by many lottery fans.

Sales of the baseball lottery hit a slump. Week after week, the rolling jackpot of $250,000 went to the unclaimed prize fund.

A public relations firm aligned with the opposition party in government fanned the flames of the sports pool controversy in the House of Commons and in the media. To add to the blows, Loto Quebec asked the Superior Court for an injunction against the use of its trademarks. (They owned the name SPORT SELECT BASEBALL.)

The National and American baseball leagues reacted strongly, requesting an injunction against the use of their schedules and club names.

Sales reached close to $1 million in the first week, plummeted to $500,000 in the second week, and after a while stabilized between $200-250,000 a week. These estimates came from the provincial lottery organizations. The Sports Pool Corporation published no statistics. They even refused to explain how the secondary prizes were calculated, for competitive reasons, they said.

SPORT SELECT BASEBALL had already received an injection of $7 million from the inheritance of the deceased Lotto Canada. Parliament voted an additional $20 million in aid, but even this transfusion didn't cure the ills; losses of up to $1.5 million were incurred each and every week.

Within weeks, the federal government called for a truce accompanied with a shameful demand that the victors pay $100 million to the Calgary Olympics. The provinces refused. Regular payments under the 1979 agreement had been made. Since the federal government could not accuse the provinces of breaking the contract, it was forced to take sole responsibility for the massive failure.

Four months after the launch of SPORT SELECT BASEBALL, the Conservative government of Brian Mulroney was elected. The Canadian Sports Pool Corporation announced its last lottery issue: September 30, 1984. In 19 weeks of play the game hadn't produced a single winner of the weekly $250,000 grand prize. For the very last draw, 13 predictors of the best outcome shared the remaining prize pool that totalled $4,852,874. Sadly, those lucky 13 were the only winners in the entire ill-advised venture.

After SPORT SELECT BASEBALL was dead, the provinces announced that the total cost of the game was in excess of $45 million. In the House of Commons, the claim that this battle had cost that much went uncontested — a political ploy to avoid release of the actual figures.

The aftermath: SPORT SELECT BASEBALL was doomed from the start. *Globe and Mail* columnist Jeffrey Simpson characterized it as a "fiscal swamp" and a "cesspool of Liberal patronage and incompetence." Another *Globe and Mail* story presented a long list of high-profile Liberals on the federal lottery's payroll. After Prime Minister Mulroney announced that the Sports Pool would be wound up, he called the patronage "unconscionable." Another newspaper put it this way: "Sports Select Baseball could easily find its place in the Guinness Book of Records, listing it under the category of the most colossal lottery loss in the shortest possible time."

To understand why the federal government went to such great extents to stay in the lottery business and willingly lose many millions is to speculate on the motivations of Trudeau, Chretien and others. Some have offered the opinion that the federal government wanted to stimulate a more visible government presence, particularly in Quebec. The hoped-for outcome would be an improved sense of belonging to Canada, counteracting the notions of being a Quebecker or Albertan. In short, to create federal institutions that promote national unity. Loto-Canada, Petro-Canada, Air Canada, Radio-Canada, Canada Post, et cetera, were all part of that approach.

But the lottery wars were over. All that remained was to agree on the details of the surrender. That didn't happen until after your lottery scribe moved to BC. Now let's get back to 1984 and report on the break-up of the Western Canada Lottery Foundation

TENTH ANNIVERSARY ... AND DIVORCE

The 10th Anniversary lottery draw was televised from the Queen Elizabeth Theatre in Vancouver. The show opened with a big orchestra and a bevy of dancers worthy of a Hollywood musical. Dave Broadfoot, one of the top comedic talents in the country, performed. The program featured a draw for a special 10th Anniversary $1 million lottery. Film clips of 10 years of the Winsday Show and notable prize winners were a highlight. And yet, all those attending were well aware that this 10th Anniversary was the end of the four-province alliance. Everyone was on edge; things were by no means clear. At one point during the show, the faces of the three "founders" appeared on the TV screen. Larry Desjardins, Bill Clarke and your lottery scribe were squeezed together in the front row to allow television a close-up. Tension was visible on our faces.

The morning after the show, a meeting of lottery ministers was convened. Alberta and Saskatchewan would have to declare whether they allied themselves with either BC or Manitoba. Bill Clarke — despite of all what had gone on — was in never-never land. He expected a last-minute reprieve and that all would go on as normal. Larry still lobbied Alberta and Saskatchewan to remain with Manitoba.

None of this bothered Jim Chabot. He was through haggling. He was through with partnerships. BC wanted to go it alone. At the evening meeting, the last thread snapped. Chabot announced BC's go-it-alone final notice. Larry Desjardins was victorious in keeping the head office in Manitoba, albeit with only half the business.

I still sense — after so many years — that Larry in some way wanted to save the head office for me so that my job would be secure in Manitoba. While he had heard rumours about my possible departure for BC, he doubted them. He finally asked me straight out: "Are you going to BC?" I told him it was true. Clarke was shocked into silence, but Larry talked about betrayal. I had a brief, emotional one-on-one meeting with Larry. I said I felt betrayed. Neither he nor the ministers nor any board member had given any thought to staff or management's fears during months of indecision. My eyes teared when the man who had given me the chance to develop lotteries in Canada couldn't see it my way. We didn't shake hands. We didn't speak for a decade.

Well before the "divorce" was a done deal, **Bob Plecas**, BC Deputy Minister to Chabot, had come to Winnipeg to talk. He offered me the job as the guru of the new lottery with the pay rank of Deputy Minister but no increase in salary. I argued that my salary had been held back by the Manitoba government under their salary restraint policies. Bob, on the other hand, explained that BC didn't want to appear to have enticed me with a salary increase. He added that Minister Chabot feared that a lawsuit might be launched by WCLF for having "stolen" its leader. I agreed in the hopes

that increases might be forthcoming. Alas, nothing resembling a raise came about until two years later.

 Another issue: the grapevine had it that the BC Premier wanted me to live in Kamloops where the head office of the lottery was to be located. I had accepted the job on the condition that my office would be in the Vancouver area. If the demand was to live in Kamloops, that would be a problem. I was too busy to deal with rumours.

It was agreed that BC would cover all moving expenses including hotel, travel back and forth, and living costs from January 1, 1985 until our Winnipeg home was sold and we were settled in our new home in Tsawwassen. My last point was a guarantee that BC would pay my legal bills in case WCLF decided to sue me for breach of contract. Done!

THE FIRST SALES MEETING

A meeting with WCLF's BC staff was planned for the day after the 10th Anniversary show. They, too, had their worries of how the separation would affect them and who their boss would be. (It was not yet public knowledge that it would be me.)

Bob Plecas decided to have some fun. While Michelle McBride was chairing the sales meeting, he waltzed in and asked if he could interrupt. I was left standing outside the door and told to wait until I was called in. Bob launched into a serious harangue of how this was to be a new era and how things would change from a sales office in BC to a formal lottery corporation. He said that the BC government wanted the lottery to be one of the leaders in the industry. In a nice but long screed he explained that such a path would require great leadership and that BC had done an extensive executive search to find the kind of leader who could guarantee the desired outcome.

By now staff were terrified about what kind of a creature would come into their lives. Bob heightened the tension by saying the new leader had arrived in town some days ago and was now ready and willing to be introduced. He walked towards the door and motioned me inside. A huge cry of surprise went up. It must have been a relief that it wasn't a stranger. All 40 people or so in the room stood and applauded. It was a moving experience.

A WEDDING AND GOODBYE

At the close of 1984, Ina and I were in Winnipeg to attend the wedding of our son **Leonard to Jennifer Mathers**. It was a grand event that needs to be told in a better tale than these lottery travails. At the end of the reception at the Holiday Inn, Dick Vincent — a staff member of WCLF — stood at the dining room door. He escorted me to my office so that I could turn in any WCLF belongings. Once in my office, he formally announced that he had been charged to get me in and out of the building. I was allowed to pick up some personal items. I requested that the rest be shipped to my BC Office. Dick Vincent took my office keys and told me that — as of that moment — personal access to the office premises was denied to me. I thanked Dick and never set foot in that WCLF office again.

BRITISH COLUMBIA 1985-1991

MANY HATS

Even though I had been relieved of the keys to the Winnipeg office on December 31, 1984, I was still the titular head of the Western Canada Lottery Foundation, and would be — as per contract — until March 31, 1985.

Apart from managing the ongoing business, the task was to ensure that the separation should proceed smoothly so that sales in both jurisdictions could continue without interruption. The major tasks were to acquire buildings and furnishings, install a Data Centre and not least, hire a hundred or so staffers.

It was confusing at times to be in charge of the British Columbia Lottery. The sales office was still operating as a division of the Western Canada Lottery. And, the division of assets such as computer systems, retail terminals and unclaimed prizes required negotiations. In those initial days, I was acting on behalf of BC but because my paycheque originated from WCLF, I had an interest in that side as well. It was a near untenable situation.

SALARY SQUABBLES

In the early discussions with **Gerry Bell** — our HR consultant whose job it was to protect us from union troubles — the arguments were about salary ranges for the new-hires and those inherited from WCLF. Gerry was very dismissive of WCLF's salary schedule which was based on Manitoba's civil service.

"You have to increase those Winnipeg salaries for the BC operation," he roared. I told him that I intended to take the BC civil service pay scale as a guide. Gerry wanted more than that. He wanted to outdo the unions. The nature of the to-be-hired jobs was rated much higher in importance by Gerry than I had established during the first 10 years. One example: the difference between delivery people and qualified sales professionals.

"If we want to keep the unions out, we have to be better than what they offer," he insisted rather forcefully. I responded that my job was to run a lottery with good people earning a reasonable salary, but paying more to keep the union out wasn't in my job purview.

The whole argument was quite strange to me because for ten years I had been hounding the lottery ministers for higher pay for our employees, only to be told to wait for province-wide increases for all employees. Now I was being bullied to pay more than I deemed necessary.

In a meeting with BC Minister Chabot, I asked for direction. Chabot just smiled. "Don't let Bell intimidate you. Follow Bob Plecas' advice." As it turned out Bob Plecas was very friendly with Gerry Bell but didn't go as far as Gerry wanted. A reasonable increase in salary for all (except your lottery scribe) was agreed upon. A real victory was that I was able to promote Michelle McBride with a substantial increase in salary to match.

IMPERSONATED

For four months I ferried between BC and Winnipeg. It was a bit of a burden to travel on Friday night to Winnipeg only return to Richmond or Kamloops in time for a Monday 9 a.m. meeting. On one of those weekly flights to Winnipeg, I was seated in 3C, the aisle seat of a DC 9. The man by the window was talkative. He kept yapping at the guy in the middle who — after some prodding — revealed that he was a Bible salesman for a U.S. religious institute. He related with great pride that once he had his foot in the door, his faith in the Lord assured him of a sale. I pretended to read a magazine but was fascinated.

 Then it was the window seat's turn to tell tall tales. "I am **Cliff Annabel** and I am the General Manager of the Western Canada Lottery," he said, extending his hand to the pious one. "As a Bible salesman, you might not approve of gambling but I assure you it is all above board," he boasted. I was at a loss what to do. If I contradicted him about his status as General Manager of WCLF, I would embarrass him. On the other hand, I was keenly interested to know how this exchange would end. Cliff rattled on about jackpots and millions in sales, but then he suddenly added that he was in charge of export sales to Japan.

I knew that a certain Cliff's Laundromat on Winnipeg's Henderson Highway was doing a large volume of lottery business for such an unlikely outlet. Rumour had it that he fronted a lottery mail-order company to Japan. After listening to the banter, I decided it had gone far enough. I leaned over to Cliff and said: "I couldn't help but overhear you talk about lotteries. Perhaps, I should introduce myself; I am Guy Simonis, the General Manager of the Western Canada Lottery."

Cliff choked visibly. Turning to the Bible guy he said: "How about that eh? I finally get to meet the big boss." At that moment the flight attendant maneuvered her cart to our row; both men folded their trays and remained silent for the rest of the trip.

DATA CENTRE

 At year's end of 1984, early in the changeover phase, your lottery scribe faced the reality that on March 31, 1985, at midnight, WCLF would disconnect the 800+ online retailers in BC. Seven hours later, lottery players were going to walk into their usual LOTTO store and expect that the familiar range of lotteries would be available for sale. They'd also be right to assume that they could encash winning tickets from the WCLF days. Our job was to see that the consumer experienced as little change as possible.

That was the ideal. The reality was that we had retailers and terminals but we had no data centre or prize payout center to handle LOTTO6/49, not to mention our new LOTTO WEST game.

Pete Morrissey of GTECH re-entered the picture. In 1982, his company had provided WCLF with an online gaming network. The purchasing rules of the British Columbia government dictated that a multi-million purchase of online equipment required calls for tenders, allocation of funds, elaborate presentations by vendors; background checks and panels of lottery technicians who would select the final supplier... and all that jazz.

Jim Chabot, the Minister responsible for the new lottery corporation was well aware that if we were to be operational by midnight March 31, there was no time for these protocols. Winnipeg would cut the cord at midnight and if we weren't ready, the retailers would be left with nothing to sell but the old-fashioned games such as the EXPRESS. For a minister of the Crown steeped in official rules of purchasing, Jim Chabot was a most practical politician.

"I am not going to make any decisions on purchases," he said. "I have asked you to get BC ready for operation with a deadline and you should be prepared to defend why you bypassed the purchasing rules of government."

Another "Absence of Disapproval" I thought but didn't say it. It turned out

that the same "Absence" was the model for commitments for the Richmond and Kamloops offices and all renovating costs. The fortunate situation was that WCLF was holding a lot of cash that was due to BCLC. This meant we could send all the invoices to **Vic Poleschuk**, the Director of Finance at WCLF and authorize him to pay the bills.

The Finance Department of BC had no clue what we were doing and Minister Chabot wasn't about to tell them. To follow the rules meant we wouldn't be ready and if we weren't ready it'd be my fault. There was only one option: Do it and don't hesitate.

A small company "BC Lottery", incorporated under the Companies Act, was used to create the initial BC lottery organization. Chabot was the single shareholder and carried the title of President; Bob Plecas, the Deputy Minister was Vice-President. The Secretary was Dale Janowski, a local lawyer in Kamloops. Chabot was apprehensive about buying the online system without any bidding procedure. He knew that WCLF bought a similar installation in 1982 without a bidding process and now I was going to do it for the second time, at a cost close to the 1982 purchase. The triad of directors of the just-incorporated private company met with your lottery scribe and Pete Morrissey in the Parliament Buildings in Victoria to discuss the purchase.

"If we don't buy this equipment now, we'll have a serious problem when Winnipeg cuts us off at midnight in March," I stated rather strongly.

After some pleasantries about really nothing, the Minister waved a dismissive hand to Pete and me and said: "Well, go and do it."

"Ahem…Minister," Pete began. "Would you care to put a small deposit down so we can build this equipment for you?"

"How much, Pete?" Chabot growled.

"Oh, a million would be okay."

Without a word, Chabot pulled out a cheque book from his desk drawer. It was a new, unadorned cheque book, no corporate imprints or logos or anything fancy. He had to write the name "BC Lottery" by hand and filled out the amount.

Pete accepted the cheque, looked at all the zeroes, and said: "I presume that this must be cheque number 1." Chabot took the cheque and wrote the number 1 in the top right corner. Pete took the cheque and smiled at Chabot: "Don't forget to fill in the stub!"

That was the first official payment by the BC Lottery. At that moment, no one would have believed how huge the lottery company was to become.

ALL'S WELL IN THE WEST

The WCLF board announced that the Northwest Territories (population 25,000) and the Yukon (population 37,000) had elected to stay on their side. Even though the population of that immense slice of the country was almost equal to the population of Kamloops, I thought it was wonderful news. BC didn't need any partners. I had had enough of working for multiple governments running off in opposite directions.

The WCLF news release also confirmed that Vic Poleschuk would become the interim manager of WCLF until March 31, when he would be named General Manager. The name Western Canada Lottery Foundation would be retained in spite of the fact that the western-most province was not a member anymore. The title would eventually be changed from "Foundation" to "Corporation" to conform to the sister organizations in Canada.

STAFFING

Competent people were needed to kick-start the new organization. I had mixed feelings about persuading WCLC staff to move to BC. Ed Reger as Vice President was a given. He had devoted his time to create a state-of-the-art data centre in Kamloops.

The woman in charge of our WINSDAY TV draws, **Susan Stevenson** had agreed to relocate and two computer genii, Gord Bigelow and Greg Marshall accepted positions to manage the online system and software. Several other staff in Winnipeg approached me for a job, but eventually bowed out due to their family circumstances. The loss of five or six key people wasn't much to the Western Canada Lottery Corporation (WCLC) but the gain was vital for BC.

THE BUILDING IN KAMLOOPS

Suffering in the cold winters of Winnipeg, Ina and I always expected that we'd spend our later years in climate-friendly BC but we always thought in terms of the Vancouver area. We had first seen that beautiful city in 1955. Since then, we often joked that we should have just stayed there with our four-month-old son Leonard, instead of going back to Winnipeg.

Within the first two weeks of transitioning to BC, the government wanted — for political reasons —the Head Office of the lottery in Kamloops and therefore the President should also reside there. I began to have belated second thoughts about our future. That weekend, watching TV news back home in Winnipeg, I saw a news item filmed from atop a hill in Kamloops. The reporter presented a woeful story of a small city in decline because of the closure of the mental hospital. Some 400 people had lost their jobs. The BC Lottery was pictured as the saviour of the town. The new crown corporation would occupy a building that housed a Woodward's store and health clinic. A library book showed that Kamloops had one of the driest climates in Canada and was the home of a highly productive but putrid-smelling paper mill. The winters brought cold temperatures and snow; the town had far fewer amenities than Winnipeg — not even an indoor-pool for this former water polo player!

When Michelle McBride, then BC's sales manager, and I arrived in Kamloops to take a look at the Woodward building, it was raining hard. So much for the dry climate! The vacated building was awful. The 'tower' above the store had been a medical clinic with cubby holes that once were doctors' examining rooms. The whole thing looked dismal but government had ordained that it would be our head office. Ed Reger, whom I assigned the task of establishing the data centre, had expanded his role to include renovation of the building and... Oh yes, and assist in recruiting staff for the Kamloops office.

When **Bob Plecas** confirmed that Premier Bennett insisted that the President must be a resident of Kamloops, I blew a fuse and flew home to Winnipeg, determined to return to the Western Canada Lottery. Joe Kanuka, advisor to the WCLC board, wisely suggested that I should not be given that opportunity.

Perhaps Ed Reger or Michelle McBride might have been asked to head the lottery instead but Bob was dispatched to Winnipeg to bring me back. I reminded him of the original offer where one of my conditions was that my home would be in the Lower Mainland. Bob agreed that this was the original deal but politics dictated otherwise. I pointed out that the Kamloops area delivered 5% of lottery market sales while the Lower Mainland accounted for 70% of the business; the rest came from Vancouver Island. Moreover, all major media contacts — TV, radio, press and advertising agencies — were located in the Vancouver area. To top it off, a meeting with government officials in Victoria, would involve take two separate flights each way.

Quandary! The President of the lottery should be at the Head Office in Kamloops but the president didn't want to reside there.

"What can I use as a reason you should live in the Lower Mainland?" Bob Plecas asked. I told him that my daughter **Cynthia** had MS and she needed regular medical attention in Vancouver. The Premier's position changed to "Absence of Disapproval." The compromise: I would get my Vancouver officer but I would also have a big executive office in Kamloops, even though it would be empty most of the time.

I would devote my time in each office as I saw fit and I could live anywhere in BC as long as it didn't affect my performance.

RICHMOND

The purchase of the Kamloops building was a done deal, albeit without staff's involvement but what about the office in the Lower Mainland?

The sales and distribution office inherited from the WCLF days, was a lacklustre warehouse located on Elmbridge Way in Richmond. It wouldn't do as the sales office of a crown corporation. The Lower Mainland marketing people and the Kamloops techies would require frequent cross-visits. Therefore, a location within 10 minutes or so from the airport would be ideal.

A new office park was being constructed behind the Delta Hotel in Richmond. It was in a nicely landscaped area and best of all, the occupancy date would be early April. Things couldn't have worked out better.

There was one minor problem. Both the Kamloops and Richmond leases were waiting for someone authorized to sign, even though workmen were already busy with installations and renovations. In "Absence of Disapproval", I signed everything and sent the bills to Winnipeg.

ED REGER

Ed Reger finished the external designs of the offices in Kamloops and Richmond and now devoted his energy to beating the architect and contractors into submission. As if he didn't have enough on his plate, he got his teeth into the interior design of the new Richmond sales office on Shellbridge Way. Again, he put his artistry and creativity to work to produce a beautiful and functional workplace that more than suited the requirements of our early beginning. Ed's capacity for work was staggering. He used the budget — all billed to the

Winnipeg account— to buy BC art for both the Richmond and Kamloops offices: paintings, sculptures, vases, plants etcetera — all modern and attractive. A sculpture called **"The Trees"** graced my Richmond office along with a beautiful sculpture of a Coho salmon. The coffee urns, cups, saucers and cutlery were identical in both Kamloops and Richmond. Even the serviettes bore the BCLC logo. The data centre was glassed in and the design by Fred Collins was so advanced that it was copied in other North American installations. The entire lottery complex spread over three cities was a magnificent achievement. Over the years, BCLC received many compliments from visitors.

My contribution to this achievement was nodding in agreement and signing documents in the correct places. Although a year later Ed departed on disagreeable terms, it must be said that if it hadn't been for Ed Reger's artistic eye and his forceful ways of meeting deadlines, the Kamloops building and its electronic contents would not have been on time nor as impressive and eye-catching as it turned out to be. I take no credit for it. It will always be Ed's baby.

WHO GETS WHAT?

Vic Poleschuk — in his capacity of General Manager of WCLC — and your transplanted scribe, acting on behalf of BC, faced each other across the table to divide the assets between the two corporations. Flanked by our respective lawyers, Joe Kanuka for the WCLC and Dale Janowski for the BC side, Vic and I were prepared for battle. There was no need. The accounting for ticket sales had always been done by the respective provinces. The money part was easy. The physical assets were more of a grey area. WCLF owned the Data Centre in Winnipeg, including software and retail terminals. Of course, there was some office equipment and draw machines in Winnipeg but we weren't about to nickel and dime ourselves to death figuring what some of this decade-old stuff was worth. BC assets located within the province included half of all lottery terminals as well as the machinery in its three regional sales offices.

We arrived at a very simple solution: "What's there is there." Which meant that whatever staff or assets were located in any of the provinces would remain there. No counting of peanuts. Joe Kanuka smiled. He loved simple solutions. Lawyer Dale Janowski thought he had been hired for what he believed to be a major confrontation. It couldn't be that easy. He struggled to make things more complicated but didn't succeed. The deal was quickly done, with everyone including the four lottery ministers quite satisfied.

WHAT SHALL IT BE CALLED?

Premier Bennett of British Columbia was concerned with logos and images. He wanted all BC Crown Corporations identified with similar looking logos — derivatives of the BC flag. A month before the start-up, I received a sketch from the Protocol Office in Victoria addressed to the "General Manager of BC Lotteries" that prescribed our corporate logo.

It was a suggestion for a stylized BC flag with the words "BC LOTTERIES" in the official font. I guess it was the same creative person who baptized the BC FERRIES and BC TRANSIT. I figured that amidst the confusion I could be creative too and without responding to anyone, I erased the title BC LOTTERY and changed the name to BRITISH COLUMBIA LOTTERY CORPORATION in the same official font. The corporate name was now similar to our sister lottery corporations in Canada. I also changed the awful abbreviation of the Corporation "BCLOT" to BCLC. I just didn't like the pronunciation: B-clot.

The altered logo was sent-off to the printers and the final copy was circulated among staff, board, media and suppliers. No one ever commented on the change, not even the Protocol Office. While I was at it and in agreement with Minister Chabot, I changed my title from General Manager to President and Chief Executive Officer (CEO). No one cared about that either. I wished raising my salary was that easy.

RECRUITING

First lottery worker hired

Kathryn Johnson can count herself among the lucky ones today.

The 28-year-old mother of two started work as the first employee of the B.C. Lottery Corporation...

The inherited sales team was a full complement, but hiring people for the Kamloops office was a major task. Ed Reger had already taken the novel step of hiring the entire graduating class of computer programmers and technicians from Kamloops Collegiate.

Several newspaper ads listed the jobs available. WCLF's organization chart was a guide. Some 70 jobs were to be filled well in advance of the opening date in order to allow time for training. Gerry Bell, our Kamloops-based employment consultant, was retained to sort and interview the nearly 5,000 applicants.

An unspoken directive was that union enthusiasts were not our first choice (nor the second). WCLF had no union and I had kept them away by "out-unioning the unions," meaning that the employment conditions were a step ahead of government conditions so that no union recruiter would find any eager takers. (It worked; after four decades there is no union of BCLC (or WCLC employees). Gerry Bell did a great job creating a competent staff. The new employees were properly trained and ready for the launch on April 1, 1985.

VIC POLESCHUK SURPRISES

During the hectic change-over period, I spent many nights at the Delta River Inn in Richmond. One night after dinner, Michelle and I entered the lobby and spotted Vic Poleschuk, who appeared to be scrutinizing the postcard rack.

I invited him to join me at the bar and we talked. Suddenly I realized the subtext: he was exploring the possibility of moving to BC. This was good news. Vic was a real professional and his presence would reunite the successful management quartet that made WCLF work. But the price of taking Vic aboard would be eternal damnation by the board of the Western Canada Lottery.

The optics — as they say — didn't look good. To a neutral observer, it might look suspicious that Vic, who negotiated the terms of the 'divorce' on behalf of WCLF, was crossing to the other side now that the deal was done.

To tell the truth, I didn't care what it looked like. I offered Vic the job of manager of the operation in Kamloops. His demands were most reasonable. He wanted the title of Vice-President, a small increase of the salary, reimbursement of moving costs and transfer of his pension. Conditions accepted, Vic accepted and was at work in Kamloops within a few weeks.

Bill Clarke, then WCLF Chairman, was quite upset about the one-sided trade and vowed never to speak to me again. (Bill and I had an emotional reunion before his death in 2000.) Larry Desjardins considered that Judas was an honourable figure compared to me. (He too, in time, relented and we re-instated our long friendship until he passed in 2012.)

Joe Kanuka was somewhat mellower. We talked regularly. He was appointed Acting General Manager of WCLC and promptly restored the badly damaged morale. He gave the managers fancy titles — six vice-presidents created — and everyone got a raise. Later Joe and I re-united when he became a legal-beagle advisor for BCLC. "Not a lawyer," he cautioned. "I am an advisor. I am not licenced to practice law in BC."

THE TRICKIEST PART

Until closing time on March 31, 1985, lotto tickets sold in BC read Western Canada Lottery. LOTTO 6/49 sales were recorded in the Winnipeg central system. The first ticket sold in the morning of April 1— issued by the same terminal — would look similar to the one the day before except it read "British Columbia Lottery" instead of "Western Canada Lottery." Those sales were recorded in the Kamloops central system.

It sounds so easy now and that's the way we wanted it to appear. The players shouldn't take particular notice the change. But what if a customer walked in with a winning ticket from a game from the previous week and wanted to cash the prize? The BC terminal could not get access to Winnipeg to prize if it was a winner. Such an incident would surely be noticed by the players.

To make it possible that the terminal could pay out a BC winning ticket sold under the banner of WCLC, we chartered an aircraft to fly a year's worth of data

 of past lottery draws (up to and including the last minute of March 31) and imported the entire batch into the Kamloops system. It worked! With

assistance of WCLF and GTECH, the change-over came off without a hitch. PACIFIC EXPRESS, a clone of the WESTERN EXPRESS carried on as the Winsday game. The releases of instant/scratch tickets were identical in WCLF and BCLC except for the colours and the name of the lottery. Bob and Nancy Dunn issued two versions of LUCK magazines — one for the West and a BC-only issue.

A HEAD START

Today many BCLC employees believe that lotteries in BC started on April 1, 1985. The truth of the matter is that on April 1, 1985, BCLC inherited a complete, knowledgeable sales staff and administrative support, a President and the most experienced lottery executives in North America, to wit: Michelle McBride, Ed Reger and Vic Poleschuk. Computer experience came from Winnipeg with Gordon Bigelow and Greg Marshall. TV show direction was Susan Stevenson's responsibility. In fact, the only new team was the administrative and technical support for the data centre in Kamloops and prize payout function. Let it be known that lotteries in BC started in October of 1974.

To the public, BCLC changed very little from what the Western Canada Lottery had presented for a decade. The only material change was that winners of very large prizes had to travel to Kamloops to collect their prize rather than Winnipeg. At the start of BCLC, the game line-up, in order of sales, was LOTTO6/49, instant tickets, SUPER LOTO, PROVINCIAL, LOTTO WEST and bringing up the rear was the oldest game, newly baptized PACIFIC EXPRESS.

FIRST SQUABBLE WITH WCLF

The 6/8/56 game called LOTTO WEST, which BCLC operated in partnership with the Western Canada Lottery, yielded $5.1 million in annual sales. Well into the first year of co-operation a dispute arose about that game.

Your lottery scribe had agreed to a bonus draw that drew 25 extra 6-digit numbers. If the player matched that winning number combination, he or she would win a Ford mid-sized car. Winnipeg did the advertising but no one — including your naïve scribe — paid attention to the small possibility that several players could pick the same set of winning numbers.

Upon my urgent request, the BCLC data centre ran a simulation of a winning number combination that was known to be popular. The sample number tested bore the fictitious winning numbers 2-4-6-8-10-12 and lo and behold there were three people who had played that combination.

There were more such spectacular combinations: for instance, 1-3-5-7-9-11, which was picked by five players. I must confess that I got a bad case of cold feet. If fate ruled against us there would be more than 25 winners of cars and we would lose bonus funds. I met with the unpolished person who had taken Vic's place as General Manager at WCLC but he laughed off my concerns. I pleaded with him, "All we have to do is publish a rule that in case of multiple winners a draw will be held among them to determine the winner." To tell the truth even your lottery scribe didn't like that idea. It was unfair. In the end nothing in the rules was changed. The draw went fine. There were no multiple winners but the relationship with WCLF was frayed. It was me, your odds-studying scribe who had upset the apple cart.

MATCH 3

One of the first BC-only instant scratch games was MATCH 3, a simple game that required the player to uncover three identical amounts to win that prize. Another version of the instant scratch line-up was called WONDERS OF THE WORLD that showed pictures of the classical wonders of the world such as the Colossus of Rhodes, the Hanging Gardens and the Great Pyramids of Giza. The game was an early financial success. Unexpectedly a note from a school art teacher asked if there was some kind of album where the children could place the respective tickets, similar to a stamp album. Michelle set out immediately to design such a collection sheet for future themes, especially for the tickets she was planning for the upcoming EXPO 86. Instant/scratch ticket images might become popular!

OFFICIAL OPENING OF KAMLOOPS DATA CENTRE

On April 1, 1985, a crowd gathered in front of the Kamloops lottery building to witness the official opening. **Premier Bennett**, there to snip the ribbon, was accompanied by his assistant Bud Smith who — thirty years later, would be named Chairman of BCLC.

The local MLA made a speech as did Jim Walsh, the grass-roots mayor of Kamloops who hailed the BCLC President "Gus Simone". The Premier finished his speech with words, "Mr. Simonis, Kamloops is now your town." I guess that put him on record as not knowing that I was living in the Lower Mainland.

LIVE VIA SATELLITE

We took new weekly "Winsday" lottery show on the road to several communities. BCTV, the originating broadcaster, loved the idea because they could use their huge mobile studio and broadcast the show via satellite. BC ticket buyers liked it because the draw time was changed from 5 p.m. to 7 p.m.

Norm Grohmann, the popular BCTV weatherman, was the host of Winsday in BC. Radio personality Sterling Faux was the announcer and, Ernst & Young's **Clark Gallon** audited the process. BCLC's **Michele Pankratz** was on set to display the drawn numbers. At our broadcast locations, Norm would visit senior citizens homes and sign autographs while Sterling was being pursued by his radio fans.

The very first live broadcast in Kamloops was well attended but since the city has a TV station, attending a telecast was not a novelty. The visits to other communities BC were huge hits.

The early shows, broadcast from all corners of the province, allowed BCLC staff the kind of luxury travel that regrettably couldn't be sustained for other business travel. With a troupe of seven, the BCTV producer, the four on-air personalities, the BCLC staff of Michelle McBride, Susan Stevenson and your non-telegenic scribe, the cost of regular travel, overnight stays, meals and extra salary was more than a one-day trip by private aircraft. It caused a bit of stir in government that these new lottery people were chartering private aircraft but it was soon put to rest when the costs were compared.

These fly-in roadshows were fun. To spin the half-hour TV show that ran from 7-7.30 p.m. into an evening of entertainment, local talent contests were added. The presence of TV cameras and producers always brought contestants and their hangers-on. The amateur performances often resembled the Gong Show but some gems emerged. Many of these performers appeared on the "live" TV show as "button pushers" of the draw machine to allow their very first TV appearance to be recorded at home.

In the summer of 1985, the show travelled to Fort St. John, Kelowna, Cranbrook, Burnaby, Victoria, Duncan, Penticton, Richmond, Quesnel, Chilliwack, Nanaimo, Prince Rupert, Armstrong, Williams Lake, Campbell River, Whistler, Vernon and Nelson. *"Winsday in BC"* proved to be one of the more popular lottery events in the province. Much of the show's success can be attributed to the enthusiasm and support that each community provided. One of the interesting facts was that in every community where the show appeared, sales of PACIFIC EXPRESS soared.

A show piece to the pre-show was a demonstration where one of the lottery balls — made of solid rubber — had its inner core drilled out and the core of another ball was filled with lead. These "fixed" balls were mixed in with the regular balls. The audience could guess how many times either ball would come up in 10 drawings. Most were stunned to witness that the "fixed" balls didn't make any difference in the randomness of the draw.

THE FLUBBED DRAW

To allow Michelle to be at home for her 32nd birthday on May 8, 1985, the Winsday in BC show originated in Richmond. Once the opening pleasantries were over and done with, the draw machines started. Sound was heard. The machinery hummed but the chromed globes that tossed the balls failed to rotate. No balls emerged. The show came to a stop. But this was live television!

I stepped on the stage to explain that we would install another draw machine. While Norm Grohmann, Stirling Faux and your cool-as-a-cucumber scribe were yakking to fill the air, I spotted **Alan Lyman** of British American Bank Note whose company had sold us the draw machines. On an impulse I announced that Alan would come on stage to explain the glitch. Alan swallowed hard, smiled and mouthed "S.O.B." at me. Fortunately for him, the producer turned to commercials. What had happened? In order to reduce the reflection of the light on the chrome trim, a stagehand had sprayed the equipment with a greasy substance that made the machinery slick and too greasy to turn.

Minister Chabot had watched the show from his office in Victoria and the next day inquired icily whether I'd bought this draw equipment without going to tender! In fact, that was correct!

LOTTERY WARS

By now, I bet you will have forgotten about the on-going **lottery wars** between the provinces and the Federal Government. The first attempts by Ottawa to re-enter the lottery business had ended in a retreat by the Feds. After the 1979 battle, the Joe Clark government withdrew from the $10 game in return for a puny $24 million. Then the Liberals came back and spent $4 million cranking out a sports-betting game that they said was a game of skill and therefore didn't contravene the 1979 agreement. Of course, it was pure baloney. No sane person would authorize a gambling game that relies solely on skill. Those who possess that skill would win every time. To countenance that kind of prattle, the Criminal Code of Canada states that a lottery is a game of chance *and* skill. Ottawa was prepared to bend and twist in order to re-gain a foothold to the field of gaming.

The way the Ottawa mandarins had conducted Loto Canada was almost beyond the ken of government auditors. In reality, the federal lottery provided a grand political slush fund for political messages exhorting how good the Liberals were. The way they could hand out all kinds of patronage through grants was political manna from heaven.

To recall: Brain Mulroney had ended the Sports Pool on September 30, 1984 but the legislation regarding games of chance was ambiguous. It needed cleaning up. It would take another lottery war before it was all settled.

LOTTO 6/49 — DOUBLE THE FUN

The flagship game LOTTO 6/49 has 13.9 million different possible combinations. In 1985, the weekly volume (nationally) was reaching 10 million plays per week which meant that the odds of a jackpot winner were increasing. To players this is a happy thought, but frequent winners meant there were fewer turnovers of the jackpot to increase the prize-pot to enticing highs. (Not to mention the extra sales that those jackpots engendered.)

To explain the problem: When jackpots aren't won the prize carries over to the next draw. Larger jackpots increase sales. LOTTO 6/49 had reached the point that there were too many LOTTO numbers sold to create frequent jackpot carry-overs. What was needed was a greater inventory of numbers to sell. The thinking was that a second draw in one week would lower the sales for each draw. A certain percentage of players would play every draw; some would stick with the traditional Saturday draw only — but the desired trade-off would be that jackpot sizes would increase.

A submission to the ILC board of directors to double the frequency of draws included the results of a similar situation in France and Germany which showed substantial increases in sales. Alas, the ILC Board, largely composed of civil servants and party supporters, remained unconvinced that people would increase their purchases. Finally, thanks to the influence of Quebec's Jean-Marc Lafaille, the required votes were cast to conduct the LOTTO 6/49 game Wednesday and Saturdays, with the Wednesday's unclaimed jackpot rolling over to the following Saturday and the Saturday unclaimed jackpot added to the Wednesday draw and so on.

The twice-a-week LOTTO 6/49 started on September 12, 1985. Within two months, total sales of LOTTO 6/49 increased by nearly 70%.

A PEACE TREATY

On June 12, 1986, Minister Jim Chabot, asked me to join him at a meeting of lottery ministers to conclude the lottery truce with Ottawa. Just because an opponent surrenders by raising a white flag it doesn't mean formal peace. A treaty needs to be signed that lists all conditions and obligations of both parties. At the conclusion of Lottery War III, the thankless task of negotiating the final terms was left to the federal government's Conservative government's **Minister Otto Jelenik,** of Olympic figure skating fame. His directive from on-high was to deliver the Liberal promise of $100 million to the Calgary Winter Olympics. The provinces magnanimously offered to pay Calgary's promised $100 million — but only on the condition that Ottawa provide an iron-clad guarantee that it would vacate the field of games of chance. It was not merely a promise, but an amendment to the Criminal Code of Canada that would make it most cumbersome for the Feds to re-enter the lottery business or operate any other games of chance. And so it was. The provinces finally obtained exclusive jurisdiction in games of chance.

The federal government's entry and disengagement from the lottery field had lasted 10 years. The departure from gaming included the statement that casinos were a provincial prerogative, a give-away that didn't receive a lot of notice at the time but that — in the decades ahead — yielded several billion dollars for the provinces.

Within months, (January 1987) the BC government established the British Columbia Gaming Commission (BCGC) to control charitable gaming, in particular charitable casinos. Its mandate was to ensure that the charities earned the maximum revenue for their pet projects. The new commission adopted a liberal interpretation of the meaning of "charitable" and permitted a wide range of non-profit, community-based organizations to qualify for casino licenses, something that would lead later to confusion, frustration and law suits. It would take another decade before provincial governments began thinking about taking over the entire gaming enterprise.

PUBLICITY? OR EXCLUSIVE NEWS?

 For four years the Saturday draw of LOTTO 6/49 had been part of CTV's Wide World of Sports. It was shown in BC in late afternoon — not the best time slot to reach a wide audience. I met with the BCTV people in order to angle for a better time. It had often occurred to me that "6:49" on the clock (11 minutes to 7), fell right in the last quarter of the popular BCTV Newshour. BCTV liked it for broadcasting both the Saturday and Wednesday draw. The deal was done on a handshake. It was a great idea until your lottery scribe received an invoice for $3,000 — the charge for one minute of Prime Time TV, a cost that would add up to over $300,000 a year. It had been made clear from the outset that the lottery was giving BCTV the opportunity to capture the thousands of viewers who wanted to know their winning LOTTO numbers. The deal included "exclusivity", which meant BCTV was the only television outlet to release the winning numbers. Other media would have to wait for BCLC's official news release. The potential charge of $300,000 was a

surprise. Print and radio media already provided the numbers for free. BCLC's position was that winning LOTTO numbers were news. BCTV held that showing winning numbers was advertising.

Month after month, BCTV invoiced BCLC $3,000 for each draw. BCLC didn't pay. When BCTV launched a court case demanding payment, we didn't immediately respond. Then a little birdie within the BCTV accounts-receivable department whispered in my ear that the station log of commercials didn't include the LOTTO draws. That meant that the station presented the LOTTO draws to the Canadian Radio-Television and Telecommunications (CRTC) as a part of its regular programming. It was extra money for them.

The finer points of the controversy were relayed to the management of BCTV. Immediately, all invoices were withdrawn. We committed to include BCTV in our regular paid advertising expenses on the condition that the free televised draws continued for years to come.

DIPPING A TOE INTO THE BINGO BUSINESS

A phone call from Deputy Provincial Secretary Bob Plecas expanded the role of BCLC. It was a small change at the time: "Control the supply of bingo paper," Bob said. It wasn't all that significant financially but it moved the lottery business a few steps into the social gaming sector.

The normal way of playing a lottery is to buy a lottery ticket at a favourite store, place it on the refrigerator door with a novelty magnet and at some point, check the newspaper for the winning numbers. That is your lottery scribe's definition of lottery play. Gambling in a social setting like a casino or bingo hall is a different experience. As your lottery scribe takes you through the evolution of gaming, you will see how this bingo-paper distribution was the harbinger for the immense gaming changes in the decades ahead.

To come back to the phone call of Bob Plecas: He expressed his Minister's concern about the loose controls on bingo. Hundreds of real and quasi-charities conducted bingo nights in church halls and recreation centres. Licensing for these events was in the hands of a government-appointed board that demanded financial reports of the bingo activities.

Of course, small bingo games had been going on for decades. They served a useful purpose as entertainment and a bit of fundraising. However, in the late

'70s, a professional aspect had slipped in. An unlicensed entrepreneur would rent a large hall and welcome small charities to bring their bingo licence. The operator then offered to conduct the bingo game on their behalf. The commercial operator relieved them of the burden of renting space and bingo equipment and volunteer commitments. When a sufficient number of charities took up the offer, it became profitable to operate a daily 12-hour business. Bingo was getting too big for loose controls.

B	I	N	G	O
3	29	45	56	68
1	19	43	50	72
11	25	FREE SPACE	49	61
9	23	31	58	63
4	27	42	54	71

One of the first moves by government was the control of bingo paper. In the days of the small church bingos, permanent bingo cards were used. Made of sturdy cardboard, the 25 random numbers of the card could be marked as "called" by sliding a small plastic opaque window over the number. In commercial bingo, a newsprint-type bingo "card" was the preferred medium. The player would mark the called numbers with a "dabber", a felt-tipped pen saturated with translucent ink.

The major BC supplier of bingo paper was a company called Bazaar & Novelty. Not a tiny enterprise, its bingo-related printing across Canada exceeded $75 million. Len Stuart, the owner of Bazaar & Novelty, was only too happy to exchange his many small clients for a single one who promptly paid their invoices i.e. the British Columbia Lottery.

To make it happen smoothly, BCLC hired Jan Slater and Bob Schwinghammer, the Bazaar & Novelty experts who had intimate knowledge of bingo operations across the province.

The volume was a surprise to all concerned. In the first year $1.8 million in bingo paper was sold. If that doesn't impress you than think about it this way: one bingo card cost less than a penny.

FIRST BRUSH WITH CASINOS

In 1984, the Province of Quebec was beginning to show interest in casinos. The old site of Montreal's Expo 67 needed an attraction to survive. At the same time, the United States was dealing with the problem of Indian tribes who used their legal status to ignore Washington's ban on casinos on native lands.

In Canada, discussions about authorizing casinos were fraught with pitfalls. In 1985, public perception was that casinos were evil places run by criminals. The idea that a government agency would run a casino was so far-fetched that it was a non-starter. Yet inside the cabinets of the provinces, the idea of licensing casinos was taking shape. Jim Chabot, asked if my international contacts included any lottery organizations that also managed casinos.

Well yes, sir!

My friend Lothar Lammers, the boss of the West Deutsche Lotterien Gesellschaft in Münster stood ready to help once again. He had been there to help me with Sports Toto in 1972 and, in 1982 with LOTTO6/49. A new casino in Hohensyburg, not too far from Münster, was about to open. Upon my urging, Lammers invited Minister Chabot and his wife Grace to the official opening to see how governments dealt with casinos. Chabot was delighted.

I mentioned to Pete Morrissey that the door was open to meet a major European lottery contact but it would involve two airplane tickets from Vancouver to Amsterdam. I told the Minister that the German casino people were paying for the airline tickets. It was a bit of a foolish conspiracy but I knew that Pete Morrissey was looking for a foothold in the European lottery market for GTECH.

And so it was that that Jim and Grace Chabot did a historical tour of Leiden, the home of your scheming scribe. Pete and Sue Morrissey joined us and when the five of us arrived at Hohensyburg Casino, Lammers laid on the hospitality, complimentary rooms and as many red carpets as he could spare.

The casino's grand opening featured Sammy Davis Jr. Grace Chabot was in awe. Jim sat far away at the blackjack table with a big smile on his face. When I asked if he liked this type of casino, he said he would apply for German citizenship in the morning.

Very late in the evening, Lothar Lammers joined our party and began describing me as the greatest lottery genius the world had ever produced. I saw the word "bullshit" written on Chabot's face. Lammers went on to say that the world's lotto organization, INTERTOTO, would have its annual conference in Rome in a few months and the Minister should be there because Guy Simonis would be elected to the executive committee of the international organization.

This was all news to me but you don't interrupt when someone is promoting your virtues. Lammers suggested — not so tactfully — that BC should host such an INTERTOTO conference in the very near future.

"How about next year, when Vancouver hosts Expo 86?" Chabot said.

But the next INTERTOTO Congress wouldn't be until 1987.

"Okay, '87 then. That's it." Chabot said. I don't think he believed any of it for a minute. But it did happen.

STEPPING ONTO THE INTERNATIONAL STAGE

When Lothar Lammers officially asked me to speak at the 1985 INTERTOTO conference in Rome, I quickly accepted and asked Vic Poleschuk to join me. Lammers felt it necessary that I should present myself to the membership with an overview of LOTTO activities in North America.

I delivered a lengthy, sleep-inducing speech. At the general meeting, despite my blathering, I was elected to the executive committee where one of my first acts was to offer Vancouver as the host city for the '87 Conference. The proposal was received by a round of applause and promptly approved. All I had to do now was ask for permission and funding from the government of BC.

As it happened, your brazen scribe was the first non-European official to be elected to the executive committee of INTERTOTO. Moreover, Vancouver was to be the first INTERTOTO Conference in North America.

As I had witnessed in Munich, the executives did not mix with the hoity-toity of the membership. Now that I was an executive, Ina and I were expected to travel in the air-conditioned bus equipped with deep-cushioned leather seats that, at the push of a button, would extend into a lounge chair.

In a step toward a more democratic future, **Richard Frigren,** my newly elected colleague from Sweden joined me in refusing to ride on the special "Presidium" bus. We rode with the membership at large. The conference itself was held in a run-of-the-mill Ramada hotel along a busy auto route, many miles from historic Rome. All evening dinners were held in places more than an hour away. We wondered why we had to travel for hours only to be served green pasta for lunch and then green pasta for dinner, again.

One afternoon luncheon, in a beautiful garden setting situated way out of town, we were served green pasta along with two little roasted birds. The seared remains were intact, still showing beaks and scorched eyes.

Although most conference goers were able to eviscerate the little tweeters, many looked on in dismay, especially a friendly couple from Münster, Ilse and **Alexander Malwitz**, our table mates at the picturesque garden pond. The maître d' handed out cardboard boxes for those who wanted to finish their lunch later on the bus. I carefully loaded my birds in the carton. Vic made some Italian prayer motions and closed the box. Alexander Malwitz made a mast of the wooden spit that had kept the birds erect and attached a napkin as a sail. We placed our newly-built burial device in the pond. Vic let Alexander set the little ship on fire. The waiters were divided— some were aghast; others smiled. One even applauded. Then we headed for the bus once more. After all, we had to get back to the hotel and get dressed — to go on the bus for a pasta dinner somewhere else — likely late and even likelier, far away.

MELBOURNE

It might strike you as contradictory that my lottery story complains about the difficulties of creating a new lottery organization yet, within the first six months of operation, your travel-happy scribe managed two overseas trips — one to Rome in summer and then a November '85 conference in Melbourne arranged by **Duane Burke**, the head of Public Gaming Research Institute He was kind in paying for my travel in return for a light-hearted speech about the travails of launching a new lottery organization grafted onto the rump of an old-fashioned scheme.

Neither Ina nor I had ever visited Australia and we were a bit intimidated by the thought of such a long flight. We scheduled a layover in Honolulu and another in Fiji where we stayed at a marvellous resort. We swam — suitably engoggled — in a bay of the Pacific Ocean that afforded a grand view of millions of multi-hued fish. It was like swimming in a huge aquarium.

The evening entertainment was a show of the Polynesian heritage where smiling Amazon-sized women clad in colourful sarongs hip-swayed their slow dances. To a critical observer, the two differing cultures of Fiji were evident. Managers, chefs, cashiers were South Asian Indians while the indigenous people did the manual work and the dancing. The emcee was an ebullient, huge Polynesian who related how in World War II Americans had protected the islands from being overrun by the cruel Japanese. The audience — enjoying the hula dances around the smudge-pot-lit pool — consisted largely of Japanese tourists. Political correctness didn't appear to hold much sway (no pun intended) with the huge announcer. "Hey!" he yelled, pointing at a large group of Japanese tourists, "This is one island you slitty eyes never got!" Ouch!

The Conference was arranged by Duane Burke and was — as is Duane's way — informal. He themed the Conference "Bringing Technology Down Under" which was really a bit of a putdown for the Aussies, who were technically more advanced in lottery operations than the U.S. I altered my speech by inserting jokes about Duane's treatment of the Aussies as newcomers to the business which made me the darling of the OZ set. Duane, as a good guy, immune to my silly gibes, and complimented me on a fun speech.

The night before our departure, Peter Gillooly, who would later become the head of the Tattersall's Lottery in the Australian State of Victoria, invited Ina and me to a surprise birthday party for his boss, Jim Fair. It turned out to be a dinner for just the four of us at one of the better hotels in Melbourne. Not a word was said about birthdays.

A jazz sextet performed during dinner. Suddenly, the bandleader announced that the Canadian guest of the famous lottery manager Mr. Fair was a well-known jazz pianist and Mr. Fair had asked that his guest be allowed to play a special song. As Peter Gillooly pulled me out of my chair, he whispered: "Play Happy Birthday." I complied and asked the jovial Australian dinner crowd to join in. They sang lustily. The tough lottery boss, Jim Fair, teared up a bit. He wished his family had been able to hear the serenade.

When I got up to return to my seat, the band-man asked the audience: "Should we ask the Canadian to play us a tune?" The crowd was game. I played

Our Love is Here to Stay with the bandleader bending over the piano to see what chords I was hitting. I managed to play the thing to the bitter end. The bandleader — no doubt completely fooled — said: "You are a great player."

Gillooly slapped his thighs in glee. "You took the piss out of him, mate," he roared. Whatever that meant.

AN ADDITIONAL RESPONSIBILITY

On the last working day of 1985, Matt Puncke —Director of the Maryland State Lottery and President of the National Association of State Lotteries (NASL), resigned his post. The membership of NASL elected your lottery scribe as President for a two-and-a-half-year term, the first Canadian to be so honoured.

I will not forget my first meeting as NASL President in Olympia, Washington in January of 1986. The main topic of discussions was the staging of NASL's convention to be held in Seattle later that year. One of my first aims was to change the name NASL which made no reference of Canadian lotteries to the "North American Association of State and Provincial Lotteries" (NASPL) The name was necessary to explain why a Canadian was the head of an organization with an American title.

The second topic was to share the hosting of the 1986 Annual Conference, between Seattle and Vancouver. The attraction was that NASPL delegates to the Seattle convention could take in the World Expo 86, where the British Columbia Lottery would have a prominent exhibit.

The decisions were all made in our favour but it was neither the name change to NASPL nor the EXPO visit that made the meeting so memorable. On the last day of the conference, the television set in the meeting hall was tuned to the launch of the space shuttle "Challenger". All eyes glanced at the screen at some point but mine happened to focus just at the moment that the space capsule blew up.

Later, reports mentioned that one of the Astronauts, a school teacher Christine McAuliffe was among those who perished. I was surprised that the Americans in the meeting were so deeply emotional about the turn of events. To Canadians, it was a terrible and regrettable accident but for our US colleagues it appeared to be a deeper loss. I guess they felt it as a defeat for their country, a sense of fallibility in a way.

When I returned to Vancouver, I announced the name change from NASL to NASPL ("Nasal" to "Nah-spell). In North American Lottery circles, I was henceforth recognized as the man who put the "pee" in NASPL.

PROVINCIAL LOTTERY: A123 - B4567-C89012

After 10-years of successfully competing with $10 lottery games, sales of the $5 PROVINCIAL game began to slacken. Various additions and changes had been introduced but it was felt a new format was necessary. Forgetting the age-old principle of 'K.I.S.S." (Keep It Simple, Stupid) the Ontario Lottery folks came up with a novel scheme that offered several combinations of numbers drawn.

Now, Dear Reader, please try to grasp the concept of the **PROVINCIAL** because many players and media people didn't and still don't. If you don't care to learn the details of this dud, go to the next topic about break-open tickets. I don't want to lose you, by inveigling you into this dumb scheme.

Here we go: The ticket featured 12 digits in three separate groups each combined with a letter A, B, or C. For example: A244 — B5108 — C97873

- For prizes of $10 the player was required to match the 3-digit-number starting with (A)
- For prizes of $100 the player was required to match the 4-digit number starting with (B)
- For the prize of $100,000 the player needed to match (A) and (B)
- For the $1 Million prize the player needed to match (A) and (C)
- There was no prize for (A)+(B)+(C).

After the first draw, a flood of letters, personal visits and phone calls came in, remarking, screaming, yelling, cursing that the 12-number combination on the ticket hadn't been drawn. Indeed, it hadn't. One inquiring journalist was Les Leyne of the *Victoria Times Colonist*. He was a good columnist who, over the years, had smelled-out many a fraud. He was a true professional and came directly to the source rather than lash out in all directions.

I spoke to him at length by telephone explaining why there was no 12-number combination. He was stuck on the notion that there was a number, it hadn't been drawn and more importantly, there was no prize attached. After a while I suggested that it might be better if I flew to Victoria to show him the print-out of all the prizes created and the fact that they added up to the promised 45% of sales when all tickets were sold.

Those last five words caused another half hour of explanation, about unclaimed prizes and bonus draws to arrive at the required 45% prize fund. That done, there was still the omission of a 12-digit-number being drawn.

I arrived at the *Times-Colonist's* office carrying an 8-inch thick, accordion-type computer print-out. To show where and how the ticket numbers were to be found, we pulled the accordion apart and spread it across the office. It was at that point the staff photographer of the took a photo of the mass of paper on the floor and it made the front page of the paper the following day. Even if you're still confused by my explanation, Les Layne's story told everyone that the game was legitimate. Naturally... that version of the PROVINCIAL game didn't survive very long.

TICKET PRINTING AND POLITICS

You didn't ask me but I'm going to tell you how the BCLC got into the break-open ticket business. There was no overwhelming presence in BC of that particular type of social gambling game. Edgar Hildebrandt and Chuck Hamilton reminded me that in late 1985 Minister Chabot had asked BCLC to create employment opportunities in Kamloops. Bingo paper had been concentrated with a single printer and now the question was: could we concentrate the printing of the millions of lottery tickets in Kamloops?

A brief research project by Vic Poleschuk and his staff showed that producing instant/scratch and PACIFIC EXPRESS tickets by themselves would not warrant a printing plant. Hence, the "Request for Proposal" for ticket printing was augmented by break-open tickets.

The problem was that none of us at BCLC had any experience with break-open tickets. We had to learn fast.

Break-open tickets or "pull-tabs" came from specialty printers in Edmonton and Toronto but the BC government was interested in attracting a national printer. The Canadian lottery ticket printers, Pollard Bank Note of Winnipeg and

British American Bank Note (BABN) were the obvious candidates. Additionally, GTECH had made some tentative moves to enter the ticket printing business.

When break-open tickets were added to the Request for Proposal (RFP), Pete Morrissey of GTECH found a printer of break-open tickets in Everett, Washington. The two companies agreed to present a joint-bid but somehow, in a mysterious move that still makes me wonder, GTECH swung its participation over to Pollard Banknote of Winnipeg.

The switch got your lottery scribe involved in a squabble between the Everett-based company and GTECH. Law suits, threats and the customary splattering of mud took considerable time to shake off, albeit without any financial harm to BCLC. With the Everett printing company out of the picture, two Bank Note companies were left: one printer experienced in break-open tickets (Pollard) the other (BABN) a specialist in instant/scratch games.

Marshall Pollack, who was at that time leading the charge at BABN, responded to the RFP in his exceptional cynical manner. He knew that the pricing of tickets printed in Kamloops required a surcharge in order to keep the printer afloat. He proposed that the tickets be printed in Montreal at the higher prices quoted by Pollard and then BABN would send a refund to BC to be divided among unemployed workers in Kamloops.

That response made it clear that BC was buying jobs in Kamloops. BABN didn't have any great interest in producing break-open tickets. This left Pollard with an assist from GTECH as the sole qualified bidder. Regardless of the additional cost of establishing a plant in Kamloops, Pollard Banknote was awarded the contract for printing instant/scratch and break-open tickets.

(Note: In the two decades that followed, the plant would print many millions of instant/scratch and break-open tickets for BC and several international customers but as I write this story, Kamloops has recently lost the lottery printing business due to the reality of economics.)

To come back to the story of break-open tickets… Soon after the decision to go with Pollard, distribution began. Throughout North America, a flourishing break-open business existed with titles such as Pull-Tabs, Nevada Tickets, Cherry

Bells, Lucky 7s, Pickle Cards, Instant Bingo, Bowl Games and Pop-Opens. In this tale your lottery scribe shall stick to the name of "break-open tickets."

To play, a break-open ticket requires a player to pull-back the perforated flaps on the back of the ticket which reveals a set of symbols. If they match the ones appearing on the front of the ticket, prizes are paid on the spot.

The distinction between a standard lottery and Break-Open and Bingo is that the latter two formats are classified as social games — played in public places like bars and bingo-halls. To keep the game attractive, the ticket price is kept as low as 50 cents. Ergo, the top prize is usually $100 or less. These games feature frequent small wins — unlike the weekly or monthly lotteries where substantial prizes are the attraction. Another aspect of the break-open is that security is less demanding. The time between purchasing, winning and cashing the prize is counted in minutes, leaving little time for forging a ticket. Moreover, the prizes are too small for crooks to bother.

A weakness of break-open tickets is that they are sold in cartons of about 3,000 tickets. That carton contains the complete game. Usually 1 in 4 tickets is a winner. Total prize pay-out per carton is often in the range of 60-70% of sales. At a given point during the sales process, it is possible that the prize amount of remaining tickets is greater than the retail value of the remaining tickets. That's when sharp players swoop in and buy all remaining tickets and take the profit. Oftentimes that sharp player is the operator of the game.

(Note: break-open games have been largely replaced by slot machines in casinos and bingo halls)

Among our BCLC sales people, **Blyth Pitkethly** got the first break-open crew together, however credit for the extensive development of break-open tickets should go to Edgar Hildebrandt. His crew included: Darry Appleton, Al Mitchell, Mark Roberts, Ken Laurie, Rick Favell, Brian Bottomley, Tom Evans, Elisabeth MacDonald and Vince Milford.

The first 6 months sales were $9 Million, but sales grew and eventually peaked at $150 million per year. Edgar should take a bow for this success.

THE CHRISTIAN COMPUTER

Accounting for lottery tickets was still cumbersome. Sales people loaded a supply of tickets in their cars. Invoices were hand-written, cheques received, tickets reimbursed and many errors resulted.

Somewhere your curious scribe learned about hand-held computers that eased inventory control and sales. Pete Morrissey of GTECH knew of a specialty bookseller in Illinois who had devised a hand-held computer system. Pete accompanied me to Wheaton, Illinois to see this device, named Route Manager, in action. The 'specialty books' that this company sold were religious tomes including the best-seller, THE BIBLE, which was available in all kinds of reproductions from soft cover to calfskin leather.

The owner was a pious doppelganger of Ted Kennedy. He showed us the details of the device, which was state-of-the-art at the time. When he asked what business we were in, I thought it best to come straight out and said "Lotteries" and for emphasis I added: "Gambling!"

He looked pained and stunned at the same time. "We couldn't be in more different businesses," he choked.

After all these years, I was hardened to prejudiced people's view of our business. "Oh, I don't think we are in different business at all," I protested. "Religion and lotteries both offer hope, except we pay off once in a while." The man had no answer. Back in the car, Pete snickered for a long time. The mini-computer proved to be a good device for us, though!

BUSINESS OPPORTUNITIES

Premier Bennett put out the call for Crown Corporations to "spin off" commercial ventures that would further enhance BC's budding computer and software sector. A few months earlier, at a meeting in Rhode Island, GTECH had demonstrated devices to play bingo on a computer screen. Electronic Bingo, they called it. This could be an opportunity to combine BCLC's Expo 86 presence with possible spin-offs the premier had urged.

 Together with Bob Plecas, the Deputy Minister and the GTECH principals, a model Expo Pavilion was designed that would be a haven for tired tourists — a place where visitors could relax in air-conditioned comfort, play bingo and become part of the computer age. Projections showed that it would be one of a few pavilions that might actually yield a profit. But, as Minister Chabot explained later, when he sought permission at the weekly Cabinet meeting, Premier Bennett (no fan of lotteries) was so angered by the proposal that he threw the beautiful Plexiglas model out of the second-floor window onto the Legislature's manicured lawn. His reaction put a bit of a damper on our entry into the age of electronic gambling.

Premier Bennett's decision also killed the idea that BCTV would house its TV studio within our BCLC Pavilion. When that Plexiglas model was thrown out the window, the process was reversed. BCLC took a section of the BCTV pavilion.

"BCTV News Hour" originated from Expo and so did our "Winsday in BC" draws. However, our presence in the studio filled only an hour or so per week. Rob Egan in Kamloops, in cooperation with the Richmond creative crew, made it fun for the constant flow of visitors through the pavilion. One of the crowd-pleasers consisted of computer screens where a visitor could punch in a set of many LOTTO numbers that were listed near the terminals. Then, the screen would show (as an example): "If you had played those winning numbers in the game "Zahlenlotto" in Austria on June 17, 1981 you would have won a jackpot of 20 million Austrian schillings."

The information was real. Our staff had established a large database of winning numbers and accompanying prizes of many different lottery jurisdictions. In the six months of Expo 86, many thousands of visitors went through the BCLC section. Premier Bennett had seen his order obeyed. Not a nickel was gambled but a heap of goodwill and understanding was earned. Perhaps the secret was that the Premier hadn't been told anything about it.

When Premier Bennett came to visit the BCTV Pavilion, he became quite agitated. He thought he had banned lotteries from Expo but we had only cancelled the active electronic bingo component. Your disconcerted scribe was expecting a dressing-down when Jimmy Pattison, Chairman of Expo 86, who was accompanying the Premier on his tour, complimented him on his astuteness in combining the attraction of his Lottery Corporation with the high-profile TV station.

BCTV's management, assembled at the pavilion, thanked the Premier, for, without the addition of the lottery, the pavilion would not be the success it proved to be. I silently thanked these saviours of my derriere. The Premier beamed and accepted the compliments as humbly as any premier should.

I don't know why Bennett was so bothered by the lottery at Expo 86. Both crown corporations, BCLC and EXPO, were his own government's creation. A week later, Bennett resigned as Premier. A year later, he was in a BC courtroom under a cloud of questionable activities at the greatest gambling establishment in the province: the Vancouver Stock Exchange. Life's like that!

CHANGING OF THE GUARD

On August 6, 1986, **Bill van der Zalm** took the reins of BC. For a second turn at the lottery wheel, Grace McCarthy succeeded Jim Chabot as lottery minister. At the very first meeting with Grace, she jokingly asked me what area of gambling hadn't yet yielded to my control. I told her about the addition of break-open tickets, bingo paper and my regret that control of casinos had eluded my grip thus far. "You'll get it, I'm sure," she smiled.

We discussed formalizing the volunteer-staffed charitable casinos that were anything but volunteer-operated. It was the same story as in bingo. Charities were given a licence to conduct a casino, supposedly in a community somewhere. While card-games were easily arranged, modern gambling games require equipment and experienced staff. Enter the entrepreneurs. They'd provide a hall, staff, roulette equipment and gear for other games of chance and all the licensed charity had to do was to hand over the casino licence and provide some volunteers to take hats and coats and count the money. There were enough licensees to fill a full-day of play in a dozen charitable casinos.

The best-known operator of these gaming places was Ross McLeod, a former midway/carnival operator who owned several Vancouver area casinos. His first venue, the Holiday Inn in Vancouver, opened in 1986. In the beginning Ross was not easy to work with. He had no experience in working *with* or *for* governments. Yet he alone — among those who were involved with such quasi-legal casinos — was straight-up in his dealing with us. One of our first deals was to supply break-open tickets to his casinos. It was a start but it took another decade before your lottery scribe's team gained control of all casino operations.

BUSTED BY... A SLIDE PROJECTOR?

In summer of '86, David Clark, then President of Loto Quebec, asked me to fly to Montreal for an urgent meeting. Well... travelling 3,200 kilometers one way for a meeting deserves a good reason but David appeared reluctant to provide one. He limited his comment to a "ticket problem." He used the word 'urgent' three times. Since ticket problems are marketing problems, I asked Michelle McBride to join me. We arrived in Montreal around 4:30 in the afternoon. A driver from Loto Quebec awaited us at the airport. "The meeting is waiting for you," the young man declared and took our bags. At the Hotel Bonaventure, David Clarke was proverbially 'twiddling his thumbs' while he waited for us to join the CEOs of the other Canadian lottery corporations. He hadn't yet divulged to anyone what the problem was.

Since the birth of modern lotteries in North America, British American Banknote had been the ticket printer of record. Their long exclusive run had come to an end when the pugnacious Chairman of ILC, Walter Struthers thundered that other printers should be encouraged to bid. He had invited Canadian Banknote Corporation — a company with great experience in printing Canada's currency but little knowledge about the booby traps inherent in producing lottery tickets — to enter a bid for printing the PROVINCIAL tickets.

Canadian Bank Note quoted a lower price for printing the PROVINCIAL than BA Banknote. The '85 version of the PROVINCIAL game was somewhat of a departure from earlier forms in that it featured a ticket and an attachment of the same size, enclosed in a 'secure' pouch. The attachment offered either the wish 'Bonne Chance/Good Luck', or a prize in the range of $10 to $1,000.

 The game printed by Canadian Bank Note had been in circulation for a few weeks so those attending the meeting quickly surmised that David's problem was with the PROVINCIAL. Then David brought out a Kodak slide-projector, turned it on and aimed the beam at the ceiling. He laid a PROVINCIAL pouch on the lens and, right there for all to see, was Bonne Chance/Good Luck. The next lit-through pouch showed a $1000 prize.

The game was compromised. With access to a supply of pouches and a slide-projector, a retailer could cash the winners and sell the losers.

At that meeting, the board decided that no further tickets would be distributed, that as many pouches as possible would be gathered up from retailers without arousing curiosity, and they would consider legal action against Canadian Bank Note.

This all implied that a new printer had to be found and rather quickly. There was only one eligible printer: BA Banknote.

Before Michelle and I left B.C, Marshall Pollack, then Managing Director of BA Banknote invited us to dinner. The dinner was amiable. Reminiscences about the early lottery days dominated the table talk. Marshall said he had heard rumours about the printing problem; in fact, he knew all about it. I confirmed that we had attended a meeting with my Canadian colleagues but provided no details of the proposed action.

Yet months later, that dinner became part of the allegations when Canadian Banknote launched legal proceedings against us claiming damages. The company contended that executives (moi) of the ILC conspired with BA Banknote to get the contract away from Canadian Bank Note. The dispute carried all the way to the doorsteps of the Court, where it was settled for an amount of money that was never publicized. BA Bank Note returned as the printer of secure lottery tickets and Canadian Bank Note was gone. More importantly, the problem never hit the headlines.

PORTUGAL

Membership in the INTERTOTO Executive Committee provided some nice perks. Twice a year, an executive meeting was scheduled in one of various member-countries with travel and hotels paid for. I found it not very difficult to weave this extra responsibility into my workload at BCLC.

September 30, 1986. Portugal was the host of one of those meetings. Pete Morrissey was aware that several European LOTTO companies were on the verge of deciding to convert to online operations. This was Morrissey's market. He asked if he could accompany me and be introduced to some of the key European management teams. Even though my European colleagues weren't too keen to see a salesman for lottery equipment at their social activities, I had the support of INTERTOTO President Richard Frigren, my Swedish colleague, who was also a satisfied GTECH client.

At the last evening of the INTERTOTO gathering, participants were bussed to Cascais, a resort on the most westerly point of Europe (farther West than Ireland). We were told — after dinner — that the Portuguese Cabinet Minister for Economic Affairs would address the gathering.

The classy dining-room featured large window-doors looking out on a beach of the Atlantic Ocean. It was a blessing that the doors were kept open, since the temperature was well above 32 Celsius. The room resembled something that might have looked like Henry VIII's dining room. The ceiling was high, thick carpets hung on the walls and, incongruously at such a high room temperature, a huge fireplace with a roaring fire. The open doors and the ocean breeze made it somewhat bearable.

It was close to midnight when the harsh unsmiling politician showed up. He had a Mick Jagger face, complete with a derisive sneer. I found it difficult to imagine he ever smiled and I was convinced he would bite if touched. The man arose haughtily and demanded that he not be overheard by anyone outside the room. All doors were sealed and guarded on the outside. The fireplace burned its heavy logs and in no time, the temperature reached sauna levels. The audience bathed in puddles of perspiration.

All this might still have had some merit if it weren't for the fact that the minister spoke in Portuguese and gesticulated like a man possessed. We looked on in awe without understanding. He made what sounded like world-shaking, pronouncements and, after a few minutes, he let his interpreter speak. The linguist's English pronunciation was not far removed from Portuguese but it didn't matter. The minister only gave him 15 seconds to translate his four-minute diatribe, before he butted in again.

Pete Morrissey turned to me. "Why are you punishing me?" he asked. "I wanted to meet lottery people but not in a sweat box. Is this a training session to meet the Finns? Will you pay my dry-cleaning bill?"

Ina slumped in her chair. She is uncomfortable with high temperatures.

It was 1:30 a.m. before we boarded the bus back to Lisbon for an hour-long trip to our hotel. Seated in the back, having discarding as much damp clothing as he decently could, Pete Morrissey demanded assurances that I would wreak revenge on my Portuguese colleague at INTERTOTO '87. I made a vow that I would lock the Portuguese lottery director in the boiler room of Vancouver's Pan Pacific Hotel. It wasn't enough for Pete. To this day he hasn't forgiven me and still expects to be reimbursed for his dry cleaning.

ODDSET

 One of the benefits of the Portugal meeting was an afternoon chat with Richard Frigren of Sweden. His company had just ended a test run of a betting game named ODDSET based on soccer. Three different gambling games were presented. One based on the total score of a set of games, another based on the number of tied games and the one of interest to your lottery scribe was called LANGEN, a list of soccer games to be played where the amount of the payout was set by the lottery.

In LANGEN a win for the home team would pay 2.17 times the amount bet. The win by the visiting team would pay 2.78 times the amount bet, and a tie (after regulation time) would pay 3.70. The bettor had to parlay a minimum three games of his choice. Chuck Hamilton, who took on the ODDSET portfolio for BCLC in the late '80s, will explain how these prices are arrived at. After the explanation by this veteran setter of odds, you could become a serious calculator of setting odds in sports contests. But you must wait until this tale gets to 1988 and beyond.

THE PICK

You may remember that, in 1986, BCLC operated a game called LOTTO WEST — a forerunner of KENO, where the player chooses numbers out of a field that offers more numbers than necessary to win.

As mentioned previously, the Las Vegas version of KENO offers a field of 80 numbers; the player can choose up to 10 numbers from among these 80. KENO draws 20 numbers. To make it easy, a player could pick 3 numbers. If these three numbers are among the 20 drawn, it's a win. That prize category can be described as "3 out-of-10 out-of-20".

LOTTO WEST was designed to acquaint the player (and the political masters) with the KENO concept. LOTTO WEST offered 8 numbers drawn from a field of 56. A player could pick as many as six numbers from the 8. For one example: picking 4-out-of-8 out-of-56.

LOTTO WEST was generating about $15 million a year, when — in spring of 1987 — the name was changed to "The PICK". In the ads, an old-time miner discussed "picking" numbers with his mule. Even though the game hadn't changed, sales doubled.

You may wonder: Why all the pussy-footing towards the *real* KENO? Focus groups had shown that KENO was perceived as "hard gambling" associated with casinos. The thought that one could play KENO at the grocery store was unfathomable to many. More work had to be done to get the public on side.

RICK HANSON & THE BINGO GAME

Rick Hanson, a paraplegic athlete, embarked on his Man in Motion World Tour on March 21, 1985, starting at the Oakridge Mall in Vancouver. Although, at the beginning, public attention was somewhat blasé, the tour soon attracted international attention. The trek took 26-months and logged more than 40,000 km through 34 countries and four continents before returning to Canada.

Hanson returned to Vancouver's BC Place Stadium on May 22, 1987 to a cheering mob of thousands after raising $26 million for spinal cord research. The adoration of crowds along the many country roads was no match for how grandly he was being hailed as an international hero in his home province.

The BC Government was pressed to add its (financial) esteem for the home-grown boy. Government policy did not allow for that kind of gift. Yet, something had to be done. Bob Plecas and I were delegated to attend a meeting with Patrick Reid, a former ambassador for Canada and Rick Hanson's father-in-law. The topic was government's contribution to spinal cord research.

Bob explained that BCLC could organize a special province-wide televised series of bingo games that would yield as much as $1 million in donations. As a diplomat, Patrick Reid was trained to keep cool but I noticed a slight facial tic which I interpreted as an adverse reaction. He didn't say anything about the proposal; he ignored it and inquired what kind of contribution might be expected from the government. He stressed the word 'government'.

Your lottery scribe spent a lot of time designing a massive bingo game but no response was ever received from the Hanson side. Sometime later, a government news release announced that government would provide $500,000 to the Man in Motion Tour.

Too bad; it would have been fun to create a province-wide bingo.

1987 THE YEAR OF INTERTOTO

May 25, 1987. A meeting of the executive committee of INTERTOTO was held in Helsinki. Ina and I made a winding trip to Finland. A mix of holidays and business had us land in Amsterdam, drive to Münster to speak with Lothar Lammers about how to deal with the INTERTOTO poohbahs in Finland, then drive to Kiel, to board a ferry to Denmark where we were to stay a few days and then take another ferry to Sweden to meet with Richard Frigren in Stockholm and then a third ferry to Helsinki to meet Matti Ahde, the new Managing Director of Veikkaus, the Finnish State lottery.

(If you deem this trip to be too arduous for your lottery scribe, do not be concerned. We had 5 overnight stays in Scandinavia. It was a lovely experience.)

The new Finnish lottery president, **Matti Ahde** was a former Speaker of Parliament. Within minutes of the 'welcome' handshake, I realized that he was intent on putting his stamp on our LOTTO and TOTO world. That was fine with me. It meant a step up from some of the old cronies on the INTERTOTO board who were only there to suck up the free travel and excellent wines.

Matti was clearly campaigning to be elected to the Board. He had my vote already. The lottery operation of Veikkaus was the most up-to-date I'd seen in Europe. (Please don't tell the Germans I said so) I was impressed with the optimistic attitude of our Finnish colleagues, although the sour looks on the people on the streets conveyed a different image. Once you got to know the Finns, you realize that they share the British sense of humour. And how can you not love a people whose national craze is the tango!

Apart from the niceties of meeting the new managing director, I was there to report on the progress of the arrangements for INTERTOTO '87 in Vancouver, only four months away. Some of the older board members (who had never been on the other side of the Atlantic) were concerned that their first Conference outside of Europe was going to be a fiasco.

Lothar Lammers and Richard Frigren put them at ease. When I finished my presentation, they were somewhat satisfied if somewhat aggrieved that the special buses, special seating and separate dining were things of the past.

Ina and I left Helsinki on my 56th birthday, May 29, 1987. While waiting in the Helsinki Airport for our flight to London, police swarmed the building. Later that night we learned that a small aircraft had set a course from Helsinki for Moscow, piloted by the German-born Mathias Rust. The teenager's aircraft had been tracked several times by Soviet air defense and interceptors. Soviet fighters never received permission to shoot him down and on three occasions he was mistaken for a friendly aircraft. Matthias landed in Red Square near the Kremlin. British newspapers blared their headlines as if World War III was at hand. Your lottery scribe and spouse were only a few meters away from where it started. We didn't think it was such a big deal.

HOSTING INTEROTO

Hosting of the 1987 INTERTOTO Conference in Vancouver, so rashly promised in Rome, was at hand. Close to 600 delegates from 65 lottery jurisdictions gathered at Vancouver's prestige hotel, the Pan Pacific. It would be the first INTERTOTO conference that featured exhibits by lottery suppliers who would support the conference financially. Up to then, the host organization generally picked up the major part of the tab.

Your brash scribe had glibly invited the world's LOTTO organizations without approval from government. For government consumption I portrayed the event as a request by INTERTOTO to hold its event in Vancouver—quite a different story from British Columbia inviting INTERTOTO to hold its conference in Vancouver.

The government finally approved of INTERTOTO coming to Vancouver but were unaware of any financial obligation other than the standard luncheon that government offered to any international conference.

INTERTOTO's slant on things was that BCLC had invited them and would therefore pay for the party. To smooth things out, I explained to the INTERTOTO executive committee that this would be a unique conference because INTERTOTO would make a profit instead of merely being a guest. This got their attention but they didn't like my rules. No free plane trips to Vancouver for members of the executive committee. No free hotel rooms either, not for anyone. No special bus for the hoity-toity crowd; in fact, no buses at all. All but one or two events would be within walking distance of the hotel. Spouses were required to pay a fee for special tours while the conference was in session. Exhibitors would pay for space at the exhibition floor. The big suppliers were asked to sponsor specific events.

These kinds of rules are now accepted practice at international conferences but at the time, the old INTERTOTO guard was aghast at this business approach. They tried to nickel and dime for little things here and there but Michelle McBride, who had no experience with their usual freebies, had no difficulty saying NO with a face that showed stunned amazement that the questioner could even think of asking for such a privilege.

Your lottery scribe also made a change to the INTERTOTO pre-conference tour, where executive committee members could visit parts of the host city that weren't part of the conference. It also had commercial overtones: We wanted to show off the ticket printing plant in Kamloops. Nevertheless, the tour for the executive committee (and spouses) included lunch at the top of Grouse Mountain and a charter flight to visit the Kamloops offices and enjoy of a mini-rodeo and lunch at a dude ranch.

INA'S AMIGO

Ina was never keen to step into the limelight at lottery affairs. She was always concerned that she would not be perfect at the job that would be expected of her, although she always was. Despite her misgivings I got her interested in a program that seemed far-fetched at the time.

Custom was that conferences delegates would stay within their own little cultural shell. Germans talked to Germans, Austrians perhaps. The French spoke to the French. There was not much mingling, especially among the spouses. Ina became part of a program that would gently nudge the crowd to meet "foreign" delegates and spouses.

Promotional gifts were the tool. Lottery organizations all over the world use promotional items to advertise their games. To describe such diverse items would fill pages. Suffice it to say that they encompass nearly every type of apparel from sweaters, hats and scarves to radios, cameras, binoculars, vodka, lighters, bags, umbrellas, raincoats. The list was exhaustive.

Each of the world's lottery organizations received a letter from your lottery scribe explaining the objective of the game. They were asked to bring current or outdated promotional items and as much they could spare. The gifts would all be used in an unusual game named "AMIGO", a very Spanish noun but also an international word. The object of the game was to get delegates out of their restrictive cultural circle. The idea received a surprisingly enthusiastic support from the world's lotto folks. A hundred or more parcels, shipments and packages were received, all containing promotional loot.

Delegates registering at the conference desk were issued a card depicting the logo and name of one of the 55 lottery organizations attending the conference. There were 55 cards. Each was duplicated 12 times for a total of 660 cards in circulation. To clarify: the card issued had no bearing on which lottery organization the recipient belonged to. In other words, a Dutch delegate might receive a card with the logo of Singapore Lotteries.

The deal was that if a minimum of six people with the same titled card would join together and come to Ina's Amigo station, they each would get a bag containing promotional material from all corners of the world. The first reaction by conference participants was lukewarm, like "Who's going to hunt around the conference to find a person with the same title card?"

Indeed, it started slowly.

Meanwhile, Ina had taken on the massive task of sorting the many contributions and creating Amigo gift bags, each of roughly equal value. At first glance, this seemed easy. But several thousands of items had been sent in. Some were cheap little gifts, other extravagant. Ina couldn't handle it alone, so family members were pressed into service to assess value, sort and distribute.

Ina and her crew worked many hours but there were few early claimants. That would soon change.

The first evening's social program featured a lottery-themed film shown at the IMAX theatre for conference attendees only. As the crowd waited for the house lights to dim, Lothar Lammers got up from his chair and turned to the audience holding his Amigo card high up in the air: "I have the card for the French LOTTO company and if you also have one like it, come see me in the lobby after the film. I'll be near the post in the back."

Richard Muller was next. He stood at the back so the audience had to crane their necks to see him. "I've got Finland!" he yelled. "I'll be in the bar in the hotel lobby, so if you have the Veikkaus card from Finland, bring your card and meet me at the bar." Eight people joined him the bar, Rick later reported. Five of them had the correct cards and three were Finns who misunderstood the whole thing and had only grasped the words "Finns" and "bar."

The next day, the INTERTOTO Daily Newspaper edited by Bob and Nancy Dunn promoted the game heavily. An "Amigo Billboard" was erected in the lobby, where people could pin notes listing meeting places for those with specific matching cards.

Wherever these strangers met, you saw them troop off together to get the loot. Ina was in her element. She was the general in charge of distribution and directed the traffic, rapping anyone's knuckles who tried to expropriate desirable items for themselves.

Now, thirty year later, old conference attendees recall INTERTOTO '87 and still smile at the excitement of the Amigo "mixer" game.

THE BIG SHOW

Behind the curtains Michelle was the driving force of the conference. The trade show floor, lunches, dinners, spousal tours and entertainment were all executed to perfection. Apart from overall responsibility for the conference, I devoted most of my efforts to co-ordinating the speakers' program.

Michelle McBride was indefatigable. She had acquired sponsors for everything imaginable. The coffee breaks were sponsored, even the cookies. The printing companies such as a Pollard, Scientific-Games and BA Banknote were vying to be seen as supporting this new approach. Minister Elwood Veitch was persuaded to make an appearance and made sure BC was the sponsor of the opening ceremony and include a display of BC talent at the closing dinner. That was another $100,000 in the bag.

Impressive support came from GTECH management, who loved our wild idea to bring one of the largest ships of the BC Ferry Corporation, the Spirit of Vancouver, alongside the hotel. From there they provided an afternoon sail on Howe Sound. A lobster dinner, sponsored by the Atlantic Lottery Corporation, offered not only those delectable crustaceans, but also a "down-east" band that had delegates dancing for hours on the ship's spacious car deck. The weather was gorgeous that day.

Our Canadian colleagues in the other four jurisdictions were also most generous in sponsoring events. Quebec offered a chic sophisticated dinner with Quebec talent and the Western Canada Lottery sponsored a western rodeo-type evening at the Plaza of Nations corral. Ontario chipped in with a special luncheon featuring a bit of the cuisine of each participating country.

Everyone assured us that that the conference was a smash. Today, veteran lottery folks still speak in glowing terms about INTERTOTO '87 and how they couldn't believe when that huge ocean-going ferry pulled up alongside the hotel, its lounges decorated with greenery and tables laid out with white tablecloths, all for their pleasure.

WIRELESS LOTTO TERMINAL

Today, it is hard to think of a world without satellite communications and wireless telephone systems. Yet in those days, lottery corporations could only sell online LOTTO tickets from terminals that were connected to land lines. Therefore, it was a real coup for BCLC to be able to demonstrate to conference delegates that online tickets could be sold from a ferry at sea. Our technical guru **Rob Egan** had collaborated with the BC Telephone system to install a radio-transmitting tower on a nearby mountaintop along the sea route. We were smart enough to allow Minister Veitch to take the bows and issue the first ever LOTTO ticket sold on the briny.

GTECH developed the technology further and made it possible for countries with inadequate telephone systems to be in the online lottery business, even if there was no online infrastructure. Its use was demonstrated when a massive earthquake caused Mexico City's telephone system to fail. Among the rubble, the only functional electronic commerce was the LOTTO system operated by the radio system installed by GTECH.

Back to the story: Sailing back to Vancouver from the Pacific cruise as the sky grew darker and Vancouver's office towers lit up, a collective sigh of regret washed over the conference goers. Guy Snowden, the President of GTECH quickly negotiated a half-hour extension. The wine flowed, the band played on and everyone experienced an afternoon that not many have forgotten.

THANK YOU TOUR IN SWITZERLAND

May 12, 1988. The members of the INTERTOTO Executive Committee were effusive in thanking your lottery scribe and staff for the success of the Vancouver conference and in particular, the cheque for $100,000 in profit for the benefit of INTERTOTO. The thank-you meeting was held in beautiful Viznau, a quaint little town in the Interlaken district of Switzerland. Its five-star hotel fronting the lake is of international renown.

The first morning, a walk to the Rigi Bahn brought us to the cog-propelled train that would haul us up the mountain. A stern man with a beard much larger than his face warranted, stood near his outhouse-sized ticket office. Even though there were no other passengers, he stared straight ahead, ignoring the line-up until he began issuing tickets at the appointed minute on the clock. If those tickets had been valuable documents, he might have been excused for the elaborate stamping, counting and recounting but they cost only 5 francs. He spoke some English but it appeared to be beneath his dignity as stationmaster to use that skill to inform tourists. After a while, he released the passengers to a kind of holding pen but not before he had punched every ticket he had just sold.

Finally, the cable-car train came trundling down the mountain. The train-man opened the door of the holding pen to admit the passengers to the platform but not until he punched the tickets for the second time. On the platform, he morphed into a security director by checking tickets (no punching this time). He got on the train along with the passengers and once aboard he went from compartment to compartment to punch the tickets yet again.

By this time, the visiting lottery group was snickering. As the cable car climbed up the mountain, we passed numerous fat cows grazing along the track. Michelle's husband suddenly addressed the officious train agent: "Do you know why Swiss cows have bells?" The man looked up. He had heard many questions, but not this one.

"Es izt ze kusstom," he said, surprised that anyone should ask.

"No it is not," Jim said. "They have bells because their horns don't work."

The man looked at him, his moustache curling into a grin. "Das ist gut!" he admitted.

After the Viznau visit, Ina and I booked a reservation at the Berghotel near Koblenz. It was a castle, high above the Rhine. The car rented by the Snowdens, our travel companions, crawled up the steep slope along the stone-paved path, built centuries before cars and elevators.

The castle's dining room was truly medieval, an echo-chambered hall with a beautiful wooden floor resembling a giant chess-board. The 15-foot ceiling and bare tiles created eerie echoes. The chairs were rigid and almost straight-backed. I felt they were unstable and were made even more uncomfortable by a thin cushion placed on the seat. The cushion was too small for my buttocks and I felt myself sliding off.

Guy Snowden was buying dinner that night so I made nice and didn't complain about the chair. In order to feel less wobbly on the chair, I decided to remove the cushion, unobtrusively of course. One does not wish to offend one's host. I raised my body an inch or so above the cushion and quickly yanked it out from under me. That is, I would have yanked the cushion out from under me if it hadn't been fastened to the seat.

It must have been quite a sight for the diners, not to mention my tablemates, to see me suddenly, without any visible cause, crash to the floor.

Ina looked surprised. "Why are you doing that?" she asked with a near-smile, as only spouses can.

What can one say?

The next morning, a walk down the steep meandering path seemed an invigorating idea. I had descended several metres when the vista of the Rhine Valley came into view, the wide river winding its way northwest. The vineyards, absorbing the spring sun, were spread out wide as far as the eye could see.

My gazing at this gorgeous spectacle was disturbed by a Texan and his bleach-blonde companion who came up from behind and looked down on me and the scenery below. "Do you know that the Bing Crosby Open golf tournament is played there?" he said pointing downwards.

I looked at him and to the vineyards below before asking: "Pardon me?"

"Yeah, I played that course last year. I did pretty well. I held my own. Do you play there often?"

I looked at the Rhine and the sloping vineyards and couldn't imagine a golf course, let alone Bing Crosby. Just before I was about to confess that I didn't know what the hell he was talking about, he bent down to tap the sleeve of my GTECH golf shirt and said: "I wish I could afford to be a member there but the fees are pretty steep."

I looked at the rim of my sleeve that read "Pebble Beach Golf Course". It dawned on me that the guy was talking about my GTECH Conference shirt from a previous conference and not the vineyard below.

"Yes, pretty steep," I mumbled and climbed back up to the castle.

AUSTRALIA: WHERE "RAPID" KENO WAS BORN

Attending the AILE world conference in Melbourne in late fall of 1988 was our chance to see how others would carry on the conference features that we had pioneered the year before. Michelle, who had taken the trip to Viznau in Switzerland, was taking care of the home front in order to allow Vic Poleschuk to join me along with the new lottery Minister Bill Reid and his wife Marion.

Because BCLC had hosted the INTERTOTO meeting the year before, we were warmly welcomed in Melbourne. The new lottery minister Bill Reid, proudly wearing his British Columbia badge was impressed with the many compliments he received about the Vancouver conference.

The atmosphere was typically Australian. The speakers were forthright and funny. (One lottery manager reported: "Last year, we stood at the edge of the abyss, but this year we'll take a step forward!") Everything ran on time and everyone was happy and relaxed.

It was a great opportunity to engage the new minister in a long chat to bring him up to speed on what lotteries were all about. Bill Reid was a populist politician who often went with his instinct rather than reasoned analysis. Regrettably, sometimes that instinct failed him.

He was all ears when Vic and I laid out the long-term plan for KENO. After being regaled on how LOTTOWEST morphed into THE PICK and how we slowly would progress to KENO, he said: "Don't shilly-shally. Change the name now and go daily." He grew more enthusiastic as we explained the details of the game.

"Let's do it" he said excitedly. "Get rid of THE PICK call it what it is: KENO."

"It isn't quite the KENO people know," Vic Poleschuk told him, "The Las Vegas game is drawn every 5 minutes."

Bill Reid, who had just okayed a major step forward, said reluctantly, "Let's be careful and take only one step at a time. Let's call it BC KENO."

And so it was! THE PICK, after a short but vivid life, was changed to **BC KENO** with the same format: 6/8/56, drawn every day but Sunday. The deal with the Minister was that no publicity campaign should accompany the launch of the new format, just information pamphlets at the point of purchase.

The public reaction was a big yawn. Sales increased by only 20% because the public took it as another LOTTO game and there were already two of those: LOTTO BC and LOTTO 6/49.

There was just one more step to get to the ultimate game: "KENO drawn every 5 minutes." Regretfully, that final step would still be seven years away.

THE EXTRA...YES or NO.

On several visits to the West-Deutsche Lotterie in Münster, your lottery scribe was intrigued by the add-on game called SPIEL 77. The format was simple. At the point of purchase of a LOTTO ticket, players could accept or decline to add a chance to 1 million D-Marks by validating a 7-digit number that was already printed on the ticket. All the player had to do was to mark YES or NO. The devil in the game was that players who said NO still had the number on their ticket. When the winning number was drawn, there would be great consternation if that number won but the player had declined to validate.

In April 1988, BC introduced an add-on game with 4 numbers out of a hundred (4/100). Whether the players chose to validate their number or not, it was staring them in the face when checking their ticket. The top prize for having all four numbers correct was $500,000. Three-out-of-four correct won $1000;

two-out-of-four won ten bucks and one-out-of-four brought a free play for the next draw. That new addition brought $16 million in sales the first 6 months

The Ohio Lottery had also picked-up the idea of a "SPIEL" game and called it the KICKER. It didn't work very well for Ohio because the customer had to ask for the extra number and if they declined there could not be any regret because the ticket — unlike the BC game — didn't display the extra number.

BILL'S PECCADILLO

Bill Reid, BCLC's lottery minister, caused a bit of brouhaha when a lottery commercial featured an actor who had worked for the minister in the automobile business. It was a funny commercial where the actor pirouetted around just to savour the fun of scratching his instant ticket. When the Minister Reid saw the ad, he yelled "That's got to go." Getting red in the face, he shouted. "Cancel it!" I objected because the ad had been paid for. Asking again and again what aspect of the commercial bothered him, he became angry and wouldn't explain his objection. When finally pressed a little bit too much, he spat, "That son-of-a-bitch (the actor) worked for me at the car dealership and stiffed me for $400." Bill was too riled-up to be reasoned with. It was a funny commercial and it would have worked well but we were forced to dump it.

PUNTO

After the worrisome days of SPORTS TOTO during the '70s, your wary scribe was ready to dip his toes again into the "pool" of sports lotteries. In September 1988, BCLC introduced a sports lottery called PUNTO. Three of the biggest North American professional sports leagues (Hockey, Football and Basketball) had already taken legal action against lotteries for unauthorized use of their games, But the Canadian Football League's Commissioner, Doug Mitchell personally visited my office to offer the league's games for PUNTO. He gave complete freedom of the use of CFL names and logos.

Above all, I wanted to avoid being bombarded with more lawsuits by other leagues. If betting on a CFL game started with no rumbling on the legal front, we would be on firmer ground to include other sports and formats.

However, there were some technical problems in designing a CFL sports lottery. With only eight teams, there were only four CFL games per week with no tie-games of any statistical relevance. The game your lottery scribe devised was terribly confusing — we treated every quarter as a "game" — but we achieved our goal of getting a toe in the sports betting lottery's business. Despite its difficult format, PUNTO produced close to half-a-million dollars in sales during the first season.

PUNTO would spin off into other versions until it was changed in 1991 to the more familiar ODDSET format. However, PUNTO shouldn't be classified as a failure. Criticism from staunch objectors to gambling was muted with respect to PUNTO, thus satisfying BC politicians that sports-betting games would be accepted by the public.

ELECTRONIC BINGO AT STARSHIP

In November 1988, BCLC launched an innovative version of bingo. The GTECH-designed electronic bingo system that never made it into that pavilion of Expo 86 was now ready to be installed at a bingo hall at Main Street and 11th Avenue in Vancouver. We titled it STARSHIP BINGO. To prove that the electronic system would change the traditional bingo parlour from a dingy den into an attractive venue, Bill Reid — who was generous to a fault but on occasion a royal pain in the behind — gave permission to create a modern bingo entertainment centre. Vic and his people made a magical transformation of the bingo hall. It was great!

At the evening launch, the trappings of searchlights, tuxedos and evening gowns created a mini-Hollywood atmosphere. Inside, subdued lighting and soft music welcomed a happy throng of civic and provincial politicians and more importantly, the leaders of charities who would eventually benefit from modernization of the church-basement game.

After thankfully brief speeches, the crowd was invited to play bingo with *our* money and not a penny of their own. However, the deal was that any lucky winners would turn over their prizes to a designated charity.

The guests raced for the gaming tables, taking only minutes to get the hang of operating the electronic equipment. Only the refilling of wine glasses could interrupt their concentration. The games were standard bingo games, the same ones as played on paper cards. There were also some new features such as automatic play and a program that offered versions of break-open tickets and instant-scratch tickets. Bill Reid was over the moon. He loved it. The most commonly asked question was, "Can we get a hall like this?" But it was only a test program, although decades later it developed into a successful "neighbourhood casino" concept called CHANCES, now situated in several locations around the province.

The launch of STARSHIP was a great success but instead of being pleased, the charitable groups sensed that government had quietly slipped a noose over their necks. If this type of bingo play became popular, government would keep the money and dole it out to charities according to their priorities. The bingo groups had been steamrolled before by government. Their fear was genuine.

Obstruction by the charities would delay the expansion of electronic bingo for years. It was only in the late 1990s, when formal bingo/casinos were authorized that charities saw the demise of their old-fashioned paper bingo. In 2019 more than a dozen such halls called CHANCES are operative in BC. But... the paper bingo game isn't quite dead...yet.

Michelle McBride contributed the following thoughts on Electronic Bingo:

"In 1988, a standard, old-fashioned bingo hall on Main Street in Vancouver, was converted to electronic. Over the years that location's bingo turnover grew from $1 million to ten times that amount. Yet, the game that is played there now is no different from its past. What was the difference?

"For one thing the ambience. With the creative use of stagecraft, lighting, paint and plywood simulating a Starship, the place looked out-of-this-world. Players seated at round tables face their individual futuristic terminal screen.

"On the terminal screen the picture looked like the same old paper bingo cards. The terminal showed as many as 12 cards. But while the old-fashioned way called for a marker ("dabber" in bingo lingo) to mark the numbers as they're called, the terminal's number flashed until it was touched by a finger. No messy colored dabbers, just technology. It is that very technology that attracts younger players to what up to then had been the game for older folks. More men began to play the game that used to be almost exclusively for women. Remarkably, with the introduction of technology, the dress and appearance of bingo players became more up-scale.

"The conventional wisdom that older people don't take to computers caused initial apprehension, but we soon learned that no particular shift in age was noted. Actually, it was a joy to see older players deal with passwords and sign-ons as if they had done it for all their lives.

"At the beginning, the 200 electronic bingo seats at STARSHIP were available for play for 100 hours per week. The overall usage was at 69% occupancy. Various bingo patterns were presented as if it were a 3-hour stage show. The amount spent per player in those three hours exceeded $40. Then, at the end, a new group of players entered.

"To provide an overall picture: Those 200 seats produced net revenue of $4 million a year. However, the system offered a solitary version: Personal play! It is a game of player-versus-machine. The terminal spits out bingo numbers that the players needs to "dab" by touching the number with a finger. It is a spell-binding game that is being played in the off-hours and between sessions.

"Everything old was new again!"

EREWHON

During your lottery scribe's term as President of the North American Association of State and Provincial Lotteries, (NASPL) it dawned on me that this multi-billion-dollar lottery business offered little to formally teach middle management the ropes — the mistakes, the perils and the pitfalls of the industry.

Your professorial scribe wanted to offer an international program for the development of middle management who generally had a much longer life-span in the business than their politically-appointed bosses. The idea was to let the students discuss and debate the same problems that their bosses grappled with. The program of actual business problems would be presented in a way that didn't identify which lottery organization had experienced these failures and/or troublesome issues.

Your lottery scribe had learned the value of case studies at the school of Industrial Management at the University of Manitoba. Students studied detailed business problems and then engaged in discussions, analysis and proposed courses of action.

Michelle knew a professor at UBC's School of Commerce who wrote case histories for his classes. She approached him to assist us in writing case histories but the prof had no knowledge of lottery situations. I contributed a dozen case studies of actual happenings in the lottery business although we couldn't name names for fear of being ostracized by our North American colleagues.

The cases had to originate from somewhere, anywhere, but in a way that the actual lotteries could not be identified. It was the professor who mentioned Samuel Butler's 1911 book about New Zealand with the strange title of Erewhon — "Nowhere", spelled backwards (well almost spelled backwards).

The EREWHON State Lottery case-history program was launched at the 1988 Orlando meeting of NASPL directors.

To avoid the impression that Canadians might have something to teach Americans, Michelle wisely urged me to introduce the course as if it had been designed by someone much higher on the intellectual tree than mere Canadians. The UBC professor would lead the discussions.

A half-day of the Orlando conference was spent on Erewhon case histories. The interest shown by NASPL wasn't very encouraging. With some notable exceptions, the average lottery director's aim was to survive the job, not learn about it.

I made the decision that BCLC would take charge of the program. It is still a surprise to your lottery scribe that I would go on to conduct international Erewhon sessions for more than 20 years. As the industry developed, I expanded the content. In 2008, only four of the original ten cases were still in use but the total number of case histories had expanded to 45.

BUDAPEST

April 9, 1989. The Hungary trip wasn't your scribe's first visit to a Communist country but I still didn't fancy dealing with their suspicious officialdom. The reason for this particular visit in 1989 was to attend an INTERTOTO executive committee meeting that would constitute the final inspection of the facilities and program for the 1989 INTERTOTO Conference in Budapest. To counteract the intrusive actions of Hungary's police state, Tibor Andor, the manager of the Hungarian lottery, stood at the Airport's customs door handing glasses of the famed Tokai drink to his arriving guests.

There were some surprised looks from my INTERTOTO colleagues when they saw that Pete and Sue Morrissey were part of my party. In those days — and perhaps even more today — lottery directors shunned suppliers of technology on the grounds that, if they were seen with them, they might be accused of something; who knows what?

INTERTOTO President Lammers was okay with the presence of the Morrisseys. He already knew Pete and Sue, but some other members wanted assurance that the Morrisseys weren't officially guests of the Association. On the other hand, the Directors of Finland, Sweden and Austria welcomed Pete and Sue with open arms and immediately invited them for additional Tokai.

A dilemma arose when the executive committee members and spouses were ready to attend an official Hungarian government dinner. Not wanting to leave Pete and Sue, I told our host that Ina and I regretfully declined the government's invitation to dinner because we were just too tired.

Unknown to our INTERTOTO colleagues, Ina and I had agreed to meet with Pete and Sue for a light meal in the lobby at 7:15 p.m. We thought it was a safe move because the official party was being picked up from the lobby at 7 p.m. for the drive to the Parliament Buildings.

At 7:15, the elevator doors opened onto the lobby. Surprise! The INTERTOTO group was still mingling about. Ina and I hastily crouched behind the large potted ferns that are omnipresent in Eastern European hotel lobbies. The official party began to move past us toward the front door. Behind the exotic bushes we shrunk some more.

Then we noticed that Pete Morrissey was standing next to the front door, reading an American newspaper. He winked at Ina and me and then held up the newspaper in front of his face. He had cut two peepholes in the newspaper so that he could watch the parade go by. After they'd gone out the door, he neatly folded the newspaper and beckoned us. I hoped the KGB didn't have a spy in the lobby; we might have been expelled for imitating their schtick.

The evening was very nice. We walked among throngs of people on the nearby square and spotted the only McDonald's in Budapest. We ate what the state banquet didn't offer: hamburgers, fries and Coca Cola.

BUDAPEST INTERTOTO '89

Ironically, the September 1989 INTERTOTO meeting had been promoted as the first INTERTOTO Conference in a communist country but history had overtaken the slogan. With the fall of the Berlin Wall only months away, Hungary was in the throes of change from dictatorship to democracy. We witnessed a few incidents where the young-ish crowd made its noisy presence known while the old guard were holding communist banners high.

Two years before, in 1987, Vancouver had been the host of the conference and the event was still fresh in everyone's mind. The Hungarians had asked for details of the highly successful Amigo game, probably with the intent of offering a similar program.

To honour our Hungarian guests, Michelle McBride came up with the idea to contribute small tins of canned salmon with a special label that read *"From your Amigos in British Columbia."* Labelling the cans wasn't as easy as it sounds. Hungarian regulations demand that there must be a special health certificate on all imported foods and all ingredients listed in Hungarian and, of course — under Canadian rules — in English.

When the labels finally conformed to everyone's regulations (so we thought) the printing was ordered. When all cartons were packed with 600 tins, the Canadian labelling police stepped in and halted the export because the label had English and Hungarian but no French, which was a Canadian packaging requirement. The shipping cartons were opened, labels ripped off and replaced with a tri-lingual message. Finally, the cartons were ready for shipment.

The idea was that the tri-lingual salmon tins would be included in the delegate welcome bags along with the gifts from other countries. However, the welcoming bags were suspiciously light weight. We thought that perhaps since that the salmon was such a unique gift, it might show up later as a surprise during the Amigo game.

On the opening evening of the conference, delegates were treated to a buffet at the Buda Palace at the top of the hill of the "Buda" part of Budapest, a magnificent dining event reminiscent of the Austro-Hungarian Empire.

Two days went by without any sight of our 600 tins of salmon. I accosted Tibor Andor, the Hungarian LOTTO honcho and asked where our salmon was. He sheepishly explained that the conference staff didn't understanding how tins of salmon got to be mixed with hats, T-shirts and scarves. In Communist countries delectable food was too valuable to be handed out as corporate gifts. The conference staff had sent the tins off to the caterer. Tibor told us that the chef hadn't been pleased with our gift. He left a message addressed to the people "from Colombia with the fish" that the next time they sold fish to a Hungarian caterer, they should send salmon in big tins instead of wasting time and money on preparing all those little ones.

HOW TO TELL YOUR BOSS HE'S FIRED

BC's Lottery Minister Bill Reid and his wife Marion also attended the 1989 Budapest INTERTOTO Conference. Bill was in great spirits. He basked in the reflected glory of the 1987 Conference in Vancouver and relished all compliments, as he had the year before in Melbourne.

Bill Reid's Deputy Minister, **Mel Smith**, also attended the Conference. Mel phoned my room on Day 3 of the conference. He had learned that the Premier would be calling Bill Reid to fly home immediately and hold a press conference at the Vancouver Airport in order to respond to accusations that he had given a juicy contract for "Blue Box" recycling bins to a political supporter without seeking alternate bids. It was not the first time the minister had done something that didn't quite match the government's guidelines.

Mel wondered when and how to tell his Bill Reid that he was going to be dismissed. Should he tell him now or later in the evening? After the cruise on the Danube? I suggested that Bill and Marion should enjoy the candlelight cruise and dinner and not be told until later in the evening.

Aboard the cruise ship "Mozart" — a major presence on the Danube for two decades — the Minister treated me as his close buddy. He kept his hand on my shoulder and introduced me to everyone on board. The fact that I had to tell him everyone's name didn't dampen his enthusiasm.

Back at the hotel, close to midnight, Mel asked me to join him in lowering the boom. I declined because that kind of horrible task was a job for the Deputy Minister. Bill called me in the morning to tell me that the Premier wanted him back in BC for an important announcement and therefore he and Marion had to leave immediately. Bill was an optimist; he was unable to anticipate a thunderstorm even if he stood, totally drenched, in the middle of it. Months later he was cleared of any malfeasance but he never stood for election again. Bill Reid: A hard-working, kind and generous soul but —on occasion — a contrary politician.

VIENNA

We said goodbye to our colleagues in Budapest and took the train to Vienna to see how Hungary looked from a first-class rail compartment. From history books, we had learned of the Austro-Hungarian Empire, a strong military and economic alliance in Napoleon's day. I'd always wondered how the cultures of Hungary and Austria could have been administered as a single imperial entity. The language, spirit and customs are so distinct.

Well...whatever unity there may have been a century ago, was gone now. First the unsmiling Hungarian border people entered the compartment to certify that we should be allowed out of Hungary. Then a kilometre farther down the track, the Austrian border guards came to check if we should be allowed in.

We toured Vienna and attended a wonderful performance of "Rosen in Tirol," courtesy of our colleagues of the Austrian Lottery.

I was looking forward to the Vienna airport— I had heard via the grapevine that the airport's pay- toilets' coin mechanism was inside the cubicle. It was true. The user had to pay to get out! It turned out to be a special section, set aside for those who didn't want to use the toilets for the common folk. It was more a room than a cubicle. But I couldn't help wondering about the poor lost soul who might go in there only to find he or she didn't have the right coins and would be forced to beg for change from under the door.

LONDON. SCOTLAND. BARCELONA. SEVILLE.

In June 1990, we left Vancouver for Great Britain to visit with the J. Arthur Rank organization in London, which had shown an interest in buying an electronic bingo system. To see what their existing operation was like, Rank offered to tour us through some of their bingo palaces.

It seemed strange that a motion-picture company was in the bingo business. But, as we learned, the arrival of television had killed attendance at theatres. To retain their value, a number of Rank's cinemas had been converted to bingo halls. That explained the magnificent Wurlitzer organs that seemed so irrelevant in the midst of a roomful of keen bingo players.

Ina and I were fascinated to see people flocking to these halls where the bingo-caller was dressed in a sparkling tuxedo. It was an antiquated set-up. Players couldn't just walk in off the street. They had to apply for membership — an administrative hassle that took two days to complete. British bingo players were not allowed to give in to an impulse.

It took three full days for us to tour the bingo parlours located in popular resorts along the Irish Sea. One might argue that if you've seen one bingo hall, you have seen them all but you must remember BCLC was paying for this tour and we worked diligently to gather all the information. My final report said that it was unlikely that our aging bingo sector would accept the electronic bingo system. They were brought up with the rituals of paper bingo. Perhaps if the younger crowd — more computer savvy — attended bingo parlours, things might change.

Once the business obligations were completed, Ina and I set out on a short tour of Scotland. The J. Arthur Rank chain delivered a bouquet of "good-bye" flowers to the rural hotel on our last overnight business stop. It was a massive bouquet. What to do? We could hardly travel around Scotland with expensive flowers lying in the back seat. I descended the creaking staircase of the Fawlty-Towers-like hotel and handed the bouquet to the heavyset young woman in charge of hotel registration. When we checked out, she was in tears — grateful

252

for the flowers, laughing and crying at the same time. "No one has ever given me flowers before," she sobbed, "and I'm already 19."

After Glasgow, Ina and I flew to Barcelona, where we stayed at the apartment of our former colleague Ed Reger. Ed gave us the run of the house and even paid for a guide to lead us on a grand tour of Barcelona's attractions. Then we set out for Seville in Southern Spain to attend the 1992 AILE Conference. At that meeting I delivered a speech about the possibility that electronic bingo could rescue the dying paper-based bingo game. I don't think anyone cared because no one followed up on my speech. (Yet, in Europe, electronic bingo is still producing substantial revenue, a quarter century after our Continental efforts.)

 The lasting memory of the 1992 AILE conference in Andalusia was the passion of the flamenco singers and dancers. You couldn't escape the Arab influence on Spain's culture, evidenced by the atonal chanting of the singers who accompanied the flamenco dancers. One must be compassionate to see the pain these performers suffer in displaying their talents. At a lunch in Jerez, the home of sherry wine, we sat close to the stage and felt the tremors of the dancers' ferocious stomping. While my thumping brain wondered whether or not the makeshift stage could stand this pounding, the boot of one male dancer went right through the floor. He sank down to his knees but extricated himself and completed his performance.

OFF SHORE SALES AND MURDER

May 14, 1991. For the second time your lottery scribe was on the periphery of a murder in lotto land. When BC separated from the WCLF in 1985, one of the unique problems (or benefits, if you are an accountant) was the so called "off-shore" sale of BC's lottery tickets. The word 'shore' was a misnomer because not many sales were made outside of North America.

Selling lottery tickets in a jurisdiction where such a lottery is *not* licensed is a criminal offense. Several BC-based agencies were part of an entrenched lottery sales group that targeted Americans using high-pressure sales tactics while disregarding the law.

The illicit scheme had begun when WCLF was only months old. The Liberal-party-affiliated Olympic Lottery distributors in BC (led by a true and upright gentleman, Guy McLellan) sold Olympic lottery tickets all over North America. When Loto Canada replaced the Olympic lottery, off-shore sales carried on. When the Western Canada Lottery took over the $10 lottery from the Feds, the business continued.

When LOTTO 6/49 was introduced, the "export" of lotto tickets boomed. BCLC had no official role in these distribution groups, but we were very much aware that some retailers sold millions of dollars' worth of tickets without a store front. No one in government, the police or the courts showed any interest in pursuing this questionable activity, largely because it was considered a 'good thing' for BC. It provided employment, profits and, more importantly, the business was conducted so cleanly, that very few complaints ever reached the ears of the provincial or federal authorities.

One of the main operators, a businessman named **Randy Thiemer** started the re-selling business in the '80s under the company name Can-Win. One of his partners was Ray Ginetti, a former stockbroker and Hell's Angels associate. Ginetti sold his share to Thiemer in 1989, but in May of 1990, Ginetti was killed in the closet of his apartment, execution style — shot in the back of the head. (It wasn't until May, 1995, when Vancouver police charged Jose Raul Perez-Valdez, of Hollywood, California with his murder.)

The crime heightened police interest in "off-shore" sales of lottery tickets. One Saturday, **Joe O'Flynn**, one of BCLC's sales people, was enjoying a libation at his local Legion. His company vehicle was parked near the Glenhaven Funeral Home on Vancouver's East Hastings, where Ray Ginetti's funeral was underway. Many Hell's Angels and other underworld types attended. Police filmed and photographed all vehicles parked near the venue.

On Monday morning Joe O'Flynn was surprised to be called into BCLC's security office, where the chief demanded an explanation for his presence at the mobster's funeral. "I was at the Legion across the street for a farewell/retirement party for a friend," he explained. Today, Joe still laughs, "That was my sole encounter with the dark side of Vancouver."

From that day on, police and politicians began to focus on illegal sales of BCLC's lotteries outside its territory. Your lottery scribe called upon BCLC's auditors to assess the volume of sales. Early estimates showed that close to $40 million per year (8% of overall BC sales) came from these off-shore activities.

Government, concerned about losing so many millions in lottery revenue, asked for ways to make this operation legitimate but there was no way. While BC's annual net profit from offshore sales was in the range of $15 million, the mark-up by the off-shore sellers netted them more money than BCLC earned.

The situation became even muddier when the US operations of Blaire Down and Al Moss were raided by the FBI. The pair was eventually jailed. Even though their merchandise originated at BCLC, no questions were asked of me. Profits aside, I was glad we had rid ourselves of this kind of business!

MUSIC '91

In summer of 1991, the wobbly So-Cred government was facing extinction and decided to put on a show to rival EXPO '86. It was to be a "Musical Year". Original estimates were that the program could be done for $12 million: $7.5 million from lottery profits and $4.5 million from tickets and sponsors.

More than 100 people were employed directly by Music '91: a fleet of eight 5-ton trucks and two 18-wheelers to haul the stages, flags, banners, signs, and giant, inflatable Pepsi cans from the principal sponsor. They produced, promoted and/or sponsored 700 concerts and festivals, some of them in unlikely places — Bryan Adams in Revelstoke, Bo Diddley and the Kingsmen in Fort Steele, the Righteous Brothers in Osoyoos, Linda Ronstadt and Natalie Cole in Whistler, Johnny Cash in Squamish and strangely, Bob Hope in Nelson.

Music '91 promotions included First Night on New Year's Eve, the Labatt's Canada Live concert series and the DuMaurier Jazz Festival. Lottery revenue provided $300,000 to convince the Canadian music industry to move the Juno Awards away of Toronto and stage it in Vancouver for the first time ever.

David Letterman's bandleader Paul Shaffer hosted the Juno Awards at the Queen Elizabeth Theatre in a star-studded show featuring the Tragically Hip, Celine Dion, and an all-star tribute to Leonard Cohen.

By the end of July, lottery Minister Howard Dirks had to dip into the lottery fund for another $5 million because sponsorship and ticket sales fell short of expectations. BCLC earned more boos than bravos for this extravaganza.

There was to be no positive legacy of Music '91. The So-Cred Party was decimated in the October provincial election. **Mike Harcourt** and the NDP won 51 of the 75 seats in the Legislature reducing the So-Creds from 47 to 7 seats.

When it was over, auditors found that Music '91 spent $26 million, of which $19 million came from BCLC. It wasn't a good deal. In fact, it might have been the worst-ever expenditure of lottery profits.

THE AIRSHIP CAPER

Jack Rutherford of Alberta Lotteries came forward to tell this tale of lottery lore. I'll let him explain:

"I was the General Manager of the Alberta Division of the Western Canada Lottery. In 1982 after a trip to England, my boss Don Hamilton (Chairman of Alberta Lotteries) was very excited about the idea of leasing a Zeppelin-type of airship and using it to promote the introduction of Lotto6/49.

The "zeppelin" was painted sky-blue and the logo of Lotto 6/49 was emblazoned on both sides. The logos of the three other lotteries, the Express, The Provincial and Super Loto were painted on the tail.

Don Hamilton positioned the airship as a novel advertising scheme to raise the profile of the existing lottery games and promote the Good Causes that the lottery profits funded. The lottery board liked it and had all kinds of suggestions for its use. As General Manager I sat stunned in the corner as this all evolved. The purpose of the operation was to increase sales of the new game Lotto

6/49, so I had to go along with it. The board approved the leasing of the airship and essentially told me to "Get on with it."

So I and my hard-working staff had to incorporate this new promotion in our advertising program. Details! Details! Federal Department of Transport regulations? Technical backup and support? Who will fly the thing? Hire a pilot? Associated costs? Insurance? Not the least of all developing a marketing and promotional campaign to piggy-back on this costly investment.

Don Hamilton left me to attend to the details. For three years we operated the airship with varying success. Our Lotto 6/49 airship attended country fairs, the Calgary Stampede, Edmonton's Klondike Days and CFL football games. It wasn't as simple as it sounds for we had to file flight plans days prior to any occasion. Most event organizers embraced our participation. Large crowds came to see the take-off and landing. The lottery got great ink and TV coverage wherever the airship appeared. However, interest lessened over time and we had to create newsworthy events. We even crashed the airship on purpose on the expressway in Calgary during rush hour. (The coverage was enormous!)

The publicity and the noise surrounding the promotional flights upset folks in government and after Don Hamilton's term as Chair ended, much of the support for the project evaporated.

I believe that all the promotions of lotteries across the world cannot approach the stir we created for that launch of Lotto6/49."

A NEW
GOVERNMENT
1991-1996

THE "EXPRESS" ENDS

In June 1991, after 17 years, the Western Canada's oldest "bearer" game, the *EXPRESS* (first named WESTERN, then PACIFIC EXPRESS) was discontinued. First bi-weekly, then weekly, it had its own half-hour television show for 11 years on Wednesday (Winsday) evening and another six years in its BC version (Saturday Night). During its run, it earned more than $50 million for British Columbia and created close to 500 prize winners of $100,000. A remarkable coincidence was that — in those 17 years — three different individuals won the $100,000 twice.

Phil Swetlikoff, one of BCLC's early sales reps adds another anecdote about the *EXPRESS*:

"In 1982 I began working for BCLC's sales department as a relief 'route person'. It those days, the $1 WESTERN EXPRESS was a hot commodity during the Hip-Hip-Hooray bonus draws. In my career of a salesman, I always had to scramble for any sale, so it was an eye opener that each sales person was given an allotment of tickets and that was it; there were no more tickets to be had.

"I assumed the "shortage of inventory" was a scheme to motivate sales people. I asked my very first customer how many tickets he wanted. The man asked me how many I had. When I told him what my entire stock of allotted tickets was, he said he'd take them all. I was overwhelmed by my suddenly acquired sales skills and went back to the office on Elmbridge to get more. To my disbelief, the manager took me by the arm and got into the car with me to retrieve as many tickets as possible from that greedy retailer. Fortunately, after seeing my anxious face, the man went along and returned the excess tickets."

CHANGE-OVER TO "DAILY" GAME

DAILY GAME After the demise of the EXPRESS, we introduced a daily online game called the DAILY, a lackluster title. It delivered $4 million in sales in its first year but sales dropped by 50% in its second year.

The remarkable thing about the demise of The DAILY is that no one working at BCLC during that period — including your diligent scribe — can remember what the exact features of that game were. One of the best guesses were that it was a $1 five-digit game that could be "decomposed" into smaller subsidiary prizes. One thing is certain: the Daily won't enter BCLC's Hall of Fame.

 A year-and-a-half later it was replaced by The DAILY3, a 3-digit type of game that still is extremely popular in the Eastern U.S. However, in the Western US and Canada it was a niche game. It picked up the slack from the DAILY and produced seven times the profit of its predecessor.

ANOTHER CHANGING OF THE GUARD

October 17 ,1991. We knew that the Social Credit government didn't really care much for lotteries and now your lottery scribe feared that the newly-elected New Democratic Party's government was even more disinclined. BCLC had to tiptoe through a lot of byways to do what needed to be done in order to keep the profits rolling in. From my experience with an NDP government in the '70s I believed that while the NDP liked lottery revenue— like many lovers of a good steak — they didn't want to be involved in what had to be done to get it.

I thought we would have a new Premier and a new Minister Responsible for Lotteries who would recycle the same old mantras:

"Lotteries are a tax on the poor."

"Exploiting gullible people who are too uninformed to look out for themselves."

"A tax on fools."

We'd just have to wait to see which of the newly elected do-gooders would be assigned to restrain our business.

 The NDP was high on promoting female participation in government. **Cathy McGregor**, a Kamloops school teacher and future cabinet minister, was appointed Chair. For the first time in my career, women constituted the majority of the board. None of them had any business experience but breathed "sensitivity" and hated "patriarchy." I am sure they painted your lottery scribe as a "fat old white guy who was tough on employees".

Based on the board's assessment, political henchmen in Victoria set out to have me removed from my post. To provide the ammunition needed to show my lack of sensitivity and male chauvinism, a consultant from Eastern Canada was hired to write a report that would justify my dismissal. It was evident that the consultant had searched high and low for "bullets" but could find little more than a comment by an Ontario colleague who described me as a "cowboy, who would go wherever he had to go to get what he wanted". There were some minor complaints by staff who had recommended a course of action on something that I hadn't accepted. That didn't seem to carry any weight.

More influential were the assurances from NDP operatives with whom I had worked in Manitoba. All testified that I was apolitical and all-round leader. BC Deputy Premier Bob Williams called me in and asked how I felt about being judged politically. I told him that I did my job the way I thought it should be done and that I hadn't had a raise in salary in four years. He laughed uproariously: "I understand your position. You would cry in your beer if you could afford one!" He sounded quite jovial so I assumed the crisis was averted.

Cathy McGregor and the other women on the board appeared to be okay with my staying on as president but were adamant about more sharing in decision-making and greater sensitivity to workers.

Listening to their philosophy, I realized I had to test their conviction to those beliefs. "Do you mean staff should vote on a business decision and if I didn't agree with the majority, their decision would be implemented? Would you then hold me responsible if it was the wrong decision?" Several of the women hemmed and hawed but I wouldn't let them off the hook. At that point Cathy McGregor won my lasting admiration.

"There is a big gap between social theory and real life," she told her board members. "Let's be practical!"

With Cathy's support, and that of **Patrick Chen** as Vice-Chairman we'd muddle through alright.

PUNTO GONE. SPORTS ACTION ENTERS.

PUNTO the sports lottery, launched in 1988 had undergone many changes in its 3-year life — all to make it more attractive to players. In PUNTO, the player had to predict various segments of a given football game. The idea turned out to be wrong. Players who didn't attend the game live or who watched it on television had difficulty finding the outcomes of the game's segments. To complicate matters, the player also had to predict the total score. Your lottery scribe has to confess that PUNTO was his idea and must count PUNTO as a major flop. Now, with a new board of directors, we could change course. We settled on the Swedish LANGEN format, which asked simply for a win, tie or loss of a dozen games. To indicate that this was a totally new game the name was changed to SPORTS ACTION.

So many years later it can be told that a bit sleight of hand was used to change PUNTO to SPORTS ACTION and make it the game that — after three decades — is still one of the most popular sports-based games in BCLC.

At the first meeting of the new NDP-appointed board of directors, where the details of sports lotteries were explained, I presented the extensive research of Sweden's sports games that had led us to introduce SPORTS ACTION. Vic Poleschuk explained the game and Michelle presented the marketing program featuring the well-known sportscaster **Don Cherry**. There was so much information being thrown at the board that the game passed without a single question.

SPORTS ACTION was in business but the use of Don Cherry as a spokesman caused discord among female board members. Apparently, Don Cherry was "Anti-Feminist" personified. The women introduced a motion to cancel Don Cherry's contract. Despite the high public opinion of Don Cherry as a spokesman, the board voted that Don Cherry had to be phased out.

We managed to drag out Don's contract for several months, much to the dismay of some of the more "progressive" females. The sales results of boastful Cherry's commercials went from $2.8 million in fiscal 1991/92 to $23 million in

1992/1993 — a ten-fold increase. In the end, politics won and Cherry was shown the door. Not that he cared; he had too many other jobs going.

WARNING! BORING DETAILS!

The Sports Action section name ODDSET— as it is today — was a simple prediction of win, loss or tie from a list of upcoming sports events. (The 'tie' in football was a final score with a point difference of 3 or less.) The player is given a choice of betting on 3, 4, 5, or 6 games. Each win, loss or tie is priced. For example: the visitor-win might pay $1.45. The home win: $2.85 and a tie would bring $8.00. The multiplied amounts of the correct outcomes became the total win. Of course, the more games one chooses to bet, the longer the odds of winning become. If you are really interested in how SPORTS ACTION works today, visit the BCLC website. You'll enjoy it.

THE SUPER 7 BATTLE

Angus Reid, the well-known pollster, accepted an invitation to speak at a NASPL meeting about his research showing that the two proposed draws (BLUE and RED) of Lotto 6/49 on Wednesdays and then another two on Saturday would yield more sales than an ILC-proposed SUPER 7 slated for Fridays.

The research had been commissioned by your rebellious scribe because he didn't like the concept of the SUPER 7 lottery which offered jackpot odds of 60 million to 1. My logic was that since week-after-week, Lotto 6/49 sales were so high and jackpot turnovers were rare, then why shouldn't the lottery organizers offer them more opportunities to play the same game rather than a different game?

Angus' research was very practical. Several focus groups were conducted. No questions were asked at the gathering. Participants were told that BCLC was testing two new games. They were given play money to buy tickets at a terminal in the back of the room. One ticket was for SUPER 7. The second was for RED 6/49. The third was a choice between LOTTO 6/49 RED and SUPER 7. The familiar game RED 6/49 won hands down.

At a meeting of the Interprovincial Lottery Board, your lottery scribe tried to sell the RED and BLUE 6/49 concept by comparing it to the dilemma faced by a movie theatre owner. A popular movie was sold out every night. The question was: should he offer extra runs of the movie or present a different movie?

The lottery executives who were part of the launch of 6/49, nine years before, were not at the helm anymore, replaced by younger people who wanted to put their own stamp on the nation's major game of chance. They championed the SUPER 7 game that within a short time would replace 6/49. My prediction was that the SUPER 7 would sell adequately but it wouldn't destroy LOTTO 6/49. That game was just too much part of life in Canada.

The name **Angus Reid** was synonymous with research and his opinion mattered. He did a great job of changing minds, but even though others (France) had successfully pioneered a Red/Blue concept, the arguments fell on deaf ears. The idea of a Red/Blue version of LOTTO 6/49 was defeated by the 7/47 newcomer, now named SUPER 7

After the defeat of the idea of competing Red and Blue Lottos, your biased scribe was anxious to prove that identical games, run simultaneously each Wednesday and Saturday, would still work well.

When the "nation-wide" SUPER 7 was launched, BCLC did not participate.

Although BC didn't have as large a population base as Canada, the success of two near identical and simultaneously drawn lotto games could still be demonstrated by introducing a second LOTTO 6/49 draw, every Wednesday and Saturday but in BC only.

BC49 IS BORN

That same year, 1992, Lotto BC, a 5/40 game that produced around $20 million a year, was changed to BC49, an obvious clone of LOTTO 6/49 that ran twice-a-week. Now we had four Lotto draws a week. Two of Lotto 6/49 and two of BC49, drawn on Wednesdays and Saturdays.

It was not noticed that with the launch of BC49, the basic principle of Lotto had been abandoned. LOTTO 6/49 was a pari-mutuel system where prize amounts depended on the number of dollars played. Pari-mutuel means dividing the prize pot among the winners. The legislative gurus didn't notice that the new BC49 was a probability game that didn't depend on the amount of participation. It was a betting game. Even if only one ticket sold and it bore the winning numbers drawn, it would pay the $1million prize. The noticeable difference was that there was no carry-over of jackpots. The million-dollar prize was either won or not! The ticket buyers liked it and it was also just fine with your smiling scribe and his board of directors.

For clarification let me explain it another way: The difference between pari-mutuel and a probability game is that the prize calculation of the probability game is not based on the amount participation but the odds of winning. If only one player played one set of six numbers in BC49 and correctly matched the winning number drawn, he or she would win the $1million prize. If the same scenario occurred in LOTTO 6/49, the winner would win 45 cents.

The price of an entry in BC49 was half of the cost of LOTTO 6/49 at the time (50 cents). Six numbers correct would win (or share) $1 million. If the player matched only three of the six numbers right, the win was $10, just as in LOTTO 6/49. BC49 would in time become identified as the RED 6/49 game. The national 6/49 was, obviously, the BLUE game.

AN ADVERTISING COUP

Our advertising genius **Steve Brook** must be credited with a wonderfully inspired advertising approach that still rings in gaming ears after 25 years. It was a riff on one of the songs from the stage success: *Annie Get Your Gun.*

Steve's creative approach was that BC49 was not merely just another lotto game but a companion, a family member— an in-house friendly competitor of Lotto6/49. The idea of the so-called competition between the nearly identical games was aimed at getting the player to buy both games. Steve hired Bill Reiter, a famous BC radio voice who spoke and sang for BC/49 and Lotto/649 along with Ann Mortifie.

It was one of our best publicity efforts, demonstrated by record sales. You can still watch the commercials on YouTube at https://tinyurl.com/y4m4rt8b.

A NUMBER OF FIRSTS

In 1992, when BC49 was launched, little notice was given that three new concepts were introduced. Not only was twinning games a first in North America but something else was added that hadn't been done before. On a single lotto ticket, one could buy the same six numbers in the RED and BLUE games, something that caught on and allowed BC49 to be pulled into prominence by its big sister, the BLUE Lotto 6/49. The third and most important feature was not given much promotion. It was the first ever "probability" lotto.

Lottery colleagues across Canada scorned the idea of BCLC going it alone with its RED and BLUE idea but... a quick check of today's annual reports in the other Canadian jurisdictions will show that a game identical to BC49 is alive and well in all provinces.

The RED game was well-established in the BC market, when SUPER7 was introduced in 1998, but it never reached the heights the promotors had envisaged. Sales ranged around the $50 million mark, about 20% of LOTTO 6/49 sales. A decade later it was replaced by LOTTO Max, the current giant of Canadian lotto games. Today, LOTTO 6/49 still hums along most profitably and clones of BC49 are available everywhere in Canada.

INTERPROVINCIAL LOTTERY CORPORATION (ILC)

You sometimes-obstinate scribe has alluded from time to time to the weird structure of ILC (Interprovincial Lottery Corporation) the organization that links the provincial lotteries. I am partly guilty of its creation because at its formation in 1976, I could not muster enough support to make it simpler than the weird structure it became.

The basic concept of a Canadian inter-governmental lottery group is very simple. There are five provincial lottery organizations that agree to administer the identical game in their respective jurisdictions and then pool the prize money. Once the game structure and administration are agreed to, the work of the cooperative structure (ILC) is reduced to figuring out the weekly prize payouts. Just for clarification, ILC is the creation of the provincial lottery organizations and not the other way around. ILC is an administrative function of the interprovincial lottery, not the boss.

The shareholders of ILC are the ten provinces of Canada.

A simple administrative structure of the five provincial CEOs could have made all the business decisions. In deference to provincial government interests, each province should appoint a non-operative representative, just to keep a ministerial eye on things. Such a design would restrict the board of directors to 10. Infrequent meetings of ministers responsible for lotteries would oversee any major changes in the ILC-based games. During the day-to-day business, only a few decisions are made by the board.

Back in 1976 when the ILC was formed, rather than opting for simplicity, the structure of the ILC became a Rube Goldberg construct. The basis for the problem began at the formation of the two founding corporations. The structure of the Ontario Lottery Corporation and the four-province Western Canada Lottery Corporation was off-kilter. Ideally, there would have been a small board of directors but the four Western provinces each rightly wanted a representative. Ontario — also rightly so — felt overwhelmed by four ministerial appointees by the Western provinces. To even things out, Ontario insisted that it too wanted four ministerial appointees, even though, these four would only deliver one opinion because they couldn't disagree among themselves. Hence the board of ILC, including the two CEOs, became an administrative monster with ten members.

Nevertheless, this ridiculous over-loading of board members continued and was even exacerbated when the Atlantic Lottery and Quebec joined.

Quebec, copying Ontario, named a CEO and four board members, so did the Atlantic Lottery. A board with very few issues to discuss now totalled 20 members. Later, when BC separated from the Western Canada Lottery, WCLC lost one seat and BC gained two members.

If you have followed this tale so far, you have now arrived at 16 government-appointed members plus the CEO of each of the five lottery corporations. Presto: 21 board members.

These 21 people constitute a "Tour Canada" program by rotating their board meetings throughout the five regions. All travelling business class, all collecting per diems.

Some will wonder why I am ridiculing this structure since I left the ILC board in the year 2000. Well, let me explain. While there 21 members there are not 21 votes. To make changes in the ILC lottery games requires the votes of the five jurisdictions. Thus, in effect there are only five votes available. Why does it take 21 people to deliver five votes?

There are 10 shareholders of the ILC, the respective provincial ministers responsible for lottery. Only they can make unanimous constitutional changes to ILC. That is not a function of the board of directors.

The jaundiced view of ILC by your lottery scribe is due to the memory of attending an ILC meeting in Charlottetown, Prince Edward Island. The total travelling time from Vancouver to PEI — one way — is seven hours.

After checking into the Charlottetown hotel late in the evening, I rose at four in the morning Vancouver time, to attend the ILC board meeting at 9 a.m. local time. The chairman opened the meeting, found there were no issues worthy of debate and, after 17 minutes, the meeting was adjourned.

I managed to get the 11 a.m. flight to Vancouver. Twenty-one people from across Canada had journeyed at government expense and briefly slept in the best hotel in Charlottetown. 63 per diems were paid out. A few of the board members who had no active role in the business made a long weekend of it.

The sad thing was that— at the time — no one cared about this crazy, costly structure. I'm not sure, but I think this set-up survives in some form even today.

(Note: While your lottery scribe bitched about it, he did cash his per diems.)

FIRST EREWHON IN EUROPE

Kingston-Upon-Thames U.K. February 7, 1992. The board of INTERTOTO gave lukewarm support to my idea of staging an EREWHON Course in Europe. Even though the members had heard about the success of the program in North America, they assumed that this was an American version of lottery management and hence utterly irrelevant to the long-established European lotto/toto organizations.

270

The whole thing might never have happened but for my friend **Charles Cousins**, who had craftily manoeuvred a lottery law through the British Parliament, up to the point where all that was needed was the approval of the House of Lords and Royal Assent.

Charles Cousins' task was to put people in place who would know something about lotteries. He persuaded the INTERTOTO board to take the lead. He convinced them that if they didn't do it, the dreaded "others", the French-oriented Association Internationale de Loteries d'Etat (AILE) would.

EREWHON was scheduled at Warren House, the training centre for a multi-national chemical company. The building was a great manor where King Edward VII once stashed Duchess Camilla's great-grandmother as his paramour. The mansion provided rooms for all 24 participants who would experience three demanding days of problem solving, enriched by the quality of meals deserving of a five-star rating.

The notion that this course was only of interest to North Americans was quickly dispelled. Attendees discussed the issues into the wee hours of the night. I was afraid that one of the attendees — a reporter for a British political magazine — had come with an agenda to discredit the lottery business in Britain before it had even started. In fact, she was captivated by meeting lottery managers from Belgium, Norway, Holland, France, and Germany and she was blown away by the scale of the sales volumes of the participating lottery organizations. Her perception of lotteries had been that of a raffle "you know...sell some tickets and then you draw a name from a barrel."

The INTERTOTO board members in attendance didn't participate but — after hours — they conceded that EREWHON might work after all, but only if it could only be "Europeanized."

"But this is international," my new-found female press-supporter exclaimed. "I saw people from five European countries sit and discuss these North American issues that were familiar to them all."

Irritated that this 'Europe-only' feeling was still in the air, I told the INTERTOTO holdouts that all I could do was to change titles and names of the

271

study cases to European sounding names but then, should it be in French, German, Spanish? or what?

"How about some British names?" the lady reporter asked. "Or would that be too North American?"

Some of the older Europeans said they understood the international aspect but I knew they didn't. They clung to the thought that solving problems originating in North America couldn't possibly be of interest to those whose lotteries were much older. The truth that North America was far ahead in the computerized administration of lotteries was difficult for them to accept.

ARUBA'S PARLIAMENT

May 12, 1992. Ina and I travelled to the island of Aruba — a part of the Kingdom of the Netherlands — where I was invited to address Parliament, all 15 members.

Aruba lies off the coast of Venezuela. Its official language — Dutch — is seldom used by the general population. The everyday language of the street is Papiamento, a mix of Creole, African tribal languages, Portuguese, English and even some Dutch. Luckily for me, the rules of El Parliamento demanded that Dutch be spoken and I could deliver my presentation about electronic bingo and lotteries in my native tongue.

The MPs were somewhat suspicious as to why a Canadian who spoke Dutch had come to lecture them on the advantage of using computerized systems to conduct bingo. One member maintained that he was anti-gambling because it creates addiction. I pointed out that problem gambling is not prevalent in bingo play; it lies with slot machines and other quick-action gambling games. Waiting days for the outcome of a lottery isn't an attractive attribute for a compulsive gambler. My arguments fell on deaf ears but fortunately for the assembly and me, he was a lone wolf.

During the break, the Deputy Attorney General (a Dutch-designated official appointed by The Hague) explained that the objections by the critic had nothing to do with problem gambling but a lot to do with the MP's financial interest in an existing illegal lottery on the island.

We left Aruba believing we hadn't made much of a contribution towards establishing a government lottery. Yet, as I write this, Aruba is the only jurisdiction in the Caribbean, apart from Puerto Rico and Trinidad and Tobago that employs an online lottery system.

OFF-SHORE SALES IN THE SPOTLIGHT AGAIN

I don't know if it was jealousy of BC's success or an effort to prevent illegal sales, but at an ILC meeting, Loto Quebec management showed up with an analysis of LOTTO 6/49 sales in BC. The argument presented by **David Clark** of Loto Quebec was that BC's share of national sales of LOTTO 6/49 was close to 17%, while the BC's population was only 12.2% of Canada. "Why such a difference?", they asked and then proceeded to point out that given the many complaints from US buyers that BC must be operating a huge "offshore" operation, i.e. selling BC tickets in the United States.

In the past, your lottery scribe had pointed out this "exception" to various BC lottery ministers but the reaction was mild tolerance rather than strong disapproval. The politicians liked the profits and no one seemed to be hurt because, it had to be said, the off-shore operations were clean. There was no evidence whatever of fraudulent marketing practices. The unofficial verdict thus far was: Wink, Wink… Don't say anything…Continue!

When protests from US officials became troublesome, Mel Smith, the Deputy Minister who monitored the activities of BCLC asked me to join him in an attempt to find a legal way to authorize off-shore sales. After pursuing every possible loophole, Mel Smith's conclusion was definitive: re-selling lottery tickets in other jurisdictions was an offense under the Criminal Code of Canada. After his conclusion was delivered to Cabinet, no action was forthcoming, leaving BCLC high and dry.

When he was in Opposition, **Moe Sahota**, a brash young NDP MLA attacked the practice of off-shore sales. Now that the NDP was in power he was determined to have the practice banned. The Legislature passed an act prohibiting extra territorial sales, with a severe penalty for those convicted of the offence. The fine amounted to

$10,000 for each ticket sold illegally. The ticket re-sellers (a handful of very active companies) weren't overly spooked and took steps to find another Canadian jurisdiction that wasn't as puritanical as BC. Guy McClellan, the leader of the re-sellers found a welcome environment in Atlantic Canada and the re-sellers continued their sales quite happily.

The effect of the ban became clear quickly. In fiscal 1992, BC's total sales of LOTTO 6/49 were $286 million. Given that the national sales grew by an average of 3%, it wasn't surprising that five years later, sales in 1997 had barely reached $291 million. In those same five years, Atlantic Canada gained net profits close to $90 million. The joke? No one ever, not even Loto Quebec, chastised Atlantic Canada for selling millions of lottery tickets illegally, nor did BC get any kudos for giving up its many millions of profits.

Your lottery scribe may be accused of feeling that BC was dealt with unfairly but let me point out that I only calculated the losses for 5 years. The illegal selling by Atlantic Canada— although very much reduced — continues until this very day.

BREAK-OPEN SALES INTRODUCED

For a long time, the distribution of break-open tickets had been handled by charitable organizations. In their attempt to broaden the market, some of these charities placed ticket vending machines in the premises of their retailers.

This move to mechanization caused a conflict with the Criminal Code which stipulated that gambling via mechanical devices was only permitted by a provincial government. Although the intent of that section of the Criminal Code meant to deal with slot machines, the definition also applied to vending machines. Of course, lawyers for the charities argued that vending machines for break-open tickets was merely a mechanized method of selling tickets. The BC Government didn't want to get into a legal debate but simply authorized BCLC to buy out and control all existing ticket vending machines and hence be the sole provider and controller of these devices. BCLC was authorized to appoint retailers who wished to use the equipment. While there was some heavy lobbying by the ticket sellers, they soon accepted the new circumstances, although they didn't like the strict controls of their operations. Edgar Hildebrandt, our ever-present break-open sales pundit and his crew made this new distribution system their own with great sales results.

HURRICAN ANDREW

Your humble scribe wants to erase any thought that he had abandoned the British Columbia Lottery in favor of travelling the globe on international lottery business. These tales of forays in foreign lands were merely interludes between running a busy corporation, staffed by competent managers and understanding ministers responsible for lotteries who felt honoured that British Columbia's "flag" was being flown around the world.

One of those travel tales needs re-telling. In late August 1992, the tropical storm Andrew, a category-five hurricane, ripped through the Bahamas and slammed into southern Florida. Although rather small in size, this intense storm became the costliest hurricane to that point in U.S. history. Damage estimates ran as high as $25 billion and 43 lives were lost. Winds in excess of 240 km/hr (149 mph) flattened entire housing developments. Hardest hit were hotels and homes within a 25-mile radius of downtown Miami. Located there were the very hotels that were to house the delegates to the 1992 AILE lottery conference

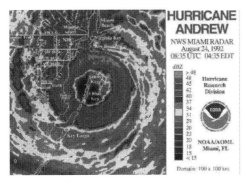

The Conference was scheduled to open a short while after the hurricane and Andrew had razed much of the tourism infrastructure. Duane Burke, who had been engaged to organize the AILE conference on behalf of the Florida Lottery, had done a yeoman's job of finding substitute conference space and hotel rooms. Duane can't really be blamed for the muddle that was to come.

The conference program itself left a lot to be desired but, given the circumstances, the fact that it actually took place was an achievement of sorts. Those who still remember it as a less successful conference forget that the host, the State Lottery of Florida, had turned its back on the conference because the invitation had been extended under a Republican administration and now the Democrats were in power.

Rebecca Paul, with a Republican background was (and still is) active in national and international lottery affairs. She had been dismissed by the incoming regime from her post as the CEO of the Florida Lottery, leaving the organization of the AILE conference in tatters. Ed Stanek, the Iowa Lottery Director, took over the leadership of the conference but it is difficult to manage an ill-fated world conference in Miami when one is located in Des Moines, Iowa.

Your lottery scribe remembers the conference well. Not only did Rebecca Paul lose her job due to a political change but my good friend **Michael Carr**, the lottery director of Michigan had also been given the pink slip. Michael quickly found employment with Pollard Banknote, negotiating instant-lottery printing contracts. Mike had always made fun of U.S. lottery directors who enjoyed the pleasantries and courtesies provided by vendors. He joked about Rebecca Paul, who said that the thing she missed most about *not* being a lottery director was that she had to light her own cigarettes and get her own drinks.

In an attempt at humour during a cocktail reception, I took advantage of the situation by making extravagant demands of Mike Carr. In turn, Mike — one of nature's innate jokesters — responded theatrically to my deliberately rude requests to round up extra chairs, peanuts, drinks, and ashtrays for our BCLC table. My personal request from Mike was a Diet Coke, no ice. I stressed: NO ICE. After others had ordered their drinks, Mike set off in the direction of the bar, his ears echoing with my cries of, NO ICE!

Five minutes later, he returned with a waiter's tray full of drinks. When he spotted me, he stopped, smiled and took a handful of ice out of the glass of Diet Coke and put it in the pocket of his jacket. He fished for ice cubes three more times before he walked up to our table and served the drinks as if nothing happened. As he sat down and joined the conversation, his jacket pocket began to drip. He pretended not to notice. It was a fun evening.

ANOTHER EREWHON IN BRITAIN

The success of the first EREWHON in England had proved that the case study program was valuable for Europeans. Yvonne Schnyder of INTERTOTO secured the same location for the seminar, the fabulous Warren House. It was to be the second Britain-based EREWHON within a year.

November 1992. Ina and I arrived in Kingston-upon-Thames on the Sunday evening before the participants arrived. Special arrangements had been made at **Warren House** to allow Ina and me to stay overnight even though no staff or guests were in attendance in the mansion. When we arrived by hired limo, the caretaker of the mansion — who lived nearby — was impatiently waiting to lead us to our room (the historic boudoir of King Edward's mistress!) He took time explaining how to open the massive, electrically-controlled, gate if we wanted to leave the building.

Ina was curious to inspect the mansion and its furnishings but after a while of nosing around we got hungry and headed for the executive chef's walk-in refrigerator. Everything was frozen. We decided to find something to eat in the neighbourhood but alas... we hadn't paid attention on how to open the big gate. After pushing many buttons randomly, the mechanism swung open. We left the gate open for fear we would never manage to get it open again.

We walked for a few miles until we found a fish-and-chip shop staffed by South Asian immigrants. The mix of accents rendered conversation difficult, but Ina managed to get them to tell us where the nearest wine shop was. By now we had lost all sense of direction. While we were standing in the middle of the road arguing about how to find the hotel, a car stopped to assist. The had not heard of Warren House but I knew the name of the street. When I said that we had walked for close to a half-hour, he told us to hop in and he'd drive us to our temporary abode.

He was surprised when we directed him to enter the driveway of the mansion with the open gate. He was even more taken aback when a police car approached and the bobby asked us what we were doing there (I assume they had been alerted by the open gate). The issue was soon resolved and we thanked the driver. In the stately dining room where royalty once dined on venison and wild boar, we ate our fish and chips and drank the Chilean wine by the light of the magnificent chandelier.

That particular EREWHON was as well-received as the first one. **Bob and Nancy Dunn** our LUCK newspaper friends from Vancouver joined the seminar. Vic Poleschuk, who had been invited to conduct a segment of the program, phoned that he was in Seattle, having missed the plane to London because he had taken his wife's passport instead of his own. He would still fly to the UK but would likely miss much of the program. I tried not to show it but your anxious scribe was nervous about holding the interest of the participants over a span of three days all by myself.

In the end, everything went well. The Europeans and North Americans intermixed beautifully and the debate about the case of a cancelled ticket carried on late into the evening. I was amused to see how my friends, Bob and Nancy Dunn, had such divergent views on that issue. It was fun to witness their inter-family squabble.

REPORT ON GAMING IN BC

In early 1993, NDP-MLAs **Dennis Streifel** and Margaret Lord, were appointed to form a Gaming Review Committee (known as the Lord/Streifel Review). The committee's mandate was to consult with charities to determine the potential impact on charitable revenue by gaming systems such as bingo, video lotteries and slot machines.

The duo visited various municipalities around the province, listened to the charitable operators and produced a contradictory report that concluded that (1) gaming will continue to be lawful (duh!); (2) charities will continue to be stakeholders in gaming; (3) government will continue to rely on significant revenues from gaming and (4) social costs of gambling are unacceptable to government. (They never identified those costs.)

When the commissioners met with your lottery scribe to reveal their conclusions, I commented that their comments were in conflict, saying the social costs of gambling are unacceptable but that government will continue rely on significant revenues from gambling. I tried to convince them of the contradiction but the irony escaped them.

278

Their Gaming Policy Review had consulted 96 stakeholders, including 20 charitable gambling associations representing the interests of a wide spectrum of BC non-profit organizations. The Review recommended: (1) to keep major casinos out of BC for fear of the negative impact on charitable revenues; (2) expand electronic bingo into other charitable bingo halls in order to enhance charitable gambling revenues; (3) explore new opportunities for charitable gambling; (4) allow BCLC to introduce 5,000 slot machines in adult-only premises; (5) protect and enhance charitable gaming revenues; and (6) introduce a new comprehensive Gaming Act. Overall, the Gaming Policy Review affirmed the importance of gaming as a funding source for more than 4,700 charitable organizations in the province.

While the government graciously accepted the report, the recommendations were neither implemented nor even considered. Government was obviously not too keen to open the gates to the charities.

As your lottery scribe writes about this review more than two decades later, he wonders how the report missed the headline the government was looking for: increased revenue from gaming. While it hid behind the idea of advancing charitable gaming, its real objective was to dedicate limited funds for charities and to keep the rest for government programs. The committee had also recommended that the "right of charities to conduct gaming" be enacted in the provincial legislature. That was a large overreach that didn't go over very well with a government hungry for more revenue.

In addition to the grab for lottery money by the charities, the British Columbia Hotel Association and the Association of Neighborhood Pub Operators petitioned the provincial government to let BCLC install thousands of video lottery terminals (VLTs) with the bulk of the profits going to them.

As the head of BCLC, your lottery scribe has to admit that as he showed interest in introducing VLTs in bars and restaurants although my personal view was that slot machines or VLTs (same thing in essence!) in such venues were unattractive. I still hold the opinion that when one dines in a restaurant or enjoys a drink one shouldn't be disturbed by the clanging and whooping of VLTs. Slot machines in a casino is quite a different situation. One may visit a restaurant for a meal and expect a peaceful ambience but going into a casino one shouldn't be annoyed that noisy gambling is going on.

The results of the Streifel/Lord Gaming Review can be summarized as follows: No VLT's were ever introduced. The legal right of charities to benefit from gaming came to nothing. The prohibition of major casinos was totally ignored. In other words: Nothing.

MADRID "UNITY" CONFERENCE

Today the world's lottery organizations enjoy membership in a single World Lottery Association (WLA) but it wasn't so neat and tidy for many decades.

On a cold, miserable February day in 1993, your lottery scribe travelled to Madrid to listen to a proposal to merge the two world organizations AILE and

INTERTOTO. Both organizations had reached the half-century mark of existence and there was a huge duplication in membership. Seventy percent of the world's lottery companies were members of both organizations. France's Lottery Director, Monsieur **Gerard Colé**, had appointed himself as leader to create a single world organization.

The marvel was not so much that a discussion about unification took place but that it had been so long in coming. Egos, cultural differences and decades of distrust caused a wide gap between the traditional state lottery organizations (AILE) and the "upstarts", the lotto and toto companies. INTERTOTO offered the most popular games and were the leaders in online technology.

Colé sent out a questionnaire to all members of INTERTOTO and AILE asking if they were in favour of a single organization. Unsurprisingly, the response was heavily in favour. M. Colé, at his imperial best, interpreted these responses as meaning that AILE should absorb INTERTOTO. To discuss his expected annexation, he called a meeting in Madrid. Representatives from Finland, Spain and France sat at the AILE side of the table with spokesmen for Switzerland, Sweden and your lottery scribe from Canada on the other.

Things didn't go well.

Matti Ahde, the accomplished Finnish politician and diplomat, understood the discussions but was reluctant to express himself other than through an interpreter, which diminished the impact of his remarks. The Spaniard on the AILE side was all too willing to let M. Colé do his imitation of a tin-pot Napoleon. Despite the insistence by your lottery scribe to talk about a merger instead of takeover, the two other members from the INTERTOTO side were bent on self-

preservation. **Richard Frigren**, who liked the title of INTERTOTO President and who enjoyed his world travel, acted as if his personal demise was being discussed. He felt that Colé was out to dethrone him. Emil Fischli, the Swiss delegate, was an excitable elderly man who — on principle — abhorred change of any kind.

Several of the delegates agreed to change the discussion from "absorption" of one organization by the other, to a merger based on cooperation and respect. However, for the overconfident Colé, it was all or nothing. He kept waving his survey responses as his mandate for the French-dominated AILE to absorb the largely Nordic/Germanic INTERTOTO.

The last chance for any fruitful discussion was sabotaged at lunch. Colé, without asking for individual wishes, ordered tournedos for all. (Tournedos are a French dish of fillet of beef cut from the tenderloin) Regrettably, the piece of meat Colé was served was not to his taste. He ordered a new serving. While waiting he informed his guests — "as a French gastronome" — that civilized people would only eat the centre of the tournedos and discard the outer area. Grizzly old Emil Fischli croaked with a mouthful that Swiss people like to eat the entire steak. Exasperated by Fischli's gauche objections, Colé reached over, took Fischli's plate away, carved out the centre of the meat, put it onto his plate and then handed the remains to Fischli, saying: "You can eat the rest." The discussion around the table grew deadly silent. Everyone looked intently at their plates, expecting an explosion of sorts, but Fischli kept on eating in silence. The spell was broken. The INTERTOTO side couldn't get out of there fast enough. After a few perfunctory good-byes, the first attempt at merging the two organizations ended in disarray.

BRITISH HOUSE OF COMMONS

One of the highlights of my career was in the summer of 1993, when I received an invitation to address a committee of the British House of Commons. I was charged with submitting a report to Cabinet on the "desirability to  implement a British National Lottery for the benefit of Sport and the Arts." The driving force behind the effort was **Denis Vaughan**, a celebrated Australian-British conductor who had begun his campaign to fund the Arts in 1987. His relentless pursuit of Members of Parliament and his many friends in the House of Lords had resulted in persuading Prime Minister John Major to convene a Commons Committee to study the matter. Denis put his musical career aside and bombarded the committee with input from various lottery executives around the world. His efforts were financially supported by GTECH.

Your lottery scribe was slated to be one of the first speakers at that Committee's session. Denis met me at Heathrow, accompanied by Charles Cousins, GTECH's man-on-the ground in London who took charge as soon as I was settled into the hotel.

Charles Cousins' initial efforts were not primarily aimed at gaining the contract to operate the lottery but rather to get legislation passed that would permit a lottery to be established. Lotteries in Britain had been illegal for 125 years. The last legal lottery had been held in 1827, when several scandals erupted and government — unable to control the hundreds of private lotteries — decided to close the door for one and all.

Denis Vaughan had started his quest when Margaret Thatcher was Prime Minister but she was no fan of lotteries. In the 1980s, she repeatedly declared that there "would be no approval of lotteries on her watch." John Major, her successor, was quick in yielding to pressure groups in sport and culture who argued that Britain was falling behind the rest of Europe with respect to government funding.

Arriving at Whitehall, I was startled to see my name on the various television monitors throughout the building that announced the starting time of my presentation. After I calmed down a bit, I entered the historic Parliament meeting room to address the assembled MPs, Lords and officials. The oak-panelled room and stained-glass windows kept me mindful of the special occasion. I had delivered this kind of speech to elected officials before, at the legislatures of Washington State, California, Minnesota and Aruba but this was the most impressive of all.

In my 30-minute presentation I was careful not to tell anyone what to do but merely relate my experience in Canada. Afterwards several of the attendees asked questions designed to promote their own interests. Few asked how the lottery was run, but uppermost in the collective mind was how much money the scheme would yield. There was no concern about problem gambling. After all, there was no greater gambling nation than Britain with its long history of pools, ponies and bingo parlors.

The toughest questions were posed by the MPs who had football pool offices in their ridings. Would the lottery kill the pools? Would hundreds of their constituents be pushed out of work? I told them no, the pools would not disappear but the lottery was sure to cause a drop in sales. The MP asked me to repeat it. I used the same identical sequence of words but very loudly which amused the crowd. Later, at a reception in the MPs' Lounge, two cabinet ministers bent my ear. But an even more memorable experience would occur the following day.

NUMBER 10 DOWNING STREET

Early in the morning Denis Vaughan phoned. "Must get ready for Number 10, Old Boy," he said. His big Jaguar was waved through various checkpoints around Downing Street. Actually, I was surprised how little security there was. A couple of steel barricades, the size of snow-plow blades, guarded the last 30 metres to the famous Downing Street dark-green door with the polished Number 10 on it.

At Number 10, as depicted in in cinema and TV scenes, a sole helmeted bobby stood guard. I asked if he would take my picture at the front door. He politely refused and volunteered that recent orders came down that pointed out that a terrorist might just hand the bobby a bomb that could explode. The bobby smirked as he related the story. He thought it was a bit farfetched, too.

Denis Vaughan was happy to take the picture but the bobby had orders to stay out of the picture. Still, one can only imagine the same scene at the White House in Washington. Would there be a single policeman or perhaps an armed platoon of marines?

The inside of Number 10 was a disappointment. I was planted on an ancient sofa and told to wait for the policy assistant to the Prime Minister. The waiting wasn't easy because the sofa sported a hernia: a spring that protruded from the seat. When I sat on the spring I could bounce up and down; when I sat next to it, I sank down and came to rest on a hard board. I'd seen better stuff along Vancouver's street curbs before the trash truck arrived.

In a tiny office, I had a most cordial discussion with a policy wonk in charge of drafting lottery legislation. When the draft law appeared a few months later, I noticed almost all of my North-American terminology and concepts had found a place in the draft legislation. It could be that vanity caused me to think that way. Never mind! I had been invited to Number 10 Downing Street to give *my* opinion. How many graduates from Leiden High School can say that?

INTERNATIONAL LOTTERY DATA BASE (ILID)

 Back at BCLC, staff had been encouraged to work on a project that would benefit the entire lottery industry. My idea was to create a repository of all up-to-date and past sales of the international lottery organizations. To make the program reach beyond the North America, I travelled to Stockholm to discuss whether the Tipsjanst organization in Sweden would accept the responsibility to be the computer-host of the European section of the ILID program.

Lottery organizations that do not have competitors within their jurisdictions feel free to exchange statistics on sales, profits and the performances of their games. At that time each organization operated within a monopoly, thus publishing sales figures had no impact on competition.

In the past, the smart lottery publicists, Terry La Fleur and Duane Burke, had each made it a practice to phone various lottery jurisdictions and collect and compile the sales results, which they promptly re-sold to the folks who provided it to them in the first place. Despite their intense efforts, participation by lottery organizations was spotty.

Both INTERTOTO and NASPL had put propositions to their respective members to help finance a database that would be accessible to all who contributed to it. The project in its proposed format never got off the ground because both INTERTOTO and NASPL wanted a sizeable up-front payment to get the project going. The lottery directors who didn't like the idea of buying a pig in a poke, demurred to finance the project and hence it stalled.

Your enterprising scribe requested that BCLC's board allow us to design an international lottery database for our own use but one that would also be freely accessible to those organizations that gave us their information. They agreed.

The North American operation of ILID (International Lottery Information Database) blossomed and, in due course, the BC-funded and operated database was handed over to NASPL which — decades later — counts ILID as one of its more useful membership programs. Your pleased scribe will say without blushing that if BCLC hadn't started the $1 Million program and delivered it for free, it might have taken a long time before someone else took the initiative.

FIRST TIME AROUND THE WORLD

In April 1993, I was delegated by INTERTOTO to inspect the arrangements for the upcoming 1994 Conference in Hong Kong. Our travel agent had a novel thought. We should buy a one-way Business Class ticket from Vancouver to Vancouver! It was quite a bit cheaper than a return ticket between Vancouver and Hong Kong. The trip to Hong Kong required four legs with a stopover at each. Ina and I flew to San Francisco and stayed a day, flew to Hawaii for two sunny days on the beach, then to Hong Kong, where we stayed five days, then on to Amsterdam for a break, and then home — all for $6,600 per person, which I hasten to say, we didn't pay ourselves.

Hong Kong was just what we thought it would be: colourful, busy, high rises, lots of traffic and pungent aromas. The staging of the conference was supervised by my long-time friend Warren Wilson, an Australian who was in charge of the lottery operations of the Hong Kong Jockey Club.

Betting on horse races is a popular activity in Hong Kong — weekend crowds of as many as 90,000 are common. The Hong Kong lottery is merely a niche in the Jockey Club's operation. Many millions of HK dollars are spent on the ponies each race day and the Hong Kong authorities limited expansion of the lottery for fear of cannibalizing the racing revenue.

The management of the Hong Kong lottery side was eager to hear about the innovations and variety of lottery games introduced in North America. While we were there, they requested that one or two of their senior people be allowed to work with BCLC in Vancouver in the marketing department. The experience so gained was to prepare for the day the Jockey Club was released from its horse-racing-only straight-jacket. It appeared that the upcoming handover of Hong Kong to the administration by Beijing weighed heavily in their decision. Yet, that change was still more than six years away.

Apart from my interest in the lottery operation, I had learned that you can't go to Hong Kong and not order made-to-measure shirts. So Ina and I followed the crowd. The shirts were of great quality and reasonable in price. I wore the prized shirts on special occasions for many years.

Ina and I had a special interest to cross over into China itself. We were so close. Our host drove us up a hill to a secluded spot where we could spot the Liberation Army patrolling China's borders. I did touch the border's electrified fence albeit for a split second. Ina stayed back in terror, afraid that I would be electrocuted and/or hanged as a spy.

The INTERTOTO inspection tour was a bit of a spoiler because we were taken to every location that that the 1994 convention goers would. Thus, when the actual conference started, we had "been there, done that."

FROM CHINA TO KOBLENZ

Our Vancouver to Vancouver trip was a world-tour of 25 days and — so far — only eight days had passed. The flight across China, India and the Middle East was long and boring but KLM deposited us safely in Amsterdam.

After a few days, we took a car for a 280-kilometer trip to Koblenz to speak at a sports betting seminar at the same mountain castle/hotel where — five years before — your clownish scribe had made such a fool of himself by pulling a chair from underneath himself and thus created a graceless tumble.

SPORTS

The sports-betting seminar, sponsored by INTERTOTO was unique, because in the many decades of TOTO operations in Europe, there had never been an educational seminar. Not that there was anything new to talk about. I delivered an insipid treatise of the unsavoury history of sports-betting in America before it was closed down in the 1900s. Sweden had some interesting ideas to share but we soon wondered what the hell we were doing there.

However, the host had a surprise for the real soccer fans. Berti Vogt, the coach of the German national soccer team dropped by for a visit. It befell to me as the senior INTERTOTO person to welcome him. I was surprised at the hero worship shown by the European seminar attendees and couldn't resist poking a little fun at Mr. Vogt in my introductory speech.

I spoke in lame German and fabricated a story about a soccer game between Canada and Germany and a dispute about which soft-drink company would be chosen as a sponsor. It was agreed that the issue would be settled after the outcome of the game. I uttered the low-brow punchline that the score was "Canada Dry; Deutschland null." I sense that you may not be laughing at this pun. Let me try to explain. To a German it would have sounded: "Canada 3, Germany 0." ("Drei" in German is "Three") Of course, the real humour was the thought that Canada could ever beat Germany 3-0. Well, you had to be there. Sorry I told you that story. Translated puns always fall flat. Even Coach Vogt who spoke English didn't get it. I looked at Ina for help but she shrugged her shoulders. When a pun needs to be explained it's no laughing matter.

KOBLENZ TO PRAGUE

After the seminar there was a party on a vessel where the amount of beer consumed could rival the water in the River Rhine. The following day we drove from Koblenz to Prague which isn't all that far if you have the nerve to join the German drivers on the Autobahn who think 130 km per hour is dawdling.

Mind you, our trip took two days because we stopped in the town of Bronau on the Austrian side of the German border. Why? We wanted to see a specific house in the village! On April 20, 1889, in that house, a young boy was born to an Austrian customs officer and his wife. The child's name was Adolf Schicklgruber. When Adolf reached the age of 21, he changed his last name to his mother's last name — Hitler. The house is unmarked today but in front of the place stands a good-sized rock that serves as a mute memorial. No information is supplied. For the curious, the address is Salzburger Vorstadt 15, and the house is very ordinary. We were in wonder how a young man from such a quiet background and such an insignificant border village could have caused such massive devastation to the world.

After Bronau, we drove to Prague. Ina took the wheel leaving me to make sense of the alphabet soup that constitutes Czech street names. We followed the sign that said Zentrum (City Centre) on twisting streets for 20 minutes until we were back at the sign of Zentrum where we had started. We tried once more, having no idea what the Czech names were for "One Way" or "Left turn." To us it was all letters strung together in no particular sequence. Ina finally stopped at a plaza and tried to find a street sign where the letters corresponded to name of the street where the hotel was located. No such luck. I asked Ina to drive onto the big market square where gypsies were sitting on their haunches, hawking their wares. To judge by the middle fingers that were raised in salute, I gathered that the street we were on was not the authorized direction to travel. The arrow signs confirmed that assessment.

In a small narrow street, we finally spotted a young man who looked like a student and might be able to give us directions in English, French or German.

"Where can we find the hotel Roma?" I asked, in my German "speaking-to-imbeciles" voice.

He turned on his heels and pointed to the door behind him: "It's right here...see the sign?" he said in an American voice.

Indeed, that was the sign of the hotel!

We thanked him and, seeing there was no place to park, we adopted the Czech custom of leaving the car parked half-way on the sidewalk. We told the hotel concierge that the Mercedes was on the sidewalk and he told us not to worry. I began to doubt that we'd ever see the car again but fortunately we were in good hands.

Our Czech hosts were old-world gracious people. The lottery manager was a holdover from the Communist days; his head looked like a dried-out pumpkin with coal for eyes, but he was most courteous. We met a young man named **Josef Tupy**, clearly the technical leader charged with bringing the Czech lottery into the computer age. In two days, we were shown nearly everything that Prague has to offer. Compared to the lavish tourist treatment we received, the lottery tour was brief. The Czechs had nothing to offer that might have interested us.

While Ina and I were tired of formal dinners, the final feast in Prague was a treat for our hosts. They reveled in their unusual situation, as it was only when international lottery nabobs were present that the cost of a magnificent dinner was no problem.

The World Ice Hockey Championships were being held in Prague at the time. During dinner, phone calls relayed the scores of the Canada-Czechoslovakia game. When the Czech team won, the night turned to jubilation. A victory over a Canadian team was a big thing for them!

FROM PRAGUE TO AUSTRIA

The next morning, a car stood ready at the front of the hotel and we were on our way out of town. We drove in the opposite direction of the "Zentrum" signs and were on the highway in no time.

In Vienna, we were hosted by the Austrian Lottery manager and treated to all the city's touristy things, including a box of the famous Zuckertorten, a cake that can set you on course for diabetes just by looking at it. Vienna was super-luxurious compared to down-at-the-heels Prague.

Our world tour wasn't ended yet. The next day we drove along the Danube to the ancient Austrian village of Krems, where an INTERTOTO executive committee meeting was waiting for us.

It was an uncomfortable meeting. President Richard Frigren talked excessively about the meeting with AILE in Spain and said repeatedly that INTERTOTO should stay independent and not ever consider a merger into a single world lottery association. The meeting hardly discussed anything else. After a long monologue Richard insisted that the meeting be extended by a day in order to endorse his view of INTERTOTO's continuance. He was enthusiastically encouraged in this stance by Yvonne Schnyder, INTERTOTO's General Secretary, who shared Richard's fear that a new structure might spell the end of her position.

Your ornery scribe did not assent to extending the meeting and left town, heading for Amsterdam in order to return home to Canada and thereby denying Richard the unanimity of the board for a motion that INTERTOTO was not in favour of annexation or merger.

A few weeks later I received the minutes of the meeting and read that the specific motion had passed unanimously. I fired off a letter to all board members re-stating my strong opposition to the policy of INTERTOTO isolating itself, especially since the majority of members of both organizations had declared themselves in favour of a single entity.

Well, writing contentious letters to fellow board members may be alright in North America, but in old Europe controversies are not discussed in public. Hatchets, no matter how bloodied, must remain buried. Surprisingly, when Richard called me, the issue was not the merger but that I had undermined his position. I told him that politesse was not an issue and that he was swimming upstream against the wishes of the majority of the membership.

Richard coolly informed me that the motion had passed by majority vote and the issue was closed. But... it wasn't closed. I vowed to carry on.

"THE CHEQUE IN THE MAIL" CAMPAIGN.

Fall of 1993. Back home again, your lottery scribe was "encouraged" by Cabinet to financially support the City of Kamloops in hosting the 1993 Canada Summer Games. **Vic Poleschuk**, BCLC's Vice President and well-known resident of Kamloops, had been named to preside over this Canadian quadrennial sports event.

As a company located in Kamloops, BCLC was prepared to make a financial contribution but handing over a million-dollar cheque in exchange for a picture of the Chairman in the paper was not a good business deal. Your lottery scribe was intent on letting it be known as wide and far as possible that lottery profits helped to make the Games a financial success.

My plan was to issue a cheque of $50 to each household in Kamloops, made out to the Canada Games. The deal was that householders could either throw this cheque in the garbage or take it to a Lottery Ticket Centre where they could exchange the cheque for a LOTTO BC49 ticket. The Canada Games would get the $50; the householder would get a free lottery ticket.

Advertising made sure that everyone knew that every Kamloops householder could assist the Canada Games. The experience with commercial mail-in campaigns is that a response of 10%-15% is very good. Since this was an offer to help the community and to get a free ticket to boot, a bigger return was projected.

The mayor of Kamloops, one of the less-quick minded city-fathers, called BCLC in a panic. He wanted to dump this crazy idea. He just wanted his million-dollar cheque. Your lottery scribe assured him that if the campaign failed, he would still get his million dollars. No, he wanted that statement in writing; he wanted a BCLC press release to that effect. Vic Poleschuk persuaded him that this would undermine the campaign to get the community involved and that he should just accept our quiet assurance that he would get his million, no matter what. He accepted our assurances but wanted his million dollars, as he wrote, "Come Hell or High Water."

As a Games co-sponsor, Canada Post delivered the 'cheques" to every household in the city at no cost. A huge image of a thermometer was placed outside the Kamloops office showing a daily rise in how much Kamloops citizens were contributing to the Games. The promotion became the talk of the town. By the time the promotion ended, cheques totalling $1,115,000 had been deposited.

When the total was announced, the mayor phoned within minutes to congratulate me on the success. He had always known it would be successful and since he had settled for a guarantee of $1 million in case of failure, he had changed his mind and was willing to accept the gesture of generosity by the citizens of Kamloops. So he said he'd anticipate cashing the cheque for the one million dollars plus the $115,000.

I felt like saying no, but the promotion had gone well. Had we merely issued a cheque of S1 Million and taken a big ad in the papers to congratulate ourselves we wouldn't have had that kind of positive reaction.

BALLS IN THE AIR!

The second idea for the Canada Games — equally unusual but not quite as successful — was to stage the strangest lottery draw ever.

BCLC, as an additional commitment, had accepted sponsorship of the Opening Ceremonies and your lottery scribe believed it would be a grand idea to distribute 49 plastic balls (numbered 1 to 49) around the attending crowd. To give you an idea, the balls had a diameter of four feet. In the centre of the field, square dancers would form six circles. At a given signal, the crowd was expected to bounce these balls onto the field, where the young costumed helpers would randomly push and rush one of the forty-nine balls in each of the six circles.

The outcome of all this would be that we would have six numbered balls from 49, for a "Special on-site BC49 draw." Six numbers would be the official winning numbers. Surely, if this hare-brained scheme worked it should qualify for the Guinness Book of Records?

The opening ceremony of Kamloops Canada Games began at 1 p.m. on Saturday, August 8, 1993. Spectators entering the stadium were given BC49 "Special Draw" tickets. If their ticket matched three or more of the six numbers "drawn" on the field, they would win a prize, right then and there.

At rehearsal, a mild breeze had blown the balls out of the circles. To make the balls heavier a bit of water was poured into the balls.

To start the ceremonies, a detachment of paratroopers from the Canadian Armed Forces staged a drop. When the paratroopers came down onto the field, the flags in the grandstand stood straight out as if painted on plywood. This wasn't a breeze; it was a strong wind aspiring to become a gale. Some of the parachutists missed their target.

"The show must go on" and so it did. When the balls were released onto the field, they flew out of the stadium like a flock of crows frightened by a shotgun blast. Several blew into the nearby hills. The crowd loved our embarrassment. Michelle McBride, who had the role of certifying that the draw procedure was done correctly, had a green flag for positive outcome and a red flag if the draw was invalid. As the balls flew into the hills, Michelle — a great trooper who knew irony when she saw it — stood stock-still, her red flag held straight by the gale. The crowd, collectively, bent over in mass hilarity.

The announcer then divulged plan B. Well before the program, BCLC auditors had drawn six numbers using the normal draw procedure and sealed the result in an envelope "Just in Case." After the laughter died down, the PA announcer announced in dramatic tones: "In case the draw cannot be properly completed, the British Columbia Lottery Corporation has pre-drawn six winning numbers." He then pompously announced the six numbers.

The applause was loud and long. If the draw had gone smoothly, public appreciation would have been one tenth as strong. Those who would consider the event a failure would be right, but in terms of marketing and making news, it was a great hit. Some of those balls were never retrieved.

PROVINCIAL COMES TO AN END

The PROVINCIAL lottery ended in September 1993. Introduced in 1979, it had made millions in profit. It had won many battles with LOTO CANADA and had suffered several embarrassing technical problems. BCLC opted to continue the game for BC-only in an online format. It continued at the rate of $10-12 million a year but petered out in 1995 when volume sank to $5 million. A good, profitable game had passed away.

HONG KONG REVISITED

October 10, 1993. The INTERTOTO conference in Hong Kong was now upon us and, this time, Ina and I travelled directly from Vancouver to Hong Kong. The organizing committee of the Hong Kong Jockey Club had asked me to be the keynote speaker. With the assistance of key BCLC members I had prepared a speech on the topic that public opinion, at some point in the future, might turn against lotteries if the market continued to be flooded with more and more games. The speech was particularly critical of video lottery terminals. Using taped video segments, 30mm slides plus singing and piano playing by your musical scribe, the speech promised to be a novel opening for the conference.

The intro to the presentation was the voice of Frank Sinatra, singing, "We stood and talked like this before but who remembers where or when" ...and when Sinatra paused for a musical break, the tape carried on with me, singing live! The content of the speech was how over the course of four centuries, there had been three waves of wild enthusiasm for lotteries only to have them shut down by public disapproval when corruption set in.

Michelle McBride, who had been in the control booth running the technical production, should have come down from her perch and shared in the standing ovation. Angus Reid, whose opinion I value, told me it was one of the more memorable speeches he had heard.

That afternoon, Chris Patton, the Governor of Hong Kong who — in 1997 — was to be instrumental in handing the rule of Hong Kong over to China, talked about that upcoming major event. His was a good speech but mine had better music and more slides. (For those who smell arrogance, I am JOKING!)

ANGER MANAGEMENT REQUIRED

Yes, I admit it; at the Hong Kong business conference, I was truly angry at the leadership of INTERTOTO. **Richard Frigren**, president for four years now, had been travelling the world on behalf of the organization— a thin veneer for holidaying. He was still obstructing efforts towards a single world lottery organization.

Your persistent scribe was determined to achieve a merger but in order to accomplish that tall order, the support of the INTERTOTO board was required. Despite the 1989 personal commitment by Richard that he would only hold the President's position for four years, he reneged. He would run again! This was no particular surprise, but now he had maneuvered it so that I would be Second Vice-President which — if the world stayed on its axis — meant that I would never gain leadership of INTERTOTO. In fact, I had been disarmed. I assure you that I didn't need the position for glory because to the BC government, friends and family, being President of INTERTOTO meant absolutely nothing to anyone in power or my family.

I failed terribly at hiding my true feelings. I was livid.

Perhaps in another setting I might have resigned but I needed the INTERTOTO board position to carry on towards the goal of one world organization. I resigned the Second VP position (It was never filled) and stayed on as a regular Director. The objective was farther away than ever.

ATLANTA TO LONDON

November 28, 1993 was the day the Georgia Lottery Corporation had chosen to start a three-day EREWHON session at Lake Lanier, north of Atlanta. After arrival at the hotel I went to bed, sensing a bout of the flu coming on. That left Vic Poleschuk and Frances Kenny to conduct most of the seminar. I lay in bed feverishly eyeing the hotel's giant Christmas light display hoping to be free of the bug by the time EREWHON was over. I had a commitment to address a gathering of bidders for the management of the emerging British lottery at the Guildhall in London, five days hence. I made it, but barely.

The London speech went okay, although I felt self-conscious. I had to address those who were interested in bidding for the contract to run the British National Lottery. The lottery was to be a licensed private enterprise and not — as I had recommended to Number 10 — a corporation owned by the state, as in North America. In my view, free-enterprise operating within a civil-service-dominated environment is a recipe for constant antagonism. Many in the audience had financial interests in the outcome of the award. I had to sail between the shoals of friendship and the rocks of dead-serious competition.

I spotted former colleagues among the audience. Ian Nielsen-Jones from Ontario was bidding on behalf of the J. Arthur Rank Group; the cheerful John Mortimer from Australia was bidding for Tattersall in Melbourne. The giant in the room was GTECH. The rest of the audience consisted of greenhorns, anxious to get a part of this juicy assignment. They were the ones who bombarded me with inane questions. I made it through the long speech which ended with lukewarm plaudits from all sides.

Afterwards, I was briefly interviewed to determine if I wanted the job of managing the British lottery under Richard Branson on behalf of his "Virgin" empire. However, as soon as his people realized my connections with Guy Snowden and Charles Cousins (of GTECH, who were among the leading bidders), I was discarded. A good thing, too. In retrospect, I would not have appreciated the assignment in London given the political conditions, although the annual pay was close to the half-million-dollar mark.

In due course, GTECH was declared the operating firm of Camelot for the first five years. I assigned a few BCLC staffers to assist in getting Camelot up to speed. Rob Egan led the fledgling company's computerized gaming system for several months. The first draw of Camelot took place on November 19, 1994 with a TV program presented by Noel Edmonds. The first numbers drawn were 30, 3, 5, 44, 14 and 22, the bonus was 10; the jackpot amounted to £3.2million.

Your lottery scribe was pleased to have had a substantial role in the creation of the now renowned British National Lottery.

A POSSIBLE MERGER POPS UP... AGAIN.

In April 1994, the AILE executive meeting was held in Paris. Your lottery scribe attended as President-in-Waiting. The nomination wasn't due to my magnificent achievements but simply because BCLC was to be the host of the 1996 AILE annual meeting. That's how you got to be president of the organization. While the task of leading AILE was of interest, my real focus remained the potential merger of INTERTOTO and AILE.

My effort to persuade INTERTOTO to take the lead in merging the two world organizations had failed. The long-term president of INTERTOTO remained opposed to a merger. A docile membership had extended his decade-long hold on the organization until 1997. In view of my approaching retirement, the window to unite the two world organizations was closing.

Your adamant scribe was convinced that if the members of both world organizations were to gather at one conference, it would be evident to one and all that both organizations had largely the same membership and, that it was the leadership of INTERTOTO that was the stumbling block to a merger.

The only flaw in that reasoning was that the Americans — all belonging to the North American organization — were not interested in the world scene. Thus, if the objective was to unite all lottery organizations around the globe, AILE, INTERTOTO and NASPL needed to get together in one place.

Where else but in Vancouver? That's where I could control the agenda.

My nomination as President of AILE was no reason to resign from INTERTOTO's board. There was no rule prohibiting leadership in both organizations. I wanted both positions because I would be able to present my views at both board tables. I pointed out to the INTERTOTO members that there was an opportunity to join the AILE annual meeting in 1996 where NASPL would also be invited to be part of what might be called a "world meet." The opportunity fell on deaf ears.

PRESIDENT OF AILE

I was elected President of AILE, largely due to behind-the-scenes lobbying by my friend **Marguerite Bourgeois** of Loto-Quebec, the General Secretary of AILE. She ruled this largely francophone institution with an iron fist. She personally had her doubts about a merger, but she wasn't as against it as the INTERTOTO leader was.

When the subject of the next conference arose, the AILE delegates were delighted to vote for the 1996 annual meeting in Vancouver and thus for its President, your lottery scribe. One organization down, two to go.

THE STATELY DINNER

Being elected as the English-speaking President of AILE didn't mean that one would be invited into the francophone executive circle. At the final dinner I wasn't asked to join the official "Head Table." The outgoing AILE president, Colé (of the carved-up tournedos) did not wish to demean his table with someone who had crossed him and whose language was not French.

All French-speaking AILE board members were provided with limo transportation to the Palais de Versailles where the banquet was held. Your lottery scribe was advised to take the bus or a taxi. Believe me, I truly didn't care. I was happy to have succeeded in obtaining the 1996 AILE Conference for Vancouver and thereby gain its presidency.

Knowing the French custom of standing-for-hours-on-your-feet receptions, BCLC Chairman Patrick Chen, Sue and Pete Morrissey, Daughter Cynthia and your lottery scribe decided to take the last conference bus to the official dinner. The bus left the historic Hotel Meurice at 7 p.m. to travel to Versailles, the location of the glorious palace of past kings of France. During my NATO military service, I had been billeted in that palatial complex of Versailles. That's why — en route to the palace — I realized the driver didn't know where he was going. When we turned the corner where we had started, I joined him up-front and assisted him in finding the right route.

We arrived at the reception more than an hour late. It mattered not. Everything was late. The reception was held in the centre of the palace garden, an area with a gravelled surface that tortured the women in their thin-soled, high-heeled shoes. The guests hadn't moved from that spot since the first bus had arrived an hour-and-a-half-ago. The wine had flowed freely but the early comers began to feel the ache of standing around. The women began to remove their shoes and we saw a lot of stork-like stances, resting one foot while balancing on the other leg. We gave silent thanks for our late arrival.

When the line finally began to move, we didn't know that the parade of 900 people would wind its way from the garden through the Hall of Mirrors to the dungeon in the cellar of the palace, advertised in the program as the "historic" dining room. It was a long trek at a pace that even a snail would have considered very slow. An elderly female guide struggled inform stragglers about the Honour of France linked to these hallowed halls. Next to her stood an itinerant gypsy woman selling instant cameras from a large shopping bag.

DINNER IN THE DUNGEON AT VERSAILLES

The banquet guests were led to the former underground jails and stables, where tables had been placed at random among the pillars, nooks and crannies. **Paul Sawyer**, a Pollard Banknote manager found a table in the corner near the 12-piece orchestra, not too far from the head table of M. Colé. It had now been three hours since we left the hotel. Thirty minutes later we finally sat down. The bewigged waiters still stood at attention, showing no intent to serve food.

At a loud trumpet fanfare, they sprang into action commencing a drill that would do the U.S. Marines' presidential guard proud. Plates were ceremoniously placed on the tables. Then, nothing!

Paul Sawyer noticed that, alongside the Head Table, four large ice buckets containing a number of bottles of wine ready for pouring. Brash as a cat-burglar, he calmly walked over and took a few of the bottles out of the bucket. He even took the time to inspect the labels. The orchestra leader spotted him and wagged his finger. Paul, experienced in how to mitigate objections, bribed him with a bottle. To the envy of our neighboring table guests, we felt a kind of thieving pride when Paul proceeded to serve the wine.

Then Paul noted that the orchestra had a crate of 12 bottles of wine delivered to the back of their stage. Paul slinked behind the riser and expropriated some more bottles. A few minutes later, he managed to look surprised and grateful when the bandleader politely brought us a bottle of his cache. We drank some more. Daughter Cynthia drank "eau minerale" which Pete Morrissey deliberately mispronounced as "eau miserable."

By the hour of eleven, the powder-wigged waters took away the plates they had earlier put down so ritualistically. Another trumpet fanfare! A good-sized but dead cow, roasted and hung upside down from a pole by its bound legs, was paraded through the hall. I am sure if the parade had slowed down for only for a few seconds, the hungry crowd would have gnawed the meat right off the carcass. Alas, the expired cow disappeared behind a door. Dry breadsticks were deposited on our table, along with jars of water, an historic moment, reminiscent of the days when the dining room was still a dungeon.

It was announced that after dinner there would be a dance in a specially erected tent at the back of the garden. Groans from around the hall were heard.

The delay was the final straw for our hungry but happy party of five. I remembered the way to the street through the back area of the palace. With daughter Cynthia in tow, we made our way to the quiet street where a French policeman stood guard. With his white-gloved hands extended, he explained that his instructions were to stop anyone from entering but had doubts about people leaving. We told him about the enforced hunger strike in the palace and asked if he could find us a taxi.

"Not at midnight," he offered. "This is Versailles, not Paris."

Suddenly a car screeched to a halt. A shoddily unkempt driver asked the "flic" what was going on. It turned out the driver was some kind of undercover cop. He said one of his friends (a suspect or a stool pigeon?) owned a miniature Renault bus. He radioed the man in harsh tones and summoned him to find us at the garden gate.

Meanwhile, Cynthia stood shivering in the midnight air. The policeman gallantly took off his uniform jacket and draped it around Cynthia shoulders. With the typical French kepi on her head, she looked ready to direct traffic on the Champs d'Elysee.

A Renault minivan arrived and we were on our way to our Hotel Maurice in Paris — at no charge! Arriving at the hotel, room service was closed. **Pete Morrissey,** shed of his formal clothes, ordered pizza from the café on the corner of the Rue Rivoli and — of course —more wine. We enjoyed dinner after all. Pete had the last word when he rose to speak of his appreciation for being personally invited by the president of this world organization to a scrumptious late-night pepperoni pizza dinner.

1996 NASPL ANNUAL MEETING

After the eventful stay in Paris, the flight from Paris to New York was most pleasant. The flight from New York to Indianapolis, the site of the October 1994 NASPL conference, was quite the opposite. It was a crowded, noisy *de Havilland* aircraft. Yet it didn't bother your lottery scribe too much because the rehearsal for my speech was uppermost in my mind.

300

The aim was to get Vancouver named as the host of the 1996 NASPL Conference. I don't recall much of the business session, since I was deep into the fog of travel fatigue. After a good night sleep, I was ready to do my spiel for a joint AILE/NASPL 1996 conference for which I had the support of the NASPL

President **Jim Scroggins** of Missouri and the incoming President Peter Lynch of New York. My presentation was supported by all Canadian lottery CEOs. Vancouver was selected as the host of NASPL 1996. Two down. One more to go.

SUPER 7 LAUNCHED IN CANADA BUT NOT BC

In June 1994, The Interprovincial Lottery (ILC) launched the game SUPER 7, a

"7 numbers out of 47" format. It was made available from Alberta to Newfoundland but not BC. It was pressure by a group of newcomers to ILC

who deemed that LOTTO 649 was on its deathbed. I disagreed and devised and launched a BC-only game called BC49 based on the 6/49 format. It was a novel approach in that a player could play the same numbers in both games. It might be cheeky to point out — after 25 years — that LOTTO 6/49 and BC49 are still prospering and have been copied in all jurisdictions in Canada, while SUPER 7 is but a memory. BCLC did join SUPER 7 three years later but the game was axed in 2009. As I wrote above, LOTTO 6/49 and BC49, after many years, are still happily chugging alongside the great new-comer LOTTO MAX.

FIRST MOVES TOWARDS A CASINO IN BC

Summer 1994. While your lottery scribe was in Paris assembling the pieces for a new united world lottery organization, out of the blue, the Vancouver Port Corporation (VPC) and Mirage Casino of Las Vegas held a press conference at Vancouver's luxurious Pan Pacific Hotel. They boastfully announced that they would build a $750 million casino complex on Vancouver's waterfront.

To be called SEAPORT CENTRE, the complex would include a 125,000 sq. ft. casino, a cruise ship terminal, sea-bus and heli-jet terminals, a 270,000 sq. ft. convention center, a 1,000-room hotel, a large retail promenade and as a token of appreciation, the nearby Woodward's Store would be converted to low-rent apartments. The proposal was dependent on the provincial government's willingness to license a 125,000 square foot casino within the complex. If that wasn't enough of a requirement, the group demanded that the provincial government should legislate amendments to the gambling laws to protect their existence as a world-class casino. In other words, "No competition."

Within days the concept was in trouble. VPC, a federal Crown Corporation, drew flack because it had not issued a public proposal and had made its decisions in private, without consulting the City of Vancouver.

Nearby Gastown merchants feared the retail complex would create a giant vacuum cleaner, sucking up much disposable income. Environmentalists decried the loss of the waterfront. Local charities feared losing income from their charitable casinos. Great Canadian Casino Company, the owners of local casinos hee-hawed for a time and told the government that they would be wiped out by the proposed casino. In short order, the project was dealt a "coup de grace" by the NDP when Premier Harcourt, despite earlier and private assurances of support, suddenly dove for cover.

Bloodied but unbowed, Steve Wynn, the owner of the Las Vegas Casino Mirage charged into Vancouver with fistfuls of dollars and a single-minded determination to get the project rammed through. In a most intense lobbying effort, his people conducted polling, appeared on open-line shows, and telephoned 35,000 Vancouver homes, promoting the project.

The group's frustration was that despite the political moves and the media's anti-casino bias, opinion polls showed that a majority of respondents supported the project.

To defend their interest, the hotel and convention organizations and the casino industry began a costly survey of the world's largest conventions to determine how many of them would come to Vancouver if there were a casino. Steve Wynn, angered by the bad vibes, flew to Vancouver where, in summer of 1994, he addressed a sold-out, $60 a plate luncheon hosted by the Vancouver Board of Trade. He told the audience that those who opposed the project were grasping at incorrect and stereotypical situations. Wynn's frank comments were refreshing but they also gave the project's opponents another target.

Insulted and upset, Wynn turned off the promotion-money tap and the SEAPORT project collapsed. Shortly after, it became obvious that the Seaport casino was not the only one in trouble. Mud was beginning to stick to the government. Premier Harcourt, wrapped in the flag of reason, tried to deflect criticism by announcing a series of stakeholder meetings which were to provide the government with an alternative gaming policy. This strategy also drew fire because the public at large was excluded. The City Council of Vancouver, already incensed by the VPC's earlier actions, picked up the cudgel and announced that it would also hold a series of public information meetings that quickly transformed into anti-casino rallies.

On October 4, 1994, the Harcourt government announced that cabinet had rejected Las Vegas style casinos for British Columbia and reaffirmed his government's commitment to a Made-in-British Columbia casino policy through the British Columbia Lottery Corporation. Another major chunk of the gambling scene had fallen in the lap of your lottery scribe.

For the time being, there would be only small charity casinos. Harcourt also said that the government would soon place 5,000 video lottery terminals (VLTs) into the province's licensed bars.

This sudden leap from the frying pan and into the fire brought his government once again in direct confrontation with the City of Vancouver, along with 40 other municipalities. They despised the idea of slot machines located in stores and pubs and banned any installation of VLTs within their jurisdiction. The BC government quietly backed off and withdrew into its political shell, only to come back later with a far better gaming policy. To be sure, your lottery scribe and his staff of Vic Poleschuk and Rob Egan had a big hand in that creation. By the way, the abhorrence of VLTs is still visible after so many years; BC is the only province without VLTs in bars and pubs.

EDGAR WELCOMES THE BRITISH ROYAL COUPLE

In August of 1994, as sponsors of the Commonwealth Games in Victoria, BCLC received a few executive passes to the CBC-televised concert in honour of Her Majesty the Queen and Prince Philip. Parking around the theatre of the University Centre was at a premium. As usual, BCLC's social animal **Edgar Hildebrandt** was drafted to drive the company passenger van. When he deposited your lottery scribe, his spouse and his colleagues on the steps of the theatre, I asked him how we would meet up after the performance. At the same time, I apologized that I had taken his ticket to the performance for Ina.

"Oh, don't mind me," he said offhandedly. "I will park the van in the area reserved for the police and I might even join you in the theatre."

There was laughter all around because Edgar had neither a pass nor a ticket to gain entrance into the building. Moreover, security for the event was the strictest the City of Victoria had ever witnessed. Even those who should be admitted might not get in.

Before individual passes to the event were issued, extensive criminal background checks had been conducted. Electronically-armed gates scanned the attendees as they entered the theatre. Police and soldiers with scary guns stood on corners and rooftops; it was all quite exciting.

Inside the theatre, the atmosphere was like a library on Sunday morning. Guests in tuxedos and expensive gowns, be-medalled officers and cabinet ministers, both federal and provincial, sat muted in their assigned seats. The invited guests stared like zombies at the empty stage in front of the red curtain, furtively sneaking peeks at the centre balcony where Liz and Phil were to sit.

Deadly silence lasted for a long time until — very audibly — creaking of the stage boards was heard. A broadly smiling man slowly strode onto the stage. Hands clasped behind his back a la Prince Philip, Edgar crossed the stage and exited at the other end, but not before he winked in my direction!

We later learned that he had parked the van in the back of the auditorium. Smiling confidently at everyone, he entered the theatre. Charmed by Edgar's politesse, the event's host, CBC's Peter Gzowski steered him toward the VIP area. It was there that Edgar noticed a briefcase on the floor which caused him to alert the security crew. It was soon realized that the briefcase didn't contain a bomb but was the property of a female RCMP agent. And so it was that Edgar became a "trusted personality" of the RCMP. He was free to roam across the stage where he wickedly grinned at us. At the other side of the stage he met the well-known NDP politician Emery Barnes. Emery invited him to sit beside him in the VIP section. Those of us especially invited to this Royal Visit sat far back in the balcony where we could spot Edgar mingling with the political elite.

KOBLENZ ... A DISAPPOINTMENT

The 1994 September meeting of the INTERTOTO executive committee was held in the Wald Hotel (Forest hotel) near Koblenz. It was a lovely venue that served an excellent German dinner. The meeting chaired by Richard Frigren was all about how he, as the President of INTERTOTO, had fought off and would continue to resist the French hordes of AILE, who were all so eager to conquer INTERTOTO. Nothing of any importance was decided at that meeting except that Reidar Nordby of Norway promoted the idea that INTERTOTO should urge its members to attend the 1996 Vancouver AILE/NASPL meeting.

Disappointed that the goal of merging the two world organizations seemed farther-off than ever, Ina and I drove back to Holland to take a KLM flight to the new Mirabel Airport in Montreal. (As your lottery scribe rehashes these memories more than two decades later, Mirabel Airport is abandoned and facing demolition, since no one could come up with a workable plan to connect the terminal to downtown.)

The purpose of our travel to Montreal was to attend an AILE executive meeting which, as its President, I was obliged to attend. I feared that a similar attitude to resist a merger would prevail at the AILE meeting. Marguerite Bourgeois, a most competent colleague, was not overly committed to a unification of AILE and INTERTOTO but she welcomed us warmly and made English the default language of the meeting.

STRANDED IN A SMOKING LIMO

Ten hours after that boring Koblenz meeting, the vast arrival hall of Mirabel Airport was "busy" with only a few dozen people strolling about. It was good news because there wouldn't be any trouble finding the limousine the AILE people had arranged to drive us to the meeting in downtown Montreal. With the promise of a limo, I felt that your lottery scribe had finally been regarded as someone-of-note in this French language-oriented world lottery group. At the time of my election in Paris, we hadn't even been invited to the President's dinner table, but now, thanks to our good friends at Loto-Quebec, we would get the kind of courtesy accorded to those who preceded me as President. (Your lottery scribe is getting a bit snooty here, don't you think?)

Waiting and waiting at the exit of Mirabel, Ina and I slowly realised there would be neither a limo nor a driver. Pacing back and forth in front of the arrival hall was in vain ... No limo! I finally phoned Loto-Quebec to say there was no limo and we'd happily take a cab to downtown Montreal. But no, the lovely Quebecois voice said that the driver of the limo would be contacted. As I hung up, I was approached by a bleached blonde of a "certain age" dressed in an ill-fitting tuxedo complete with a skewed bow tie. She asked in her best English if we were the "Sea-Mo-Nee" people. We confessed to being members of that tribe. Blondie was to drive us the 50 kilometres into town.

The limo would have been a new one in the years immediately following World War II, but now it smelled funny as we strapped ourselves in for the trip. The smell got stronger as we progressed. When white smoke began to curl from underneath the dashboard, our driver decided to pull off the highway with rush-hour traffic whizzing by at 120 km per hour. She got on her black nyloned-knees and gazed under the car. She gave up and radioed her boss, who said he'd send a replacement limo. The driver threw our luggage onto the grass strip and ordered us out of the car.

For a few minutes the traffic whizzed by until it slowed to a crawl due to an accident up ahead. This afforded the stalled drivers a better view of stragglers standing next to a smoking limo. Most expressions were of the kind that suggested that if we were vain enough to hire a limo, we deserved what we got. Rescued at last by a newer limo, we arrived at the hotel just in time to see the members of the executive committee depart for an expensive dinner downtown. This time we happily dis-invited ourselves and had long leisurely showers followed by dinner. Ina ordered a salmon entrée; a hamburger for me

Before retiring we turned on TV coverage of the Quebec provincial elections. The leader of the Party Quebecois, Jacques Parizeau, was elected Premier. What a memorable day that September 12, 1994!

The business meeting was unique for AILE because your lottery scribe caused the business language to be English, rather than the 40-year old custom of French with English translation. Since all but one delegate from Africa were fluent in English, it caused no problems. The main topic of discussion was how the 1996 AILE meeting in Vancouver would be conducted. Marguerite Bourgeois gave full support to my tentative plans to include participation by NASPL members which made for an easy meeting. I didn't mention the possible participation of INTERTOTO. Best to save that for another day.

306

OVER AND UNDER AND ALMOST OUT

Let's get back to the lottery business. SPORTS ACTION — BCLC's brand of sports lotteries — started its new season in 1994. The new betting game added to the schedule was called "Over and Under." The game is really simple. BCLC publishes the predicted total combined score of say a basketball game and the bettor choses whether that prediction is "Over or Under." To illustrate, BCLC's setting "the line" of a certain basketball game is 195.5 (the .5 is to make sure there is no tie). Now, you must bet whether the actual result will be Over or Under. Under BCLC rules, players couldn't just predict one game, they must predict a minimum of three. The amount of the win is dependent on the amount bet and the number of winning predictions.

On October 27, around noon, **Sam Hui**, BCLC's sports-betting specialist peeked around the door of my office and whispered that there was heavy betting on basketball in Over and Under. Not a little bit, but six times the normal volume. Sam and his people, who had set BCLC's "line" stressed that they had done nothing different from the previous year. Upon staff assurances that everything was alright, I allowed sales to continue, but after lunch the value of bets was increasing rapidly. Something was wrong! But our people kept on insisting there was nothing wrong with the "line." Things looked quite dangerous to me. If the outcome of certain games overturned our predictions, BCLC could be on the hook for 40 times the value of bets accepted.

High-volume, sports-lottery retailers were contacted to find out what kind of player was investing so substantially. The answer was that some of the heavy bets were placed by Vietnamese and also, surprisingly, university students. Large betting amounts are sometimes used to launder drug money. Even if these characters spent a little more than they won, the winnings would be still be "clean."

An exposé that BCLC was being used to launder drug money wouldn't be good for BCLC, nor would paying out huge wins to disreputable characters. I decided to stop all betting on Over and Under.

The Kamloops radio station — generally supportive of our efforts — was on the phone immediately. In a live interview, I said that I didn't know what caused the unusual increase in betting but it might be that we were targeted as a means of laundering money.

All hell broke loose. The media heard "gambling" and "money laundering" and zeroed in on those words. Of course I shouldn't have used those terms; it was just a supposition after hearing about Vietnamese characters betting on basketball. I had goofed with my loose remark. Badly!

That afternoon the Legislature's Question Period was buzzing with questions about money laundering.

 The Minister for Lotteries, **Elisabeth Cull** called your worried scribe in a rather excited state. To add to the melee, the RCMP visited my office within 30 minutes, blaming me for throwing a spotlight on their investigation of drug dealers. The media took a different slant and proclaimed that BCLC had smeared all those players who won a prize in Over and Under as possible crooks. The Minister took to the air to explain I had made a remark without the benefit of knowing the facts. In short, I was painted as a dumb bastard.

Apart from the crazed hullabaloo, there was still a lot of money at risk. Sports Action staff worked with the BCLC Data Centre and analyzed the risk every time another basketball result came in. CTV reported that a group of regular sports bettors had maxed out their credit card and had invited the TV cameras to be with them to watch the basketball game so that the moment of their big win could be featured on the evening news.

By 9:30 that night, with one California basketball game to go, we were on the hook for $8 million more than we had taken in. The big bets were all on "Over." The final score of that last game was "Under." (Sighs of relief!)

We had dodged the bullet. If the actual score had been "over," it might have been "over" for your lottery scribe's employment. I couldn't help but think about that long-ago night when St. Louis upset Montreal in hockey and I had told Ina "Never again."

The prize payout was still four times the amount of the bets, but that was within the acceptable range. It wouldn't cause much of a blip over the entire season. The next day, our security people asked the RCMP to attend the prize payout centre when winners — known for their activities in the illegal pharmaceutical trade — picked up their winnings. Unsavory as they were, we had to pay them!

The Minister of Finance, a bit of a nervous Nellie, sent in a retired CPA to audit our odds-setting policies. The NBA rules had changed from the previous season. It was now possible to earn three points for a basket from an outside position. Our Sports Action people had assumed that this would make no difference since the rules were the same for both teams. It was a logical assumption but the erroneous public perception was that if a basket, or field goal, is made outside of the two-point arc, it would benefit one team but not the other. Over the years the scoring statistics have borne out that our crew's assumptions were correct. As predicted, at the end of the financial year the total payout percentage of prizes paid was no different from statistical norms.

On a final note: The net profit from Over and Under was so small that the board of directors agreed with my recommendation that this type of basketball betting be de-activated. After an eight-year hiatus it has now returned to the BCLC Sports Action line-up with no problems.

THE BLUE MOUNTAINS

In late fall of 1994, Australia's New South Wales asked for a three-day Erewhon course. Vic Poleschuk had offered to come along to assist in the seminars even though the trip would only be a short week at "Down Under."

Ernie O'Keefe of the New South Wales Lottery treated Vic and your lottery scribe royally and treated us to a tour of the Blue Mountains before we settled down for our three-day seminar. The Blue Mountains offer spectacular scenery, plant and wildlife. Ernie O'Keefe told us that the name Blue Mountains comes from the blue haze that hovers above the mountains and that the mist is produced by the oil from the plentiful eucalyptus trees. Trees create smoke? I looked it up. It's true!

The blue haze blanketing the mountains is created in the atmosphere when dispersed droplets of Eucalyptus oil combine with dust particles and water vapour to scatter refracted rays of light. Make a note of that gem. You never know when you'll need an ice-breaker at a boring party.

The experience of presenting EREWHON to the Aussies was quite different from the sessions in Europe, where voicing an opinion was more stifled. These Aussies were exuberant. As part of the EREWHON course, study groups are required to design a new instant lottery. It couldn't be a copy of anything that had been done before. In Europe — generally speaking — this revelation was received with a dull panic and a sense of impossibility. Not so in Australia. In the evening, the challenge was introduced and the next morning FedEx delivered emergency packages from various Australian lottery offices that included some key components for their planned designs.

One memorable, humorous game design was called the "House of Windsor." It spoofed Prince Charles and Diana, made fun of the Queen Mum for her penchant for gin, and mercilessly mocked Prince Philip for his dalliances. The game was clever and parodied the other theme games so perfectly that it won the highest score, which annoyed two students who were avowed monarchists and heckled the winners.

FINLAND

It was still cold in Finland on May 14, 1995, when Michelle McBride joined me to conduct an EREWHON in Finland. The hotel was a quaint, out-of-the-way resort along a frigid arm of the Baltic Sea. In scanning the menu posted on the dining room door, I saw fish, fish, and fish. For breakfast, lunch and dinner. Dried fish-snacks were available at the bar!

When I approached the owner/manager of the hotel about the omnipresence of fish, he admonished me jokingly (?) not to be like Helmut Kohl, the German Prime Minister who at a recent official dinner at their hotel asked: "What's with these people and their fucking fish? I hate fish." The hotel manager laughed uproariously at his use of the American epithet. I did not tell him that I concurred with Helmut Kohl's remark. Old stiff-necked Helmut was braver than I would be in expressing his malevolent thoughts about fish.

The Finnish EREWHON students were mostly young managers who approached the seminar with awe and, I suppose, trepidation. The session turned out to be quite different from EREWHON in the Blue Mountains of Australia. The Finns, I know — with noteworthy exceptions — are utterly devoid of humour. They find it difficult to engage in frivolous conversations or to display any variation from the norm of formal Finnish behaviour.

I believe my EREWHON audience viewed your lottery scribe's style of teaching through humorous incidents, as if the director of the asylum had just joined the inmates. It is not for nothing that a well-known Swedish proverb has it that the definition of hell is heaven with Finns in charge of entertainment.

By the end of the third day, at the evening dinner and farewell, the young executives unwound and tackled the task of consuming stunning amounts of vodka with great diligence. Calla Nyberg, one of the very few Finns who is able to produce a wide-open grin, brought-in a jazz-loving, professional bass player from Helsinki. He and your musical scribe played all the old jazz favourites on the luscious grand piano in the lobby. It redeemed the dullness, the cold and the fish although I didn't drink any vodka that night. I had to keep up with that great bassist.

A SPEECH 15 KILOMETERS FROM HOME

In August of 1995, the European Association of State Lotteries held its annual conference at the Dutch coastal resort of Noordwijk. The seaside town is situated a mere 15 kilometres from the home of my youth. As a child, I had always admired the big "Huis ter Duin" the luxury hotel on the coast of the North Sea. I often imagined how rich these people were who could afford to stay there.

I was to speak before the international gathering of 66 European state lottery organizations, advertised as the "lottery guru," from Canada (I didn't originate that term "guru"; that's what the program said). It was just another business speech but the real reason for my attendance was to promote the '96 World Meet conference in Vancouver.

Richard Frigren, was still hesitating to participate in the world conference but I was confident that he would relent. The performance in Holland went well and enthusiasm to attend in Vancouver was evident.

SYDNEY, SOUTH NEW WALES

October 10, 1995. Another round of globe-trotting by your intrepid scribe and his spouse landed us first in Sydney. Mike Howell — the genial general manager of the New South Wales Lottery — took us under his wing and conducted a tour of the scenic corners of that great Australian state. This was our third visit to Sydney and this tour, especially through the small towns along the Eastern coast, made such a delightful difference from the traditional Harbour Tour and the oohs and aahs over the Sydney Opera. We learned some

strange sounding place names. I remember Wollongong as one of those tongue-twisters. After a delightful three days of fun and teaching we took a four-hour flight to Perth, a beautiful city along the coast of the Indian Ocean where the 1995 INTERTOTO was being hosted by **Jan Stewart,** the charming leader of the Western Australian lottery.

PERTH, WESTERN AUSTRALIA

Originally, Ina and I intended to drive from Sydney to Perth but the 4,000-kilometre trek through that lonesome territory called "The Outback" did not appeal to us. We were told that one particular stretch was a ruler-straight 250 kilometres where the only required driving skill would be to dodge a wandering kangaroo and we might not see another human being for many hours. So we flew instead. In Perth we were met by Jan Stewart who took us to the Burswood Casino and Hotel, the site of the '95 INTERTOTO Conference.

Despite my obstreperous stance at the previous INTERTOTO Conference in Hong Kong, where I refused the demotion to Second Vice President, Jan Stewart gave me the opportunity to promote the cause of one single world lottery organization.

I had already ensured that the 1996 AILE conference in Vancouver would be joined by the North American Association of State and Provincial Lotteries annual meeting, where the speakers' program would intermesh. In Perth, I invited INTERTOTO to join the special conference, thereby making it the first true gathering of the world's major lottery organizations.

Richard Frigren was still fearful that such a close cooperation might lead to a merger that, in turn, would cause the disappearance of the INTERTOTO organization. He had, of course, good reason to be concerned because that was exactly what I had in mind. However, it was difficult for him to continue to ignore World Meet '96 in Vancouver because three quarters of the INTERTOTO membership would be there as members of AILE.

At the Perth trade show, our BCLC booth promoting the '96 Vancouver Conference, attracted a high level of interest. After totaling up the many responses, we estimated that a crowd of 1,400 delegates and spouses would attend, compared with the normal attendance of a world gathering of 800. Your lottery scribe became hopeful that a unified world organization could be a reality by the start of the year 2000.

 My business speech to the assembly was on a tepid topic that even I didn't care about. A huge laugh came when I spoke after the introduction by the lottery minister of Western Australia, a fine gentleman called **Max Evans**. His accent — combined with extremely rapid speech — was so foreign to most non-Australian attendees that they looked at each other for interpretation. My speech began by saying it was the first time an INTERTOTO Conference featured five official languages: French, German, Spanish, English and whatever language it was that the honourable minister Evans just spoke.

From the peal of laughter, it was obvious that I wasn't the only one who couldn't decode the "Strine" language (A fun Australian dictionary defines "Strine" as the language spoken by 'real' Australians). After I stepped down from the dais, the minister approached me, jokingly wagging his finger and speaking to me in Strine where the only two words I could decipher were Kinneder and Trantaw, which I assumed to be the names of my country and the capitol city of Ontario.

Jan Stewart was aghast at my ridiculing her minister but Max laughed the loudest. It was a memorable moment.

In those days, INTERTOTO would devote a whole program day to a tour for all delegates and spouses. In Perth, the wonderfully kind organizers arranged a trip to a real Australian ranch complete with cattle and ranch hands. From experience we knew that it was best to take our own transportation to and from these events. Otherwise we would be left in the caring hands of the organizers who would decide the length of our stay.

BCLC chairman Patrick Chen, who had accompanied Ina and me to the conference, rented a car with right-hand drive and we prevailed on him to follow the buses out to this working ranch. Upon arrival, the first person we ran into was the Chairman of the China Welfare Lottery, a certain Mr. Chen. I took great delight to introduce my Chairman Chen to the Chinese Chairman Chen. They chatted in Mandarin for a while and smiled a lot. I asked Patrick: "What did he say?"

"He wanted to know what village I was from. I told him I was born in Calgary and my grandfather was born in Vancouver but that I believed my great-grandfather came from Hana, in the province of Hunan and he said he knew of the village and the family."

These Chinese folks have long-time connections!

The picnic at the Western Australia ranch will be forever burned in my memory. Flies. Flies. Flies, almost as pervasive as fish, fish, fish in Finland but much more annoying. I had seen these Australian sheepherding hats with little floating balls suspended from the brim but I thought it was just a weird decoration. Immediately I wanted a hat like that because the motion of the little balls kept the flies off your face. Not ten flies or twenty or thirty — hundreds of hungry flies would swarm around your head, not to mention your picnic plate. It was a great party and... we got out safely.

SINGAPORE: ONE "FINE" CITY

On October 28, 1995, we flew from Perth INTERTOTO Conference to Singapore. A "fine" city, our GTECH host Raymond (Ray) Leung joked. There is a fine for dropping paper on the sidewalk, a fine for not wearing a mask when suffering a cold and a fine if you drive to the neighbouring country of Malaysia with a tank of gas that is less than full. Singapore has been cited as the most over-regulated country/city on the globe, yet in all the global surveys about happiness, the people of Singapore are found to be happiest of all (Perhaps they'd get fined if they voiced what they really thought).

After checking in at the famous Raffles Hotel, Ray showed us the bar made famous by the eminent writer Somerset Maugham and widely acknowledged as the original home of the Singapore Sling. A century-old Raffles tradition demands that when a peanut is cracked open, the shells are thrown onto the floor. Ina, who wasn't aware of the tradition, thought we had chosen the filthiest bar in town; I don't think she believed the story about the tradition. One thing that Somerset Maugham didn't tell you in his book is that every half hour a servant with a broom and dustpan shows up to reduce the height of the mess by a couple of centimeters or so.

The next day Ina and I were guests of honour at the annual Singapore horse racing event, a splendid occasion, with top-hatted gents, formally dressed ladies, tuxedoed waiters and a lavishly attired military band leading a marching regiment of Ghurkhas. Ina and I felt we cast in a historical drama.

The next morning, we left for London but not before Ray presented a silk tie and silk to me and a silk scarf to Ina! We were most appreciative of the gesture. The gifts probably cost less than an ounce of Johnnie Walker Blue.

CANADIAN REFERENDUM ON SEPARATION

October 30, 1995. Leaving Australia, I wanted to get some Dutch and British pounds for the rest of our trip. I tried at least four different ATMs in Sydney but none of them accepted my debit card. I would have to try in Heathrow. While we were flying to London over India and Pakistan, the people of Québec were voting whether their province should remain part of Canada.

Eager for news, we disembarked the Boeing 747 at Heathrow, where we asked the first airline employee we saw if he knew about the referendum.

"Canada won by a hair," he announced cheerfully.

The ATM at Heathrow proudly showed a sign that Canadian Dollars were back in circulation. That explained the unwillingness of the Australian banks to offer us a currency exchange.

Ina and I were pleased that Canada would survive to continue to argue about Quebec's place in Canada for at least another generation or two.

CLUB KENO

Settled back in the BCLC routine, your travel-weary scribe was called to the office of the Minister of Finance, Elisabeth Cull in 1995. She had been briefed on my recommendation to replace the current KENO with a draw every 5-minutes, a change that — according to your lottery scribe — would yield a 400% increase in profits. I sensed that the Minister feared to learn too much about gambling, a topic she abhorred, because she didn't ask any questions. Her only demand was that there be no publicity. I assured her we could get the job done without any adverse public reaction.

Learning from the KENO experience in South Australia, your lottery scribe knew this change would be a real money-maker. It had taken almost a decade to get KENO accepted by the public as a game played other than in a casino.

The essence of KENO is that more numbers are drawn than it takes to win; thereby the player gets to choose his or her own odds of winning a prize. "Choose an easy way to win: you can win a little. Choose to make it difficult for yourself: you can win a lot."

Back in 1985, ten years before, I had launched LOTTO WEST. It was a keno format but we didn't dare call it that, since the KENO name alone would arouse the anti-gambling crowd.

Only now — years after the introduction LOTTO WEST — did we have the nerve to call the game by its proper name. The lawyers, wary of possible legal action, strongly urged us to call it CLUB KENO to distinguish it somewhat from the Vegas game. The change of name didn't do anything to increase sales but the name KENO was now out in front.

1. How many spots (numbers) do you want to play?

1	2	3	4	5	6	7	8	9	10
11	12	13	14	15	16	17	18	19	20

2. Pick your numbers

1	2	3	4	5	6	7	8	9	10
11	12	13	14	15	16	17	18	19	20
21	22	23	24	25	26	27	28	29	30
31	32	33	34	35	36	37	38	39	40
41	42	43	44	45	46	47	48	49	50
51	52	53	54	55	56	57	58	59	60
61	62	63	64	65	66	67	68	69	70
71	72	73	74	75	76	77	78	79	80

KENO in its most popular format calls for 20 numbers to be drawn from a field of 80, providing more opportunity for players to assemble their own favourite set of numbers; a participant could play as few as 4-out-of-20 or as many as 10-out-of-20 and everything else in between.

Minister Cull's condition to have no publicity was not really a problem. To make the change from BC KENO to CLUB KENO all we had to do was nearly double the prize payout percentage, increase the game's field to 80 numbers and increase the frequency of drawing from once a day to 216 times a day (18 hours at 12 draws per hour). Moreover, we would start selling the game at 600 additional outlets including licensed bars and pubs.

Surprisingly, for a lottery-adverse government such as the NDP, the proposal was approved by a small committee of cabinet.

The name change didn't require massive advertising. The new name CLUB KENO just appeared out of the blue. Using in-store point-of-sale material and a write-up in *Luck Magazine*, the game became an immediate hit. Later, comparing year to year sales, CLUB KENO produced more than 10 times the profit of the game it replaced.

Because the introduction was done without any fanfare, there was not a whisper of criticism. Any lingering fears on our part disappeared when actual experience showed that the new keno game did not appear to increase the prevalence of problem gambling.

A few battles were fought, especially with my home city of Delta, BC. Their complaints were based on a misunderstanding by local politicos who didn't do their homework. Vaguely aware that KENO was played in Las Vegas and casinos had slot machines, they deduced that KENO had to be a slot machine. Delta didn't want a casino with slot machines. Still we had to go to court to get the Delta ban of KENO dropped. (Delta wound up paying all court costs.)

Despite the success of this fast-paced KENO game, no lottery organization in Canada could persuade its regulators to let them operate a 5-minute KENO game in retail locations and bars.

Today KENO still operates in BC and will celebrate its 25th year in 2019. And as I write this, Delta Council is avidly promoting a new casino with 400 slot machines and several dozen card tables near the Massey Tunnel.

PREMIER HARCOURT RESIGNS

The Vancouver Sun published a cartoon showing a mock gravestone with an inscription that blamed the BC Premier for the Nanaimo lottery scandal. It took just 15 days for the cartoon to prove prophetic for the hapless Mike Harcourt. On November 27 1995, the 52-year-old politician told reporters gathered in the basement of the BC legislature that he would resign as soon as his party chose a successor. "A new leader who will be free of some of the baggage that I have been harnessed with," an emotional Harcourt declared.

Even his critics found it a noble decision to give another leader a chance to rescue the NDP from impending oblivion. "Faced with a succession of disabling controversies almost since his government won election in October 1991, Mr. Harcourt has done the right thing," said Gordon Campbell, the Liberal Leader of the Opposition. The NDP stalwarts were happy because their election chances were improved. For most other British Columbians, Harcourt's departure caused months of indecision and policy drift. A successor would find it difficult to restore the party's standing in time to avoid defeat in the looming election.

For Harcourt, a lawyer, it was a dispiriting end to nearly a quarter century in pursuit of political consensus. In 1991, he led the party to a landslide victory over the Social Credit party, which had been left discredited and demoralized by the forced resignation of disgraced premier Bill Vander Zalm. In contrast to the So-Cred record, Harcourt promised clean, open government and an end to British Columbia's history of poisonous, partisan politics.

That good feeling lasted just seven months. In May, 1992, there were allegations that the Nanaimo Commonwealth Holding Society (NCHS), an NDP association had diverted bingo revenue supposedly meant for charity, to political purposes. Harcourt denied any links existed between the NDP bingo and his party — but ordered a provincial investigation into its affairs.

The Nanaimo Commonwealth Holding Society (NCHS), a non-profit group masterminded by David Stupich, an NDP MLA, sold lottery tickets and operated charitable bingo games with the proceeds going to the party's objectives instead of local charities. It had been a scandal that refused to go away. Like a virus that the government could not shake, the NCHS controversy, dubbed "Bingo-gate" by colourful columnists, kept returning to public attention as a series of investigations that shed an ever-more penetrating light on the society's

318

activities. The NDP-appointed auditor disclosed that the NDP-linked Nanaimo society diverted funds earmarked for charity to a party propaganda newspaper and used charity revenue to pay for BC delegates to attend a national leadership convention in Winnipeg. It also violated NDP policy by disguising the source of hundreds of thousands of dollars in corporate donations. In practice, the report declared, the Nanaimo society had "acted as a hidden bank for the NDP."

Harcourt reacted by naming yet another party committee to examine the auditor's report — a waffling response that seemed finally to crystallize his own party's mounting impatience with his leadership. Asked the same day by reporters in Victoria whether he had considered stepping down, Harcourt snapped: "I'm not going to resign. I believe what I've done is right. I'm prepared to be judged on that." Pressured by his NDP colleagues, Harcourt resigned, on February 22, 1996.

By then, quitting had been on Harcourt's mind for months. He later acknowledged that he had been toying with stepping down ever since May because mounting criticism of his leadership had "taken its toll on me personally, on me politically and most importantly on my family."

FAST FORWARD: In 1999, Dave Stupich who had been the mastermind of the "Bingo-gate" scandal faced 64 criminal charges of theft, fraud, forgery and breach of trust. He pleaded guilty to fraud and running an illegal lottery, involving the misappropriation of about $1 million from the NCHS. He was penalized with two years in jail but was allowed to serve his sentence with electronic monitoring at his daughter's home in Nanaimo. The NDP repaid $115,000, a fraction of the millions of dollars that had been siphoned away.)

WHO IS NEXT?

Leading the roster bidding for Harcourt's job was Employment and Investment Minister Glen Clark, aged 38. Aggressive and intelligent, the former

labor organizer was a hawk among cabinet leftists. As Finance Minister, Clark was the author of the NDP's first two, hugely unpopular budgets. But he had not yet shaken off his tax-and-spend image. The future looked like an up-hill battle for the NDP. The Liberals outpolled the NDP 2 to 1 in an Angus Reid survey. Despite all of that, on February 28 1996, the membership of the NDP elected **Glen Clark** as its leader.

AHEAD: A COMPLETE GAMING CORPORATION 1996-2000

STATE OF BCLC

While spinning this tale, your lottery scribe has told you all kinds of things about BCLC but hasn't spoken about the growth of the BCLC operation. Well, here's the update. In January of 1996, the sales network consisted of 2,200 online retailers, 100 off-line sellers and a social gaming network of 640 bars, cafés and restaurants where Club Keno and break-open tickets were sold. Sales for 1995/96 were close to $800 million. We were now gunning for $1 billion in sales before the year 2000 and a lot more if we were charged with the development and operation of casinos in BC.

NAPA VALLEY

In spring of 1996, **Frances Kenny**, the ablest of assistants and your lottery scribe travelled to San Francisco to conduct an Erewhon seminar in Napa. Frances had booked a one-story hotel, far away from the enticement of nightclubs and sophisticated dining because — as at every Erewhon — the participants are inundated with problem solving from morning to midnight for most of the three days and they absolutely must not be distracted.

The attendees were a mix of Canadians and Americans who engaged in spirited the group discussions in their so-called "consultant offices". These rooms faced the hotel's front garden — a pleasant view of the rich display of California flowers. (In February, that was a rarity for most Erewhonians)

By mid-morning on the second day, the pleasant study atmosphere changed when a backhoe appeared and started digging in the garden in front of the Erewhon discussion rooms. Frances ran to the management offices to demand an immediate halt of operations to protect the training program but the owners countered that the backhoe had been booked long before Erewhon was scheduled. Frances was not to be deterred; she demanded refunds, discounts, whatever! The owners — who were also proprietors of a small winery down the road — appeased her by bringing in cases of California chardonnay, the contents of which were evenly distributed among the discussion rooms.

Each group had six students and got six bottles. Frances cautioned them to preserve the nectar of the gods for the evening. Moreover, it would have to last two days. The seminar attendees, however, reasoned that the backhoe might not come back the next morning and they needed to get the loud digging machine noise out of their heads. Now!

At the end of every morning and afternoon session, a debrief brings resolution to the group discussions. One couldn't help but notice that the noon-hour repartee was much more spirited and garrulous than at any other Erewhon. However, in the afternoon, the discussion resembled TV news clips of stormy sessions in the parliaments of Taiwan or Guatemala, where deputies climb over their desks shouting at colleagues while others need to be restrained from committing acts of violence. It was a bit like that, but all in good fun.

A young man from Ontario slipped into a Fred Astaire song-and-dance act while making his point; a woman from Washington State, so shy at the outset, stood on a chair to loudly defend her solution to the case of the cancelled ticket.

During dinner, Frances checked the discussion rooms and reported that enough wine was left to fuel the midnight-oil-burning session where each group would create an instant scratch game "from scratch", so to speak. One could only speculate what wild designs might come out of that.

Indeed, the group presentations of proposed new games were in a class by themselves. One group presented their game concept of the "luck" of getting pooped on by birds. Various prize categories were in direct relation to the respective points of the drop, if you catch my drift. On top of that, the group was dressed in old clothes covered in grey and white splotches.

The farewell dinner was at the winery of Robert Mondavi — as if these happy seminarians needed more wine.

INSTANT SCRATCH GAMES

Your lottery scribe has referred a few times to scratch-off tickets as one of the important money earners of the BCLC lottery portfolio. The reason for not talking about every single new issue is that scratch tickets are ever-present but very few names of the games lived very long. In my time, more than 130 different scratch games were brought to the market. That kind of presence deserves more comment than this tale has offered so far. In the period of 1983 - 2000, more than $1.6 billion worth of scratch tickets were sold.

INSTANT SCRATCH-ITS

In the '80s, European lotteries started noticing the success of instant/scratch lotteries in North America. The idea of instant games aroused not only their curiosity but an incentive to replicate the profits from this "new" lottery within their own organizations.

Your lottery scribe was invited by the German lottery to a seminar in Münster, where product managers of several Northern European lotteries came to hear what North America had learned about instant games.

I hope you may be interested in reading my presentation to that seminar. This article contains everything you'd want to know about instant games. If you would like to skip this tale about how scratch games work, feel free to advance to the next subject... but perhaps you should take a little peek?

WHAT DO YOU CALL THOSE THINGS?

The oldest form of an instant game is the German "Losbrief", a folded piece of paper, which when opened, reveals either a prize or the rather curt comment "LEIDER NICHT" which literally means: "Sorry, nothing!" A Teutonic dismissal not very pleasing to the player, one might think.

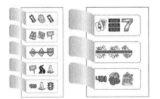

A technically more advanced format of an instant-win game is the "break-open" or "pull-tab" game. When the flaps on the back of the ticket are opened, symbols such as cherries, lemons and oranges (or other creative icons) are revealed. Perhaps three cherries might yield a top prize of say $50 while three lemons may bring a smaller prize. With three or more window flaps as part of the ticket, the enjoyment of play is somewhat more pleasant when compared to "Sorry, Nothing!". As your talkative scribe will go on and on about instant scratch games in this section, the discussion about those pull-tabs will show up again farther down. Just wait for it.

The name to describe the lottery game where the outcome is already known but the players must reveal the result in some way, has gone through several names. In the early '80s the name was "instant" which referred to a closed pouch or a latex-covered ticket that, when scratched, revealed a win or loss. When the majority of instant tickets became scratch-off tickets, the name "scratch and win" became more prominent. But when tickets were introduced that featured extended play those games could hardly be called "instant."

One of the more time-consuming scratch games is "**Crossword**", a ticket that features a standard crossword grid covered with latex where spaces must be scratched to reveal letters of a word.

First released in BC in June of 1998, those types of time-consuming games like "Crossword" reached a total of $29 million in three years, which represented almost 16% of scratch tickets sold during that period.

Today's scratch-off/instant game offers more stimulation than the earliest versions. Graphics, color schemes, ticket sizes, themes and game variety, even smell, produce a rich set of ingredients for a game that relies on impulse buying.

When the Western Canada Lottery launched its first instant games in 1982, annual sales in BC were around $5 million. When I retired (January 1, 2000) scratch-ticket sales for the previous year had reached $180 million.

SO WHAT'S THE SECRET?

If you ask a cynical person why lotteries are popular and the answer will likely be that people are desperate and want to win big to "relieve their hopeless lives." (Or any other dramatic variation upon that theme.) But when asked to explain the phenomenon of scratch-off ticket success, where the top prizes are around $5,000 to $10,000, those critics are at a loss.

So what *is* the attraction? There is no 'Dream Prize'. Not even a prize that will make any great impact on people's lives other than perhaps, a nice vacation or some new furniture. Playing instant games cannot arouse the hope of becoming rich. One must ask, "If the size of the prize is the prime factor in the attraction of lottery tickets, why do instant games have such appeal?"

Many will suggest it's instant gratification. Your contrary scribe disagrees. Instant gratification implies impatience. The inability to wait. To hate delays. "Must have it now!" This character trait is related to gluttony, envy and lack of self-control. That is not an issue with a scratch-off lottery ticket.

The answer to the success of the scratch-off games is to be found in a more positive human trait than instant gratification. Curiosity is a better description. Curiosity is nature's way of learning. Curiosity is to play. To test. To explore. To find something of interest or value. It is curiosity that causes people to learn by experience. Watch two puppies engage in a pretend fight learning how to attack and defend. Watch a toddler's intense drive to walk or crawl to an object that has aroused his or her curiosity. A kitten does not even need a mouse to get excited. Chasing a ball of wool or its own tail will do. Curiosity never stops.

Curiosity requires an anticipated reward. Unanswered curiosity is frustrating. There must be a realistic expectation of a new experience or new knowledge. The shorter the period before the outcome is known, the more the enjoyment rises. On the other hand, when the outcome is delayed, (e.g. monthly draws) the excitement fades. The short period before knowing the outcome also feeds the impulse to play again and again.

Instant tickets are a discovery game with a possible reward. Under a thin cover of latex may await something of value. It attracts interest and attention.

Buying an instant ticket is hardly ever a planned purchase. It is a safe bet that few shopping lists have ever included a reminder to buy a scratch ticket. But... a big but...to create the impulse to buy a scratch ticket, it needs to be noticed. It must arouse curiosity. Therefore the game must be openly displayed. Instant lottery tickets hidden in a drawer will not sell. When displayed, the game must have appeal. Therefore titles, colours and themes are important. As an aside, the player shouldn't be misled. If the game is named "MONOPOLY" and shows the parlor game's logo, the player expects some similarity to that familiar concept. If the game has no relationship to the real MONOPOLY, it will be a major turn-off. It will fail.

While a favourite numbers game of Lotto will be played for many years, players tire of scratch-games more quickly than any other lottery. The player does not get weary of playing scratch-off games in general, but they do get tired of specific games. This is natural. With repeated effort and little success, the urge to change one's luck with another game is obvious.

To avoid those turn-offs, games must offer intermittent success in order to delay frustration. A winner in one-of-four tickets or at worst one- out-of-six is necessary to keep the game going for an extended period.

One of the ways to delay the 'tiring' of the game is to create different looking tickets within the same game —variety within variety. For example, in an instant game with the theme of 'Winter Sport', the pictures within that issue may offer twelve different sports. To be sure, there is only one prize fund for the game. While such a multi-image game is colorful, its purpose is to delay the "tiring" factor. Players will reason: "Well, I tried "figure skating" several times but I have not yet tried that "ski-jumping" ticket.

Sometimes, for reasons unknown, games have a lifespan of many years. That game can be brought back, successfully, time and time again. In BC the game 'Gold Rush' has been issued again and again over the years. If we only knew what the secret of this longevity was, we would have created more.

DISPLAY: A player of an instant game should have the freedom to select a particular ticket. The retailer is an important factor in that free choice. A retailer who reaches under the counter, produces a scratch ticket from a hidden supply and hands it over to the customer is a scratch-lottery killer. If retailers only knew how this action displeases the players, they would shed this terrible habit. If a ticket — so presented — is a non-winner, it raises suspicion of the retailer.

Instead, the entire range of tickets should be displayed (under a glass cover for security) so that the customer is able to buy the ticket that he or she selected. No player should ever be handed a ticket, "Here, take this!"

Seeing the ticket displayed is not all that's required. If at first glance it is not interesting, the impulse to buy is likely to end right there. The visible qualities of the ticket can be expressed in color, shape, name or theme, graphics and in some special cases, aroma.

Game designers must consider price, prizes, frequency of winning and play value — the process of discovering the prize. An example of poor play value is a single spot which, when scratched, reveals the answer. It's efficient, accurate

328

and understandable, but it is too quick and is poisonous to the success of a game. The best solutions let players win or lose slowly.

COLOR AND GRAPHICS: Ask the experts who design packaged goods. They know about the attraction of color. Just as the brightest, liveliest colors attract the bees, so will the visual sensation of instant games attract the lottery player.

A lottery ticket is a document that could yield a substantial financial return. If the ticket looks like it is printed on a cardboard cereal box combined with badly drawn cartoon characters, and pastel-pale, Sunday-morning-newspaper-cartoon-colors, it will not be an appealing game.

TICKET QUALITY: It is wrong for a game designer to opt for cheap-looking tickets in order to get the lowest possible bid from a printer. When game designers think nothing of raising prize fund percentages by 20% or more, it is difficult to understand why they would skimp on the quality of ticket printing when a cost increase of 1% spent on ticket printing will yield a far more marketable product.

SHAPE OF TICKET: Most scratch tickets are a standard size with some creative exceptions made possible by die-cuts. Tickets shaped in the form of Santa Claus' boot were successful in the Christmas period. Images of Volkswagen Beetles have had their day of fame in the die-cut hall of fame.

Oversized ladybugs and 45 rpm records have been among the most unlikely but noteworthy die-cut tickets, all aimed at catching the eye of the impulsive buyer.

TITLES AND THEMES: More than a thousand instant/scratch game names have been registered over the past decades. All to prevent boredom. Many successful themes are copied by other lottery jurisdictions. Themes include sports, gambling, money synonyms such as moolah or bananas, precious metals like gold, silver and diamonds, treasures, riches, wealth, banks and vaults. Not to mention outlandish themes like "Read my lips" and "Let's do the wild thing."

From time to time a scent has been added to the scratch tickets. From a candy smell for Valentine tickets, coffee, peppermints and even bacon! Scratch 'n Sniff never got the top endorsement of the buyer. It sold, but didn't increase sales a great deal. It does serve as a short-time novelty. (Some retailers who absorbed the smell in their clothes, hated it when they came home.)

GAME DESIGN: The prime directive is that the player must be entertained. An instant lottery ticket does not deliver a positive experience at least 75% of the time. That is a frequency of winning a prize of 1 in 4 which still means that 3 out of 4 times is a non-winner. What else can be offered? Play Value is a concept not easily understood by a logical, practical personality. Such practical lottery people say "Let's give them result fast." Wrong!

In my saying 'wrong', the reader should not conclude that a waiting period of hours before knowing if you won or lost would make an excellent instant game. We are talking a maybe 20 seconds of play value. That's all.

"COMING CLOSE." The player should also get the feeling that he or she *almost* won. In the game format called 'Match 3' there are six latex covered spaces. Each spot, when scratched, shows an amount of money. If there are three identical amounts, you win that prize.

If an inexperienced game designer places a different prize amount in each of the six areas, he or she is dead-wrong. By doing so, the process of losing is speeded up, when slowing down is a requirement. It is far better to put two similar amounts in the grid area as often as feasible. Any player who scratches two squares of $10,000 is excited to think that one more scratch may yield a $10,000 prize. The same feeling for a $5 win. Such a close loss represents play value. Hence, *"Coming Close"* is a very important play value and should be built into the game design.

"Scratch-off bingo" takes the process of extended play further. It takes considerably longer play than a standard scratch game, sometimes five or six minutes or more. This constitutes added play value for those who like to take the time to play. Other extended-play values are popular, Monopoly and Crossword, to mention a few. All have the same attribute in common. Play time!

PRIZES: The size of the prize is not directly proportional to the success of *instant* lottery games. Instant scratch games will not change your life. That spot is reserved for Lotto games. The two games have totally different appeals.

In a standard instant game, prizes in the range of $5-$10,000 are quite acceptable unless that market has been spoiled by frequent higher prize amounts. Of course, the size of the prize make does a difference but several experiments have shown that a small top prize with more prize money devoted to the lower tier prizes will likely be more successful than a large top prize with fewer bottom prizes.

During one test period, three different $1 tickets were on the BC market at the same time. The "WINTER GAMES" ticket featured images of Olympic winter sports with top prizes of $ 10,000. Close by in the retailer's display case, was COLD CASH offering a $ 5,000 prize, while a third game called BANCO had a top prize of $1,000. All three games did well but the BANCO game with a lot of smaller prizes proved more popular because the odds of winning any prize were far better than the other two. By the way, the other two sold reasonably well.

Prizes in the "middle" of the prize list look nice on advertising pamphlets but game designers should not put a lot of prize money in the middle range. As an incentive to buy the ticket, the mid-range prize means very little. No buyer focuses on the mid-range prize. By all means there should be some middle prizes, but a lot of small prizes are what make the scratch/instant lottery a success. It may sound cynical but $2 and $5 prizes are not really prizes to take home. Insiders call them "short-term loans." Ten dollars may entice the player to walk away with the prize. However, winners of $2 or $5 invariably turn those winnings into new tickets. The phenomenon is called "the churn," a name borrowed from stock-brokers.

A "churn" example: A player buys five $1 tickets and wins $2, which he/she turns into 2 more tickets, one of which wins $5, with which the player buys five more tickets that yield a $2 winner, which when the $2 is re-invested in two more tickets turn out to be losers. The player's result is that a total of $5 worth of tickets yielded nothing; nada! That is correct! However, the lottery's accounts show that $14 worth of tickets were sold and $9 was paid out in prizes and that is correct too! That is the 'churn' in action.

ABOUT PRICE: In the early days of instant scratch tickets the conventional thinking was that if instant games are really an impulse item then the price should be of such low value that the decision to buy should be a whim of the moment, a bit of fun.

When your lottery scribe wrote this presentation years ago, he wrote: Spending one dollar is an impulse; five dollars is a decision. Early on, five dollars for an instant ticket was considered out-of-line. But as inflation slowly nibbled away, the two-dollar ticket made its appearance. To overcome buyer resistance $2 tickets were introduced featuring two games on the same ticket although all prizes came from the same prize allocation. In an administrative sense it was really one ticket but the player perceived it as two one-dollar tickets presented

on one ticket. It was a bit of a subterfuge but it assisted in raising the general price. The $5 and $10 ticket broke through the barrier of price resistance by the same method: five ways to play on one ticket and a big main prize of a $100,000 or more. Illustrated here is even a $30 instant scratch ticket.

A small issue, sometimes overlooked, is that instant ticket sales should be able to be completed with one bill or one coin. A $2.50 ticket which requires a minimum of three currency units (A $2.00-dollar coin or bill and two quarters). This multiple output of money tends to detract from the impulse. One monetary unit for one ticket is the right way to go.

PRIZE FUND: In the early days, scratch lotteries had a standard prize fund dedication of 45% of sales. In some U.S. jurisdictions lottery law mandated such a percentage. However, game designers soon looked to slot machines for the secret of "churn." After all, a slot machine is a just machine version of an instant game. Prize dedication for slot machines is about 80%-90% of sales.

Remember this: Frequent winnings are the attraction to keep on playing but the initial motivation is winning the prize. Early instant game-designers were loath to follow the lessons of the slot machine. To test the waters from time to time and to let the players get a feel for the more frequent win-experience, 'ratchet' games were introduced. These games — issued infrequently and not advertised as such — offered as much as 80% in prize funds. The object of the 'ratchet' game was somewhat devious. The idea was that once the players experienced the high payout success and thus increased their success, they would continue to do so when regular prize funds came back. One does not hear much about 'ratchet' games anymore. Players are a lot smarter those days.

However, prize fund percentages have been steadily rising over the years and that is where a debate begins. Retailers want higher dollar sales to increase their commission. Lottery management want higher overall profits.

The question becomes: Will there be an increase in *net* profit when extra money is dedicated to the small bottom prizes and thereby increase the frequency of winning?

An example: When the prize fund is raised from 45% to 60%, gross profit is reduced from 55% to 40%. (Forget about commissions for a second.)

An issue of 10 million S1 tickets at a 45% prize amount yields a gross profit $5.5 million. But, to achieve that same $5.5 million gross profit while offering a 60% prize fund, the lottery must sell 14.7 million tickets (including the cost of printing extra tickets) just to break even. *Almost 50% more tickets must be sold!*

Game designers must balance the wish for higher sales with those of profit. Do not discount the possibility that once the market has a taste of high-frequency-win games, it will be difficult to go back to more profitable games.

There is a certain misalignment of interests in these high-prize percentage games. The players win more, the tickets printer earns more, the retailer earns more but lottery management must create a huge increase in sales or risk a reduction in the profits they have become used to.

SPECIAL EVENTS: As I write this, a few North American lottery organizations have not yet embraced the idea of designing tickets for special days. Yet, such a promotional issue can be quite effective. While the selling periods for Father's Day and Mother's Day tickets are short, the low ticket price makes these issues an attractive casual gift. (

Valentine's Day is another such gift-giving event, especially in conjunction with gift card companies who were quick to produce greeting cards writing witty sayings like: "It's not the thought but the money that counts."

FREE TICKETS AS A PRIZE: "Win a Free Ticket" is a phenomenon dating back to the early days of instant games. The argument was: "What does it matter? It's a prize and doesn't cost anything." Not true! The ticket printer charges for those "free" tickets and the retailers want commission for selling them. Moreover, free tickets dilute the prize fund. Most players don't appreciate a free ticket. In a game of chance getting your own money back is not considered a win. More combative players can even consider getting their money back to be a slap in the face.

Because the instant game has been positioned as a butterfly — a whimsy — players do not always pay a whole lot of attention to detail and hardly ever read the instructions (that are often printed in mouse-sized print). Therefore, a sudden change in the format of "how-to-play", is risky.

For example: For years BCLC featured instant games of a "Match 3" format, then suddenly introduced a game where the play area consisted of an outer ring of six small circles with a small circle in the center. If you matched the amount of the outer circles with the amount in the center circle, you won that amount. In other words: "Match *two* identical amounts and you win." Simple? No sir! Conditioned for years to match three amounts, many winners discarded their winning ticket in the belief they had to match three. Only 75% of the prizes available were cashed, despite the explanation on the ticket, TV ads and the point-of-sale material.

On another occasion, an extra 'tear-off' portion of the ticket was issued as a "consolation" game. The extra chance to win went unscratched by thousands of players. The moral: In designing instant games, be cautious in stepping off the well-traveled path.

Here's another innovation that looked promising but proved to be a disappointment! Capitalizing on the popularity of professional sports, game designers created a ticket for football fans where the total points scored in each quarter of play needed to be scratched. All the player had to do was to add up these points and if that total exceeded the points the other team had scored — a result that was also covered with latex — the player would win a prize.

It was as close to the reality of football one could get and yet the game did not live up to expectations. The major difference between real live football and the instant game was that in the stadium the scoreboard would add up the total points for the player but in the scratch game, the player had to add the scores by himself or herself. Simple addition appeared not to be within the skill set of many instant players. (Not to mention the retailers) It was a misadventure that saw 40% of the prizes remain uncashed.

PROBABILITY GAMES

A probability game is where each and every ticket could be a winner. All the symbols any player needs to win are on the ticket, along with a lot of other symbols that are NOT needed. Scratching only the spots that contain the winning symbols make it a random outcome. The player is of course restricted to making a limited number of scratches; otherwise he or she would go on scratching until all covered combinations were found. Scratching more spots than allowed renders the ticket invalid.

You would be surprised how many players scratched the correct number of spots and found a winner only to have some curious child or a nosy spouse find the stashed-away ticket and scratch covered spots before the ticket owner could stop them! (Or at least that was the excuse made by many players) There were many claims of such instances. Of course those prizes weren't paid out.

The overriding condition for the design of a probability game must be that all winning combinations cannot be identically placed on every ticket. If the location of the numbers was always the same, one buyer could purchase many tickets and scratch the same positions on the ticket. Still, if tickets are printed in groups with identical patterns and then mixed in with other groups, it is still possible that someone will detect the pattern and exploit a weakness. Your lottery scribe's advice to game designers: Stay away from probability games. It's not worth the risk.

Applaud yourself. You survived the tedious lecture of instant/scratch-off lotteries. Let's go on with our tale.

JAZZ IN THE DESERT

In March of 1996, your lottery scribe and his spouse needed a holiday from all the business travel so we flew to Palm Desert CA, where friends gave us the use of their condo, situated along a golf course. Ina was most content not to be obliged to conform to other people's agendas. But one can stand relaxation only so long before the urge to get back to real life returns

Our "duty" wasn't far away. GTECH had chosen the resort at Indian Wells for their '96 Users' Conference. This confab surpassed all Users' Conference before and after. The first evening was "Dinner with the Stars." With a reception around the pool and many celebrities in attendance. Two of Bing Crosby's sons were among the crowd, as well as Harvey Korman and his buddy Tim Conway, Brenda Vaccaro, Mary Crosby...I forget many of the others. Every table had a "celebrity." Your lottery scribe's table was "graced" by Lou Ferrigno, otherwise known as The Hulk, but he soon left to sit with his showbiz buddies and a good thing it was; he was a terrible bore.

The audience was kept in the dark as to what the evening's major entertainment would be. When funny-man Red Buttons, the MC for the evening, came out we knew it was going to be first class. Liza Minnelli and her entire nightclub act of dancers, singers and orchestra performed a fabulous show of dance and song.

The next night's outdoor concert was too cool for many, but for your musically-inclined lottery scribe, it was magical. Atop a windy hill in the Desert Playground Park, the Count Basie Orchestra was in concert. Just for those at the conference! The breeze was strong and one had to situate one's self in the right position to get the impact of the 22-piece big band featuring none other than the great blues singer Joe Williams.

It was a wonderful experience for Ina and me to sit in the middle of the exciting sound that — decades before — we had listened to in Holland on our scratched 78 rpm records. Many listeners went looking for warmer spots but Ina and I stayed in the cold air until the very end.

Later that evening, the Ike Cole Trio played classic jazz tunes at the bar's hotel. In a brash moment I asked GTECH president, Guy Snowden, if he could persuade the trio to let me "sit in" for a few tunes. The pianist was most polite in letting me take his place. I had played the song Route 66 many times and it made me almost sound good when I sang and played that version with the backing of the outstanding bass and drums players.

By now, the thawed-out musicians of the Count Basie Orchestra had shown up and gathered around the trio's bandstand at the bar. I did Route 66 once more but at a much faster tempo. The drummer of the Count Basie band had found a FedEx carton that sounded just like snare drum when he played with his percussion brushes, which seemed to have been stashed inside his inside jacket pocket. The trumpet player, with his muted horn, added some great licks.

Ike the piano player was pleased. "That's the tempo my brother played at," he said after we finished.

I stupidly said: "Who's your brother?"

He looked at me questioningly. "My brother Nat Cole — Nat King Cole."

I turned away in embarrassment and asked a young musician: "Is this true?"

"Yeah sure," he answered. "I am Ike's producer. I am married to his niece, Natalie Cole."

Ina and I sat down together to listen to this impromptu jazz session that seemingly went on and on. It was one of the memorable moments in our lives.

HUNGARY

Barely a month after the Count Basie and Ike Cole experience, I presented an Erewhon seminar in Hungary at a typical East European hotel/spa along the shores of Lake Balaton, a famed holiday region. It was still cold in early May, much in contrast to the heated discussions inside. Several lottery directors of former Communist Bloc countries did not share the Western philosophy that companies could discuss their problems openly. The power of the Communist state to punish its citizens was something they understood well but why a company should talk about their screw-ups was a mystery to them.

One of the first problems discussed at any Erewhon seminar was when a retailer requested the lottery office to cancel a ticket that his lotto terminal had issued but the customer didn't actually buy it. The lottery corporation took the ticket purchase out of the list of paid bets and instructed the retailer to destroy the ticket. For whatever reason, the retailer failed to destroy the ticket and sold it again. After the draw, the computer system declared that there was one proper winner who had won $4.2 million. The problem was that the holder of the cancelled ticket also had the correct six numbers.

To clarify: Two apparently winning tickets were in circulation. One was issued properly; the other was a cancelled ticket. The fellow who had bought the cancelled ticket said that he wasn't aware that the ticket was not valid.

Does the lottery pay both claimants $4.2 million or do each of the two ticket holders get $2.1 million? On the other hand, it could be decided to give $4.2 million to the proper ticket-holder and $2.1 million to the holder of the cancelled ticket. Or should the $4.2 million go to the official winner and nothing to the holder of the cancelled ticket. (As the official rules say it should be).

The reaction of the Hungarian participants was remarkable. Communists stuck to the rules. "Give the holder of the valid ticket the $4.2 million and tell the other man to stop bothering us," was the determined response of the Czech Lottery president who received a nice round of applause from his cohorts.

Participants from western Europe feared public backlash if they ruled so harshly and suggested $4.2 million for the official winner and $2.1 million for the holder of the cancelled ticket on the basis that the ticket was sold as being valid. ($2.1 million is all the second "winner" would have collected.)

The lottery manager from Brazil had a completely different view. He was the only seminar attendee who advocated giving both claimants $4.2 million. When asked why he was so overly generous with the lottery's money, he said: "In Brazil, I would pay both people because the lottery does not want any controversy. If there is an official dispute, there will be a government investigation into the lottery's affairs and God knows what they might find."

It was a revelation to see the "rules" attitude in eastern Europe contrasted with a hint of corruption in Latin America and the "iffy" position of western Europe.

In case you wonder, the proper answer is that the lottery should turn over the $4.2 million to the judicial system and let the courts decide: A solution that deflects any blame from the lottery organization.

HELSINKI

After the seminar in Hungary in May of '96, travel took your scribe to Helsinki for a board meeting of INTERTOTO, where Matti Ahde, president of the Finnish National Lottery, Veikkaus was a gracious host. Checking into the hotel, Matti told me to get dressed for the Helsinki Opera, an institution for which he was on the board. A great number of excuses not to attend sprang to mind, stimulated by my intense abhorrence of opera. I sleep much better in bed than in those narrow theatre seats. However, the performance was an upbeat version of the Barber of Seville. I attended and was pleasantly surprised!

The next day's business meeting was filled with banalities as only Europeans can master with such aplomb, but that evening's entertainment was most pleasant. Matti caused a marvelous grand piano to be brought into the dining room, to be played by a pianist who resembled Harpo Marx. He was only the accompanist, not the star. The featured soloist was a gorgeous female violinist who recently had been featured in the centrefold of the European version of *Playboy* magazine.

On this occasion she wore rather modest apparel, but watching her still made the performance of the classics more enjoyable. Once the professional artists had taken their bows and gone home, one of the lottery guests, a female lottery attorney from Iowa became overly emboldened by the high-octane Finnish vodka. She gave-in to her burning desire to live her dream of performing Broadway tunes before an international audience.

The INTERTOTO board members took great delight in witnessing my agony as I was dragooned to musically accompany this young woman on that beautiful piano. Her performance was spirited but was not in synch with her use of different musical keys within the same tune. Her lyrics were unacquainted with the original text. Nonetheless, the Finnish vodka-fueled lottery audience gave her a rousing "Bravo!"

THE PREMIER CALLS ABOUT CASINOS

On May 29, 1996, my 65th birthday, Premier Glen Clark's NDP party quite unexpectedly won re-election in BC. Barely four weeks after the election, your apprehensive scribe was summoned to the Premier's office for a discussion about casinos. Clark acted the jovial boss but I felt there was always a bit of a wolfish aura about him, an eerie feeling that he might pounce at any time.

We talked a bit about the history of charitable gaming in the province. In 1969, changes to the Criminal Code of Canada allowed the provinces to license games of chance. In early 1970, British Columbia established a Gaming Licensing Branch to license charitable organizations to conduct casinos. In those early days a charitable casino could only be conducted in conjunction with a social event such as dinner and dancing. The bet limit was $2 and only a maximum of six blackjack tables were approved, although an unlimited number of roulette wheels and wheels-of-fortune were allowed.

However, these games were not allowed to be conducted from permanent sites. The rules were intended to keep professional operators away. Staff and card dealers had to be volunteers from the ranks of the licensed charity. As time passed and no problems arose, private operators came on the scene, offering a permanent a location for those licensed charities, where they were able use the operator's gaming equipment and seating for a rental fee.

Premier Clark was aware that I had attended the national minister's meeting in 1986 where the authority to manage and conduct casinos was transferred to the provinces. He listened politely to my tedious tale as to how those innocent casinos originated in community halls with simple casino games turned into commercial establishments.

In summer of 1986, the provinces took over licensing of charitable casinos. One of the earliest operators was the Great Canadian Casino Corporation headed by Ross McLeod and Fred Glasgow.

Premier Clark told me that government would soon make slot machines legal so that revenue for charities could be increased. My response was that allowing charities to operate slot machines might prove an uphill battle because the Criminal Code stipulated that only a government entity could manage them.

He shrugged off my comment and moved on to the topic for which he had invited me, namely, how to proceed with the idea of destination casinos— a tourist attraction with a commercial casino attached. It was obvious to the Premier that the primary attraction was the casino, with the "touristy thing" a secondary consideration. Although he conceded that a classy hotel in the right location could be a tourist attraction.

 Clark had just returned from a Premiers' Conference in Dawson City, where he had played a slot machine at the "summer-only" Klondike Casino. He mentioned Barkerville, a BC hamlet in the Chilcotin area that had a gold-mining history and wondered if a summertime casino might work there. Barkerville (named after the famed miner Billy Barker) was a BC-owned Heritage Property and Park as well as a National Historic Site. Clark thought that Barkerville was an authentic, unique world-class heritage experience and might be the right place for a destination casino. He appeared to be a bit put-out when I pointed out that Barkerville drew less than 90,000 visitors a year and 60% of those were children. He then proceeded to lecture me on the reality that once inoffensive casinos were accepted, bigger casino operations would become more politically palatable. Lesson learned!

A month later, I met with the Premier again. He told me his NDP caucus abhorred the idea that casino games would be operated by government, a most undesirable concept for the NDP. Premier Clark must have kept Barkerville in mind because over the next few months his people kept reminding everyone about the possibility of a small touristy casino in a place such as Barkerville.

 (Note: A casino like that came eventually about. In 1999, the Billy Barker Casino was established as a "Destination Casino" not in Barkerville but — 70 km away — in Quesnel BC, a town with a population of 22,000. In the new millennium, the attractive establishment featured a hotel and casino with 134 slot machines in combination with 6 gaming tables. It annually earned $9.3 million in profits for the BC government.)

But... back to 1996. The left-leaning members of the legislature —thinking about casinos operated by government employees — perceived casinos to be a corporation like the BC Ferries where all staff from the kitchen to the souvenir shop were unionized and paid high wages. A government employee dealing Black Jack was not a very appealing scenario for the NDP. So clearly, Premier Clark was looking for another way to operate casinos.

The premier appeared to be encouraged by my view — contrary to what was taking place in Quebec — that BCLC should control betting in the casino (in order to satisfy the requirements of the Criminal Code) but leave all other functions to private service providers.

He asked that I repeat my spiel to his executive assistant who came in from an adjoining room. I suggested again that BCLC should *not* employ blackjack dealers, cocktail waitresses, kitchen staff or other service functions. As long as BCLC controlled the legally required gaming activity, most tasks of running a casino could be done by private operators on contract. I simplified the concept by comparing the casino to a corner store that sold lotteries. The building, store, staff, and inventory were the responsibility of the owner. BCLC's function was to place its lottery equipment in the store and control all gaming activities.

Clark seemed to like it and asked: "Can the BC Lottery Corporation handle such a project or should there be a separate crown corporation?" My view was that there was no need to create separate a crown corporation. Clark grinned at that. I repeated that BCLC considered casino play just another type of gaming to be added to its portfolio of gambling activities.

Within the confines of the NDP caucus, the old faction of the NDP who had opposed gambling so strongly for so many years fought a losing battle. A lot of internal haggling took place but eventually legislation was passed that allowed the BCLC to "manage and conduct" slot machines in charitable casinos with the revenue split between the charities and government.

That decision created a problem. The charities were licensed to conduct table-games within a charitable casino and right beside them (because it had to be so, according to the Criminal Code) BCLC was managing and conducting slot machines. It was a complicated arrangement that was open to possible judicial intervention. The law said that profits earned in a charitable casino must accrue to charitable purposes and yet, the government wanted a slice of that revenue. But... more about that legal controversy later.

HONOURED?

PUBLIC GAMING RESEARCH INSTITUTE

In June of 1996, Ina and I travelled to Boca Raton, to attend a session of the Public Gaming Institute, where your humble scribe was to be honoured with the Institute's "Lifetime Achievement Award" for my work in advancing government lotteries.

The title of "Lifetime Achievement" is far more impressive than the ceremony that accompanied it. My dear friend, Duane Burke — the heart, soul and body of the Gaming Institute, whose organizational skills were always a bit wobbly at such affairs, wasn't at his best that evening. One of the lottery directors, concerned about the informality of it all, went to the lobby flower shop to buy a bouquet of flowers for Ina. At the brief rite, your lottery scribe was presented with an etched glass bowl of such an imposing dimension that it caused Ina to wonder aloud how we could take this award back to Vancouver.

Ed Stanek, my lottery colleague from Iowa, who had been buttonholed to present the award made a funny, light-hearted speech wherein he commented that the bowl was beautiful. However, he expressed "great regret" that the bowl carried an inscription with my name, something that would seriously depress its value at a Vancouver garage sale.

WORLD MEET '96

September 1996. The project that BCLC had been working toward for so long was finally at hand. Close to 1,400 delegates from across the world gathered in the Vancouver Trade and Convention Centre to participate in the largest lottery conference to date. Officially, the Conference was an AILE conference but NASPL had agreed to hold its annual meeting simultaneously.

A few months before WORLD MEET '96 began, INTERTOTO President Richard Frigren had still not committed to having his organization join the conference so that the title "WORLD MEET" would become factual. I appealed to his Scandinavian colleagues, who were sympathetic to the aims of a single world lottery organization. We will never know what words were exchanged but Reidar Nordby of Norway called to say that INTERTOTO would be part of World Meet '96, provided it was given equal status as AILE and NASPL. Since I was president of AILE, past-president of NASPL and a director of INTERTOTO, this was a given. The INTERTOTO logo was to be shown side by side on everything that carried the AILE and NASPL logos.

The World Meet organization went into action. During the previous 18 months, the hard-working BCLC crew had recruited more than 60 speakers on a wide range of topics. BCLC staff ensured that they came well prepared and ready to use the latest audio-visual aids provided. With so many delegates and such diverse interests, five "streams of learning" were created, which meant that delegates could choose from among five different subjects throughout the conference. Several sessions were repeated so that delegates wouldn't miss out. In later years that innovation was copied but in retrospect five streams proved to be too many and future programs settled on three streams.

WORLD MEET '96 is fondly remembered by many for its educational and networking opportunities. The real benefit, in my view, was that AILE and INTERTOTO were finally talking to each other. The resistance by Richard Frigren had been diminished and now the INTERTOTO board of directors were more supportive of a merger. The path forward to a single world lottery organization looked much smoother for your aspiring scribe.

ROUTE 66

Opening ceremonies of these types of world lottery conferences are usually a dreary affair. It is a hoary tradition that the chairman of the conference reads the list of member countries attending.

The WORLD MEET '96 team created an hour-long show featuring musicians, dancers and singers that "read the roll call" by performing songs related to the provinces, states and countries. My colleagues, from Ireland, Norway, Sweden, Czech Republic, Australia, Finland, Atlantic Canada and Quebec acceded to my pleadings to present their personal musical tribute. It was an event that may not be equalled soon.

But what of the United States? We couldn't possibly introduce 39 lottery companies and get away with one song. Yes we could! A musical-arrangement of the song Route 66 was pre-recorded, which allowed your lottery scribe to write new lyrics that included the name of lottery states in North America. Despite having no great voice for singing, your lottery scribe worked up the chutzpah to perform the seven-minute-long lyrics. I tell myself that the song was a great hit. The performance can still be found on YouTube under "Guy at World Meet 96". https://tinyurl.com/yxsfh3wa

In November of 1996, the INTERTOTO board convened at Rome's top-rated Hotel Hassler. Situated at the top of the Spanish Steps overlooking Rome, the hotel served the finest dining for those who care for that kind of extravagance.

On the opening evening, in order to be part of the posh crowd, Ina and I endured the long dinner ritual. As crude Plebeians who didn't fancy the meagre but exotic food portions, we sneaked out of the hotel after dinner and found the nearby McDonald's restaurant below the "135 Spanish Steps". The brass plaque outside indicated that McDonald's hamburger chain had paid for the restoration of the famous location. (The Spanish Steps are a set of steps climbing the steep slope between the Piazza di Spagna and the Piazza Trinità dei Monti.) Your travel-wise scribe and spouse didn't visit McDonald's for the culture but the Big Macs and fries were excellent.

The bombshell at the next-day's meeting was the announcement that Richard Frigren was no longer employed as a lottery director.

The Swedish government had merged Richard's Tipsjanst Lotto-Toto company with the old state-owned Penninglotteriet that was headquartered in the town of Visby on the remote Swedish island of Gotland. As part of the merger, Richard was required to move from cosmopolitan Stockholm to Visby. Nearing retirement, Richard did not accept this directive and resigned.

According to the INTERTOTO bylaws, this meant Richard also had to resign as president of INTERTOTO and the Senior Vice-President would take over. You will remember that at the INTERTOTO Conference in Hong Kong, I had haughtily declined the office of Vice-President.

As the board digested the startling change, I announced a little bombshell of my own. Marguerite Bourgeois — the de-facto leader of AILE — had left Loto-Quebec to take a position in the private sector. This meant AILE was rudderless.

In the film *High Society*, Bing Crosby and Frank Sinatra sang, "When the moon and stars are aligned with Jupiter and Mars," good things will happen. This was such a moment. The merger of the two world lottery organizations was suddenly much closer.

Without arriving at a decision of what the next step would be, the official meeting at the Hotel Hassler was adjourned and continued — informally — at a secondary site: the bar! I didn't join. I stayed with Ina in our hotel room. Barely ten minutes later the phone rang. I was asked to join the crowd at the bar.

Vice President Matti Ahde of Finland, speaking on behalf of the INTERTOTO board of directors, put the question through his interpreter rather officiously... "Would Guy Simonis be prepared to assume the Presidency of INTERTOTO leading up to the 1997 INTERTOTO Congress in Berlin and when there, would he stand for re-election to the Presidency of INTERTOTO?"

I agreed to take on the Presidency of INTERTOTO, while still holding the office of Past President of AILE and with the condition that the INTERTOTO board would support the "merger of AILE and INTERTOTO on mutually agreed principles and respecting the culture of both organizations developed over a half-century." (I had rehearsed this pompous declaration in our hotel room.)

Your lottery scribe immediately moved to create an Implementation Task Force (shades of Manitoba in 1973) with membership drawn from AILE and INTERTOTO. The group would consider the issues and make recommendations for the steps to create a new world lottery organization. The make-up of the Implementation Task Force was to be viewed as being equal.

From the AILE side, it was important that a francophone member be named. **Michel Ansiaux**, the cocktail-hour-happy director of the Belgian Lottery, was an obvious choice. His prime value was that he wasn't from France; therefore, he wouldn't be automatically resented. A Nordic delegate from AILE was my Finnish opera-loving colleague, Matti Ahde. Iowa's Ed Stanek accepted the appointment to represent North America. From the INTERTOTO side Reidar Nordby, who had persuaded Richard Frigren to be part of WORLD MEET '96, was the first choice. Although he had sincere doubts about the merger, Friedrich Stickler of Austria joined as well.

The new General Secretary of AILE, Lynne Roiter of Loto-Québec was an automatic choice as was Yvonne Schnyder, INTERTOTO's General Secretary.

A lot of work ahead lay ahead.

DESTINATION CASINOS

At the end of November 1996, when your travel-weary scribe had barely returned from the Rome meeting, I was summoned to meet with NDP Deputy Premier **Dan Miller**, who told me that cabinet was again considering "Destination Casinos."

This concept was quite distinct from the existing charitable, city-based casinos. "It'll be akin to Monaco," he smiled. I thought he meant a type of sedate meeting of tuxedo-clad gentlemen and gowned-ladies rather than the glitzy, gambling factories of Las Vegas. "We want a destination resort casino geared to well-off tourists that will go a long way to relieve BC's financial woes," he added. I must have looked doubtful because he added that the plan had the support of Premier Glen Clark.

In mid-December, the government announced that that it was exploring the introduction of "Destination Casinos" and that the outline of the concept would be forthcoming within a couple of months.

By early January 1997, the model was introduced and public reaction began to bubble immediately. As expected, many voices were raised against what was seen as "Las Vegas of the North."

On January 25, just hours before the start of a street-rally opposing destination casinos, Premier Clark ruled out a Las Vegas type of casino for BC and promised he wouldn't force expanded gaming on communities that didn't want to be part of it. However, the very next day he declared that he was still interested in expanding gaming activities — including the introduction of slot machines in existing charity casinos. He emphasized that BCLC would be responsible for managing and conducting slot machines. Just to clarify the confusion: BCLC was to run slot machines but not the table games' operation, which remained with the charities.

In February of 1997, a Lottery Advisory Committee (LAC) was created which included your lottery scribe. At the first meeting it was discussed how to implement the province's new gaming initiatives, which — although the news release gave no hints— would cause a significant expansion of gaming. That particular news release made repeated references to the protection of the charities' income, which was a bit misleading because the changes meant more revenue for government and a freeze of the profits for charity.

When the new Gaming Policy was announced publicly, a lot of words poured out but the essence was that government would take over all gaming operations and the charities could cash cheques totaling $130 million annually, but they were out of any involvement of gaming operations.

THE END OF CHARITABLE LOTTERIES

For your lottery scribe that decision was the end of a long trek. In 1974, when I became the head of the Western Canada Lottery, charitable organizations were the sole operators of gambling. They operated the sales function from A to Z and earned substantial revenues that they did not consider a government grant but rather compensation for hard work.

Their first loss of status came in 1976 when commissions were reduced by as much as 50% followed by further reductions in subsequent years. Control of break-open tickets was taken away. Charities were weaned of bingo by the introduction of the electronic version. The biggest change came when online gaming was introduced in 1982 and their function as ticket distributors was taken over by BCLC. Now, 25 lucrative years later, charities were out of the gaming business entirely.

For your lottery scribe, the survival of this long, nasty war with charitable lottery distributors was a reward in itself. Now, my efforts could be concentrated on the remaining opponents of provincial government-controlled gaming, the municipalities.

CITY OF VANCOUVER OBJECTS ...THEN BANS

On March 25, 1997, Vancouver's City Council decided that gaming expansion wasn't just for the provincial government to decide. In its view, the people of British Columbia should decide about casinos through a "meaningful consultation." The question would be whether "the public" wanted more gambling or not.

Vancouver City Council wanted a provincially initiated comprehensive Gaming Act that left them practically in charge. In their opening paragraph, the provincial minister responsible for lotteries and gaming was advised that Vancouver opposed the introduction of slot machines.

A month after that pronouncement (April 22), Vancouver City Council decided that it should put controls in place to counter negative consequences of gambling: specifically, the expected increase in compulsive gambling and criminal activity. To that end Council passed a by-law to prohibit slot machines in Vancouver. Furthermore, Council demanded to determine any increase in betting limits and expansion of casino hours.

With that legislation, the city of Vancouver became (and still is) a pain in the neck for those who wish to gamble in the city. The whole thing was all a bit of ineffective show business because adjoining municipalities were lining up to welcome the new gaming opportunities.

GETTING UP TO DATE

With all these rapid changes, your lottery scribe needed to become an expert in casino management. Not overly familiar with casino operations, I arranged to meet with the "guru" of charitable casino gaming, Ross McLeod. Ross's chain of charitable casinos (now: Great Canadian Gaming Corporation) was the dominant organization in BC and had provided casino services to many licenced charities. Ross was a charming and knowledgeable man.

At the age of 18, while attending the University of Victoria, he began his career in the amusement and entertainment industry by purchasing amusement games and taking them on the road. Later, Ross teamed up with Freddie Glasgow, a "carny" who had built his career in fairs and exhibitions.

In 1982, McLeod ran midway games at the Pacific National Exhibition, BC's annual fair. The legal underpinnings for those early casinos was the Criminal Code with respect to fairs and exhibitions under the aegis of the Federal Department of Agriculture. (You may recall that in 1986, when Jim Chabot was the BC minister in charge of gaming, the Feds transferred control of casino games to the provinces).

Ross McCloud was no slouch. When the provincial government opened the door for licensed charities to run small casinos, he quickly took the initiative.

His business model morphed into a "casino service provider", where professional staff ran the games in permanent facilities on behalf of charitable licensees. In order to retain the image that the charities were running the casino, volunteers were recruited to help sell bingo cards, welcome players, provide janitorial services and... of course... collect the net profits.

In fact, Ross McLeod's business was a commercially run casino, on behalf of charitable licences. To be sure, everyone was quite happy. The charities collected money, without much work. The operator was satisfied with its share of revenue and government collected a tidy licence fee.

Several charitable casinos were established in the mid '80s and early '90s:

- February 21, 1986. The Holiday Inn Casino in Vancouver.
- June 1, 1986. The Nanaimo Casino, the first permanent charitable casino on Vancouver Island.
- Fall of 1986. Charitable casinos in Kamloops, Kelowna, Vernon, operated by Jacee Schaefer; then Great Canadian Casino and subsequently Fred Glasgow's Lake City Casino company.
- Jan 15, 1987. Billy Barker Casino in Quesnel (originally the Royal Casino)
- May 1, 1987. The Red Lion Casino in Victoria.
- June, 1987. The Richmond Casino in Richmond.
- July, 1987. The Langley Casino.
- June 1987. The Royal Diamond Casino, 750 Pacific Blvd in Vancouver
- September 1987. The Grand Casino, 735 SE Marine Drive in Vancouver
- June 1986. The Wagers Casino; (later Hollywood Casino in Prince George)
- 1988. The Guildford Casino, 15269 104th Avenue, Surrey, (Closed in 1994 and replaced Newton Casino)
- 1992. The Mayfair Casino in Victoria.
- 1992. The Mandarin Centre in Vancouver.
- 1992. The Royal Towers in New Westminster.
- 1994. The Renaissance Casino in West Vancouver.

SLOT MACHINES BUT NOT TABLE GAMES

In March of 1997, BCLC took charge of slot machines in charitable casinos. Licensing and control of table games such as Blackjack, Craps, Fortune, Pai Gow, Mini Baccarat and Roulette remained with the BC Gaming Authority. That two-headed control of BCLC and the Gaming Authority caused not only management problems but legal problems that later on would create serious complications.

On the technical side, our people at BCLC learned a lot about slot machines. Vic Poleschuk and **Rob Egan** did a great job of evaluating and selecting slot machine suppliers, popular slot machine games and slot-management systems that provided central control.

Ultimately, Bally Technology and Williams Gaming became the suppliers of the new equipment. The machine types were a mix of 25 cent and one-dollar plays, offering twenty different games. Payouts of all slots were similar, but the make-up of the prize table varied. Even though the prize payout percentage was nearly identical, the different themes made the image of the machines appear as if offering different chances to win.

The distinction between what BCLC was doing in the administration of slots and how stand-alone slot machines were operated in the past became a bit of a squabble with the folks at the Gaming Authority. The old guard didn't grasp that BCLC's slot machines were not open for manipulation, which was the bane of stand-alone slot machines. BCLC controlled all slot machines from the Data Centre in Kamloops, thereby excluding any outside interference. This was quite distinct from a single stand-alone slot machine that could be manipulated by a person of criminal intent.

It was a complicated technical issue but my explanation to the political masters convinced them that BCLC's slot machine operation was secure.

BINGO AND SLOTS

In March of 1997, the BC Government authorized the BCLC to "manage and conduct" slot machines in the province's charitable casinos. While the focus was on slot machines, the concurrent permission to expand electronic bingo received little notice.

For years, BCLC had been the sole distributor of bingo paper. BCLC's first venture into electronic bingo was the 1988 installation of electronic bingo terminals at Starship Bingo on Vancouver's Main Street. In 1997, BCLC's bingo role expanded with an additional six electronic bingo halls. A total of 84 charitable bingo licensees were allowed to join in a province-wide bingo game called SUPER STAR LINKED BINGO to be conducted by BCLC.

Linked

Linked Bingo is in effect a bingo game played simultaneously in many separate locations. In keeping with its mandate, BCLC provided the electronic systems to run the game. Computer-driven printers, creating bingo cards on the spot, were placed in each location. Nights of free demonstration bingo sessions were launched in October of 1997, offering merchandise prizes in lieu of cash.

I'd love to tell you that when it all went "live", it all worked just fine. Alas participation was so huge that the system crashed at the very first official Linked-Bingo game. The opening $50,000 jackpot prize had to be postponed for a few weeks. After that, a nightly routine minimum jackpot of $20,000 became a permanent feature in BC's electronic bingo operations. The initial months of operation yielded over $10 million in sales. As this this tale is written, Linked Bingo is still in operation.

THE END OF CHARITABLE GAMING LOOMS

Remember when I told you that this weird dual control at the charitable casinos might cause complications? It did. Separate operations by two organizations were being conducted at each casino: table games on behalf of the charities and slot machines by BCLC. To the player, though, it looked like a single operation.

In the opinion of your lottery scribe, the issue of dual control was a strange but done deal until it suddenly it wasn't. In the view of government (and the charities), BCLC ran the machines at a charitable casino because the law said so and not because it was the preferred route.

BCLC doled out the revenue from those slot machines: half to the charities, half to the government. That — precisely — was the point of the legal "no-no." The law says that revenue earned at a charitable casino is for the benefit of charities. The fact that government was raking in half the profit that legally belonged to the charities became a real problem.

More about that issue later but you can guess how that turned out: the government changed the legislation so that it could retain *all* the profits.

REQUEST FOR PROPOSALS FOR DESTINATION CASINOS

Let's get back to the idea of BCLC-operated Destination Casinos. On July 31, 1997, the BC government issued a Request for Proposal for Destination Casinos. It laid out the conditions, including revenue distribution and the process of how this expanded gaming would unfold. All the stuff that had been hinted at before. The deadline for submissions for a license was November 1997. An astonishingly quick 41 proposals flooded in. In a follow up, ten of them didn't have the necessary municipal support and another eleven were sent back for more information. It took a while to assess all that. Meanwhile your lottery scribe had other battles to fight. I'll come back.

SINGLE WORLD ASSOCIATION GETS CLOSER

On August 29, 1997, on a sweltering hot weekend, one of the decisive meetings of the Implementation Task Force was held in Lisse, a small Dutch town, five kilometres north of my parental home in Sassenheim.

After a 10-hour flight from Vancouver, I arrived at the Lisse hotel trying to adjust to the nine-hour time difference and the 32 degrees Celsius humidity. The only relief was a big fan that rearranged the air in the bedroom.

The Monday morning meeting of the Implementation Task Force had to decide on some crucial matters and how it was going to be reflected in legalese text. As the chairman of this group, I had to deal with many biases and personal conflicts. One of the most bruising decisions was which one of the two Secretaries-General was to emerge on top?

 **Lynne Roiter** of AILE had a shorter tenure in lotteries than Yvonne Schnyder and was AILE's General Secretary on a part-time basis. She wasn't afraid of losing her job at Loto Quebec where she occupied the legal chair but I imagine she felt somewhat edgy about being sidelined and perhaps losing prestige and influence in the world of lotteries.

In contrast, INTERTOTO's General Secretary, Yvonne Schnyder, conducted a guerrilla battle to scuttle the merger. She had been employed at INTERTOTO for 25 years and feared the changes that a merger would create.

Yvonne's strategy was to demand changes that would clearly be unacceptable to the AILE side while Lynne Roiter's was trying to make the best of a thorny issue and find a way to achieve a mutually acceptable merger. Yvonne desired AILE's oblivion which would leave INTERTOTO in sole command. That position would negate the whole deal. I understood Yvonne's concern but her strategy caused me dismay.

With the assistance of my dear friend, Joe Kanuka, the Regina lawyer, a draft set of Bylaws was prepared that would govern the new association. The working title was World Lottery Organization (later changed to World Lottery Association). The proposal, with minor alterations, was adopted by the Implementation Task Force and was now headed for approval by the entire INTERTOTO board of directors meeting to be held in Berlin.

ELECTED PRESIDENT OF INTERTOTO

September 6, 1997. The drive in a brand-new SAAB from Amsterdam to the Berlin meeting of INTERTOTO was much shorter than I had imagined. This was my first visit to the capital city of the nation that had attacked my home country of Holland in 1940.

Ina was taken by surprise when she entered the regally adorned auditorium of Berlin's Congress Hall. The flags of 64 nation-members of INTERTOTO flanked the ornate walls. Miniature national flags were displayed at the respective individual delegates' tables. The sight of so many countries' delegates gathered in one room in order to elect her husband as the head of this world lottery gathering even impressed my spouse.

The nomination of **Guy Simonis** as President of INTERTOTO was unopposed. My inaugural speech dealt with the advantage of creating a single world organization. The membership applauded in all the right places and voted to dissolve its 50-year-old INTERTOTO in favour of a merger with AILE. It felt a bit strange to be authorized to terminate the association that had just elected me.

It was now left for the AILE membership to approve its own dissolution at its Congress in Buenos Aires the following year. A lot of details still needed to be dealt with — egos to be stroked, wounds to be healed.

The duty of the incoming President of INTERTOTO is — by protocol — to preside over the final dinner, not that this entitled my dear spouse and me to any special seating. That job was reserved for the Berlin organizers.

One of my tasks at the dinner was to honour the outgoing president, Richard Frigren, but somehow that fact had slipped the mind of the Berlin host, Hans-Juergen Reisinger. Instead, he called on Yvonne Schnyder, INTERTOTO's General Secretary, to say something nice about her retiring boss. I put my nice speech back in the pocket of my jacket. It wasn't a speech that expressed the cruel reality, but truth is not expected at such occasions.

A short address, a handshake and a peck on the cheek was all that Richard got. Yvonne then announced that Marianne, Richard's wife, was to be presented with a bouquet of flowers, whereupon Yvonne stared into the audience, shielding her eyes from the stage lights as if looking for a florist far away on the horizon. Alas, the flowery tribute didn't materialize, whereupon Hans Juergen grabbed a pot of decorative chrysanthemums that ringed the stage and handed it to Mrs. Frigren.

 But then it was my turn to be embarrassed. The hired emcee returned to the stage and was ready to present the newly elected president of INTERTOTO... Mr. **Warren Wilson** of Australia! Some folks in the audience, who didn't have any idea who was who, applauded lustily. The emcee stared into the audience, expecting someone to stand up. I certainly didn't rise to my feet. Neither did Warren. My friends and colleagues quietly winced in sympathy for this goof-up, but Warren — ever the rambunctious Australian — was slapping his thighs and laughing his head off. The emcee was hauled off the stage, to have her ears filled with my whispered name. Then she mispronounced my name as Simone Guy.

Lothar Lammers, the Past-Past President of INTERTOTO seated nearby, approached the head table to see what he could do to repair the gaffe. He came back shrugging his trademark shrug.

"Reissiger doesn't want to apologize," he said. "It's the emcee's fault. She couldn't find her notes before she made the announcement. She had asked a Berlin lottery employee: 'What's the name of that big bald guy there?' The answer was Warren Wilson."

THE FIRST OFFICIAL VISIT: BRATISLAVA

Berlin, September 13, 1997. It was 50 years to the day when I started working for a living at the Netherlands Railways. I don't think that many of today's generation may be able to celebrate such a lengthy working period and I wasn't finished yet. I mentioned the anniversary over our quiet morning coffee but Ina didn't think it was much of an occasion.

After breakfast, the Saab took us through the streets of East Berlin onto the Autobahn toward the once lively city of Dresden. The view, with its endless rows of monotonous concrete apartment blocks so overly present in the Communist Paradise, was depressing.

Our final destination was Bratislava, the capitol of Slovakia, where I was invited to conduct a seminar on instant/scratch games. It was impossible to travel in a straight line towards the City of Bratislava because — at that time — Western European car rental agencies didn't allow their cars to be driven in former states of the USSR. The exception was East Germany, because it was now a part of a unified Germany. The reason for the ban was that criminal groups of the former Communist countries were ready to steal any reasonably new car and ship it to somewhere in the East or chop it up for parts, with no traces left. The policing in these countries was either inadequate or corrupt.

We were forced to skirt both the Czech Republic and Slovakia who had recently separated and now, arriving in Austria, we finally got within reasonable distance of Bratislava.

We parked the Dutch-rented Saab in the Vienna garage of the Austrian Lottery. Helena Ursulova, one of the smarter participants in Erewhon at Lake Balatan in Hungary, drove us the final 90 km to Bratislava. It was only a one-hour car ride but a huge cultural leap. Between the German language and Slovak tongue, only a dozen words are the same. The outlook, food and work ethics differ so widely that the question arises: When these people settled here a 1,000 or more years ago, at what point did they stop and say: "We remain here. This is where Slovak nation ends and the Germanic culture begins?"

We stopped at the corner where Austria, Hungary and Slovakia meet and sat down for a coffee and mused about the fact that between the Netherlands and Germany there is no distinct language boundary.

As one travels east from the Dutch coast, the local accents and expressions slowly change. By the time one reaches the German border, the people on either side speak exactly the same dialect. It then goes on changing until it resolves in High German but not so between Austria and Slovakia and Hungary. They are each totally different.

The change from German to Slovak became even more complex when further down the road the border with Hungary came into view. Centuries before there had to have been three tribes with different cultures and languages facing each other, not to mention the Czechs, 50 kilometres further down the road. The countries have always been plagued by political and cultural problems. Fascinating!

Sorry about this non-lottery prattle!

A HIT IN SLOVAKIA

In Bratislava, the seminar on instant/scratch tickets went okay. It was a plodding event but it achieved its goal. The management of TIPOS, the Slovakian Lottery, treated me as a wiseman having descended from the mount. They would have covered us in frankincense and myrrh if we'd let them.

The hotel lodged us in the presidential suite with a wide window facing the Slovakian Parliament Building. Ina was supplied with US $300 in Slovak currency to shop for souvenirs while I was introduced to the Minister of Finance, who provided a complete rundown on the Slovakian economy. I hopefully nodded in the right places and smiled when he presented me with a special edition of the new Slovak constitution, personally autographed by the Prime Minister. (Bit of a show-off here.)

That evening's dinner was followed by a jazz concert in the hotel's nightclub featuring Dixieland music. Our host, having been informed of my amateurish piano playing, ordered the band to let me play a few tunes. The bandleader faked rapture while I performed a dreadful imitation of Errol Garner accompanied by the excellent Slovak musicians. It appeared to Ina and me that the plaudits were fake but then the restaurant staff appeared from the kitchen and applauded. The young busboy even whispered to me in broken English that he liked my music better than the Slovakian stuff.

We were a hit in Bratislava!

The next evening's dinner was to be an exploratory outing of our own. We were given the names of the three top restaurants in Bratislava. Much to the dismay of the political mandarins of Slovakia, we chose the newly-opened Pizza Hut. My obviously deficient taste buds voted the huge pepperoni pizza to be the best dinner of the week.

At our hotel, a lot of European diplomatic activity was taking place. Limousines were arriving; flunkies were bowing and scraping. We overheard one Dutch diplomat speaking our native tongue explain that he was part of a European fact-finding mission to assess Slovakia's fitness to become part of the European Union. So all that ceremonial stuff wasn't for us...too bad.

On the final evening, we were set to experience the folklore of Slovakia. The destination was a "typical" Slovak village called Lemburg. In a walk through the old streets, I noticed a decrepit church with its cenotaph inscribed with German Gothic lettering. In the neglected cemetery were gravestones bearing the names of Germans who died before 1944. Even the town's name Lemburg was German. I asked where all the German people were. Helena Ursulova, our guide for the entire three days, said that after the war the German speakers had been driven from their land and pushed into East Germany without compensation. She smiled contentedly while relating the story.

At that "typical" Slovakian rural hotel/restaurant, the music was supplied by a Hungarian gypsy band playing their instruments at a wild and wonderfully high tempo. A local comedian, who appeared to greatly amuse our hosts, delivered a lengthy monologue in excellent Slovakian. Afterwards, our interpreter explained that the performer was a nephew of the lottery director and had been shanghaied to entertain the foreign guests.

At the close of the evening the comedian produced a bazooka-like instrument from which he managed to produce a wailing sound that is used to call sheep home from the meadow. He referred in mangled English to my "excellent" musicianship and pulled me onto the stage to blow the thing. I managed to produce a pig-sounding squeal or two. Then, to great fanfare, a much bigger version of that horn was brought in and — presto! — I was now the proud owner of my own five-foot fujara, the deluxe version. (Dictionary: Fujara: originated in central Slovakia, serves as a large folk shepherd's flute)

Ina's first reaction was that it was nice gift, but how do we get it home? When we first examined the car, we noted a slot for stowing skis in the trunk via the back seat. Those Swedes think of everything. Driven to Vienna by our hosts, we stowed our baggage and the 5-foot fujara in the SAAB and drove the 1,100 kilometres to Holland in 13 hours. At the BC lottery office, the ever-inventive Frances Kenny made arrangements to transfer the shepherd's flute from Holland to our home in Tsawwassen, where it still hangs on the wall, ready for a flautist, in case the sheep fail to come home one night.

WHERE IS GOTLAND?

After a short stay in Holland, Ina returned to Vancouver. Your apprentice flautist, accompanied by the ever-ready Frances Kenny, flew to the town of Visby on the island of Gotland in Sweden, where a four-day lottery seminar was scheduled for a group of Scandinavian lottery people. While the conference was successful by the low-excitement standards of our hosts, the highlight was the final dinner at a centuries-old pub. During dinner, our bare table fish-and-bread feast was raided by Vikings dressed in full battle gear. I was handed the sword of a "fallen" Viking and told to defend myself. Geez... I could hardly lift the damn thing, never mind hold it in a fighting stance. Your rude scribe has made some petty remarks about the Swede's lack of excitement but these Gotland Vikings knew how to party. It was a great evening!

Visiting Visby is like exploring a theme park with its narrow streets and the big wall. The Hanseatic city is arguably the best-preserved medieval city in Scandinavia and since 1995, it has been on the UNESCO World Heritage Site list. Among the most notable historical remains are the 4 kilometer town-wall that circles the town center and a number of church ruins. We visited the ruins of a 1200-year-old church of which the missing parts were replaced by modern glass walls and Swedish interior. Unusual and fascinating.

BOSTON

September 29, 1997. Our son Leonard was waiting at the NASPL Conference hotel in downtown Boston. At first, I didn't recognize him; he had a neatly coiffed goatee that made him look like the well-known hypnotist Reveen.

At the exhibition we got into a confusing misunderstanding. Len and I were checking out the vendor displays when a gentleman approached us and said, "I just spoke to your son up there; gee, he is a nice young man and very competent." I shall not easily forget the look on Len's astonished face. It was between wonder and worry.

"So where did you meet my brother?" Len asked the man, thrusting his ID badge at him. "Over at the GTECH booth," the man mumbled, slowly realizing he was into something he wouldn't be able to finish. "You are Guy Snowden, aren't you?" he said to me, walking backwards now.

"No, I have the same last name as my son here," I said pointing at Len.

It wasn't the first time that I had been mistaken for **Guy Snowden,** the boss of GTECH — not because we resembled each other but perhaps because of the name Guy and the initial S combination. Two years earlier, at a NASPL meeting in Washington, DC, an NBC television camera filmed me while listening to the speeches. Later in the afternoon, entering a washroom, I was filmed once more. When I exited the toilet, the camera's red light came on again. Then an NBC reporter stepped into the scene and said: "Congratulations on the city's proclamation declaring this to be your day!"

"Are you talking about the City of Vancouver?" I asked incredulously.

He sneered at what he believed to be an evasion. "The reason we are here is to talk about David Smith."

It now began to dawn on me that they were pursuing a story that GTECH Vice-President David Smith was about to be charged with financial misdoings, all rumours as far as I knew. I decide to play along:

"David Smith is the corporate lawyer for the Atlantic Lottery Corporation. I know him well and the rumour is that he will shortly be appointed to the Bench in New Brunswick." (This was a true!)

The reporter reached over to read my ID badge. "You are not Guy Snowden," he said in an accusing tone.

"No, he is with GTECH," I said helpfully.

He mumbled under his breath something that sounded to me like "Shit."

360

LOTTERY ADVISORY COMMITTEE

I'd better return to talk about the lottery job I was getting paid for. To refresh your memory: in October of 1997, the BC Government announced the creation of a Lottery Advisory Committee (LAC) to formulate the province's new gaming policy, which hinted at a huge expansion of BC gaming.

The members (commissioners) of the existing lottery-licencing authority were correct to think they were being ignored. All six resigned. To their chagrin public reaction was that the commissioners were acting like spoilt children. In fact, they were being sidelined for being too closely identified with the interest of the charities and thus obviously antagonistic to the new government policy.

In October 1997, after having paid little attention to the concerns of the charities, the BC Cabinet passed an act titled "Gaming Proceeds Distribution Regulation," that guaranteed the profits earned by the charities in the 1995-96 would be paid out in the next fiscal year at the same amount plus 5%. Revenues would flow through a new entity called the Provincial Charity Trust.

The Act made it abundantly clear that that the charities would not get a single nickel from the profits of the new destination casinos.

After the government had bitten that bullet, the Lottery Advisory Committee undertook a province-wide information campaign to explain how this new gaming regime would impact charities. Your lottery scribe was too involved with BCLC issues to spend a lot of evenings in community halls to explain to the charities, in the most evasive terms, that their involvement in lotteries and casinos was at an end and their new role was reduced to applying for grants from lottery profits.

Many charitable organizations, tired of haranguing their volunteers to assist in running lotteries and casinos, were relieved. However, the professionals who earned good salaries from running charitable gaming were adamantly opposed. The explanations by LAC at the various community meetings were difficult because bruised egos and fading employment opportunities caused the affected people to hurl insults at the speakers.

Fortunately, BCLC's V.P. Michelle McBride and PR person Jan Carinci were up to the task. BCLC's representatives did their best to assure the charities that gaming funds would continue to benefit their causes. However, the charities became quickly disillusioned and felt that the Lottery Advisory Committee was not truly consulting or listening to their concerns but rather "used" them to "sell" the policy to the broader charitable community and to soothe opposition. Of course, they were correct in that assumption. It was a PR offensive.

DETAILS ON DESTINATION CASINOS

Peter Clark, the chairman of LAC wasted no time digging into the file on destination casinos. Proposals were invited that would have to be evaluated from several perspectives. While your lottery scribe was the official spokesman, Vice-President Vic Poleschuk, and Director Chuck Hamilton were BCLC's representatives on the casino project. Poleschuk was given a lot of freedom to steer the process.

While BCLC, as a corporation, welcomed the casino business, I personally didn't care for casinos, just as I personally don't care for lotteries. The BCLC board was aware of my devotion to leading the business but not being a great aficionado of its products. My defense to those who thought I was the wrong person to lead the lottery file, I resurrected the hoary premise that men could never be successful brassiere salesmen because they did not use the product themselves nor could non-smokers be in charge of Imperial Tobacco.

I didn't object to gambling; I just wasn't a devotee. Perhaps my lack of personal enthusiasm for gambling was all to the good; it made me cautious, rather than a rabid fan, eager to plunge into every new gambling scheme.

400 SILENT SLOT MACHINES

While the members of LAC were still discussing casino minutia, the installation of slot machines had begun. On October 21, 1997, 191 slot machines were installed at Great Canadian Casino's Surrey location. Please keep that Surrey installation in mind until a few paragraphs from now when your lottery scribe comes back to an unpleasant happening.

On October 23 1997, two days after the Surrey installation, 214 slot machines were on their way to be placed on the third floor of the Mandarin Centre in Chinatown at 611 Main Street in Vancouver.

The next day newspaper reports accused the casino of "sneaking in slot machines under cover of darkness". Today, **Dave Gahdia,** the manager still hates the reference to subterfuge. "When you park an 18-wheeler, 50-foot trailer on Main Street at night, it's hardly a secret," he said. But the bad news was that, when the City of Vancouver learned of those slot machines, it immediately insisted on their removal. After considering the issue, the BC Supreme Court ruled on December 19, 1997 that there had to be agreement between the City of Vancouver and provincial government before slot machines were installed. The City Fathers of Vancouver refused to accept the slot machines. Vancouver won! The slots went dark. Twenty-three days later, they were removed.

Today, decades later, I could sympathize with Vancouver's perspective for not wanting those "one-armed bandits." Slot machines are extremely lucrative and sometimes a problem for gamblers with addictive personalities. During a 24-hour shift they require little oversight and the machines retain an average of eight per cent of all money wagered.

Playing slot machines requires no real skill and can captivate some gamblers for hours. Banning slot machines was a no-brainer for Vancouver's overly socially-minded City Council. They argued that slot machines would lead to an increase in the number of people with gambling problems. Perhaps so, but the sale of alcohol and (now legal) drugs have its problems too. Vancouver City Council opposed a casino in 1997 but doesn't object now.

CANCUN? CANNOT!

November 12, 1997. **Hector Morales**, the manager of the Mexican lotto organization had convinced INTERTOTO to stage its 2001 convention in Cancun. It would be a historic international conference if the merger between INTERTOTO and AILE was a done deal. Your lottery scribe had serious doubts about the ability of Senor Morales to create a successful event. He was a charming man but didn't have a practical bone in his body.

Along with the General Secretary of INTERTOTO, my duty was to inspect the facilities and management skills for the Cancun conference. Especially so because the lottery headquarters was in Mexico City and had no presence whatsoever in Cancun, a thousand miles away.

The inspection visit was a combination of two INTERTOTO commitments: the scrutiny of the conference site and — unrelated to the assembly —the staging of an Erewhon seminar in Brazil.

The Mexican lotto corporation appeared to bring very little to the proposed Cancun conference. The organization was totally focussed on its own operations and had absolutely no idea of the scope of the lottery sector beyond its borders. Their concept of hosting a conference was akin to a circus that came into town, put up its tents, performed a show and then left. Mexico's role would be to watch the show.

Instead of explaining to INTERTOTO how he would organize the conference, Senor Morales recited the attraction of Cancun's beaches and the good time that would be had by all. It did not enter his thoughts that Mexico was expected to stage the overall program: arrange for speakers, lunches, dinners, registration and a long list of other obligations.

As inspectors on behalf of INTERTOTO, Yvonne Schnyder and I found no evidence of competence to run even an ice cream stand but enjoyed the hospitality: the evening at the Mexican folk ballet, the evening at the Latin jazz club, the art colony in Coyoacan. The atelier and home of Frida Kahlo, Mexico's famous painter was a special treat.

Cancun, is situated on a spit of land sticking out in the Gulf of Mexico. Yvonne and I rated the location to be a most unlikely place for an international conference. A dozen huge American hotels were situated along the narrow beach. Each hotel had a huge pool for those who didn't care for salt water and featured an extremely loud and powerful music amplification system that blasted Mexican rock music into the stifling heat. INTERTOTO had voted to hold this 2001 conference in Cancun but I wished the whole thing would disappear somehow. My hope was that the 2002 conference planned for Jerusalem would be easier to manage! (ha!)

I told Hector in a harsh way that Cancun as a location and the poor assistance by the Mexican lotto company was unacceptable. Mexico being the host of the conference was denied.

Hector Morales finally confessed his real interest in the conference. He needed the conference for his political survival. There would be a national election in early 2001 and a real possibility existed that, for the first time in history, a labour-minded government might be elected. Hector — a nice man but a product of an elite environment — would lose his job unless there was some very important reason why he shouldn't.

He still didn't grasp the situation. Too bad! Nice man!

SAO PAULO

November 23, 1997. It was time to forget about Cancun and travel to the Erewhon seminar in Brazil which was to be held at a resort some 40 kilometres south of Sao Paulo. Hector Morales and his assistant Jorge Salazar had paid their Erewhon fees as students and joined the long flight to Brazil's largest city.

The trip was uneventful. While waiting at the Sao Paulo passport control, **Dr. Judith Saldana**, a statuesque woman who would be our interpreter, had just arrived from Mexico City and joined our growing group of Erewhonians. Chatting happily, we approached the customs booths. Four travelling companions got through in no time but the passport of the fifth one — your lottery scribe's — was detained.

It took a long while before a senior officer came to tell our interpreter that Senor Simonis would be refused admission to Brazil because his passport lacked the required visa.

"Were you not required to show your visa when you left Canada?" Judith Saldana asked.

"Well no, because I had a ticket for Mexico and no visa is required for entry into that country," I said.

"Well, how about when you checked in at the airport in Cancun?"

Mexican airline people would know that Mexicans can enter Brazil without a visa but were likely not aware of visa requirements by Canadians. Despite much arguing, bureaucracy prevailed. I was refused permission to enter Brazil and had to wait for a plane that could take me anywhere but not anywhere in Brazil. The Brazilian immigration people were kind enough that the location of my arrest would be in the first-class lounge of Varig Airlines. Looking down from the huge window, I could see my travel companions in the hall arguing with the customs and immigration people.

After I was left for a couple of hours of drinking coffee laced with Kahlua, Yvonne Schnyder and Judith Saldana entered the first-class lounge to speak to me under the watchful, coal-black, eyes of a guard.

The ladies brought their Erewhon study papers and were making notes in order to conduct the Erewhon seminar without me. In the midst of this sad exercise came the news that I would be sent back to the U.S. on a nine o'clock flight that evening.

Yvonne and Judith left and I found myself all alone in a huge lounge with the lights dimmed and a gurgling Coke dispenser.

I couldn't be aware of the efforts by my travel companions to set me free but they were busy. It was a Saturday morning, the start of a long summer weekend in Brazil. The passport office in Ottawa, contacted after great effort by Yvonne, reported that no passport was ever issued to a Guy Simonis (of course not; my passport reads Gerard Simonis, something they didn't know). Hector phoned his friend, the mayor of Mexico City who had political connections in Sao Paulo.

In response to a call from the mayor, the Brazilian immigration officer promised to get a minister's permit for a four-day emergency visit but the problem was that the minister was away on a long weekend in Brasilia, the capital of Brazil. The Mexican consulate was alerted; somebody phoned somebody else who knew someone and seven hours after my incarceration in the First-Class Lounge, I was free to enter Brazil... for a limited time.

As I stepped out in the fresh air, the first thing I noticed was a huge outdoor sign that proclaimed in Portuguese: "When you travel, use your Visa" over a picture of the well-known credit card.

The seminar was one of the most energetic Erewhons. Participants from eleven South American countries screamed their opinions at each other. Dr Saldana's translation couldn't keep up. Finally, a hybrid language evolved with interwoven expressions in English, Spanish and Portuguese (and French when needed). To everyone's surprise the seminar was a great success.

366

The day and time of departure from Brazil was stipulated by my captors. I had to be out of the country by 4 a.m. There was no chance to see anything of Brazil but our host was determined to create a Brazilian event for the last evening. An amazingly talented rumba/conga/salsa band was engaged to play jazzy Latin music.

It was a summer evening under the stars and the local drink was coconut milk straight from the nut, with a little rum added. At least that is what I was told. Like Cinderella, I had to leave the party at midnight to get to the Sao Paulo airport before the 4 a.m. red-eye flight to Atlanta. I hung around the bandstand as long as I could. Suddenly, realizing that I hadn't packed anything, I rushed to my cabin...well, let me re-phrase that. I stumbled to my cabin, because that coconut milk contained more rum than advertised.

With a sloppily stuffed travel bag I lurched back to the party to say good-bye. Yvonne had the wisdom to ask if I had my tickets and passport. The documents had to be somewhere but not on my person. I evidently wasn't answering their questions satisfactorily because Yvonne and Judith grabbed my bag, put it on the bandstand, found the documents and placed them in my hand. "Hold them!" Dr. Saldana commanded.

I must have watched all this with some interest because all I remember is that a lottery employee fastened my seatbelt in the corporate van. Someone retrieved the boarding pass after wresting it from my grip. The plane arrived in Atlanta at an ungodly early hour. A single person was waiting for deplaning passengers. It was my son Leonard!

It was Thanksgiving morning 1997 in the United States and indeed I was thankful I to be with my Georgia family.

BCLC LOSES ITS COURT CASE

On December 19, 1997, the Court ruled that the City of Vancouver had acted within in its jurisdiction in tossing out the slot machines.

While the BC Government and Vancouver City Council clashed about casinos at the political level, your sneaky scribe moved quickly to install another batch of slot machines. The targeted locations included a small 4,000 square foot operation in New Westminster on the top floor of the Royal Towers Hotel plus the charitable casinos in Kamloops, Kelowna, Vernon and Prince George. None of them could have more than 30 gaming tables and 300 slot machines. (Those small numbers were expanded later.) These communities were quite happy to accept the slot machines.

TROUBLE RETURNS

In December of 1997, trouble came a-knocking again. The BC government was being sued by the Charity Gaming Association of Nanaimo, acting on behalf of 78 charities on Vancouver Island. They challenged the distribution of slot machine profits earned in charitable casinos of which the government took a percentage. BCLC lawyers had recommended the sharing of slot machine profits between government and charities. Those legal beagles now told us that the charities had a good legal point.

A bit red-faced, they explained that the revenue of charitable gaming should go to charitable causes. Profits raised at a *charitable* casino could not be confiscated by government in order to enrich its coffers.

SHARING REVENUE WITH CHARITIES NIXED

Months later, on January 14, 1998, the Supreme Court of BC ruled on the Nanaimo issue. It declared that the government's plan to share slot machine profits with the charities was a violation of the Criminal Code and that the revenue earned from those slot machines should go — in its entirety — to the charities. The Court observed that the new government policy would facilitate an unparalleled expansion of gaming in BC, thereby enabling the government to take the largest piece of the profit.

The government was in a dither. The ruling was unexpected. Government had collected $24.5 million from slot machines and now the court said they had to give it back to the charities. Government first argued that they couldn't return the money because it had been turned over to its own "charity" (hah-hah) i.e. the Department of Health and Education. Everyone knew that argument wouldn't hold water.

A press release of that period of time showed that the rage of the charities humbled the stance of government.

The Vancouver Sun headline read: BC CHARITIES TO RECEIVE ADDITIONAL $24.5 MILLION

"VICTORIA- January 28 1998. In accordance with the recent BC Supreme Court decision, charities will receive $24.5 million in addition to the $9.1 million due to them in payouts by the end of January, Employment and Investment Minister Dan Miller said today. "I have instructed my officials, to begin the required actions to ensure these funds are paid out as soon as possible."

Miller then asked Frank Rhodes, a Deputy Minister, to immediately meet with charitable organizations to discuss the impact of the court decision and to seek ideas on a new mechanism for gaming revenue distribution.

Miller was quoted: "It is important to remember that the provincial government's initiatives in gaming were developed openly, transparently and in consultation with charities. Our regulatory change in November was designed to ensure consistent and increased revenue levels to give much-needed stability to the charities."

Afterwards in the safety of his office, your lottery scribe was given the government's view that the best solution was to legislate the charities out of the gaming business; take direct control of gambling, keep all the funds in the Treasury and pay-off the charities in any way that cabinet saw fit.

The recipients of the $24.5 million greatly enjoyed their victory but the government had had enough of the bitter battles with the charities. The role of charities in the operations of gaming in BC was on death row.

As governments do when they want to change things, the BC government established another review, headed this time by my favorite senior civil servant **Frank Rhodes**, a man of sterling reputation who handled things wisely.

Many non-profit groups feared, and rightly so, that the Rhodes Review would recommend that charities be removed from all gambling operations, putting them squarely in the hands of BCLC.

To compensate the charities, a provincially funded "Trust" was to be created in order to disburse funds to non-profit organizations — a concept was dubbed as the "Community Chest model."

369

An ad-hoc committee of charities, calling themselves Charitable Gaming Information Systems (CGIS), rose to oppose Frank Rhodes' recommendations.

Having listened to the contrary views, Rhodes recommended that a White Paper be created and distributed for public comment. And so it was.

The comments received made it very clear that the charities believed that gaming revenue was their property — their endowed domain. You may get the impression that the charities were naïve and rather condescending but since beginning of lotteries in BC, government had used the charitable aspect as a "beard", a ruse, to gain the public's acceptance. That false front was now not needed anymore. The public had endorsed gambling, indeed enjoyed gambling, and the revenue to the charities had grown too massive. The time had come for the government to take over, limit charitable funding by doling out grants for genuine charitable causes and dedicate the rest to government programs.

Comments on Frank Rhodes paper were not overly flattering.

One of the former lottery regulators told your lottery scribe: "The mandate of the Lottery Advisory Committee (LAC) was to put this new gaming policy into place come hell or high water. To do this, it needed an organization that would give the appearance of consultation but the critical path for government policy was already established. The views of the charities were not considered." (Well, he had a good point there.)

A former BC Gaming Commission staff member was quoted as: "The Gaming Commission was opposed to the gaming expansion, particularly the expansion of electronic bingo. Nevertheless, LAC went ahead, ignoring the directions by the Commission. As a result, the commissioners resigned because they felt they "could no longer serve the interests of charities." The writer obviously didn't understand that the Gaming Commission was appointed to serve the interest of Government of BC, not the charities. Well... for your lottery scribe many painful obstructionists were removed!

Betty Gilbert, Executive Director of the BC Association for Charitable Gaming was really upset: "Ever since the loss of commission sales for lottery tickets in the 1970s, charities in British Columbia have been scared to death of the Lottery Corporation... it seems they just used charities to build up the gaming business and when that was done they kicked us out the door."

Wendy Smitka of the Business Council of BC, non-profit organizations said: "The system is a stepping-stone for the government's operation of gaming and will remove the ability by non-profit agencies to decide for themselves what the local community needs."

In the opinion of your lottery scribe, Wendy was correct. And it was all for the best, as the years ahead would prove.

SURREY COUCIL TURNS ORNERY

Let's go back to the time when BCLC installed 191 slot machines in the Surrey casino operated by Great Canadian Casino Corporation. Upon a complaint by Surrey Council, a judge's order delayed the operation of the machines. In February 1998, the City of Surrey introduced a zoning bylaw with respect to slot machines. The official reason for the bylaw was to "minimize the negative social impacts of gaming on the residents, businesses and workers in Surrey" or in other words "We want a slice of the profits."

At that early Surrey Council meeting, where the zoning issued was debated, the lawyer of Great Canadian Casino pooh-poohed Surrey City Council's opinion that the introduction of slot machines would lead to problem gaming and that the citizenry would face dire consequences.

He questioned why slot machines are such a major concern when there are other addictions equally as damaging. "Almost half the Canadian population is overweight," he quoted from a paper issued by Ottawa's Health and Welfare. In the light of the ravages inflicted by obesity, should the Council perhaps pass by-laws to help prevent citizens' addiction to excess food?"

"Nearly 8% of the population are alcoholics," he noted from his research. "Should Council regulate the number of drinks served in bars and pubs?" He further argued that a Harvard Medical School study showed that problem gamblers constitute only 3.5% of population — compared with 8% for alcoholics. Participation in many forms of entertainment, such as racetracks, pubs, sports parks, can result in troublesome consequences."

"The problems of over-eating, abuse of alcohol and participating in hazardous activities are the by-products of living in a free society in which our citizens can exercise their choice within the law."

371

He concluded his presentation by stating that Council should consider his remarks and to acknowledge that the majority of the citizens of Surrey expressed their interest in playing slot machines in their own city.

The council listened attentively and passed a bylaw banning slot machines!

(A year later, Surrey Council changed its mind when the Province offered the Council — and all other affected municipalities —10% of the profits earned within their jurisdiction Then, of course, the objections faded away except for the left-leaning Vancouver City Council which didn't allow a slot machine until 2005 — and then in only one huge casino.)

BCLC appealed the decision.

The Superior Court held that the Surrey zoning by-law had the effect of prohibiting slot machines. The Court ordered that Great Canadian Casino cease operating slot machines in the Surrey casino. The 191 slots in Surrey went silent. Now, Vancouver and Surrey were without slot machines, although other types of gambling carried on in their respective charitable casinos.

BCLC DIDN'T QUIT

After the Surrey decision, BCLC's lawyers convinced the Great Canadian Casino Company to assign its lease of the casino premises to the Lottery Corporation, and — so armed — on May 29, 1998, BCLC commenced proceedings against Surrey.

In that court case, your lottery scribe argued that the Surrey zoning by-law did not apply to the Lottery Corporation and requested that the earlier Court Order prohibiting slot machine gaming in the Surrey casino should be rescinded. The outcome? The Courts said NO!

WHO CONTROLS THOSE SLOT MACHINES?

An earlier hassle with the City of Surrey had been about whether slot machines in a charitable casino were being operated within the Criminal Code. The Code says that slot machines cannot be operated by anyone other than by the provincial government. The reality was that slot machines in charitable casinos were operated by a private operator under an agreement with BCLC, an agent of the Crown. The judge found that the BC government had illegally delegated its power to manage and conduct slots to the Surrey Casino. The legal question now became: Is the operation of a slot machine controlled by BCLC or the casino operator?

To your lottery scribe, the question was answered by the fact that BCLC owned all the slot machines at the casino. Those machines were connected to the BCLC Data Centre in Kamloops, where BCLC controlled the payouts and only BCLC personnel had access to the controls inherent to the operation. The location and hours of operation were determined by BCLC. A BCLC service technician had to be present during the hours of operation. If any unauthorized interference occurred, the system would automatically be de-activated.

In short, BCLC's argument was that it controlled the slot machines and the role of the casino operator was limited to opening the machine "drop buckets" and depositing the money in a BCLC-designated account.

Allow me to explain how the operator received its earnings: The operator i.e. the "service provider" received a commission of 28% of the slot machine's net revenue (which means the money left after prizes). This is quite similar to the lotto store where BCLC owns the machinery and the retailer deposits the money in a designated bank account, less his or her commissions. Apart from these arrangements, the casino service provider was authorized to provide food, beverages, other enhancements and retail services. Just like the store.

If you understand the similarity between the storekeeper and the casino operator, you are smarter than quite a number of politicians who believed that casinos were the owners of the gambling operations.

That misconception was fed by the popular designation of "casino operator." In order to clarify the roles, the title of the casino's relationship to BCLC was officially changed to "service provider."

Surrey's legal objection to slot machines was based on the alleged "illegal delegation" by BCLC of "managing and conducting the equipment." The City argued that the operator (Great Canadian) supplied the business plan, management skills, premises and operational and executive staff.

The judge agreed with Surrey that the operator was a participant in creating profit for the casino. In the judge's view the agreement between BCLC and the operator was not simply a rental agreement but a profit-sharing scheme (meaning commissions) that came very close to delegating provincial powers to the casino operator.

But, he added, profit sharing was not enough proof that the casino managed operations. The real issue was whether or not the province was the "operating mind." After hearing all the facts, Mr. Justice Leggat concluded that the service provider (i.e. the casino) wasn't "the master" with respect to operating slot machines. "The service provider might offer some ancillary services but the installation, technical support, monitoring and setting of games and payouts are all controlled by BCLC."

Finally, we had won the main issue. Phewwww!

In April of 1998, the BC Government announced a new model for gaming as described by your pleased and gloating scribe.

The announcement put BCLC in the driver's seat for near exclusive management and conduct of all gaming in the province! Horse racing was still far away. It was still the domain of the Federal Ministry of Agriculture.

DESTINATION CASINOS ANNOUNCED

Something new to your lottery scribe was the concept of Destination Casinos. Proposals were invited. The word "Destination" meant there had to be a tourist attraction attached to the casino. The proposals received would be evaluated from several perspectives.

Casino evaluation was by no means a single decision-making process by me and my staff. The idea was that the Lottery Advisory Committee would assess our staff's rating of the proposals and make recommendations to cabinet.

After working at this for a few weeks as a member of the four-person advisory committee (LAC), I was surprised to learn that our committee was told NOT to make recommendations as to which casinos should be approved. The committee would only supply information to cabinet. Politicians would evaluate the bids and decide. This turn was unusual and somewhat ominous.

My fear that something was not right was confirmed months later. The entire destination casino project was a political battle fought way above the heads of us civil servants. The issue became city versus province, cabinet versus

374

caucus, casino promoters versus gambling opponents. We, poor but faithful servants would have to wait to see what became of all this jockeying.

On May 14, 1998, the BC government announced that three Destination Casinos were approved in principle:

- Casino of the Rockies. St. Mary's Indian Reserve - Cranbrook. The casino was allowed 30 gaming tables and 300 slot machines. Its approved resort proposal showed a 124-room hotel, lodges, restaurants, a conference centre, an 18-hole golf course and other amenities.
- Jack O'Clubs at Wells BC (near Barkerville) was authorized to have seven gaming tables and 125 slot machines

- Motor Vessel Pacific Aurora was allotted five gaming tables and 35 slot machines. It would cruise from Prince Rupert to Vancouver in the summer and between Prince Rupert, Victoria, Seattle, Nanaimo and Campbell River in the off-season.

Another 34 proposals were left to review. As a member of the Lottery Advisory Committee (LAC). I can tell you, that only a few of the original proposals under review warranted an approval-in-principle stage. Thirteen of those original proposals were located in the Lower Mainland, none of them in the City of Vancouver. In my view most of those remaining proposals where amateurish efforts.

(Note: Of the three proposals that were approved... **Casino of the Rockies** went broke and is now operating under new and more competent owners. **The Jacks O' Clubs** never materialized but morphed into an attractive casino in Quesnel not too far from Wells and Barkerville. The **Motor Vessel Pacific Aurora** proposal never amounted to anything.)

SOMETIMES THEY WERE AFTER ME

You may wonder what your lottery scribe did as President of BCLC when he wasn't off gallivanting around the world. Well, apart from managing a province-wide enterprise, there was always something afoot when the news cycle hit a dry spell — a time when media are looking for colorful stories.

In summer of 1998 BCLC found itself in the limelight. Well not so much the corporation per se but rather its "colourful" president a.k.a. as your lottery scribe. The timing for a good juicy news story was ideal. It was a peaceful period for BCLC; the lotto games produced their jackpots and the CLUB KENO game brought in millions annually. Destination Casinos were in development. The administration was well in hand.

The daily media were inactive on the lottery file but *VANCOUVER MAGAZINE* produced a dramatic piece quoting unnamed former BCLC employees that "working at BCLC was akin to toiling in the salt mines".

Those complainants who assailed their former president (Moi) evoked images of Attila the Hun. Apart from my admission that I don't suffer fools gladly, there wasn't a great deal of substance to the story. However, it got more absurd when an anonymous complainer alleged that I had installed "live cameras" in the men's and women's washrooms to spot idlers.

Another anonymous but more damaging slur claimed that your faithful scribe had awarded a multi-million-dollar contract for GTECH lottery terminals without calling for tenders. The implication was that I was on "the take." Some reporters have a particular ability to report facts in such a manner that the issue looks corrupt. The facts were that BCLC had joined with the Ontario Lottery Corporation in a joint purchase of lottery terminals. Ontario called for the tenders and the BCLC and Ontario Lottery staff cooperated on the details.

Two BCLC board members travelled to Toronto to evaluate the agreement that BCLC would purchase lottery terminals in tandem with Ontario. After being informed in detail by the board of the OLC, the BC board members approved the purchase. BCLC would get the benefit of better pricing, due to a larger purchase. Yes, it was literally true that BCLC hadn't officially asked for tenders; that part of the administration had been left to Ontario. After completion of the deal, I received a letter from the BC Government's Purchasing Bureau complimenting me on my "innovative approach that yielded substantial savings."

Nevertheless, after reading the magazine's accusations, NDP lottery minister Elizabeth Cull appointed a team of investigators to check out the story. They discovered that the lowest bidder — a largely unknown company — provided a substantially lower price than the winner, GTECH. The financial sleuths zeroed in on that issue and made it the primary finding in their report.

However, I was able to point out that after the company's response to the Request for Proposal was issued, the low bidder had gone bankrupt. The report to the Minister of Finance was a bit blah-blah; nothing substantial was found but one of their recommendations was that next time we shouldn't look for savings but go by the book and pay whatever is offered by the lowest-cost supplier! Yes... bureaucracy can contradict itself in many ways.

The whole thing would have ended there if it weren't for the covering letter of the findings to the Minister. It said that significant errors in procedure were found. However — the actual report — submitted along with the letter, said that NO significant errors were found. I knew that the Minister would read the covering letter and not the report. I asked the audit team for a retraction. They wouldn't concede their error but allowed that I could write an explanatory letter stating that I disputed the content of the letter to the Minister. I not only wrote a strong protest but insisted that if the report was ever made public, my letter of protest should be included.

Months later, a reporter from the *Vancouver Sun* obtained a copy of the report under "Freedom of Information Act" but my explanatory letter was not attached. When the reporter approached me for comments in search of a possible high-octane exposé, I produced my explanatory letter. The result was that the *Vancouver Sun* blasted the Minister for supplying incomplete information. That is the problem with working for government. Whatever you do will be re-visited in hindsight. Fortunately, I had anticipated the problem by establishing my strong exception to the report.

MICHELLE MCBRIDE QUITS

It was a sad day when Michelle McBride walked in to my office and presented her resignation. She had been offered the position of Vice-President of GTECH and would leave for Rhode Island within the month. I felt a loss. How can one not, after working together more than two decades? She had joined the Western Canada fledgling lottery 23 years before as a newbie secretary and had developed into a strong sales executive, rising in the ranks to Vice President. Michelle has a great intuitive management style and guided BCLC through some difficult times. A natural leader who was adored by her staff!

For me, Michelle's departure was a major blow. I lost a friend and a colleague. But for Michelle it was a beginning of a new career that — in the years ahead — would bring her international fame. Without her support, your lottery scribe might not have withstood the storms that threatened to engulf our early lottery years. She is a force to be reckoned with.

LONDON, GLASGOW AND THE WORLD CUP

June 10, 1998. Inspection of the facilities for the 2000 AILE Conference brought Ina and I to London and Glasgow. Arriving two years in advance of the event might be for naught because — technically — events in 2000 would not my responsibility. I'd be retired from BCLC by that time. Glasgow was scheduled as an AILE conference but it would turn into the World Lottery Association conference if the 1999 INTERTOTO meeting in Oslo agreed to the merger.

Our British colleagues were so certain about the unification that they referred to their Glasgow event as the WLA founding meeting. Ina and I decided to take a bit of a holiday in Britain. Starting in London in a rental car, we toured the coast that was originally settled before by the Angles from Denmark and the Saxons from Holland.

We slowly made our way north, eating at pubs, which, I think, offer the best food in Britain. Every evening we found ourselves in a pub with a World Cup soccer match on the "telly" attended by a boisterous crowd of madmen. In one small town pub called the British Lion, the locals had gathered to watch Brazil versus England. Attending the game at the stadium wouldn't have been much different from what we experienced in the pub. Yelling, whistling, booing and singing (not to mention, drinking) created a constant roar. Alas, England lost. We expected riots and misery to ensue, but fortunately the second match of the evening brought the defeat of France by Romania. France's demise revived the happy atmosphere of the Brits. Ancient rivalries are not forgotten.

The actual inspection was unsurprising. Glasgow isn't a glamorous location but the plans and facilities for the conference were solid and proper. On the way back to London, along the coast of the Irish Sea, we learned more about Scotland. In Oban's oldest pub, we joined the locals in mourning England's loss to Portugal and suffered along in the agony of seeing France beat Russia. By the time we got to Wales, England was out of the World Cup. When we finally flew to Amsterdam, we were fully aware of England's soccer fans' insanity.

FLORENCE

July 12, 1998. After a weekend in Holland visiting friends and relatives, we flew to Florence for an INTERTOTO meeting. A side meeting of the Implementation Task Force in Florence had been productive but the meeting of the full INTERTOTO board had no discernable purpose other than to get together in Florence's best hotel and enjoying an exquisite evening dinner in the mansions of the famed Medici family. Fortunately, the expensive tab was largely absorbed by Lottomatica, one of Italy's lottery suppliers.

The Medici dinner was very "18th century" with white-wigged attendants, candle light and strains of delicate harp music. We were told that patronage by the Medici clan was responsible for the majority of Florentine art. During dinner, Ina went on a quiet reconnaissance and found that the chateau's bathroom offered an upscale electric hair dryer and a can of Old Spice which spoiled her illusion of the Golden Age of the Medici.

Now at this point in this lottery tale, your lottery scribe should bore you with the ebb and flow of the debates leading to a merger of the two world lottery organizations, but while there was a lot of hot air at this meeting, nothing of consequence developed. The next day's events proved to be more amusing (and more expensive.)

VISIT RELATIVES FOR ONLY $1000-A-DAY

July 15, 1998. On the INTERTOTO meeting's free day in Florence, Ina and I decided to take a drive to visit relatives in Italy's rural Viterbo. The cheapest rental car was a Daewoo, a Korean-made car we had never heard of, and — in hindsight — we would have preferred to remain ignorant of. My cousin had a summer place on the outskirts of a small village close to the Autostrada. We knew it was a modest place where they absorbed the glorious sun that hardly ever shows its face in Holland's frequently damp summers.

After wasting a full hour of trying to drive out of Florence's suburbia we found ourselves at the spot where we started. Things were looking up! However, when we found the correct highway, the Daewoo became the day's woe. It made noises as if out of breath and seemingly very desirous to slow the pace. Ina, my chauffeur, was kind and slowed down to 100 km/h, which — in

Italy — is considered obstruction of traffic. Almost two hours behind for our visit, we found the cut-off to the town where our cousin Jan would be waiting.

In our haste to get to the village, Ina did not notice that the railway crossing was literally a crossing of the rails. There were no wooden beams between the rails to make a road! Despite a series of awful bangs, the Daewoo still stumbled into town. We spotted Jan's frantic wave from the piazza bar. Any worries that he might have been bored waiting for us were dispelled when we found him behind three empty beer glasses. His enthusiastic welcome made us forget the cursed Korean vehicle.

Jan volunteered to drive the Daewoo to his home located on a sunny hilltop. To everyone's dismay, halfway up the hill, the Korean conveyance surrendered to the Italian countryside. It just died, in the middle of a bend on a narrow country road. We pushed the dead vehicle onto a property that belonged to an unshaven and annoyed-looking Italian, resplendently dressed in sweat-stained undershirt and baggy trousers. He looked at our efforts but didn't utter a word. We just left it and hitchhiked our way to our cousin's home, where we settled down for a short rest before we set out to look for a repair shop in town. There was a repair shop but because it was Italy and it was mid-summer, it didn't take much translation of the handwritten sign to figure out that the garage would re-open in September.

We phoned the rental company and asked what to do. Should we perhaps phone the carabinieri, the police?

"No. No! No! No Policia!" the voice screeched back. "Where eez zee car?"

Well, it was on a bend on a small, unnamed road outside a town the name of which escaped me at the moment. The information was good enough for the man to suggest abandoning the car and leaving the keys in the "glove box."

Ina and I had come so far to visit with our cousin and now after barely 90 minutes we were panicking about how to get back to the INTERTOTO meeting in Florence. Jan's car had only two seats, not because the car was built that way, but by removing the back seat, he had to pay less in road taxes and it provided more room to stow stuff on their 2,500-km treks to and from Holland.

Train! Travel by train! That was the answer!

But this meant that we had to travel to Rome and transfer to another train to Florence with only minutes in between. I used Jan's cell phone to call Yvonne Schnyder in Florence to tell her our car had broken down and did she have any ideas how to get back to the INTERTOTO meeting?

Twenty minutes later she phoned to tell us that she had arranged an Alitalia flight from Amsterdam to Florence that evening. "Why?" I asked in stunned amazement.

"Are you far from Amsterdam?" Yvonne asked.

"Yeah, a couple of thousand kilometers. We are near Rome."

I could hear Yvonne swallow: "How can that be? The read-out of my phone read that you called from the country code 31. That is Holland!"

I explained it was my Dutch cousin's cell phone located in Italy. Minutes later, she phoned again to say it was important that the INTERTOTO meeting should be held as planned and that we should take a taxi. The local cab driver was ecstatic when he heard our destination was Rome! The fare would be $500 U.S. Yvonne said that Lottomatica agreed to add the taxi cost to their hospitality account. No out-of-pocket expense for INTERTOTO or me! Lucky for us!

All we had to do was get in the cab, travel to Florence and the desk clerk at our hotel would pay the fare. In Italy, there is no correlation between the highway speed signs and the actual rate of speed of vehicles. It would have been no use to tell the driver to "step on it" since there was no more room between the accelerator and the floor to step on.

It was well after dinnertime when we arrived at our Florence hotel. The cabby raced to the concierge to collect his bagful of liras. The concierge stared at the driver without saying a word. He put his index finger beneath his left eye and pulled down, showing an enormous bit of white eyeball. I don't speak Italian but I understood it to mean: "Are you shitting me?"

He counted out the equivalent of $500 and shoved it at the taxi driver, who slipped into the role of someone who was bewailing the departure of his dearly beloved mother. He crawled into a near fetal position on the lobby's sofa, wailed and pointed at me. The concierge pointed at the exit and threatened to call the police. With appropriate music it would have resembled an opera scene.

After freshening up a bit, we joined the rest of the conference participants at a restaurant on the ancient Florence plaza, where the maître d' snobbishly decided that we were too late for service and with the greatest reluctance, allowed us to consume the offered dessert. We had an exciting day; we had seen our relatives for 90 minutes but the expensive cab ride was paid for so what was there to complain about?

It turned out that we could complain when — one month later — we received our Visa statement. It included a car rental charge and damages for a total of 1.5 million lire ($1,500). We tried arguing by long-distance in Italian but gave up after four tries. Our little trip had cost $10 per kilometer.

MONTECATINI

After that expensive meeting in Florence we traveled to Montecantini, a tourist haven located at the foot of the Pistoia Mountains. We were not there for the 14th century baths and spas... but rather to lead an Erewhon seminar. Attending the seminar was an eclectic mix of Europeans and North American lottery people, including two members of the BCLC board of directors, both NDP devotees who — in principle — saw lotteries as a social evil. They had wrestled with their conscience to accept a holiday in Italy to learn about gambling, but quickly relieved themselves of their principles and travelled in style.

These British Columbians were apprehensive that your lottery scribe might transform them into frenzied gamblers but their fears were assuaged, not by me but by the enthusiasm of the participants from 14 different countries, of which 10 were governed by socialist parties. I can tell you that it became a lot easier to deal with the BCLC board now that two newly converted gaming "experts" were on my side.

BUENOS AIRES

In November of 1998, Ina had enough of travelling and decided that I should go to Buenos Aires alone, especially because I had foolishly agreed to deliver speeches in the Netherlands and Britain, only three days after the AILE Conference in Argentina. While shaking hands with the many Spanish-speaking delegates the day before the Buenos Aires sessions began, I became aware of the great distinction between various South Americans. The Mexicans consider themselves closest to Americans and deem Argentineans as supremely arrogant and mainly focused on retaining their dominant Caucasian heritage. While

Columbian, Chilean and other delegates were of obvious native South American ancestry, there appeared to be very little indigenous blood among the delegates from Argentina.

I was quickly informed by friends that Argentineans consider themselves to be at the top of the heap. Despite my laughter at their intolerant views, I became the trusted ear for many weird jokes about Argentinean haughtiness.

"Why do Argentineans open their windows during a thunderstorm and stick their heads out to look at the sky? Because they think God is taking pictures of them!"

In turn, Argentineans believe people from the South American states are ignorant peasants. The Portuguese-speaking Brazilians are regarded as resembling the Irish — jolly, irreverent and party-loving. For me, it was a quick immersion in South American identity politics.

What they didn't realize was that my task was to get them all on-side in order to approve the merger between AILE and INTERTOTO. At a pre-vote cocktail party of Latinos, the lottery director from Spain — who automatically holds the post of Secretary General of all Spanish and Portuguese speaking lottery nations — leapt into action as my lobbyist. Dragging me around the cocktail circuit, he introduced me to many bronzed, dark-haired, mustachioed men with names I couldn't repeat within seconds after hearing them. Let me correct that. I could remember their names from the printed membership list but the custom is that the mother's last name is added when being officially introduced. This led to some confusion. To be introduced to Senor Mario Martinez-Martinez makes you wonder whether that's his actual moniker or someone being helpful by repeating his last name. Some of those names resemble rhymes like my Mexican colleague Hector Morales-Coralis.

It was also hard to recall the names of the lottery organizations. Several of the South-American countries have more than one "national" lottery. Argentina has five! Peru has three. Mexico is merely a piker with two.

Speaking of Mexico, Hector Morales the director of the Mexican National Lotto and TOTO introduced me to his counterpart, the General Manager of the Mexican National Lottery — an institution founded in the 1700s. His last name was **Salomon** and his Brylcreamed hair and bird-flew-up-your-nose moustache, were a match with his haughty attitude. From here on, I shall refer to him as Salmonella, because he was poison to the merger.

Delegates from the 75 lottery organizations were seated behind tables featuring nameplates with their long titles when the 80 marchers-strong Presidential Guard drummed themselves into the audience with an ear-deafening din. The parade wasn't well-rehearsed, for there was not sufficient room for the delegates plus the orchestra. As the Guards marched relentlessly forth, tables were hastily moved and the delegates squeezed against the walls.

The ruckus suddenly stopped. A government official uttered a welcome in Spanish. This is largely an assumption on my part because the interpreters who would have translated his speech had been evacuated from their booths.

I must further suppose that the densely-packed crowd was probably very excited to learn that "Senor Presidente" Simonis would address the conference but before that, the squished audience was advised have a coffee in the foyer in order to allow the Presidential Guard to stage an orderly retreat from the hall.

"Be back in 10 minutes," the chairman admonished in his best English.

Forty-five minutes later, when I finally got to speak, the audience was reduced to a quarter of the original attendance. Nevertheless, I delivered my stuff pretending that someone was truly listening.

My closing paragraph was that the delegates could indicate their approval of the proposed merger by applause. The applause was there but whether it was real or relief that it was time to visit the bar, will never be known.

ONE MORE VOTE TO GO

At the closing of the Buenos Aires business meeting and according to tradition, the host of the next AILE Conference would become the chairman of the next gathering. Glasgow had been chosen for the year 2000. **Tim Holley** was the Managing Director of the National Lottery of the United Kingdom and he graciously turned the assembly's closing meeting over to me in order to obtain the vote to approve the merger. It was unanimous. The vote meant that AILE was committed to disbanding itself and become part of the World Lottery Organization and that the Berlin meeting in 1999 would be a joint-meeting for INTERTOTO and AILE.

THE LONGEST DINNER EVER

Our Argentinean hosts announced that the highlight of the conference would be the closing dinner with the promising title: "Feast of the Argentine." Any inquiries as to what this feast might be and its length in hours were fended off with a smiling, "Sorpresa!"

At 6 p.m. conference-goers were bussed to a huge air-conditioned tent where tango music poured loudly from the speakers. Smiling servers urged trays of finger food upon new arrivals. The hustling of food never did abate, appetizers and drinks kept on coming. The Europeans and North Americans began to wonder if this cornucopia was the signal that a dire famine in the offing and that food should be stockpiled. After 90 minutes of tacos, tequenos and tangos, the big dining doors opened.

Immediately, national entities formed aggressive cliques in order to sit together. There was a reserved head table for AILE notables but it was occupied by well-dressed squatters of unknown origin who may or may not have been associated with the event. It didn't matter — they were obviously unfamiliar with the meaning of the English-language sign "Reserved".

The Argentine Lottery President Senor Olme, his family, friends, hangers-on and associates had secured half a dozen tables in a fine location. From afar he waved jovially as your scribe and my colleagues searched for a table in the back. However, our location — at first judged to be a distressed area — turned into a blessing when a tower of loudspeakers next to Olme's table exploded with raucous tango music. It was the beginning of a 60-minute parade of 20 different tango-crazed couples — each from a different region of Argentina — performing their particular interpretation of the tango. To be clear: not 20 couples en masse, but each separately.

To any observer, it was clear that no one in the huge room was paying the slightest attention to the dancers. By 10 o'clock, the supply of finger food had ebbed. The tangos thankfully faded by 11. Suddenly a series of lottery commercials were shown on a big screen to the absolute disinterest of hundreds of guests, most of whom might have been employees of the Argentinean Lottery— they certainly weren't conference attendees.

Patrick Chen, BCLC Chairman and my table companion, was ravenous. "It's almost midnight," he moaned, "I didn't have any of those appetizers before dinner and now there is no food in sight. Can you do something?"

As I passed the stage in the hunt for food, any food, I heard the emcee call my name. He waved me onto the stage but since I had no idea what was being said, I waved gaily back and kept going. I heard later that I was supposed to present a trophy to some Buenos Aires TV advertising producer. In the chaos and din, nobody cared.

I must have followed the right trail because at the kitchen door I nearly collided with waiters carrying silver trays. I didn't expect much in terms of food, but Patrick Chen, who expected dinner, was disappointed. The dish of pasta, interspersed with spinach was nicely arranged but it didn't have much caloric value so by 1:30 a.m., the BCLC contingent decided to find a cab and go back to the hotel where GTECH had promised an after-dinner nightcap.

The GTECH hospitality suite was already well-populated with early deserters from the spinach-pasta. The GTECH hostess was persuaded to order hamburgers and fries from room-service in sufficient numbers to feed the burgeoning crowd. Never had a serving of hamburgers and fries been so mouth-watering. The jazz was entertaining and cleared our musical ears from all those tangos.

By 2:30 a.m. additional delegates straggled back from the front to tell us there had been a lavish dinner and a great Caribbean Show.

For your tired scribe it was time for bed! The flight to Holland would leave in the afternoon and it would take 18 hours. Fortunately, I had reserved my favourite seat — 2B — in business class and could sleep most of the way.

In the morning, at brunch I sat with German delegates who had stayed awake for the very late dinner and talked about the Caribbean Show. "It was great," my seat mate said, adding that the final dinner, when all the lights went out, the waiters carried-in huge flaming steaks on barbecue plates, something that topped just about anything he had ever seen.

"What time was that?" I asked in surprise.

"Oh we left before the dancing started at about five," he said. "Only the Argentineans stayed for the dancing."

"How many were there?"

"Oh, a few hundred or so. None of them conference goers, I think!" he said, yawning widely.

FLIGHT RESERVATION GONE

The Buenos Aires Airport was a mess. The United Nations Conference on the Environment ended on the same day as the AILE conference. The KLM flight to Amsterdam via Lisbon was one of three direct flights to Europe. It took an hour to reach the check-in counter. To my great annoyance, the clerk told me my seat had been given away to the Dutch cabinet minister for the environment, the Honorable M. Pronk, who was booked to travel two days later but had decided to go home early.

The KLM computer had found me to be the only non-European passport holder on the flight and therefore the least risky customer to piss off. I showed the clerk my passport showing my nationality at birth. She was a nice Dutch-speaking woman and was close to tears of embarrassment. My choice was to either go nuts and create a scene or accept reality and maybe survive the flight in tourist class.

The KLM woman was so grateful for my unusually gentle behaviour that she gave me a wink and handed me two boarding passes with adjoining seats in economy. She had seated me in a small section with a bathroom just around the corner. I tried to hypnotize myself that I was comfortable and relaxed as I slumped into a sardine-can position.

A few hours into the flight, I walked into business class and there were my colleagues from Holland, Germany and France happily chatting with their premium beers in hand. They took an unpleasant delight in my misfortune.

I did survive but once arrived safely in Holland, ensconced in my mother's old living room I dreamed about a secret revenge on Minister Pronk.

I got no response to my written tirade to his Ministry but the PR folks of KLM sent me some lovely special porcelain statues of famous buildings in the Netherlands plus a free trip anywhere within Europe.

A MILESTONE AND THE 45-YEAR-OLD PREDICTION

Let me side-track you here to mark a special milestone in time for me.

In May of 1954, a couple of weeks after Ina and I arrived in Canada as immigrants, Walter Scott Wright — who many years later would be President of Manitoba's Court of Queen's Bench — told Ina and me at a social evening at his home, that we shouldn't fear our future in Canada. He said he admired our determination and that in his view your lottery scribe would end up as the head of a multi-million-dollar enterprise. It sounded far-fetched then — likely a lot of flattery intended to buck us up. But Justice Wright was right; I did preside over a company with a billion dollars in sales, on January 22, 1999.

On that memorable day, at 10.15 a.m., the computer screen on my office desk showing "live" annual sales, clicked from a nine-digit sales number to 10-digits, indicating that a billion dollars had been reached. It was a special moment for me but then looking at the screen half an hour later the billion had grown by tens of thousands of dollars more and I realized that it was just a point in time and life would go on. At the end of the fiscal year — March 31, 1999 — the sales number stopped at $1,261,494.000.

(In 1972, when your lottery scribe began his lottery journey, the first year's sales of the sports lottery were just under $250,000.)

AUSTRALIA'S GOLD COAST: A SHORT BREAK

The lottery folks in Queensland had requested an EREWHON seminar. The Australians, more than any region loved Erewhon. Those who attended the session in the Blue Mountains of Australia, a year or so before, had raved about the experience. The setting for this March 1999 Erewhon was the Coolum Resort north of Brisbane, where the G7 countries planned to have their meetings a few months later. The trip was most pleasant and provided a relief from the difficult casino developments back home and the hassles of forming a single world lottery association.

Ina and I were welcomed at the Sydney Airport by my ever-efficient assistant **Frances Kenny.** She had flown a contorted route in order to save money. Without a moment of rest, a car was rented for the 1,000-km trip north of Brisbane. We could have traveled by air but the lush countryside and perhaps the opportunity to spot a kangaroo in the wild was the appeal.

The drive started out fine but after a few hours a white mist began to emanate from the air conditioning vent. The technical expertise of your lottery scribe caused him to dismiss the fog as the effects of that strong industrial-type of air-conditioning, required to cool the Australian summer heat. My technical opinion might have been turned out to be true if it hadn't been for the fact that we were sweltering in a stinking car. My skill in diagnosing automobile ailments was undermined when the car hiccupped to a standstill, hissing menacingly.

Frances Kenny located a phone and we were soon rescued by a dealership in a nearby town. Our car was exchanged for a better model at no charge; the company's service was excellent. However, with respect to making good travel time, it wasn't that great. Five hours after leaving Sydney Airport, we had only covered 100 kilometers. After having a coffee and a sandwich at a cute roadside diner where Frances chatted with every single person in the joint, we continued on our merry way.

A half hour later, Frances commented on the irritating brightness of Australian summer and realized she wasn't wearing her expensive sunglasses. They'd been left on the counter at that jolly diner! The way *out* of town had been easy but there was no assurance we'd ever find our way back. Frances was distraught. But we did locate the diner and as soon as she walked in, the owner — who couldn't help remembering this chattering Canadian jaybird — hurried over to hand her the sunglasses. Hugs and air-kisses ensued.

The Erewhon at the fabulous Coolum Resort was wild and wonderful. While Frances and I had a great time, Ina was bored to tears. She was locked in a posh resort, miles from anywhere and surrounded by hoity-toity shops that only featured Louis Vuitton, Gucci and Prada.

My readers may wonder why I write about the things around the Erewhon sessions and not the lectures themselves. Well, the thing is these sessions aren't all that different. The same problems are solved, the same arguments presented and the joyous windups after three full days of intense involvement are always a high point. Participants reflect their cultural outlook. South Americans are bombastic but receptive; Eastern Europeans conniving for advantage; Northern Europeans introspective; Southern Europeans are suspicious; Australians high-spirited; Chinese quiet but intensive; Africans argumentative; Israelis querulous; Japanese aggressive; Americans litigious.

After leaving the Coolum paradise we accepted the local wisdom and took the inland-road back to Sydney rather than the lush coastal roads. Not only did we fail to see a single kangaroo, we hardly saw anyone or anything, except in a weird town called Tamworth, Australia's headquarters of Country Music. We discovered a 12-metre high, gold-plated statue of a guitar on the side of a huge guitar-shaped swimming pool. It was fascinating enough to entice us to spend the night there on the trip back to Sydney Airport. It was a good tour of an empty vastness.

MERGER HASSLE IN LONDON

May 21, 1999. Another meeting about the merger was scheduled for London. Facing the reality that the two old associations would finally disband in favor of a single organization, the old-guard of INTERTOTO started dragging their feet. The latest controversy was how to divide administration tasks between Basel and Montreal. The fears of the General Secretary of INTERTOTO could only be laid to rest if the Montreal office was abandoned, leaving Basel in full control. This didn't sit well with the AILE bloc. The ideal solution had to be meaningful for both sides.

My plan was that the INTERTOTO office should handle the common business of a trade association, i.e. member inquiries, seminars, conferences, information and publications, while Montreal office could easily handle support functions, such as legal issues, convening board meetings, financial controls and continue as a liaison with diehard AILE members.

INTERTOTO pushed their original position to have all functions in Basel with Montreal housing an "industry library." In other words, a return to the idea of INTERTOTO swallowing AILE.

Yet there was another major issue to deal with. The much-discussed draft bylaws made it clear that the new association was an association of the world's lottery corporations, not countries. AILE's old rules specified that each *country* would be eligible for membership. This would be fine for a national lottery such as France but not for federated countries like Germany, Canada, Argentina and the USA who devolved their gaming authority to provincial and/or state lotteries.

These proposed rules riled the French, for France had one lottery company with one vote while Germany — that devolved its lottery operations to their "landers" — would have 16 votes. I had personally experienced the AILE rule when BCLC was allowed pay its "national" dues but when it came to a vote at the annual meeting, five Canadian votes would have to be delivered as one.

I explained to the unitary states that the U.S. and Canada combined could have as many as 41 votes but since these state and provincial lotteries didn't have that much in common, there was no problem. I won the day by proposing that for any 'major' vote, a majority of 75% was required so that none of the "blocs" could control the agenda.

But there was still the issue of control of the purse strings.

Indulging my ever-shortening emotional fuse — I decided to throw a tantrum. While the Austrian delegate kept sniping at North American control, I threw papers across the table and stormed out yelling: "I quit! I have carried this load for two years and it appears that compromise is impossible."

Europeans are used to long, dreary meetings but dare not disturb decorum. This display of rudeness startled them. The meeting broke up with the saboteurs of the merger on one side, and those who wanted a single association on the other. The latter group was in the majority. Matti Ahde and Tim Holley (UK), ever the politicians, shuttled from one end of the room to the other. Given my bad-mannered outburst I found myself alone in a corner. When Tim and Matti approached me, I insisted on complete acceptance of the proposals of the Implementation Task Force. No compromises!

Tim Holley, his arm around my shoulder, dragged me back to the obstructers. Subject to some adjustments in the proposed constitution — that I didn't particularly like but could live with — the meeting concluded on a positive note. My greatest supporter, Matti Ahde, was critical of my outburst. He called it "unparliamentary". We agreed to disagree. When faced with persistent stubbornness, I tend to explode and then wait to gather up the pieces. It's not nice, I know, but it has often won me the day.

Never mind: We were set for final the vote in Norway in September of 1999.

MALTA

May 23, 1999. After the dust-up in London, Ina and I travelled to Malta, where the lottery companies of Europe were gathering. The structure for the new World Lottery Association clarified that the regional organizations of Africa, North America, Latin America and Asia/Pacific would be "umbrella" members of the world entity, so a European association was required.

The humble working title was "European Lotteries", a name that proved to stick. Amazingly, there had never been a Europe-only lottery association.

The initial stance by France and Spain was that the new European association would be a group of countries. That annoyed the 16 German lottery organizations because they would get only one vote. The rules of the World Lottery Association allowed each individual member organization one vote. Countries that had more than more than one lottery operation were in favour of "one organization / one vote."

The warring factions would have to compromise. It promised to be a boisterous spectacle. The country of Malta was a great spectacle all by itself. Ina and I wandered the old streets, seeing a cross between Europe and North Africa, Christian and Arab.

The host lottery was most gracious in providing us with a limousine and a driver; we saw every ruin, fortification and glorious site of this remarkable blend of Africa and Europe.

My speech to the Conference made it clear that a single European association was required. The unitary states of Europe accepted the new way of doing things but when the merger was agreed to, the German lottery managers behaved badly and made a spectacle of themselves and let one single person deliver the 16 votes, just as the French had expected. It was a crude move and created unnecessary dissension.

WHAT ABOUT YOUR LOTTERY SCRIBE?

Meanwhile I had to jockey for my own place in the overall scheme. I had informed the BC Premier that I would retire from BCLC the day the calendar changed from 1999 to 2000. If the merger would come about in fall of 1999, I would have only four more months in office as the Founding President of the World Lottery Association because the bylaws — yet to be approved — provided that all members of the executive committee had to be active lottery general managers.

I needed at least a full year at the helm to steady the ship. At the end of the meeting of the Implementation Task Force where my dilemma was discussed, a clause (unanimously approved) was inserted that made it possible for me to serve until the first anniversary of the new association. Therefore, I would be the Founding President in office from the formation in Oslo until its first annual meeting in Glasgow in fall of 2000.

COLONEL GADHAFI INTERVENES

While all this was going on in Malta, the trade show of the lottery suppliers was in a state of confusion. The majority were US-based corporations. Rumors of trouble wafted through the meeting hall.

Unexpectedly, the Americans were suddenly leaving the conference, but why? In the exhibition hall, the GTECH booth — among others — was being dismantled. The GTECH cocktail party was cancelled. What happened? Finally, it was confirmed that the U.S. Embassy in Malta had cautioned the American companies that the conference hotel — the new four-star Hotel Valetta — was owned by Colonel Gadhafi of Libya. Under "Trading with the Enemy" regulations, any U.S. firm or individual dealing with Libya or Gadhafi could be subject to severe penalties.

To the rest of the delegates, the issue seemed rather disingenuous but everyone holding an American passport cleared out of the hotel, returned home or found another place to stay. Although darkened by American politics, the launch of the new European lottery association was a done deal.

OH, THOSE MEXICANS...

 May 31, 1999. Members of the Implementation Task Force who were present at the Malta conference flew on to Helsinki to discuss the last niggling details. One of the first items was to deal with the waffling bid by Hector Morales of Pronósticos para la Asistencia Pública (Mexico's lotto and toto organization) to host the 2001 World Lottery Association's annual meeting in Cancun. He'd been given several opportunities to pronounce either a final commitment or a decent withdrawal but he failed to do either. He had come to Finland empty-handed once again.

In a private meeting, I told him bluntly that his bid was null and void. Mexico would not host the 2001 meeting in Cancun. Instead, the WLA would entertain Israel's offer to host the conference in 2001. I gave Hector an opportunity to speak to continue his bid (in which case his bid would be shot down and publicly taken away) or he could announce that difficulties had arisen and that Mexico had to withdraw. In that case, we would all be most sympathetic and bemoan the Mexico's ill fortune.

The Mexican didn't understand the escape clause, not because of his poor English but because of his lack of common sense. I took away his opportunity to speak and told the gathering that Senor Morales of Mexico had informed us that his country couldn't fulfill its commitment and had withdrawn its bid to host the Cancun Conference. He looked stunned about this blunt statement but nodded agreement... slowly.

Then it was time for new bidders to perform their dog-and-pony show to host a conference. The Aussies put forth Adelaide for 2002 and made a grand presentation, pouring Australian wine for all and extending an invitation to a dinner cruise on a nearby lake. Good stuff!

The Chairman of the Israeli State Lottery**, Mr. Katz-Oz**, made an impassioned plea for Jerusalem. Matti Ahde, the politically savvy Finn, whispered to me that Jerusalem had not been accepted by the United Nations as the capital of Israel. He feared that hosting WLA's conference in Jerusalem might become controversial in government circles. Even though the situation in Israel was peaceful at that time, who knew what 2001 might bring?

Lynne Roiter, the General Secretary of AILE, was emotionally committed to see the conference in her religious homeland. However, the consensus of the meeting was that WLA, in its early days, was fragile and should avoid any controversy. While there might be misgivings about Jerusalem, only Israel was prepared to fill the Mexican-caused void.

And so it was that Jerusalem was chosen, although it was not a ringing endorsement.

After the meeting, I was accosted by Senor Salmonella, he of the Mexico's centuries-old state lottery company, quite distinct from Hector Morales' outfit. Salmonella had not been invited to any meeting. I think he just traveled all the way to Finland to see what was happening to his competitor in his quest to obtain the Cancun Conference. He appeared to be most pleased that his Mexican colleague had been forced to withdraw Mexico's candidacy.

When I asked him what he was doing in Finland, of all places, he responded that he was bringing a gift from the President of Mexico for the President of Finland. He showed me a small box, wrapped in plain brown paper, the size of a paperback. In a confidential whisper, he declared that the President of Mexico would be pleased if I allowed him to attend the meeting of the Implementation Task Force. I told him it was not possible; the meeting was a closed session.

Salmonella became agitated and responded that he would hold a press conference in Rome to reveal what a sleazy operation this new lottery association was.

"Why Rome?" I asked. He mumbled something about the Pope but by that time I had dismissed his ramblings in order to attend to other issues.

When the meeting ended, I retired to our room and found a gift on the pillow. It was Salmonella's package for the President of Finland, with a note that since Finland's President wasn't available for his presentation, I could keep the gift for myself. It was a book with black and white photographs of public statues in Mexico with a descriptive text in Spanish. I filed the book in the metal container provided for such purposes located underneath the wash basin.

HILTON HEAD

In late summer of 1999, GTECH, our supplier of electronic lottery gaming devices, hosted a Users' Conference at the splendid resort at Hilton Head, South Carolina. GTECH's customers came from all corners of the globe. With severe thunderstorms in the area, the welcome party was relocated from the beach to a big tent where a Bee Gees tribute band played their surfer hearts out. What happened next? Guests were supplied with water-squirting bazookas, called Aqua Guns. Huge containers of water were brought in for ammunition.

With so many nationalities present, the ensuing tribal war was worthy of a sociologist's treatise. The Germans attacked together, clearing a path through the throng. The French looked disdainful but stayed in their chairs to watch and inflicted the incidental liquid swat when combatants came too close.

A delegate from Mainland China built a defensive fortification out of upturned tables and squirted anyone within his range. A Korean who hadn't said a word for the entire conference transformed a kitchen dishtowel into a war-like bandana and crept along the walls and under the tables to ambush selected victims with a whooping war cry. He appeared to be the happiest participant!

Reclining in beach chairs, Ina and I surveyed the carnage with a loaded water pistol hidden under a towel. There must have been some respect for my status because we were not attacked. The mayhem lasted for close to an hour.

The next day, in a business session, the senior GTECH people approached me about taking a position with GTECH as director of staff-training of their world-wide lottery sites. Once I had officially retired from BCLC, it would be something to think about.

PREMIER CLARK IN TROUBLE

In August, 1999 while your lottery scribe was attending the World War of Water Guns in South Carolina, Police knocked on the door of a modest home on Anzio Drive in Vancouver's east side. At home was Mrs. Dale Clark, a teacher, and her two young children. Three officers from the RCMP's commercial crime unit showed a search warrant. They were looking for evidence relating to her husband's granting of a charity casino license. Also on hand were a reporter and a cameraman from BCTV.

An hour into the raid, NDP Premier Glen Clark arrived at his family home. To avoid the cameras out front he slipped into the house through the back door. However, the television news crew had another camera in a van in the alley behind the premier's house, which caught the disturbing image — shot through the van's window — of the Premier pacing outside and looking perplexed.

Dimitrios Pilarinos, a neighbour of the Clark's, was being investigated for running an illegal gambling operation known as The Lumbermen's Social Club at the North Burnaby Inn, a strip club favored by members of the Hells Angels. Steve Ng, the inn's owner, was a business partner of Pilarinos. Together they had applied for a casino licence.

Pilarinos had a friendly relationship with the Clark family. Their children played together. A contractor by trade, he had built a sundeck for Glen Clark at his Anzio Drive home and at their family cottage near Penticton. The police believed the decks had been gifts from the contractor in exchange for favourable consideration of his casino application. During the raid at Clark's home, police deliberately (or accidently) missed a stack of cancelled cheques made out to Pilarinos for extensive work on his property. Clark's lawyer delivered the stack to police believing the evidence of payment for work would exonerate the Premier.

After the raid, Clark said that before the casino evaluation had started, he had emphatically instructed his staff "to ensure I was insulated" from any matters relating to the casino application submitted by his neighbor. Aides distributed a memo, written by **Adrian Dix**, (then Clark's chief of staff and now (2019) a current cabinet member of the NDP government) stating the Premier's acknowledgment's of Pilarinos as a

friend and his request to be recused from the process. The memo, with its sloppy punctuation and misspelling of Pilarinos was back-dated July 17, 1998. It was a set-up by Adrian Dix and it would become an infamous incident in the province's history.

Clark resigned as Premier after police confirmed that he was the subject of an investigation. He was charged with breach of trust and accepting a benefit of more than $10,000. After a lengthy trial, he was acquitted on both counts, though the judge admonished him for his "poor judgment" in hiring Pilarinos. The judge described Clark's misbehavior as an "act of folly."

Under oath in BC Supreme Court during Clark's trial, Adrian Dix admitted that he had deliberately backdated the memo to help his Premier.

Pilarinos was convicted of fraud and influence peddling and committing breach of trust, a criminal offence.

Clark was acquitted of all criminal charges by the Supreme Court of British Columbia on August 29, 2002 with Justice Elizabeth Bennett ruling that while Clark had unwisely left himself open to a perception of unethical behavior, there was no solid evidence that he had actually done anything illegal.

But I can't shake the memory of that meeting of the Lottery Advisory Committee (LAC) when I was told the committee shouldn't make recommendations as to who might or might not be eligible for a casino license.

THE 25th ANNIVERSARY OF LOTTERIES IN BC

Peter Adamo one of the early employees of BCLC tells us one of his memorable promotions in this special year

"One of the most successful promotions by BCLC was the Hey Wagon (from the ad campaign "hey… you never know"). You must imagine a semi- trailer full of professional sound and lighting equipment plus a full-sized game show set. Now add a second semi-truck towing a complete mobile performance stage and a power generator with enough power to light a village. It created a performance stage 40 feet wide by 40 feet deep and towered nearly 4 stories high.

"This show-biz caravan employed two drivers, two sound engineers, lighting engineer, production manager, stage technician and me as emcee. The team rolled into town on a Friday morning and would be up and ready for a concert or gameshow in eight hours."

"From the lawn of the Legislature to the festivities of Lumby Days and from the outdoor stage at Bella Coola to the sophistication of Whistler, the "Hey Wagon" visited many communities, all to celebrate 25 years of government lotteries in BC."

The way Hey Wagon worked was based on Monte Hall's "Let's Make a Deal" Players could win their way into the game for a chance to drive away a brand-new Ford Escort. Three brand-new Ford Escorts were parked in front of the stage, awaiting the winning contestant to try to start the car they had selected through a number of choices.

On the stage, there were three doors. The contestant was invited to choose a door and when the door was opened, he or she faced three cupboards to choose from. In each of the three cupboards were three small metal tubes. The participant was asked to choose one of the three tubes. Each tube contained a car key. The contestant then took a key to one of the three cars and…. if that car started, the lucky winner could drive it home. If the car failed to start, the BCLC auditor who had inserted the working key (before the show) in one of the tubes produced the key and started the winning car. It convinced the audience that the contest was legit.

The lottery chances to win were simple: The choice of the door was 1 in 3. The choice of the 3 cupboards raised the chance to 1 in 9. The choice of the three tubes that contained a car key elevated the chance to 1 in 27. In picking one of the three cars made the odds of winning a car 1 in 81. Not bad for a $15,000 car.

In some towns there would be several thousand spectators cheering at the moment of starting of the car. Of course, not every show produced a winner but when it did happen, the crowd including the winner went crazy. Peter Adamo the emcee of the "Hey Wagon" recalls giving away two cars in one show and the next day there was a long lineup of potential contestants. In that celebratory summer of 1999, eight winners drove their Ford Escort home.

THE PARADOX OF THE "THREE DOORS" ODDS

This anecdote is for those of you who are mathematically inclined. It is little-known in lottery circles that the choice of three doors, based on the Game Let's Make A Deal is a mathematical paradox. When a contestant choses Door #1 and the emcee (who knows where the winning key is located) opens Door #3 where he demonstrates to the contestant that it is a losing key, the conundrum for the player become should he or she change to Door #2 or stay with door #1. Is it to the player's advantage to switch doors?

Logic says there is no advantage to switch. But there is. The first door has a chance of 1 in 3 of winning. Once one of the doors is eliminated, the chance to win becomes 2 in 3. You will win twice as often when you change doors. Think about this! Suppose there are a million doors and you pick Door #1. Then the emcee, who knows what's behind the doors, will always avoid picking the door that has the prize. Say that door was for example #777,777 (or any other number) When you could see that, you'd pick that door pretty quick.

They key issue is that the emcee is not choosing random doors. He avoids choosing the right door. By doing that he has created new odds in the process.

If you don't believe me, try the game yourself with Styrofoam cups and a hidden penny. You'd have to do a substantial number of tries to observe that the odds are in favour if you pick the other cup (or the Door# 2) when you are faced with the choice.

RELATIONS WITH NO ELATION

"Oslo Relations" was the theme of the September 1999 combined INTERTOTO/AILE Conference in Oslo. The final vote for the creation of a world lottery organization was at hand.

The voting was unusual because so many delegates were carrying two votes — one as a member of INTERTOTO, the other as a member of AILE. I nervously wriggled in my seat overlooking the somber-minded membership. The first vote was to disband INTERTOTO in favour of the new World Lottery Association (WLA). It carried unanimously.

An identical motion by AILE received near unanimous approval with one vote abstaining. INTERTOTO and AILE were dissolved. The World Lottery Association was born! The executive committee, a carefully blended slate of directors, nominated by both sides of the aisle, was elected. Since I would retire as President of BCLC within a few months, a special "rider" to the bylaws was passed, allowing me to be president of WLA until the end of the next conference which meant that my election as a founding president of the WLA was a foregone conclusion.

Well, there is it was. **The World Lottery Association** was a reality. Years of badgering, cajoling, pleading, and bartering had finally led to a single association. The ever-on-going battle of the French versus the Germans was transferred to the European association. At the world level — no doubt — there would arise other head-banging situations.

After a few more housekeeping issues, the general assembly was adjourned. A new era had begun. I had requested from our Norwegian hosts that something symbolic should be staged to mark this important passage. Reidar Nordby had arranged an indoor fireworks display in the meeting hall in order to celebrate the merger but... nothing happened. The world meeting adjourned with the delegates wondering if that was all there was.

When I met Reidar in the hallway, he said. "Oh," he said, "my staff delayed the fireworks until the final dinner."

Matti Ahde of Finland thanked Reidar and the newly appointed executive members repaired to a special corner in the hotel bar and toasted their achievement. My colleagues on the implementation task force had devoted two years of travel and meetings to hammer out the agreement. I reflected on the old saying: "It is not the final destination that matters, it's the journey."

THE LAST HURRAH

Frances Kenny and Barry Auliffe of BCLC joined me at an Erewhon session in "Haus Krickenback" — a conference centre in a remodeled German castle. At the opening reception Alexander Malwitz, my fine German colleague, had rented an elaborate "Lord of the Castle" costume complete with plumed hat.

Your freaked-out scribe was required to wear the get-up while welcoming the Erewhon participants to the castle.

The opening ceremony was great fun and the ensuing sessions were successful, although — given German reserve — not as animated as Australia.

During the final dinner, I was quietly absorbed in self-reflection — this was the end of my career in lottery management and in a few months I'd retire from my post. But no one at the Erewhon session paid attention to my miserable attitude. The party was on! So what could I do? I joined in the revelry!

Frances Kenny was in great spirits. She was serenaded by the seminar goers to a heartfelt rendition of "She's a Lady". She deserved it. She had been the lively spirit of many Erewhon session and this one was very special for her.

TIME TO SAY GOODBYE

Upon my return from Germany, I formally notified the BCLC board of my wish to retire as of midnight December 31, 1999. I had chosen that special time and date to celebrate the unique calendar change from 1999 to 2000.

Several board members urged me to stay on to finalize the casino development but I felt it was time to go. I was 68 years old. The lottery and casino programs were solid and in the good hands of Vic Poleschuk. "Destination casinos" needed an energetic driver to see it through. Thus far, Vic had handled the casino business very well. Together with Doug Penrose and Rob Egan, he was handling the difficult file with aplomb.

PIER 21 THE NASPL GOODBYE

The Dutch immigrant ship "Waterman" had docked at Pier 21 in Halifax on March 10, 1954, to disgorge 700 Dutch immigrants looking for a new life in Canada. Both Ina and I were among that crowd. We still remember walking down the gangplank into the immigration hall wondering what kind of life lay ahead.

September 14, 1999 — a business life-time later, we stood again at Pier 21, looking at the photographs of those who had arrived before us and the many who came after. A huge wall of engraved plaques with names of those who arrived here was a prominent feature.

We were in Halifax to attend the annual meeting of the North American State and Provincial Lotteries, the final one for me as a lottery chief. Thirty-eight lottery organizations were now NASPL members, compared to my first meeting in 1975 when seven lottery directors in North America met to compare notes. At that time none of us knew how many complexities we would face. I leave it to others at the NASPL organization to tell the story of its amazing growth. My two-year presidency in the mid-'80s was certainly a career highlight for me.

As a goodbye, NASPL had arranged a nice ceremony where Ina and I were recognized by the 1000 or so attendees. Ina received flowers and your lottery scribe was presented with the latest Sony digital movie camera. I delivered a much re-written speech that found great favor with the audience.

My speech harked back to Pier 21 of 45 years ago when we stood there facing a new country and new opportunities. Now, standing here today, in the same place, saying good-bye to and being honored by my North-American peers was an emotional moment. I alluded to the Dutch proverb that says: "When you are born for a dime, you'll never be a dollar." It means that people of humble origins should not get uppity and expect to rise above the station of their birth. Canada had more than rewarded us for our efforts. On behalf of Ina and me I thanked our colleagues "for honoring us and make us feel like a dollar."

As Ina and I made our way back to the table, I saw more than a few tears.

THE ROYAL CITY STAR

On October 6, 1999 the first Destination Casino opened in BC — a river boat purchased from a Louisiana company. She was dubbed "The Royal City Star" and was to ply the waters (on non-windy days) of the Fraser River. The future of the Royal City Star didn't shine too bright.

Most of us at BCLC realized that the "destination attraction" of touring the Fraser River was a sham. People came to gamble and weren't overly excited to be at a casino that would float away from the parking lot and keep them captive for the length of the tour.

We knew the floating casino would likely be permanently moored as soon as the political interest focused elsewhere. The operation eventually moved to a building and after remaining tied up for a few years, the vessel disappeared from the New Westminster waterfront without fanfare. The Star closed its casino doors for the last time on December 9, 2007.

GOODBYE AT HOME

Even though my retirement was set for December 31, there were so many unused holidays that your lottery scribe could take the final three months off as a vacation and not return to the office.

My loyal BCLC staff arranged a private dinner at the Hotel Vancouver where colleagues from far and wide came to say good-bye. The head table consisted of our entire family including a very pregnant Cynthia and her husband Rick. Leonard made a difficult trek from Atlanta to be there.

The World Lottery Association organized a board meeting in Vancouver so friends from across the world could attend my retirement "do". More than 300 people: family, suppliers, business friends and government colleagues sat down for an excellent dinner. Cathy McGregor, a cabinet minister and former Chair of the BCLC spoke eloquently as a friend, boss and referred to the many millions of profits the government had earned from lotteries over a quarter of a century.

My successor, Vic Poleschuk acting as MC presented a long list of colleagues eager to speak. Your prideful scribe must confess that he urged Vic to include everyone who wished to say something, so I must accept the blame for the speeches that proved much too long for comfort. I thought that our **daughter Joanne's** speech on behalf of the family was best, although I might be biased.

Many of the well-wishers at the final dinner made it a point that in retirement I was now "free to travel". They didn't realize that staying put for a while instead of hanging around airports and hotel lobbies was a wonderful thing to look forward to.

Free of the lottery's responsibility, I pored over old Annual Reports to summarize what had been achieved. What was the bottom line?

In 1974-75, the BC government received $5 million in profits from lotteries. In my final year 1999- 2000, it pocketed a hundred times as much: $521 million. In my 25-year term the lottery had netted well over $4 billion.

For your retired scribe a new chapter was about to unfold.

CONSULTANT AND LECTURER 2000-2012

LONDON

After a couple of months of enjoying nothingness, your lottery scribe, freed from the chains of day-to-day management, began his travels around the world doing that thing that is termed "consulting." I like the definition of consultant: a person who borrows your watch, tells you the time, pockets the watch and bills you for it.

In my capacity as the non-paid president of the new World Lottery Association, I kept a close eye on WLA's development while paying gig was as an "advisor/consulting/teaching guru."

NATIONAL LOTTERY
COMMISSION

On March 11, 2000, I arrived in London to conduct a one-day Erewhon session with the National Lottery Commission, the UK government's regulating body that oversees operation of the National Lottery and other licensed gaming. It was a lovely bit of irony that at least 25 of the initial staff of the British National Lottery had been trained by our BCLC staff and now I was being asked to enlighten the people who were their overseers.

Even though these board members were convinced that their knowledge of lotteries was the reason for their appointment, their interest in debating the condensed version of EREWHON was high. The opening hour was spent erasing prejudices and misunderstanding about lotteries, such as the old saws that the poor are the main consumers of lotteries and lotteries lead to compulsive gambling. After muting those thoughts, I began to work on convincing the majority of the attendees that their role was to monitor and direct lottery activities rather than micro-manage the day-to-day affairs. It is a difficult job to keep bossy board-members from telling staff how to do their job. One may always hope they will listen.

A couple of tight-lipped board members couldn't be wedged from their view that their presence on the Lottery Commission was to obstruct the expansion of lotteries. With that negative attitude I was certain that the government wouldn't let them survive very long on the board. To their bewilderment, I informed them rather forcefully of my opinion about their obstruction, which silenced them for the rest of the day. In retrospect the session was very worthwhile for this interesting and responsible group.

The case of the cancelled ticket, explained in earlier chapters, threw a spanner in their up-to-now polite debate. Two opposing camps quickly evolved into a shouting match with one group defending the legal position and the other fearing a political disaster if the legal position was maintained. The group that wanted to pay everyone involved in the situation calmed down after I explained the dire consequences of their behaviour as good Samaritans. I was pleased to note that the session raised the apprehension of the many pitfalls that might await them as guides of the British Lottery.

JOHANNESBURG

After that intense session I jetted-off to Johannesburg. Old friend **Charles Cousins** of GTECH had asked me to conduct an EREWHON seminar for the newly-hired executives of the soon-to-go-online South African National Lottery. The structure of the new organization was built along the lines of the UK National Lottery, i.e. not a government operation but a private operator licensed for seven years. The operating company was named UTHINGO. Their corporate construct was a combination of politically aligned interests in South Africa plus the dominant US technical partner, GTECH.

Your provoking scribe began harping at the 7-year-limit license. What would happen if the licence was not renewed after seven years? Would 10,000 retail computer terminals be discarded and find a new use as boat anchors? Would the big main-frame computers be sold as scrap? Would 500 experienced staff members be put on the street? Would a new licensee be forced to buy the used equipment? Would the departing licensee be reimbursed for all the development over the many-years term? No one had the answer but the slogan of the South African lottery commission was "Carry On. Don't Ask Questions."

The EREWHON sessions were attended by staff members of both the operator and the regulating commission. This provided a unique opportunity to caution newcomers to the lottery business to NOT fall into the trap of favouring the player at the expense of the legal rules and regulations.

This bending the rules in favour of the lottery player was more pronounced in South Africa than anywhere else. The standard opening debate at all EREWHON seminars presents the case of two seemingly correct winning lotto

410

tickets whose owners would share the $4.2 million jackpot-prize. However, one of those tickets had been cancelled and voided by a retailer, something the buyer had no way of knowing.

(To save you from searching back to when I mentioned this before, here's how it could happen: A player orders a ticket but leaves the store before paying. The store keeper either has to pay for the ticket or cancel and destroy it. But if the cancelled ticket is not destroyed... and eventually sold to another buyer, the problem arises.)

The question: What should the lottery organization do? The legal answer is: There is only one winning ticket and the holder of that ticket must be awarded the entire jackpot. The holder of the other ticket — printed in error and cancelled — is entitled to a refund of the amount paid for the ticket.

The application of that stern rule upset the South Africans. I should explain that there were only two white faces in the 28-person class. The two hard-nosed guys in charge of security were Afrikaans-speaking Boers who sympathized with the non-winner but who understood the inflexible rule.

One well-educated young woman said: "This is the kind of treatment we black people have been subjected to for centuries and now we are supposed to treat our own people this harshly?" I countered her argument by pointing out that the rules were the same for all lotteries across the world regardless of colour. It was fascinating see these young people beginning to realize that being in charge meant having to make unpopular and even seemingly unfair decisions.

Some of the more combative attendees argued that the lottery should pay the full jackpot to both ticket holders. When I asked why the National Lottery was brought into being, they said it was to assist in funding the Government's Department of Health. I asked if they thought it was fair that this important program should be punished with a loss of $4.2 million due to their irrational decision to pay someone who was legally not entitled to it.

A lot of head-scratching ensued. I was watching an inner struggle that must bedevil all formerly oppressed people when they are suddenly empowered to affect the lives of others. "I thought this was going to be a fun job," the young female leader said. "But it looks as if there is pain here as well."

They argued late into the evening and finally came to terms with the issue. As the days unfolded, they slowly became more protective of the integrity of the lottery and the realization that they were its guardians rather than the advocates for the player. For your lottery scribe this EREWHON seminar was one of the most rewarding.

The nicest part for me personally came when our remote conference site, Hotel Sparkling Waters near Rustenburg, was suddenly placed under military guard because the top brass of the South African Defense Force dropped out of the sky for a high-level conference.

At the noon-hour break, one of the Air Force officers offered me and my colleagues a closer look at the big Sikorsky helicopter parked outside the seminar room. The senior pilot offered a flight over the area. The big war machine has two big doors that are seemingly never closed. When strapped into a folding seat, one's body is open to the elements. The noise and draft were both overwhelming and exhilarating.

The area of Rustenburg is one of the most rare geological formations on earth. The pilot maneuvered the copter very closely to the highest peak of the barren red-rock mountain. When I say "very closely," I mean less than one meter between the copter and the top of the rock. The altimeter read 6,500 feet (around two kilometers) above sea level. The co-pilot climbed out of his seat, hooked himself onto a thick cable, stepped over my feet, leaned out of the aircraft and touched a small outcropping with his finger. I saw a fossilized imprint of a fish, a sole or flatfish. It was wondrous to me that eons ago, fish were swimming where I now sat in the sky, strapped in a whirlybird.

Back on the ground, the seminar that had begun in controversy was now being embraced by the students. What impressed me were the serious opinions expressed during the discussions. There was no glibness. No jokes. These people were convinced they were building something of importance for their country.

Before the flight back, the Lottery's security people invited me to the Sun City casinos adjacent to the Pilanesberg National Park. In the splendid park I discovered that while the animals roam freely, visitors are locked in a wire-enclosed pen. The animals come to look at the caged spectators.

DUBLIN

October 12, 2000. A nine-hour flight from Johannesburg got me to my brother-in-law's home in the Netherlands. After a restful weekend, I flew to Dublin where I was to address the board of directors of An Post (Post Office)— operators of the Irish National Lottery. **Ray Bates**, the lottery director and a good friend of many years had a difficult board with an attitude similar to the young South Africans. Ray had lectured them on the realities of lottery rules but he needed an outsider to confirm his assertions. I can confirm that the Irish are tough to convince when their assumptions are being challenged but I think Ray and your lottery scribe made good headway. It seemed to me there was acceptance of our position.

NEW ORLEANS

The last destination on this long trip was a Public Gaming Institute seminar in New Orleans organized by the ever-enterprising couple of **Doris and Duane Burke.** Duane had kindly seen to it that Ina received a flight from Vancouver to New Orleans to accompany me home for the last leg of the trip. The reason for my attendance? Duane wanted me to assess a last-ditch attempt by Mexico's lottery director Hector Morales to host the Cancun conference that — in reality — was already lost to them.

It was obvious that the Mexican lottery people feared the upcoming July presidential elections, where the opposition party led by Vicente Fox would likely win the popular vote and sweep Hector and his mates out of their comfortable offices. These pleasant but naive people believed that a commitment to host an international conference would save their hides. They didn't know or believe the cruel rule in politics: Win by the sword and die by the sword. They were goners but didn't realize it.

The one disturbing bit of news from the Mexican side was that "Salmonella" — the manager of the century-old government-lottery in Mexico — had convened a press conference in Mexico City where he cast aspersions on WLA, alleging financial mismanagement. The press release was cleverly written in order to raise the smell of corruption without making a specific accusation.

413

Moreover, the man had written a letter to members of the South American Lottery Association CIBELAE, making similar remarks.

I didn't understand why that Mexican was doing this other than to escape Vicente Fox's incoming steamroller. Proclaiming that someone else is corrupt is never a good defense to camouflage one's own deportment. I was not overly concerned, but this man had to be taken care of!

SAN DIEGO

In the process of creating the World Lottery Association, the suppliers to the lottery business had been kept at arms-length. Now was the time to bring them into the fold, for they — the suppliers — were a large source of funding for the WLA operations.

A couple of months after the New Orleans meeting, I asked the WLA executive committee to meet with lottery suppliers in San Diego to talk about the new ways and — as a side issue — discuss Salmonella's charges of corruption. I had invited this strange martinet to come and face the people whom he was slandering. To either his credit or his inanity, he showed up.

At the meeting, I isolated him by seating him so that he had to face the executive committee with no one around him. The committee appeared nervous about the pending confrontation. I started out gently and suggested that we were taken aback by Salmonella's attacks and since he hadn't supplied any facts to back his allegations, he could now present his findings.

The agitated Mexican launched into an incoherent mishmash of odd remarks, the gist of which was that he was the most powerful lottery director in Central America and we had ignored him and dealt with Hector Morales, his lotto colleague, whom he said, was corrupt.

I told him there was time for him to substantiate his remarks about his colleague but first things first: what were the alleged corrupt activities of the WLA? Again, a storm of words followed so fast that even the experienced interpreter had to remind him to slow down and speak in a more orderly manner. He didn't and kept on ranting.

In a change of approach, I offered him an escape. I said I understood his position. I confessed that in my career I had also taken positions that I shouldn't have and once out on that limb, it is difficult to climb down. I added that everyone in the room had also been in such a bind once or twice. I added that we understood that irritation might have gotten the better of him and, if so, we would let the matter be and proceed to more positive discussions.

He not only didn't accept my opportunity to save face, the idea seemed to enrage him even more. It was almost time for lunch. In order to cool emotions, I adjourned the meeting. During lunch he spoke quite animatedly with the director from Spain and a Spanish-speaking member of our host, the California Lottery. "Salmonella" appeared to be in good spirits.

After lunch I resumed questioning him on specific allegations, even repeating his accusations in detail. Was it personal gain? For me or my colleagues? Was it extravagant expenses? Theft? Lies? What? He had nothing to offer but a verbal monsoon of Spanish words strung together that sounded impressive when heard but contained none of his assertions in the translation.

Then, unexpectedly, in the middle of his rant, a TV news crew entered the room and filmed various members as they were speaking. The German WLA board member Hans-Jürgen Reisinger was the first to react.

"Who are these peoples?" he asked.

Of course, I had noticed the video crew but assumed that it was a California Lottery effort to show them basking in the glow of international attention but — when asked — the California Lottery representative denied any involvement. But then the camera man, upset by the rancorous debate, showed his identity card of the Tijuana TV Station in Mexico, 30 kilometers down the road.

I looked around the room. "Which one of you hired this TV crew?"

All eyes turned to Salmonella.

"Did you bring the cameras into this closed meeting held specifically to explain your unwarranted charges?" I asked.

Only when several committee members pressed him, did he offer the weak response that this was a public meeting and he had to defend himself publicly. I admit I was angry. I told him it was not an open meeting and that he was a rude, ill-mannered man who abused our hospitality. He had betrayed the principals of civilized people; he ought to be ashamed of himself.

Rebuking him some more I added: "I have given you every opportunity to substantiate your accusations. As president of the World Lottery Association, I will notify the cabinet minister responsible for lotteries in Mexico of your unacceptable behavior and I shall write your colleagues in South America that you were invited to explain your accusations and failed to do so."

When it comes to relations between Northern American organizations and South Americans, Spain is always the mediator. I prevailed on the lottery director from Spain to explain the board's feelings in Spanish, just so there would be no language barrier. I expected our Spanish colleague to mollycoddle the Mexican and tread the middle ground. Instead he gave him superb shit.

"Chairman Simonis gave you an elegant opportunity to bring this matter to a close — you chose to make matter worse," the interpreter translated.

Salmonella launched into his final diatribe. He was livid and shook with rage and pointed at me. "You will regret this," he spat at me. "Mark me; you will!"

Yvonne Schnyder, who had watched these proceedings with trepidation, showed fear. "I want to leave," she said. "I want to get out of San Diego."

Not only Yvonne felt like this. So did the television crew.

Matti Ahde, the Finnish Director eased the tension. "We should repair to the bar," he suggested jovially. Salmonella remained all by himself in the room.

Months later, when Vicente Fox was elected, Salmonella was the first one out the door. No one since has heard anything about his whereabouts.

ATLANTA

Most of the international participants in the San Diego board meeting had combined their stay with the NASPL annual meeting in Atlanta where our hostess was Rebecca Paul, now head of the Georgia Lottery. My role there was to explain the structures and policies of the World Lottery Association and to provide a preview of the planned program of the 2000 Glasgow meeting —the first full-fledged meeting of the WLA.

The Wyndham Peach Tree Hotel lobby was crammed with hundreds of guests. It was NASCAR week and anyone not from the South or who isn't a NASCAR fan is considered a "sissy from up north."

 **Rebecca Paul** told me that the hotel's biggest suite had been reserved for me. She found this honour so exciting that she accompanied me to the classy digs. Indeed it was chic, with sofas and three bedrooms and a well-stocked fridge with enough Coca Cola to satisfy the entire WLA Executive Committee. I dumped my bags on the bed and accepted Rebecca's invitation for a drink at the bar. It was all very comfortable after the tense confrontation in San Diego.

After the drink, I returned to my room to unpack my bags and wash up a bit. The room key didn't fit, but my fumbling alerted someone inside. The door was jerked open by an ugly face that was straight out of the cast of the movie "Deliverance".

"What y'all want man?" the man croaked, his beady eyes boring into mine.

"This is my room" I offered tentatively.

"Well, come on in and let's have a talk about that!"

The room was in near darkness. Another bozo sat on the sofa sucking a tube of beer while two others scavenged through my newly delivered pizza. A hostile aura pervaded the room. I began to fear that these strange-looking guys with their atrocious accents were part of a lynch mob sent by Salmonella to "make me regret" my actions!

It turned out that they were four near-religious NASCAR fans from rural Mississippi who were in town for the big event. Having found no room at any hotel in Atlanta, they convinced the Peach Tree hotel to sell them my "Executive Suite." The backwoods man repeatedly showed me his "paid in cash" receipt while moaning that even the one-quarter cost of the room would buy him a room for a week at any motel in Mississippi.

When called to deal with the issue, the hotel manager suggested that I could settle for a smaller suite and give these poor ragamuffins a bed for the weekend. I agreed, relieved that Salmonella would have to wait for his revenge.

GLASGOW

A few months later, on May 29, 2000, my 69th birthday, Ina and I arrived in Glasgow to conduct an EREWHON for GTECH's European employees. This was the third seminar I had done under contract with GTECH. These "in-house" EREWHON seminars were different. Over the discussions hung the entrenched GTECH corporate view that very few employees dared to oppose. Yet, the difference in perspective between the East Europeans and those from the West and Nordic companies was quite noticeable. The Eastern people were overly secretive and manipulative. In contrast, the Westerns were too liberal in favoring the player despite the established rules.

More importantly the first annual meeting of the World Lottery Association was only a couple of days away.

THE FIRST WLA ANNUAL MEETING

CAMELOT, the British National Lottery operator hosted the meeting in Glasgow. In my capacity as President of the new association I was to lead the proceedings and then, at the conclusion of the conference, hand the gavel over to Reidar Nordby, the nominee for President who would be elected by acclamation.

But first there were the fine accommodations for Ina and me. Our assigned hotel room was something we didn't quite expect in gloomy Glasgow. It was the Royal Suite. The only thing amiss in the palatial chambers was the glass shower-door that shattered on the first day and wasn't repaired until tradesmen were available five days later. Luckily, there was another shower stall and two more bathrooms. Our request for room service of hamburgers and "chips" was sniffed at by a condescending waitress clad in the frilly costume of a French maid. Her Scottish brogue felt totally out of place. Yet the delicious typical British repast of chips was delivered in style, wrapped in an old newspaper.

Tim Holley, the boss of Camelot, had gracefully made his driver and the official car available so Ina and I could go wherever and whenever we wanted. Ina got quickly used to that perk.

Business-wise, everything was in place. For your world-weary scribe, presiding over a congregation of 1,400 delegates from 85 lottery and supply companies was by now an easy routine. The annual meeting went smoothly, except for when Hans Juergen Reissiger, the Chrysanthemum Lotto Emperor

418

from Berlin, caused a little grief by pointing out misplaced commas and other minutiae of the documentation. As usual, he managed to annoy most of those present. Despite his minor interjections, the meeting went very well and all objectives were met.

One of the senior Camelot people whispered to me that at some point I would be thanked for my efforts for leading the creation of the World Lottery Association. The place and time of the ceremony were not explicitly stated but it was supposed to be at the well-attended luncheon, where the winners of the WLA advertising awards were announced.

I spent the luncheon concentrating on a witty speech which would be one of my last official remarks on the international scene. However, the lunch was fueled by a lot of the best French wines , ran overly long and came to an untidy end without my having delivered a final farewell.

After lunch, the pleasantly tipsy crowd was to reconvene in the big hall for video presentations by the promotors of the upcoming WLA meetings Jerusalem (2001) and Adelaide in 2002. I blame it on the win — the majority of the crowd absconded to rest and/or try out their rented kilts for that evening's formal Scottish dinner.

Out of loyalty to me, a handful of friends showed up for the travelogue videos. Several snoozed during the video and others sneaked out halfway through until, in the presence of a handful of diehards, it was time for me to be thanked for my efforts in establishing the World Lottery Association. In a few kind remarks, **Reidar Nordby** thanked me and announced the institution of the WLA's award. It was to be named The Guy Simonis Lifetime Achievement Award — an honour to be bestowed every two years to a deserving lottery executive. It was a great moment for Ina and me.

Reidar, who realized the lack of warmth of at that business session, interrupted the evening's well-rehearsed closing gala to restate his earlier kind remarks but in a more colorful manner. The World Lottery Association's Lifetime Achievement Award in my name was endorsed by a standing ovation.

At the start of the main course, Reidar called upon me to "Toast the Haggis", the traditional Scottish dish historically prepared using sheep's "pluck" (heart, liver, and lungs), minced with onion, oatmeal, suet, spices, and salt, mixed with bouillon and boiled in the animal's stomach for approximately an hour, as the provided speech notes said.

I whispered to the emcee that I would do the toast in my best acquired Scottish accent but I wouldn't eat nor even pretend to taste the haggis. The emcee said he would embarrass me openly if I balked but I said I would respond that I had a full stomach with another well-known Scottish dish — a McDonald's hamburger. He relented and gallons of a great whisky were swallowed by the more than 2,000 diners and spouses in repeated toasts of the haggis.

I delivered my little farewell in the promised faux Scottish brogue.

It was a good goodbye.

SWINDON

Even though Ina was urged to stay for the next part of the trip, she departed from Heathrow on a direct flight back to Vancouver. She'd had enough and wanted to go home.

With Frances Kenny in tow, I drove into the English countryside to find Swindon College, located in the ceremonial county of Wiltshire in South West England. It was there that INTERTOTO regularly staged its language courses and where I was to conduct a three-day EREWHON session.

It turned out to be an argumentative session but the school's environment was not as conducive to group interaction as the intimate locations of many of the other seminars had been. There were a number of Dutch participants, one of whom got so terribly drunk on the first day that he missed the remainder of the three-day event.

At the closing dinner, the drunk insisted on getting his "certificate" attesting to the fact he had participated. His colleagues pleaded with me to issue the document because denying him would signal to his boss that he failed.

"Precisely," I said, "It would be an insult to the other recipients. You can't earn an EREWHON certificate by lying on your bed in a stupor." I refused to issue it. I was told later he had earned a serious rebuke from his employer.

LEIDEN

The third leg of this lecture tour led me to the Netherlands for a seminar on sports lotteries at the Holiday Inn in Leiden, the very spot where — in the '40s and '50s — your lottery scribe swam in summer and skated in winter. It was just about a kilometer away from my old home. It was a bleak visit. Your lottery scribe's parental home had fallen to make room for an industrial complex. Only my kindergarten was still there.

The sports betting seminar was scheduled to coincide with the European Football Championship: Euro 2000. Each afternoon at 5 pm the seminar broke up to watch the first of two evening soccer games in a hall especially reserved for that purpose and amply stocked with various intoxicants so as to better facilitate the expression of inspired, scatological criticisms of referees and hapless footballers.

Twelve soccer nations were represented at the sports betting seminar and, although rivalry was fierce, a friendly, joshing atmosphere was maintained.

The Dutch lottery treated us with tickets and transportation to attend the Portugal-Romania game at Amsterdam Stadium and the next day's game between Netherlands and Yugoslavia at the Feyenoord Stadium in Rotterdam.

Your sporting scribe reveled in being part of the immense sea of orange-clad fans. Whenever the excitement on the field sagged, 50,000 voices sang traditional Dutch songs at decibel levels only attainable by fanatic soccer fans.

CHICAGO

For the fourth leg of this journey, KLM delivered me to Chicago where a group of GTECH employees had gathered for a three-day EREWHON session. I must have been tired because nothing in particular stands out in my mind except for one older, self-confessed cynical employee who said at the start that he was bored already, had seen and done it all. Afterwards however, he came up to thank me and to say that this was the first training session he truly enjoyed and added that — apparently a surprise to him — he had learned something.

When I got back to Vancouver, I'd been on the road for a full month. But I wouldn't be home for long. If this was retirement, I sure could use a rest.

CONNECTICUT

In mid-July of 2000, Ina decided to join me at a GTECH-sponsored EREWHON in Southbury, Connecticut. As an accomplished driver she had navigated the maze of Prague, the left-driving roundabouts in England and the freeways of America but had never navigated the streets of New York. Renting a car at JFK, she drove through the clogged streets of New York to Pennsylvania and into Connecticut to a boring audience of GTECH office staffers who would rather hang around the pool than listen to my diatribe.

But think of it this way. It was a paid holiday. The GTECH honcho barbecued hamburgers for us at his Connecticut home and on the way back we survived the streets of Yonkers and Jamaica and experienced the New York State Freeway at peak hours, a terrible misuse of the word "free." Otherwise, quite a nice relaxing work week.

SACRAMENTO

Late summer of 2000 was spent writing columns for Public Gaming Magazine and conducting an EREWHON in Sacramento, California, with Ina driving up and down Interstate 5. The participants of the seminar were all staff members of GTECH. As your lottery scribe has noted before when seminar attendees come from the same employer, there is little debate. Participants will toe the company line and the debate is difficult to stimulate. The leader of the debate (moi) then must assume the role of contrarian which in turn diminishes a good argument. However, these Californians made it interesting.

ZANDVOORT

In October 2000, GTECH organized an EREWHON in Zandvoort, a North Sea beach area near Amsterdam. It went off without a hitch. These EREWHONs were beginning to roll off the assembly line. If a seminar didn't end in prolonged applause it meant I had failed. So far so good.

On the last day of the session, Ina arrived in Amsterdam to join me for a 2,100-km drive to the ancient Spanish city of Toledo. This time the EREWHON was arranged by the World Lottery Association.

TOLEDO

The plains of Spain were without rain and were as boring a landscape as the Canadian prairies before the snow flies. The heart of Toledo was a charming, historic old neighbourhood surrounded by a new and ordinary city. Our host, the Director of the Spanish Lottery, who had become one of my great supporters after the San Diego dust-up, was proud to show the city of his birth. "Toledo is a city with the greatest wealth of monuments." he told us. It is called the "city of three cultures" because Christians, Arabs and Jews lived peacefully together there for centuries. Behind its stone walls, Toledo preserves a cultural legacy in the form of churches, palaces, fortresses, mosques and synagogues. The differing architectural styles make the old quarter an open-air museum, a World Heritage Site.

Of course, the seminar participants were expected to tour the Alcazar of Toledo, the fortress built by the Moors that still dominates the skyline of the city. On this hot day, Ina and I saw the long steep stairs and decided that an ice-cold Diet Coke under the massive trees in the city square would be an equally interesting cultural experience. Much to the horror of our Toledo guide, who deemed Spanish culture to be superior to North American barbarians, we sat down in the plaza in front of the cathedral, a place jammed with Spanish teenagers munching on McDonald's hamburgers.

The WLA-commissioned EREWHON in Spain was a far better experience than the GTECH- sponsored seminars. In Toledo, there were representatives from North America, Poland and Latvia in the east, Scandinavia in the north, Netherlands from the centre, Senegal from Africa and a liberal sprinkling of Italians, Spanish and Portuguese. There was a real excitement debating with colleagues from other nations, exchanging views with people who worked in different cultures. Dearly held principles were frequently swept aside by the onslaught of new ideas. Toledo was an Erewhon to remember.

JOHANNESBURG AGAIN

A month after the return from Spain, Ina and I set out for the fourth overseas trip of the year 2000 and my second visit to South Africa. Ina had skipped the first visit but I persuaded her that she should see that part of the world at least once.

The first South African lottery game had now been operational for some time. Teething problems caused the Uthingo management to request a three-day EREWHON with the field staff. These folks were having a tough time working in a difficult retail climate. Well-lit outlets such as Shell and Esso

stations proved to be solid points of sale but most of the Mom and Pop retail stores operated in dimly-lit, dangerous neighbourhoods. Impoverished retailers had to contend with at least four problems not very evident in the First World: criminals, inexperienced players, untrained employees and the occasional cop asking for protection money.

Statistics showed that Johannesburg and Durban were the main centres of criminal activity. At the earlier EREWHON seminar in South Africa, the lottery staff displayed great sympathy with "victims of the system", no doubt a holdover from the era before apartheid.

The culture of the lottery company Uthingo was that the lotto was a financial source for good things to happen. It would bring pleasure to many and suppliers and retailers would find that doing business with the lottery was a desirable business relationship.

The first South African EREWHON, a year or so before, had shown that middle management was worried that being in charge meant having to make unpopular decisions. Sales of lottery tickets at retail stores were one of the first tests of their resolve to do things legally and responsibly.

Within days of the launch of the lotto, petty thieves focussed on lottery stores. There was cash to be had and instant/scratch tickets to be stolen. A high percentage of retailers claimed that stick-up artists had robbed them of their day's lottery take. They regretted tearfully that they couldn't pay the lottery for the tickets they had sold. They also confessed that the lottery was a good product for them to sell. They wanted to continue offering tickets to their customers. If only the lottery company would just forgive them the amount that was stolen from them, they would carry on!

In keeping with the overwhelming sense of protecting the underdog, Uthingo had established a policy that if lottery money had been taken in a robbery, Uthingo would forgive that amount provided that the robbery incident had been officially reported to police.

Not many of our First World colleagues who attended EREWHON sessions had worked in an environment where robberies are a daily event. To their cynical eyes, it seemed that a policy of paying for lost revenue might just be an incentive to fake robberies. A retailer might ask a brother or cousin to enter the store wearing a mask and demand all the money in the lottery till, only to later split the loot, knowing that the lottery would make up the loss. Even if the storeowner was an upright citizen, as soon as he left the store, his employees could stage the same rip-off and the amount would be covered by the lottery.

The question put to me was how this problem might be solved while remaining in good standing with the retailers. Before I met with the sales staff, Charles Cousins, GTECH's man on the ground in South Africa, asked me to "toughen them up" — meaning that the Uthingo sales staff and their middle management should drop their charitable attitude and become more cynical— treat the retailers as contractors rather than dependant clients. It was a tough battle. The sympathy for "victims" was bred into the employees' souls. They felt that enforcing strict rules would make them "oppressors."

 Perhaps more practical steps would help. The Director of Security **Dawid Muller** — who had been a senior police officer in the days before apartheid — suggested a steel strongbox could be built into the retailer counter. The box would be securely fixed and would ring an alarm at Uthingo's data centre if an attempt was made to dislodge it. The installation of the box would be secure enough that it would take at least five minutes for any robber to get the box out in the open, but not ready to open. That would take a special key by Brinks' truck drivers. That expensive solution still wouldn't solve the entire problem of cash shortages because the retailer could still claim that a customer ran off without paying. But it did bring some relief.

The discussions were rewarding but no fun for Ina. We were lodged in the "luxury suite" at the same Sparkling Waters resort where the earlier seminar was held.

The "luxury hut" was a cement structure with a thatched roof that contained a big bed and a strange low sofa on which Ina could plop down but could not get up without a helping hand. No businesses, houses nor stores were within walking distance. The nearest store was in Rustenburg, a half-hour walk away. The game park with its wild animals was closer. It was very peaceful place except for the strange night noises.

When the seminar was at an end, we toured the game park in a military troop carrier, open on both sides with a canvas top. One could look from the sides but not skyward. When we slowly rounded a bend in the red-clay road, four slim brown-and-tan-spotted tree trunks appeared beside the vehicle. Ina stuck her head out from under the canvass roof and saw a young giraffe looking down at her. Neither of us had any idea that these magnificent beasts were so very tall. It looked like their height reached four meters. Later we saw his papa (One didn't have to look too far up to determine the gender), who was taller still. We were told this "little" giraffe was only two years old.

We drove alongside a gaggle of ostriches that ran as fast as our vehicle without seeming to exert themselves. These huge birds were at least eight feet tall and must have weighed close to 300 lbs. They cannot fly but are very fast runners. Our guide said that, contrary to popular belief, ostriches do not bury their heads in the sand. If threatened while sitting on her nest, which is literally a hole in the ground, the hen presses her long neck flat along the ground, to blend in with the background. The male ostrich is likely a member of the old Mormon Church since he has from two to five spouses.

At the house of the local game warden, your adventurous scribe made a near-fatal error by placing himself between a mother ostrich and her ugly baby. The idea of taking a picture was quickly abandoned when the mother high-stepped toward me, hissing fiercely like a broken steam pipe. The game warden yelled: "Get behind the baby." I did as told and the ostrich wandered off looking bored. Neither Ina nor I were bored. We were trying to calm down.

A PAID AUTHOR

In early summer of 2001, GTECH informed me that the number of EREWHON seminars for GTECH would be reduced. Instead I was asked to develop instructional CDs on the topics of game design for lotto, instant, keno, numbers games and sports betting. I was given 18 months to complete the job. Fees remained as generous as usual. Well, this was great news—being paid for

426

what I had planned to do on my own time in the expectation of selling such a training program. In addition, all expenses incurred would be reimbursed. Such a deal! To end the seminars for GTECH I did two more EREWHONs: in New York State and Rhode Island. They were both quite non-inspirational.

ISRAEL

Mifal Hapais

Prime Minister Ariel Sharon's visit to the Temple in Jerusalem in late 2000 had caused Yassar Arafat to declare the Intifada, starting a series of riots and terrorist attacks on Israel. Night after night, TV news presented pictures of unrest and violence. The WLA membership was becoming

increasingly concerned about holding the 2001 Conference in Jerusalem. Several members, vendors and delegates let it be known that they would not risk travelling to the Middle East. In June 2001, on behalf of the WLA, I conducted a three-day seminar for Mifal Hapais (Israeli State Lottery) in Tel Aviv.

It was a gesture towards Israel to soften the blow that the country was going to lose the WLA conference, now only months away. At that late date it was difficult to find another host country to assume responsibility. WLA arranged with NASPL to host a joint annual meeting in 2001 as was done in '96 in Vancouver. The new conference site was to be called World Meet 01 to be held in New Mexico.

The Israelis were upset. They lived with the fear of terrorist action every day and saw nothing unusual in the current bloody conflicts but the decision was final. I think they understood but they didn't like it.

Holding the conference in the United States promised a safe and peaceful environment. The WLA membership and associates were happy about the decision. The joint annual meeting in September of 2001 promised to be a great get together and most importantly, absent of war-like experience!

TEL AVIV

Immediately after conveying the crushing news to the Israelis, the EREWHON seminar in Tel Aviv began. Although I was experienced in conducting this type of session, I was unable to control the Israeli participants. When a topic was raised that wasn't foremost on their minds, they waved me off as a pesky fly and insisted on what *they* wanted to talk about.

Flexible enough to go with the flow, I carried on. However, as soon as a controversial issue was touched upon, they began to shout and yell at each other in Hebrew, a language liberally sprinkled with throaty "g" sound that I believed only the Dutch could produce. These weren't gentle disagreements. The flamboyant discussions were carried on with only a few inches between the noses of the debaters. Then, suddenly there would be peace while the various participants were likely ransacking their minds for a new controversy.

I felt I was failing badly but at the end of the first day some of the orthodox participants with their distinctive appearance of curly locks, beards and yarmulkes told me it was a most interesting day! I think that any day they can argue so vehemently is a good day.

Under duress I promised to explain BC's Red and Blue lotto games. Finally, I had their full attention. Not so full that they wouldn't interrupt me at any point but their interjections were not that hostile. Maybe it was because the topic was new to them and they had not formed an iron-clad opinion. These people wore me out! All day long they made me think on my feet and in my sleep, I re-played the debates over and over.

The second day, at lunch, I tried a different approach. Instead of joining the class for a kosher meal, I walked barefoot on the beautiful beach behind the hotel. The weather was warm and the sky a beautiful blue, but there were only young Israelis and no tourists. The beach chairs and cabanas outnumbered the bathers 50 to 1. Tourism in Israel was suffering!

On their free day, the lottery people offered Yvonne Schnyder and me a guided trip to the Dead Sea. We were cautioned that the trip was scheduled to travel through the occupied territory of Westbank and part of Jerusalem.

The guide, Mischa, was a jovial character who spoke with a wonderful Brooklyn-Jewish accent although he had never been to America. He answered every question with a question but when we crossed the pre-1967 border into the Westbank, he became less jovial and much more alert. We were now in Palestinian country, or "Occupied Lands" as the Arabs maintained and the Jews denied, arguing that the land had been theirs for millennia.

Even without the border post, we would have known it was a different land. The green olive fields were gone. No trees, no orange groves that bloomed so lushly in Israel; this land was sand, stone and low creeping vegetation begging for water. The Arabs walking the roads looked unkempt although their housing seemed okay— contrary to what we heard in North America, that Arabs were huddled in camps, living in squalid conditions. "Most of these people are Israeli citizens," Mischa explained. "More than a million Arabs hold Israeli citizenship." I now understood why all the hotels were operating on the Sabbath. The Arabs are the only ones who work on the Sabbath, keeping tourism operative during Saturdays and Holy Days. These Arabs might have been designated as Israeli citizens but their land and their villages did not resemble the green fields and attractive homes along the Mediterranean coast.

When we approached Jerusalem, western-style houses and cafes appeared. Civilization returned. After a brief tour through Jerusalem, Mischa announced the trip was to go through the arid zone on the way to Qumran where the Dead Sea Scrolls were displayed in a special museum.

During the trip I began to grasp the difference between "arid" and "semi-arid". Semi-arid was if even a single sprout of foliage raised its head. Arid meant...*nothing but stone.* And boy, Qumran was arid and — at 42C, so hot that not even our late-model, air-conditioned car could fight it.

Qumran was an oven. However, to preserve the Dead Sea Scrolls, the temperature in the museum must be kept at a constant 19 degrees Celsius. As we stepped from the desert into the icebox; I felt dizzy but after a few minutes, the eyes and the body got used to the cool temperature and the extremely dim lighting. I marvelled at the Dead Sea Scrolls written long before the birth of Christ and written in the same characters of today's Hebrew. The sect that wrote these parchments, the Essenes, must have been hardy people to live and write in this furnace.

To cool off a bit, the Dead Sea was not far away. The startling thing is: One has to descend very steeply to get down to the salty sea. The lake — once part of an ocean — is 300 metres (1,000 feet) below sea level and so much water has evaporated over the centuries that the salt content of the water is dense enough to keep a person afloat without moving a muscle.

The swim, or rather, float, wasn't refreshing because the water was too warm. Your lottery scribe (pictured here) found it strange that he could "lie" in the water. My body just couldn't stay in a vertical position. I had heard stories that you could read a newspaper in the Dead Sea while lying on your back. I tried reading the map in that position and indeed I could.

Several big hotels on the Dead Sea offer mud baths rumored to have curative effects because of the concentration of minerals. I didn't care for the elderly people covering themselves with a coat of black mud dug from the bottom of the sea. I decided to pass on the mud application.

Then suddenly it was time to return to rainy Vancouver. It had been a wonderful experience, both in terms of the rich history of the area and on the business side of spirited debate. I admired the country of Israel. I feel sorry for the Arabs outside of Israel whose third-generation offspring — 50 years after the war — still hover in camps, still carrying the label of "refugee" that, in my view, only their grandparents were entitled to. Sometime in the future they must face the facts that waiting for a solution for 50 years is about time to get off their behind and do something with their lives. No matter how much they wish for an opportunity to return to non-Jewish Israel, it isn't likely to happen.

THE BRIDGES OF MADISON COUNTY

September 4, 2001. For an Erewhon in Des Moines, Iowa, Ina and I made the 6,000 km round trip by car, visiting the Dakota Badlands and touring the country roads of South Dakota and Nebraska. One of the surprises of the visit, apart from the historic Badlands, was the hotel in Des Moines where the seminar was held.

We stayed in the Madison Suite, a name that didn't mean much to us. It was decorated as a Mid-Western rural home of the '50s. The 19th century treadle Singer sewing machine immediately caught my eye. Ina stuck her nose in the old-fashioned ice box. When we noticed the portraits of Meryl Streep and Clint Eastwood, the lights went on. Scenes of the movie The Bridges of Madison

County had been filmed in that room and the décor had been retained for the enjoyment of guests. Ina enjoyed it in a functional way. She used the country table for her ELNA sewing machine that she had brought with her to break the boredom while I was conducting the three-day seminar.

A surprise of the Erewhon session was the unusual attendance by a trio of female administrators of the Dutch State Lottery, one of which was a native Leidenaar. (A citizen of Leiden, my home town) She was amazed to find herself in a town in mid-America with another born burgher of her home city. She doubted my declaration of our common birthplace but when I launched into the unique flat twang of Leiden, she responded in a hysterical laughing response and in the same accent. Her Dutch companions were also intrigued to find a Dutch seminar leader and kept responding in Dutch to the annoyance and/or laughter of their Erewhon colleagues.

I wouldn't have bothered to insert this minor encounter in Iowa if it weren't for the fact that — after the seminar — these Dutch women were heading for a for a week holiday at New York's World Center Hotel. Their second day in New York became known by the unforgettable date "9-11." I never did find out how they got through the attack.

ALBUQUERQUE

October 12, 2001. The World Lottery Association annual meeting of 2001, originally scheduled for Jerusalem had been cancelled, due to bloody terrorist activities in Israel, and relocated to Albuquerque because the USA was considered a safe country. Imagine the distress of the registered delegates when New York and Washington were attacked by Al Qaeda (9-11). Two weeks after the attack many delegates to that WORLD MEET 01 decided that air travel was a scary proposition. With attacks in both WLA-chosen countries, one couldn't help but feel that World Meet 01 might be an ill-fated affair.

Ina and I made arrangements to meet our German lottery friends Alexander and Ilse Malwitz at the Los Angeles Airport. We arrived a few hours before they did but we were not allowed to pick them up at the arrival hall because access to the airport was reserved for licensed taxis only, lest some terrorist drive up in a truck with bombs and do bad things. We eventually found our colleagues. After a day's drive along US I-10, we spent a couple of nights at the Palm Desert home of Bob and Nancy Dunn before making our way to Albuquerque.

The conference was rather dull and uninspiring. The Americans acted as boys whistling past the graveyard, trying to stay cheerful in a fright-induced situation by pointing to their Old Glory lapel pins. We thought they were overdoing their patriotism but then we had to understand that no one ever before had ever attacked Americans on their home soil.

After the conference, which featured a mass congregation of manned air balloons, we were on our way back to Los Angeles, when Alexander asked us stop in Tucson to visit the immense graveyard for hundreds of de-commissioned aircraft. A guided tour bus drove us around for the half-day tour. Alexander was in heaven. On the other hand, Ina and I learned more about American aircraft than we ever wanted to know.

QUEENSCLIFFE

April 2002. Adrian Nelson, my former colleague at Tattersall's Lottery in Melbourne, had requested another EREWHON for a new cadre of Australian lottery managers. The World Lottery Association arranged for comfortable travel arrangements with stopovers in Hawaii both ways. Who could say no?

The seminar was in Queenscliffe, a fishing and holiday village along the coast, south-west of Melbourne. It was a good seminar without surprises. The Australians — being the high-spirited people they are — made it a happy and stimulating event.

On this trip I failed to realize that I was in the Southern Hemisphere. Out for a walk in early afternoon, your adventurous scribe got lost in the small town that featured a quirky traffic pattern. I knew I had gone in a southerly direction so if I oriented myself to the north, I'd find my way back. As any boy scout will tell you, you are northbound when you can see your shadow in front of you. If the sun is in your face, you're a heading in a southerly direction. So I turned my back on the sun and marched on until I realized I hadn't been in that area before. Then it dawned on me that Australian boy scouts are told that when the sun is in your face you are northbound. I knew that of course, but the penny had failed to drop. Just like the last time when I made up my mind that I would take note of the direction of the swirl as I flushed the toilet in Canada and then compare it to the eddy "Down Under." On every trip to the Australia I had failed to conduct that experiment but this time I did and yes, the water swirled opposite the way it did in the Northern hemisphere.

LONDON

May 21, 2002. Reidar Nordby, now President of WLA kindly appointed me to chair the nominating committee for the elections to the WLA executive committee to be held at the Adelaide conference. After having exchanged dozens of emails, London was chosen to be the site of the final meeting of this nominating group. As coincidence (ha!) would have it, the London meeting was at the same time as the FIFA World Cup, just as lottery meetings happened in 1998 and in 2000.

In three days, I managed to see eight televised games of the 2002 FIFA World Cup in the company of very partisan colleagues. At one of the evening dinners, the committee members amassed a betting pool of some £200. The bet was who would win the Cup. I bet Brazil and was declared winner of the pot, but the banker (who shall not be named) took the pooled money home and your lottery scribe didn't receive his winnings until two years later and that after many comic challenges and phony ultimatums.

ADELAIDE

November 17, 2002. Your lottery scribe was asked to speak at the 2002 WLA conference in Adelaide. Ina said: "You go. I'll stay home." During the stopover in Hawaii, I was assigned the same room in the Waikiki Outrigger as in April, even the weather was the same. This travel to Australia was getting to be a bit of a bore. (Not really!)

Adelaide was a new destination to me. It is a nice city with tree-lined streets and orderly traffic. In fact it is a huge, beautiful village. Even its financial centre is located in a park setting. The population seemed to be as diverse as any Canadian city. Yet, the tourist pamphlet announces proudly that three-quarters of Adelaide's population is of British ancestry.

The conference was well-organized but not very exciting, including my tepid contribution. I accepted the emcee role in order to stimulate a panel of so-called experts into livening up their musings about lotto. I failed. My only contribution to brighten the proceedings was delivering some stale wise-cracks that fell flat. However, there was one bright spot. Reidar Nordby's presidential hotel suite, which had a marvelous grand piano whose ivories were tickled by

433

your musically inclined scribe until the participants ran out of gas, booze or songs to sing, whichever came first.

PERTH

It had been seven years since my last visit to Perth. This beautiful coastal city is just about as far away from Vancouver as you can get. My speech was to dwell on "Security", since the business meeting was exclusively devoted to that unexciting topic. I am convinced that security chiefs in the lottery business are chosen for their quality of being utterly devoid of any sense of humor. The speech began on a serious note but when it became clear that I was preaching to the choir, I dug-up old horror stories where the security department had been an absolute pain in the ass and then caused havoc with disastrous results. I shared the story of the Western Canada Lottery draw in 1975 when six mailbags full of entries in the lottery were never deposited in the draw drum because of a lapse in security. To the audience's astonished ears, I confessed that I had found the perfect solution by burning the late-arriving entries in a farmer's field and then keeping quiet for years.

I rehashed the old story of the lottery's lawyer insistence on making the winners' cheque payable to a "nom de plume" rather than an identified winner which led to a lawsuit that cost many times the amount of the actual prize.

"Security" had also caused an instant/scratch game to be withdrawn from the market with a substantial loss in 6-figures because a slide projector could reveal what prizes lay beneath that latex paint that covered the winning symbols. Even if a person had access to such a machine and bought thousands of tickets, the fact remained that all the losing tickets still needed to be sold.

The audience seemed to be upset because I told stories so contrary to how they viewed their particular responsibility in the lottery business but they sat up and took notice. There was little laughter.

Right after that session, the conference attendees sailed out of Fremantle Harbour on a cloned Dutch "tall ship" from the 1800s called the "**LEEUWIN**

(Lioness). Under full sail, we flew across the waters of the Indian Ocean. I never realized how fast such vessels can go with just the power of the wind. It was a delight. You learn something new every day.

ROODEPOORT

In April 2002, the staff of the South African Lottery had nearly two years of experience. Anyone who couldn't hack the demanding routine had been replaced, resulting in a far more sophisticated group. Although they were smart and educated, they were new to the world of lotteries and its pitfalls. Thus, another EREWHON was requested. There were still some naïve people in the group but, on the whole, it was a more realistic collection of young university grads than the cast of previous EREWHON students. I felt flattered to be asked for a third session.

We were housed in a beautiful resort near Roodepoort, 80 kilometers from Johannesburg. The discussion groups sat around the flower-rimmed terraces and the sessions only moved to the indoor lecture room for the general debate. The resort was in the centre of a small-sized game park that was populated by giraffes, peacocks, "spring-bokken" and zebras. To enter the EREWHON plenary meeting room, one needed to pass through a small lobby where coffee and cookies were available all day.

While handling a heated discussion, I became suddenly googly-eyed, stared at the doorway and stopped speaking in mid-sentence. The participants, wondering what was going on, turned to the back of the room where a 15-foot giraffe stood licking coffee drops from the saucer placed underneath the tap of the urn. After that, he (it was obviously a "he") chomped a few chocolate chip cookies and wandered off contentedly. The owner of the resort knew which giraffe it was because there was only one that had become addicted to the caffeine jolts. (Picture: Your lottery scribe gazing at the tall coffee drinker.)

After the completion of the EREWHON, I attended a meeting of the l'Association Africaine des Loteries d'Etat, the African AILE. AALE is the French-language based association of state lotteries in Africa. The South Africans, who live in a country that has 11 official languages — none of them French — made the conference a largely English-speaking affair much to the dismay of delegates from the former French colonies who had never had to wear headsets to listen to a speaker at an AALE gathering. This time, they wore the headphones almost continuously as South Africans threw their weight around by scheduling only one French-language speech at the entire conference.

I sneaked away from the speechifying to fulfill daughter **Nadine's** request for certain colourful gemstones she wanted for her collection. Visiting the many gem stores in and around the hotel didn't yield the stuff itemized on her shopping list. One of the conference organizers offered to help me. Just before I walked onto the podium for my speech, she handed me the shopping bag with the stones. I stored it under the lectern. Alas by the time I ended my speech it had disappeared. I returned to the stage in order to ask if someone had taken the bag in error. The conference lady went in a no-no-no waving mode. Such crass behaviour was not deemed to be in good taste. If I were to even hint that something was taken unlawfully, I would offend the conference goers and accuse all of them of stealing. Better that the conference lady should go out and buy new stones. She did and refused payment. I had been robbed in Africa but it had not been admitted to. The second batch of stones looked better than the first. Nadine was happy!

GRANADA

In fall of 2003, **Alexander and Ilse Malwitz**, our friends from Münster joined Ina and me on a car trip to the WLA Conference in Granada, Spain. Starting in Amsterdam it took two days to drive to Arles, the "largest" city in France, inhabited by 50,000 people in an area of more than to 800 square kilometers.

When Alexander insisted on visiting the famous Arles cathedral, Ina and I excused ourselves and consumed delicious ice-creams in a park-like setting along the beautiful river Rhone. Accompanying our travel companions to the cathedral would have violated my personal pledge (The one I made in 1980 after visiting a dozen Japanese temples in three days) to never to visit an ancient place of worship again. Arles is a beautiful city. It is obvious why Vincent van Gogh left chilly Amsterdam to establish his home here.

436

After a couple of days of joyful travel, we arrived in Catalonia, Spain and stayed in a coastal town that looked familiar to us. Belatedly it dawned on Ina and me that we had visited the town of Sitges twelve years earlier when we were on our way to an AILE conference in Seville. Were we getting old? Did we travel so much that we didn't remember where we'd been?

All in all, driving from Holland to Granada had been an enjoyable four-day trip. Ina saw much of historic Granada, including the Alhambra, a massive fortress and palace from the period when the Arabs controlled Southern Spain. Meanwhile, the WLA annual meeting had become a bit of a travelling circus. Same people. Same speeches. Same exhibits. Only the location changed.

One of the positive developments to come out of Granada was a long discussion with Jean-Marc Lafaille, the former president of Loto-Quebec. He had the idea of co-authoring a book on the components of gaming, a topic that — to our knowledge — had not been addressed before. We agreed to exchange published columns and speeches we had written over the years. I didn't think we'd ever get around to writing a book but what harm was there in talking?

Well, we talked and talked some more, and in the following months, a book appeared. *Lotteries! Dissected and Rearranged* was published and purchased in bulk by most lottery organizations. It was a success.

LEIDEN

June 20, 2003, your travel-crazed lottery scribe travelled to Holland to conduct an EREWHON in Noordwijkerhout on the North Sea coast, a community only a few kilometers from my birth-place in Leiden.

I have written about various EREWHON sessions and this one was no different. Exuberant Australians mixed with a happy threesome from Thailand, a hassle of argumentative Dutchmen, a few Italians and even a wild man from England made for a great mix, especially the last evening, when the Thais — teetotalers all — warbled their way through Frank

Sinatra's "My Way." Urged to sing a Thai song, they said they could only do so when clad in their native dress. To create their sarongs, they wound themselves in tablecloths and performed a fertility dance on the table. You had to be there!

SOUTH AFRICA

Ina wasn't in the mood for another South African visit, so in October 2004, my fourth visit to that continent became a solo trip. The WLA-sponsored EREWHON seminar was held at a hotel that had seen better days. It was another South African resort, just outside Johannesburg, with round thatched huts masquerading as hotel rooms.

The seminar was far from the best and perhaps the eeriest. The participants were divided in two groups: employees of the South African Lottery and officials of the regulating agency. The inherent hostility was evident.

Uthingo, the lottery operator, had recently hired a corporate spokesperson, a former South African entrant in the Mrs. World contest. I don't know whether this South African lady gained the top title but she attended the informal Erewhon sessions dressed as Queen Nefertiti of the Nile. Instead of Nikes, as was the accepted footwear at the seminar, she wore golden slippers. Her neck was being strangled by copper nails of some sort. After she complained that this international event should have been held in a five-star hotel, I had a little talk with her, explaining that I had strongly suggested this type of informal environment. After that she came down from her high horse and dressed down to tailored blue jeans and a blouse specked with little gold stars.

When the first Erewhon session began, four participants from Ouagadougou, the capital of Burkina Faso, were still missing. An hour later, two new white Mercedes arrived and four women in full-colour African floor-length

dresses strolled into the lobby, followed by three huge males dressed in African-art inspired shirts. They expected to be addressed in French and asked if the conference would pay for their cabs. Two disappointments for them in the first two minutes. Seeing there was no alternative, one of the men produced a wad of cash and paid the cabbies.

Immediately after that, another financial hassle ensued — four people had registered and paid the required fees but seven people had showed up. When that was settled, all seven informed me that they wouldn't attend the first-day sessions because they were going to travel to Johannesburg to shop.

I explained that EREWHON was a continuing course: one day's sessions would segue into the next. I suggested if they wanted to go shopping, they should go for three days — i.e. get with the program or leave. After a long discussion with WLA's hired interpreter, it was announced that the men would attend and women would take limos to Johannesburg.

Finally, the sessions began.

The interpreter was a delight. He was deep into the discussions about lotteries and had forgotten all about his role as a translator. He felt that he was a lottery director now! He argued with the Burkina Faso group whose proposed solutions, although loudly expressed, were far removed from reasonableness.

The Burkina Faso group wasn't quite as arrogant when they heard the reasoned responses of the South African participants. They countered the opinions of their host's students with an avalanche of meaningless words, but their B.S. didn't carry the day. The South-Africans laughed at their naiveté.

A new design for an instant game is always the closing segment of each three-day EREWHON. The discussion groups were urged to include some humor to their respective presentations. One group created a lottery game based on food delicacies of rural South Africa. In an attempt to win votes from the other groups, they had shopped at the nearest village and bought pig's feet and salty meat strips of an unnamed animal. Fatty fingers left traces in the workbooks.

At the appointed moment during their presentation, the doors opened and hotel waitresses served the delicacies that matched the themes of their lottery game. At the presentation's end, a dozen carafes of local berry wines were brought in, causing some participants to suggest the contest be stopped and the pig-feet group automatically be declared the winner!

The Burkina Faso group redeemed themselves by presenting a game relating to the dances and chants of their native songs.

The next day, several of the seminar attendees joined me on the flight to Durban on the coast of the Indian Ocean to attend the World Lottery Association annual meeting.

DURBAN

November 11, 2004. Durban's Conference Centre, site of the 2004 WLA annual conference, is a state-of-the-art building situated amidst a crime-ridden slum that fronts the beaches. On the first day, looking out from my well-appointed suite, I spotted a local market with dozens of stalls selling everything from rugs to drugs. It was worth a look. When I walked out of the hotel, a security guard, dressed in neat civilian clothes stopped me, pointed at my Rolex and shook his head. When I turned around to go back to the room to stash the watch, the man called me back. With his hand patting his bum he said: "No wallet, take just enough change to buy a little something."

When I noticed several lottery colleagues who returned to the hotel were nearly fainting from the near 40-Celsius heat, the thought occurred to me that staying in the air-conditioned hotel might be a better idea. My colleague Jean-Marc Lafaille, who had just checked in, persuaded me to spend a few hours discussing the progress of our lottery book-in-progress. Discussing is too polite a word. It was more like yelling, pounding fists and intense debate.

Later that evening reports circulated that a GTECH employee, strolling along the beach, had been robbed and beaten and was taken to the hospital. Staying in the hotel appeared to be the best chance for survival.

The opening dinner featured the obligatory, boring speeches. The emcee was "Queen Nefertiti of the Nile" of EREWHON fame. For five minutes, she acknowledged a long list of people with titles, from the premier of the province to presidents, directors, even local city councillors. She gave a special warm welcome to the WLA's Founding President, who had brought the two organizations together. All the other worthies had risen when they were announced, so when my position was announced, I scrambled to my feet but she suddenly announced: "Reidar Nordby Jr." I sank back into my chair. My seatmate and friend Charles Cousins, who was the guiding hand behind the conference, looked perturbed.

440

At roll call the following morning, Charles winked at me when the first order of business was an abject apology by Nefertiti of the Nile. Yes, it's true. I am not good at hiding my hurt feelings.

The two-hour roundtable discussion with leading lottery directors went well, although there was a sticky moment when in the midst of a spirited debate, the serene delegate from India, in his most pompous, speech-making voice, stated that he desired to comment. To that point he hadn't said a word. To my surprise he opened his briefcase to extract a written speech. I was aware that at other sessions that this man had made 15-minute speeches in an impenetrable accent, droning on while the hall emptied.

As he rose and scraped his throat to commence his speech, I cut him off and snapped: "No, not here. Not now. This is a spontaneous debate no notes, no prepared speeches."

The audience grew deadly silent. Someone had dared to challenge a member from a visible minority. The accepted thing in a world conference is to suffer every fool gladly, no matter how much he or she upsets the flow of events. When I got the discussion back to order without the boring reader, Ray Bates from Ireland was busy writing a note. He arranged for someone to hand the epistle to me. It read: "I love you!"

Later, after the session ended, I approached the Indian gentleman, half-apologized for my stern reaction. He reached for his briefcase and handed me his non-delivered speech. Those who were still around giggled, but the Bombay blatherer smiled contentedly.

My final contribution to the conference was to present a glowing tribute to the winner of the "Guy Simonis Lifetime Achievement Award" at the final dinner — to my old friend and mentor Lothar Lammers.

By three o'clock that afternoon, I felt less than 100%. I thought it was the stress of that morning's marathon session and the preparation for the evening tribute. I went to the room to rest and when I was about to leave for the dinner, Ina called from Vancouver, where it was early morning.

"I had a sense that you were not feeling well," she said, "Are you okay?"

I assured her that I was fine, but I lied. It felt as if a big stone was lodged in my stomach. Fortunately, my presentation was the second item on the agenda and was scheduled to be delivered just after appetizers were served to the 1,000 or so delegates and spouses of the conference. I hovered near the washroom, where Michelle Carinci found me. In the midst of telling her of my discomfort, I was called to the stage.

From the dais, I could see my face as it was projected onto the large TV screens that were placed around the room. I felt nauseous. About halfway through the speech, I knew I had to finish fast or vomit. I didn't finish.

There, before the multitudes and projected on huge TV screens, I was shown live, vomiting profusely! Around the dais, the floor was a mess. The audience was stunned. No one moved except Michelle, who ran towards me from the back of the hall. I pulled the microphone stand out of the mess and placed it in a clean area. The cleaners moved in to swab the floor. After a few minutes, I returned to the cleaned dais and apologized to the audience and said I wasn't feeling well before to the dinner but that I remained in order to pay tribute to a friend of 30 years. I added that I felt I should finish my speech and to the surprise of the audience, I did.

When I finished, I called Lothar to the stage. His first words on the stage were: "How are you, Guy?"

Equally inanely, I answered: "Fine."

He read his prepared speech as written and did not refer to the incident. It was weird! Backstage, they cleaned my jacket and shirt, took the mops and brooms to finalize the clean-up while the audience was served their soup.

Afterwards Jean-Marc Lafaille took charge of your wobbly scribe and brought me to my room. A doctor diagnosed food poisoning but that didn't make sense to me.

The next day, Jean-Marc had a commitment in Capetown, **Mona**, the Norwegian conference supervisor for WLA, was assigned to attend to me.

When a doctor showed up — a nice young Indian man who insisted on calling me "Goy" — he listened to my story and whisked Mona and me off in his dilapidated Honda to the hospital in a colourful shopping street of the Indian sector of Durban.

The Indian hospital was primitive by North American standards but very clean and staffed by nurses who — on my floor — seemingly outnumbered the patients by a ratio of three to one, all full of smiles and ever willing to help. At one point five of them were in my private room to chat.

The X-ray verdict was bowel obstruction and doctor's orders were: "Eat nothing. No liquids. No food. Just lie there for 36 hours or 48 if necessary. The following day I was discharged at noon, in time for my flight from Durban-Johannesburg-Amsterdam at 5 p.m. However, first I had to pay the X-ray bill of around 800 Rand ($160).

The cashier couldn't connect with the Visa office so I signed a promissory note that would eventually reach Visa. From there, I was directed to the cashier for the hospital stay. The bill was close to 6,000 Rand ($1,200). I handed the clerk my Visa card who phoned for authorization. He gave my Visa number, listened, slammed down the phone and said: "Your Visa is cancelled."

The young Indian doctor nearly had a fit. "I brought you in, Goy," he panicked, "If you don't pay, I am liable for your expenses."

I told him he could trust me and I would send the money from Canada. He looked at me as if he had heard that one before. "Have you no cash card, Goy?" he inquired with great urgency.

I did have a Bank of Commerce card and a Dutch Banking card and they would be good for $600 each, I hoped. All that was needed was an ATM machine. The young doctor sprang into action. He knew of a bank a few streets away. The armed guard at the bank demanded to see my passport before I could enter. I didn't have my passport but I had my wallet. The big guard said that with so many credit cards I didn't need to enter the bank; I should go to the ATM around the corner. At the side of the bank, an armed guard watched over a row of three adjacent ATMs, two of them riddled with bullet holes and the third with a line-up of Durban citizens who eyed this bald white guy accompanied by a redheaded movie-star type dressed in white with suspicion, interest or greed...or perhaps all three.

I hadn't eaten for more than two days; the temperature was around 40, the humidity high. I felt faint.

"We are not going to do this," Mona declared. "We are going to the conference centre where there is an ATM and it is air-conditioned."

"May I come with you?" Doc asked. He probably thought might not get paid.

The cool air of the empty conference centre was heavenly. I tried the ATM machine with my Dutch card. It had listings for the equivalent of Rand — R100, R500 and R1000. I knew I needed $600. In my misery, I pushed 600 and, of course, received 600 Rand. I had made a mistake. I would have to wait at least an hour to get more money from the Dutch bank account. I made no such error with the Canadian card. We were now $200 short. Mona had a card from her bank in Norway and she managed to extract the $200.

The doctor stuffed the bundle of Rand bills in the pockets of his pants and said: "Good-bye, Goy, I must run."

Back at the hotel, Mona took it upon herself to guarantee that WLA — who had a running account— would be good for the extra amount owing on the hotel bill. Then it was off to the airport, where I was put in a wheelchair and hauled onto the baggage elevator together with the passengers' meals.

I slept across the entire African continent and didn't awake until flying over Rome. I stayed in Holland for a few days to get back to normal and to prepare for the remaining 10-hour flight home.

LAS VEGAS

In Las Vegas, in February 2005, the Public Gaming Institute inducted five old friends — Guy Snowden, Ed Stanek, Jean-Marc Lafaille, Lothar Lammers and

444

your lottery scribe — into the Public Gaming Hall of Fame. To make a holiday out of it, Ina and I traveled by car along the California coast with the intent to turn inland from Los Angeles. Unfortunately, the rain never ceased and when we learned that the coastal highway was washed out farther south, we turned east because the Mojave Desert was supposed to be warm and dry. Our expectations were dashed. The low spots farther down on the road to Quartzite, Arizona, had turned into rushing lakes, where level of water frequently rose above the top of our headlights.

We made it to Las Vegas where the weather was cold and the Bellagio Hotel huge. The distance from our room to the meeting area was more than one kilometer. The ceremony wasn't much. For the speech, I presented a segment of the soon-to-be published book I had co-authored with Jean Marc Lafaille. Along with the other speeches, it was met with polite indifference. The meeting ended with the presentation of inscribed fruit bowls to the five Hall of Famers. Another garage sale item?

HAMAR

August 22, 2005. There was some doubt whether I could lead the September EREWHON in Hamar, Norway, because two weeks earlier I suffered another one of those damned bowel obstructions. This one landed me in hospital for three days and although it delayed my departure, I did make it to Norway in time.

If I had to vote for the friendliest, most productive EREWHON, this would be it. Part of the success was the setting. The familiar Hamar Hilltop Hotel hosted the entire seminar. The huge lobby/tea room featured four quiet corners with a circle of comfortable leather club chairs. Each of the Erewhon discussion groups was assigned a cozy corner, illuminated by a crystal chandelier. Coffee and cookies were on stand-by during deliberations.

The participants were from twelve different countries: a sprinkling of Americans, Italians, Spaniards, Portuguese and Dutch. The Finns were of an unusual kind; they were outgoing and cheerful. The Brits were sarcastic and, as always, the Aussies were the merrymakers. The best thing for the EREWHON success was that the participants were bussed in from Oslo and therefore had no transportation to visit the local nightspots (If there are such things in Hamar, where all solid citizen go to bed early.)

The responses to the lottery issues were wonderful. Most of the attendees had been in the lottery business for quite a few years, which made the debates much more interesting.

MEXICO REDUX

Since 1997, any effort to stage a WLA annual meeting in Mexico had run into difficulties. The attempt at a 2001 meeting but had to be cancelled late in the game. The newly-elected Mexican government offered to try again in 2006. Again, the site would be in the holiday resort of Cancun, a strip of American hotel chains on the Gulf of Mexico.

Mexico had invested billions in this tourist magnet and wanted to promote it to the world. Mexico's proposal was accepted and hundreds of delegates registered to attend but in mid-October — only weeks before the conference was to start — Hurricane Wilma thundered in from the Atlantic basin and nearly destroyed Cancun. The WLA made a solid and quick decision to postpone the conference until after the New Year's celebrations, but when later it became evident that Cancun could not recover in time, the conference was moved 300 kilometers in-land, to the city of Merida, the capitol of the state of Yucatan.

MERIDA

In February of 2006, Ina and I flew to Merida via Mexico City. At the WLA conference it was "old home week" again — an entire slate of familiar faces plus the newly appointed Mexican delegates.

For all the problems that had befallen Mexico's bids to host a conference, the Merida conference turned out to be great. In retrospect, that city was a better choice than Cancun, given the tropical beach would have been just steps from the conference site, attendance at the sessions would surely have suffered. The conference was elegantly housed in the Hotel Tropicana. Merida is a clean, attractive metropolis of close to a million people, yet relatively unheard of on the world stage. Amsterdam, Oslo and Copenhagen have less than a million people and yet are world-famous. Not many of our colleagues had ever heard of Merida, a city founded by Spanish missionaries in the year 1572.

We were told that the city's industry for centuries was sisal, a tough marsh-reed from which all strong wipe-your-feet doormats are made. The sisal barons of yore built many beautiful mansions in streets around our hotel. Every day, Ina and I found time to walk the magnificently-treed boulevards and admire the lush flowers.

INA MEETS THE FOX

The Merida conference was opened by Mexico's President, Vicente Fox. Ina was thrilled to be a few feet away from his commanding presence. Your less-than-modest scribe could have bragged that he spoke right after El Presidente, which was true, but my trifling monologue was scheduled after the coffee break when the President had left. The following day, I headed another panel discussion on an even less interesting topic. The audience seemed as un-thrilled as I was. I realized I had spoken too often of these lottery issues and I decided that this type of presentation/lecture should be the last.

My third address, delivered in a gorgeous park setting at the closing gala, was a tribute to the outgoing WLA President Reidar Nordby, accompanied by humorous slides,. My speech listed the good he did over the years for the association and his generous attitude toward me. I knew the presentation hit home because of the plaudits afterwards.

PRAGUE

September 9, 2006. Out of the blue came an invitation from the slightly tarnished **Ales Husak** (pictured centre), the managing director of SAZKA, the Czech lottery. Ina and I were to attend the opening of the Prague Ice Hockey arena designed to world-hockey specifications.

To your lottery scribe, Ales Husak was a garrulous, friendly guy who had once visited our Tsawwassen home with his father. Ales was opinionated and argumentative but knew very little about the intricacies of lotteries and bets. My agreeable impression of Ales was not the same as his Czech critics, who railed at his extravagant salary and his grandiose financial rewards to staff and board members. A published report shows an accounting of his expensive ways:

- Average monthly salary: $45,000 CDN
- Severance pay under contract (Est $45.5 million CDN) was not paid
- Business cars, including a Bentley and a Hummer: $1.6 million CDN.
- Statues and paintings located in Sazka arena $2.1 million CDN.
- One year of wages at the arena: $33 million CDN.

This decadent expenditure of lottery profit was a major loss to the Czech sports associations who were entitled to receive that lottery revenue.

On the evening after our televised arrival in Prague, a reception was held in a castle, the name of which escapes me. The impressive building was obviously intended to cater to foreign visitors. The formal reception was held in a gilded mirror-clad ballroom where bewigged hostesses dressed in 17th century garments lounged on sofas and elaborate chairs. A string quartet played the kind of music that would transport the guests back to the days of such courtliness. As if that wasn't too much of a cultural shock, your lottery scribe was inveigled to transform the string artists into a jazz quartet to accompany me on the piano. It went wonderfully well if one measures by audience participation.

After consuming much finger-food and fine Czech-produced champagne, guests were urged to go outside into the garden where medieval warfare weapons were to be tried.

On offer were battleaxes, halberds, war hammers, bows and arrow, pikes and spears. I chose the battle-axe but after a strong heave it fell to the ground before it even approached its target. **Ina**, my dear gentle spouse chose the cross bow and successfully hit the target but the force required to release the arrow, damaged her shoulder muscle, a painful feeling that still bothers her from time to time.

The following day a small group of former WLA executives was invited to lunch at an elite restaurant — a place where the maître d' announces the next course with a flourish before the formal-dressed waiters bring in the food in a theatrical fashion. Ina and I counted the number of aperitifs, food and wine but we stopped at 22 when we were only halfway through the four-hour lunch. The meal was so lengthy that — at the end — the somewhat (!) inebriated group only had time to rush back to the hotel to dress for that evening's formal dinner.

The next day, Ales Husak, the great spender, led his entourage of several hundred guests to the Prague Railway station where a vintage 1940s train stood puffing in a cloud of black smoke mixed with white steam. A military band performed familiar marches.

The mood in the train was already in a state of bacchanalia when the train huffed its way into the Czech rural area where the same band (who followed the train in a bus) marched us into a historic local eatery where we were offered a feast of local foods. The dining room's bare benches were uncomfortable but the local wine was excellent. It was late in the evening when buses took us back to the real world.

On the closing day of the Czech visit, the official opening of Prague's ice hockey arena was attended by current and past executive members of WLA but... only those who were in Ales Husak's good books. It was the most gigantic opening celebration your humble scribe and spouse have ever attended, then and since.

If the exceptional concert was not enough of a festive event, the halls of the hockey arena featured many culinary corners where thousands of invitees indulged in fine foods of Central and Eastern Europe.

As special guests, we were invited to view a demonstration of the modern way to dispense Pilsner beer. A humongous stainless-steel tank, the size of a gasoline-tanker truck held the Pilzner beer. A maze of tubes fed the 15 beer stations around the complex. Nearby, two trucks were awaiting their contents to be syphoned into the system the moment the supply ran dangerously down.

The evening gala was attended by thousands of SAZKA lottery retailers, staff and international colleagues. The featured entertainment was a band called the *Leningrad Cowboys*, a Finnish rock band that performed rock and roll covers of well-known songs. They wore exaggerated pompadour hairstyles and long, pointy shoes. They made quite a spectacle even before singing a song. After the Cowboys, a splendid musical presentation by the Russian armed forces entertainment group took the audience by storm. The magnificent concert included the 80-man Red Army choir, a 45-piece orchestra and a dance ensemble that performed a range of music including folk dances, olden-days tunes, hymns, operatic arias and popular music. Your musically inclined scribe and Ina delighted in great performances of *The Volga Boatmen's Song*, *Katyusha*, and *Kalinka*.

While Ina and I shook our heads at the profligate spending by the Czech lottery, we were secretly pleased that we'd been part of this fabulous festivity. It was truly an affair to remember.

SINGAPORE

On November 10, 2006, daughter Joanne and I left for a strenuous trek to Hong Kong followed by another hop to Singapore where the annual meeting of the World Lottery Association was to be held. The first ceremony was to honour **Yvonne Schnyder**, who was leaving her post as Secretary General of the World Lottery Association. My old colleague Lothar Lammers had been invited to deliver the "Thanks-and -farewell" speech for the young lady he had hired in 1972. The speech of the 80-year old veteran was received with big applause for the pioneer of the modern lotto game.

At one of the business sessions, I was scheduled to deliver a discourse based on Max Weber's view of rational and irrational actions insofar as they related to the mystique of games of chance. Weber was a German sociologist, philosopher, jurist, and political economist whose ideas profoundly influenced social theory and social research. I had done a lot of reading of his rather dry tomes and found some nuggets that applied to gambling.

While I believed the topic was of interest, the audience was more interested in the bread and butter of lottery management than the sociology with respect to gambling and the human impulses behind it.

One particular dinner has stayed forever in our memory: the only non-fish course was a super-sized chicken that was presented "en toto" on a huge board in the center of each table with great fanfare. When I say "en toto" I mean the bird had been de-feathered and disemboweled but everything else was still intact including the claws, eyes, neck and beak. How to share that among 8 guests seated around the table?

Soon, the problem was resolved. A red-cloth head-banded waiter removed each platter one at a time to a side board and — with a banzai cry — attacked each bird with a cleaver and until the carcasses had been hacked to bite-sized bits. The platters were then replaced in the centre of each table for guests to share in the smithereens. Face with the chicken/bone/beak melee, Joanne and I had already lost our appetites. Needless to say, the Chinese delegates loved the presentation.

BUCHAREST

June 15, 2007. The EREWHON sessions that your lottery scribe had developed and enhanced since their inception in 1988, ended in Romania. I'd been at it for close to 20 years. At age 76, it was enough EREWHON for me. From an initial set of five discussion cases, the curriculum had expanded to more than thirty topics. It took three full days of 8-hour sessions for the participants to work their way through the material and that didn't include the evening sessions where the course demanded the groups develop new concepts in instant-scratch games.

 Ina and I arrived in Bucharest a few days early to meet with the Director of the Romanian Lottery, **Lilliana Ghervasuc**, a most courteous woman who, in addition to being president of the Romanian lottery, was a member of Romania's Parliament. After checking us in at the excellent hotel, she took Ina and your scribe to a wonderful picturesque park, where a formal British Tea was served along the lake's shore.

Later that evening son Leonard and granddaughter Danna joined us on this final EREWHON course located in Mangalia, a tourist town on the Black Sea near the border with Bulgaria.

Granddaughter Danna, then 18, was there as a reward for graduating from high school and son Leonard had taken the last opportunity to find out what his Dad had been teaching all these years.

Lottery managers from Switzerland, Britain, Italy, Bulgaria, Australia, Netherlands, Ghana, and Germany and of course Romania attended. It was a good group. The debates were substantial and rewarding. The outstanding memory of this last seminar was that — in late evening — the seminar attendees took over the pool at the small Black Sea beach and enjoyed a great bash that lasted into the early morning.

WHY YOU SHOULD SIGN YOUR TICKET

A lottery ticket purchased from a retailer is a "bearer document" which means whoever presents the ticket is the winner. Legally, the unsigned document belongs to the person who presents it for payment, just as a $10-dollar bill is the owner whoever holds the bill. The holder of a ticket can "own" the document by writing his or her name on the back of the ticket. At that point, it is no longer a bearer document.

Despite the warnings ad nauseam that players should sign their name on the back of the tickets, it wasn't being heard. Failing to sign, one risks losing one's prize should the unsigned ticket fall into someone else's possession.

Another point: Ticket holders, who ask the retailer to check their un-endorsed ticket, are in danger of being cheated. All a crooked retailer has to say to the inquiring customer who asks if the ticket is a winner, "Your ticket is not a winner." The customer goes away satisfied and the retailer is free to write his own name (or that of a proxy) and cash the winning ticket.

In 2007, a journalist of the Vancouver Sun wrote an article that BCLC's lottery system (which is practically identical to most others around the world) was compromised. A formal request for information by the journalist revealed that dozens of retailers had won large prizes over the years.

In the newspaper story, a dozen of these retailers were named and excoriated for stealing winning tickets from innocent players. In response, the minister responsible for lotteries, an ornery, uninformed impulsive man, claimed BCLC's system was fraught with loose controls that paid prizes to people who weren't legitimate winners.

Although no legitimate claims of fraud or even hints of misdoing were ever received, but that didn't bother the politician. He fired BCLC president Vic Poleschuk, who had toiled for the lottery for 32 years. Shame on that politician!

Shortly afterward, I made a speech in Kamloops before an audience of lottery colleagues, determined to revitalize the downed spirit of my former dear colleague.

He appreciated my efforts but likely not as much as the truly substantial amount eventually paid to him by the BC government for wrongful dismissal.

KENTUCKY

September, 2007. The combined annual meeting of NASPL and WLA was held in Louisville, hosted by the effusive WLA President Arch Gleason. Ina, who loves driving, suggested we should travel there by car which meant an 8,000 km return trip.

After the long trek to Kentucky, your lottery scribe was to deliver a speech at the retirement of the head of the Iowa Lottery, Ed Stanek. The speech was ghost-written by **Kenneth Brickman**, the noted legal beagle of the Iowa Lottery and humorist of renown. The story was about varmints in Ed's home and the efforts to euthanize them.

I have made many speeches in my career but seldom have I heard as many roars of laughter. I have a bad habit of giving no credit to others when I can safely absorb the plaudits for myself. The audience's wonderful compliments were warmly received by your larcenous scribe.

MONTREAL

My final lottery speech took place on September 25, 2012 at the combined annual meetings of NASPL and the World Lottery Association in Montreal. The invitation was courtesy of my dear friend Lynne Roiter who — as I write this— is President of Loto Quebec.

This last speech was to celebrate the entry of my former Norway Lottery colleague, Reidar Nordby, into the ranks of recipients of the "Guy Simonis Lifetime Achievement Award". Reidar was pleased with my speech welcoming him to the circle of outstanding lottery leaders in the world. He particularly loved the gift of the inscribed harmonica — a present of the World Lottery Association.

I took the opportunity to pay tribute to the 2012 passing of Lothar Lammers — my early tutor — who had been so instrumental in reaching out beyond his European-based association to embrace lottery companies elsewhere in the world. Lothar was one of the first to foresee the creation of the WLA.

EPILOG

Looking back on my 40-year journey in the field of lotteries, I feel part of a truly pioneering effort. I am blessed to have been chosen to lead the early development of what is now a huge financial industry. I hasten to credit and thank the fifteen Western Canadian cabinet ministers who governed my lottery actions during my career and who gave me the freedom to operate within extended bounds — a privilege that few civil servants in the world have enjoyed. I especially want to acknowledge those cabinet ministers who were most influential in the progress of lotteries and my career: Laurent Desjardins of Manitoba and James Chabot of British Columbia.

In the early '70s the lottery business in Western Canada was a shunned stepchild of governments. The direction your lottery scribe was given was that lottery management should do what it had to do as long as it kept government and politicians out of trouble and minimized their visibility. Of course, good news, such as an upstanding citizen winning a nice prize or the announcement of a lottery grant for a popular cause, were always occasions for government ministers to be front and centre.

When lotteries began to yield notable revenues, the lottery administrators receive only a little credit. And during the few moments of public disapproval, politicians went into a strange denial, claiming that the lottery wasn't really their favourite program.

I felt — and still do — that success was ultimately achieved despite some political winds that continuously blew against early initiatives. In the '90s, that perspective turned. Politicians realized that the public wholeheartedly approved of lotteries, and that they were here to stay.

When retirement came in the year 2000 and I entered the world of consulting and lecturing; my feelings about that transition were mixed. It was a shock to be no longer in charge of managing the business and I missed the sweet satisfaction of introducing new games of chance. I have to admit that it pained me that someone else was going to do what I still wanted to do, but at age 68, having to deal with the political crap that surrounds managing a crown corporation was the deciding factor in saying goodbye.

I enjoyed being a consultant, but in 2008 I let that go too. These days Ina and I pass our time keeping up with friends and colleagues — at least those who are still alive!

I read regularly about the lottery business and continue to be amazed by the industry's unrelenting growth.

I hope you enjoyed these stories. Thanks for reading, and don't forget to buy your lottery ticket!

Made in the USA
Lexington, KY
30 July 2019